PSYCHOPATHY IN ADOLESCENCE AND ITS CONSEQUENCES IN ADULTHOOD

What becomes of young people who display strong psychopathy traits? By combining cutting-edge research with interviews from over 500 incarcerated youth assessed for psychopathy and involved in serious, violent offences, this book investigates whether they are destined to persist in crime throughout their lives. Evan McCuish explores not only long-term offending patterns but also psychopathy's influence on relationships, employment, substance use, and mortality. Through this, the text clarifies the meaning of the clinical construct of psychopathy and debunks myths and misconceptions popularized by the true crime genre. This allows readers to more reliably interpret the accuracy of popular culture descriptions of psychopathy. Synthesizing over 100 years of research, this book makes sense of major debates in the psychopathy literature and contributes new knowledge to the field through empirical analysis. It is ideal for students, scholars, and practitioners in psychology, criminology, social work, and law seeking further insight into this intriguing disorder.

EVAN MCCUISH is an associate professor at Simon Fraser University, Canada and is the Principal Investigator for the Incarcerated Serious and Violent Young Offender Study. He is the recipient of the American Psychology-Law Society Outstanding Dissertation Award and the American Society of Criminology Division of Developmental and Life-Course Criminology Early Career Researcher Award.

PSYCHOPATHY IN ADOLESCENCE AND ITS CONSEQUENCES IN ADULTHOOD

EVAN MCCUISH
Simon Fraser University

Shaftesbury Road, Cambridge CB2 8EA, United Kingdom

One Liberty Plaza, 20th Floor, New York, NY 10006, USA

477 Williamstown Road, Port Melbourne, VIC 3207, Australia

314–321, 3rd Floor, Plot 3, Splendor Forum, Jasola District Centre, New Delhi – 110025, India

103 Penang Road, #05-06/07, Visioncrest Commercial, Singapore 238467

Cambridge University Press is part of Cambridge University Press & Assessment, a department of the University of Cambridge.

We share the University's mission to contribute to society through the pursuit of education, learning and research at the highest international levels of excellence.

www.cambridge.org
Information on this title: www.cambridge.org/9781009273084

DOI: 10.1017/9781009273053

© Evan McCuish (2026)

This publication is in copyright. Subject to statutory exception and to the provisions of relevant collective licensing agreements, no reproduction of any part may take place without the written permission of Cambridge University Press & Assessment.

When citing this work, please include a reference to the DOI 10.1017/9781009273053

First published (2026)
Cover credit: Ekely via Getty Images

A catalogue record for this publication is available from the British Library

A Cataloging-in-Publication data record for this book is available from the Library of Congress

ISBN 978-1-009-27308-4 Hardback
ISBN 978-1-009-27304-6 Paperback

Cambridge University Press & Assessment has no responsibility for the persistence or accuracy of URLs for external or third-party internet websites referred to in this publication and does not guarantee that any content on such websites is, or will remain, accurate or appropriate.

For EU product safety concerns, contact us at Calle de José Abascal, 56, 1°, 28003 Madrid, Spain, or email eugpsr@cambridge.org

Contents

List of Figures	page ix
List of Tables	xii
Preface	xiii
Acknowledgments	xx
List of Abbreviations	xxi
Structure of the Book	xxii

1	**The Elusive Definition of Psychopathy**	1
	Chapter Goals	2
	Definitions Matter	3
	Early Descriptions of Psychopathy	8
	The DSM and Its Failed Attempt to Clarify Psychopathy as a Mental Disorder	11
	Contemporary Descriptions of Psychopathy	16
	Chapter Summary	25
2	**Psychopathy Debates, Myths, and Misconceptions**	27
	Chapter Goals	27
	Debate #1: Is Criminal Behaviour a Trait or Consequence of Psychopathy?	28
	Debate #2: What Is the Structure of Psychopathy?	30
	Debate #3: Is There a Successful Version of Psychopathy?	36
	Debate #4: Can Self-Report Tools Measure Psychopathy Reliably?	40
	Debate #5: Do People with Psychopathy Traits Change?	43
	Myths and Misconceptions about Psychopathy Perpetuated by Popular Culture	50
	Chapter Summary	58
3	**The Incarcerated Serious and Violent Young Offender Study**	59
	Chapter Goals	59
	ISVYOS Research Design	61
	Sample	63
	Procedures	64

vi　　　　　*Contents*

	Control Variables	66
	Measuring Psychopathy	69
	Assessing Psychopathy among Incarcerated Youth: Lessons Learned through Interviews	72
	Manifestations of Psychopathy Traits from the Interpersonal Factor	74
	Manifestations of Psychopathy Traits from the Affective Factor	80
	Manifestations of Psychopathy Traits from the Lifestyle Factor	83
	Chapter Summary	87
4	**The Reliability and Validity of Psychopathy Measures**	**89**
	Chapter Goals and Analyses	90
	PCL:YV Reliability	91
	PCL:YV Validity	93
	Chapter Summary	114
5	**Psychopathy Traits in Adolescence and Persistent Offending through Adulthood**	**116**
	Chapter Goals and Analyses	118
	Measuring Persistent Offending	120
	The Importance of Understanding Persistent Offending	125
	Psychopathy and Persistent Offending	127
	The Measurement of Offending Persistence Using ISVYOS Data	130
	Are Psychopathy Traits in Adolescence Associated with Persistent Offending in Adulthood?	131
	Do Youth Psychopathy Traits Predict Offending for Everyone?	135
	Psychopathy Traits and the Perpetration of Harmful Offences	137
	When Do Psychopathy Traits Fail to Predict Persistent Offending?	140
	Chapter Summary	148
6	**The Underexplored Costs of Youth Psychopathy Traits**	**150**
	Chapter Goals and Analyses	150
	Measurement of Social Outcomes	151
	Measurement of Health Outcomes	156
	The Relationship between Psychopathy Traits and Informal Social Control	159
	The Relationship between Psychopathy and Prison Peer Networks	165
	The Relationship between Psychopathy Traits and Substance Use Issues	175
	The Relationship between Psychopathy Traits and Early Mortality	177
	The Consistency of Findings across Alternative Representation of the PCL:YV	182
	Chapter Summary	182
7	**Understanding the Relationship between Psychopathy and Offending**	**185**
	Chapter Goals and Analyses	186
	The Psychopathy-Offending Relationship within a Cumulative Disadvantage Framework	189

	The Psychopathy-Offending Relationship within a Criminal	
	Propensity Framework	190
	Measurement and Developing the Mediation Model	191
	Case Study: Illustrations of Mediation	194
	Does Informal Social Control Mediate the Relationship between Psychopathy and Convictions?	196
	Does a Negative Criminogenic Network Mediate the Relationship between Psychopathy and Convictions?	198
	Does Substance Use Mediate the Relationship between Psychopathy and Convictions?	199
	Are the Findings Reliable?	199
	A Better Understanding of the Relationship between Psychopathy and Offending	202
	Chapter Summary	206
8	Psychopathy and Treatment Effect Heterogeneity	208
	Chapter Goals and Analyses	209
	Hypotheses Regarding Treatment Effect Heterogeneity	210
	Psychopathy and Treatment Effect Heterogeneity	214
	Social Resistance as Fourth Hypothesis on Treatment Effect Heterogeneity	215
	A Case Study Illustration of the Social Resistance Hypothesis	218
	Testing the Interaction between Psychopathy and Social/Health Outcomes	223
	Chapter Summary	229
9	Birth Cohort and Period Effects: Implications for the Relationship between Psychopathy and Offending	232
	Chapter Goals and Analyses	233
	Measuring Cohort and Period Effects	233
	An Overview of Birth Cohort Effects and Their Implications for Psychopathy Research	236
	An Overview of Period Effects and Their Implications for Psychopathy Research	239
	Does Birth Cohort Membership Moderate the Relationship between Psychopathy and Offending?	241
	Do Period Effects Moderate the Relationship between Psychopathy and Offending?	246
	Psychopathy, the Ecological Context, and Implications for Criminal Legal System Practice	248
	Chapter Summary	250
10	Psychopathy Traits and Responses to Incarceration	252
	Chapter Goals and Analyses	253
	The Origins of the Pessimism Regarding Psychopathy and Responsivity to Punishment	255
	Psychopathy, Treatment, and Reasons for Optimism	257

The Incarceration Experience and Its Impact on Reoffending	258
Evaluating the Impact of Incarceration on Reoffending for Youth with Psychopathy Traits	259
Implications for Treatment and Intervention	261
Chapter Summary	266

11 Concluding Thoughts   268
    What Is Missing from the Book?   268
    Summarizing and Synthesizing the Chapters   273
    Final Thoughts   281

References   284
Index   321

Figures

4.1	PCL:YV correlated four-factor model	page 97
4.2	PCL:YV hierarchical four-factor model	98
4.3	PCL:YV hierarchical three-factor model	99
4.4	Expected response functions indicating the probability of scoring a "2" on the given PCL:YV item	106
4.5	Graphical LASSO network graph of the PCL:YV	109
4.6	Bootstrapped differences in strength centrality across the 20 PCL:YV items	111
4.7	Correlation between PCL:YV total scores and other measures of psychopathy	113
5.1	Example of the output from semi-parametric group-based modeling	123
5.2	Conceptual description of the causal influence of psychopathy traits on offending	129
5.3	Probability of different criminal legal system outcomes at each year of age	132
5.4	The relationship between PCL:YV total scores and the probability of conviction (Panel A) and incarceration (Panel B) at each year of age between ages 18 and 40	133
5.5	The relationship between PCL:YV total score scores and the probability of conviction (Panel A) and incarceration (Panel B) at each year of age between ages 18 and 40 for male and female participants	136
5.6	The relationship between PCL:YV Total scores and the probability of conviction (Panel A) and incarceration (Panel B) at each year of age between ages 18 and 40 for Indigenous, White, and Non-Indigenous participants.	138
6.1	Hypothetical ego network of social ties between "h" and their alters on a prison unit	155

6.2	The relationship between PCL:YV total scores and a person's CRNA-based informal social control rating in early adulthood	162
6.3	The prison-based criminogenic social network of "Chris" measured between ages 18 and 23	168
6.4	Combined ego networks of all positive tie criminogenic peer networks in prison	170
6.5	Relationship between PCL:YV scores and positive tie degree centrality	171
6.6	Prison-based conflict tie network	172
6.7	Relationship between PCL:YV scores and negative tie degree centrality	172
6.8	Combined victimizer ego networks among the ISVYOS PCL:YV Cohort	173
6.9	The relationship between PCL:YV total scores and a person's CRNA-based substance use rating in early adulthood	176
6.10	The relationship between PCL:YV total scores and the probability of mortality by the end of the study period	180
7.1	Conceptual model examining the mediating impact of informal social control on the relationship between PCL:YV total scores and conviction frequency in adulthood	192
7.2	Sensitivity analysis of the adult conviction frequency outcome and CRNA informal social control mediator	201
7.3	Sensitivity analysis of the adult conviction frequency outcome and CRNA informal social control mediator	201
8.1	Graphical depiction of the difference between mediation (top) and moderation (bottom)	209
8.2	Examining the interaction effect of psychopathy traits and informal social control on the rate of convictions in adulthood	225
8.3	Relationship between PCL:YV scores and positive tie degree centrality	226
8.4	Relationship between PCL:YV scores and negative tie degree centrality	227
8.5	The relationship between PCL:YV total scores and a person's CRNA-based substance use rating in early adulthood	228

List of Figures

9.1 Macro-historical environmental characteristics in the Province of British Columbia, Canada — 235
9.2 The distribution of PCL:YV total scores across participants from different birth cohorts — 242
9.3 The distribution of convictions across participants from different birth cohorts — 243
9.4 The relationship between PCL:YV total scores and convictions across birth year — 244
9.5 The relationship between PCL:YV total scores and convictions across different birth cohorts — 245
9.6 The distribution of PCL:YV total scores across participants who were incarcerated under either the Young Offenders Act (left) or the Youth Criminal Justice Act (right) — 246
9.7 The distribution of convictions across exposure to specific youth justice legislation — 247
9.8 The relationship between PCL:YV total scores and convictions across exposure to specific youth justice legislation — 248

Tables

1.1	Contemporary descriptions of psychopathy	page 19
2.1	Key terminology when discussing the structure of psychopathy	31
2.2	Clarifying points of confusion regarding psychopathy	52
3.1	Non-exhaustive description of information included within CORNET administrative data	67
3.2	Ratings for Case Studies from the ISVYOS	73
4.1	Description of PCL:YV items	94
4.2	Fit Indices for different confirmatory factor analysis models	100
4.3	Estimated PCL:YV item parameters	103
4.4	Convergent validity between the PCL:YV and the MACI Psychopathy Content Scale and CAPP-IRS	112
5.1	The costs of persistent offending	126
5.2	Description of false positive cases	142
7.1	Mediation test of cumulative disadvantage (PCL:YV total scores)	197
10.1	The effect of changes in incarceration on changes in reconvictions	261

Preface

As part of my graduate student training at Simon Fraser University, I worked as a Research Assistant for the Incarcerated Serious and Violent Young Offender Study (ISVYOS). I spent more than a thousand hours interviewing over 300 incarcerated youth from the Province of British Columbia, Canada. These interviews were conducted for research purposes and were not in court proceedings. This meant that the information participants provided was confidential unless they made a direct threat to hurt themselves or someone else. Participants were not your typical youth. In fact, the youth who participated in the ISVYOS are unlike most youth involved in the criminal legal system. For example, in the United States, youth who are sent to custody often are involved in relatively minor offences. In fact, some youth are incarcerated for status offences (i.e., an offence that would not be a crime if committed by an adult) such as failing to complete homework (Cohen, 2020). In contrast, youth who experience incarceration in British Columbia tend to be involved in particularly serious or violent offences or have a history of repeated contact with the criminal legal system.

To illustrate the severity of the ISVYOS sample, about 30 of the youth I interviewed were incarcerated for sexual offences. Another 30 were incarcerated due to their involvement in a homicide offence. One of these youth, Michael, was convicted of second-degree murder (i.e., a deliberate but unplanned offence) after he stabbed an adult male. While incarcerated for this homicide offence, he hoarded various canteen items that he used to bribe others to perpetrate violence on his behalf. Several years later, as an adult, Michael was involved in the murder of a gang member. During the commission of each offence, Michael was not intoxicated nor was he suffering from any delusions or hallucinations. He was fully aware of his actions and their consequences.

I spent about 30 hours interviewing Michael and reviewing his correctional file, which included pre-sentence reports detailing his family, educational, and behavioural history as well as psychological assessments detailing his mental health. Interview and file information was compiled to assist with the scoring of the Psychopathy Checklist: Youth Version (PCL: YV; Forth et al., 2003). Compared to other ISVYOS participants, Michael scored below average. How can someone who is as violent as Michael *not* be a "psychopath"?[1] Given the absence of intoxication and delusions, it may seem intuitive to equate his behaviour with psychopathy. After all, psychopathy is associated with a lack of empathy, and homicide involves a lack of empathy. But does that necessarily mean that Michael should be considered a "psychopath"?

One of the main motivations for writing this book was to debunk myths about psychopathy. These myths are commonly perpetuated by various forms of media. One such myth is the notion that involvement in extreme violence implies that a person is a psychopath. To debunk this myth, it is important to draw a distinction between states and traits. States are situational and fleeting (e.g., anger after being cut off in traffic). Traits are observed across different contexts and are stable over time (e.g., general aggression). A lack of empathy, for example, is a core psychopathy trait. States in which a person displays a lack of empathy do not imply psychopathy. In fact, a lack of empathy in certain contexts can be a healthy coping mechanism. Health care workers who can regulate their empathic responses are better able to avoid distress, burnout, and compassion fatigue (Decety et al., 2010). For some people coming from extremely disadvantaged situations, low levels of empathy in certain situations may be a protective mechanism that should not be conflated with psychopathy.

For Michael, his lack of empathy was limited to his criminal offences (e.g., a state rather than a trait). He cared deeply for friends and family and was empathetic towards them. In the community, Michael was shy. He enjoyed cooking for others. His attempts to manipulate others were restricted to his prison environment (i.e., a state rather than a trait). In fact, in the community, he was more likely to be the victim of manipulation from older, gang-involved family members and so-called friends. His first homicide offence was in defense of a family member who was being abused by an older male involved in drug trafficking. His second homicide offence was directly influenced by gang-involved peers who preyed on Michael's suggestibility. At an early age, Michael was diagnosed with fetal alcohol

---

[1] Because psychopathy is a dimensional construct, I avoid terms like "psychopath" and prefer terms like psychopathy traits to identify instances of clinically relevant levels of psychopathy. The term "psychopathy traits" is also less stigmatizing.

spectrum disorder, which can result from prenatal alcohol exposure. Fetal alcohol spectrum disorder impacts executive functioning, which is responsible for impulse control and planning. Like other forms of intellectual disability, youth with fetal alcohol spectrum disorder tend to be easily influenced by peers and family members, and this can lead to elevated levels of criminal behaviour (Corrado & McCuish, 2015). In essence, many factors influenced Michael's involvement in extreme violence, but psychopathy was not one of them.

Beginning a book on psychopathy by describing someone who scored relatively low on the PCL:YV may seem puzzling. However, a goal of this book is to communicate how psychopathy is described in the academic literature. To do so effectively may require first breaking down some myths about psychopathy and, in some cases, engaging in a process of unlearning. Surveys of laypersons indicate that when people think about psychopathy, one of the most common words that comes to mind is criminal behaviour (Helfgott, 2013), and it is not uncommon for laypersons to believe that all psychopaths are murderers (Smith et al., 2014). Michael's background was introduced to illustrate that psychopathy and criminal behaviour are not always perfectly linked. I have been teaching undergraduate and graduate students about psychopathy for over a decade. The most common sources of information they rely on to learn about psychopathy include true crime podcasts, television shows, YouTube videos, and popular psychology books. These sources tend to use case studies involving extreme violence to illustrate examples of psychopaths, even if there is no evidence that the perpetrator was characterized by psychopathy traits (e.g., callousness, pathological lying, and manipulation).

Although psychopathy traits may be disproportionately observed among people involved in extreme violence, as illustrated by Michael, psychopathy is not a prerequisite for extreme violence. Further, although psychopathy traits are disproportionately observed among people involved in crimes like homicide (Fox & DeLisi, 2019), most people with psychopathy traits do not engage in extreme violence. Nevertheless, it is these types of offences that get sensationalized by the media and subsequently linked to psychopathy. For example, in April 2020, a mass shooting in Nova Scotia, Canada, resulted in the death of 22 people (Public Safety Canada, 2022). I was interviewed about the shooting by a journalist from a national news organization. The journalist repeatedly posed leading questions about whether the shooter was a "psychopath." I spent about an hour explaining what psychopathy is, what it is not, and that the lack of information on the shooter's personality characteristics meant that I could neither confirm nor deny the relevance of psychopathy. None of this information was used in their story. A Google search of "Nova Scotia Shooter Psychopath" returned over 400,000 results. As of January 2025, there is no publicly documented evidence that the shooter in Nova Scotia received a formal psychopathy assessment. Instead, the assumption was often made that, because of the severity of the violence, the shooter must be a "psychopath."

To be blunt, popular culture depictions of psychopathy get things backwards. Violence, even extreme violence, is not particularly strong evidence that the perpetrator is a psychopath. Academic research in disciplines like forensic psychology, correctional psychology, and criminology has taken an interest in psychopathy because it is a strong predictor of chronic, serious, and violent offending. Said differently, there is little that can be learned about psychopathy by narrowing in on extreme violence, given that the criminal behaviour of people with psychopathy traits rarely rises to this level of severity. Focusing on extreme violence risks overlooking many people with psychopathy traits. However, much can be learned about the risk of offending by studying psychopathy.

Whether it is university students or the general public, there are good reasons why people tend to learn about psychopathy through the media, including the true crime genre, rather than peer-reviewed papers. For one, people want to know how events such as the April 2020 shooting in Nova Scotia could occur. Psychopathy offers a convenient and comfortable explanation for extreme violence. Psychopathy is a convenient explanation because people may feel uncomfortable pushing back against the idea that there is sufficient evidence to call the shooter a "psychopath." Pushing back against such an idea can incite accusations of showing sympathy toward the perpetrator or excusing their actions. Psychopathy is a comfortable explanation for extreme violence because the term communicates to an audience that the perpetrator is fundamentally less human. This framing allows the public to feel more at ease knowing that it is easy to detect and avoid psychopaths. The convenient and comfortable nature of psychopathy as an explanation for extreme violence has given rise to YouTube and TikTok videos perpetuating false information on "how to spot a psychopath" and that detecting psychopathy is simple (e.g., "@drjaleelmohammed" on TikTok). Psychologists are not immune to holding pseudo-scientific views on psychopathy, especially if these views can be monetized on social media. Unfortunately, YouTube videos and other sources in popular culture and the media are often more accessible and less dense than the academic literature. This highlights the need for psychopathy research to be communicated in ways that are both scientifically rigorous and broadly accessible.

The case study involving Michael showed that not all youth involved in extreme violence have psychopathy traits. However, what about other forms of offending? Are all youth with psychopathy traits destined to be involved in offending at a high rate over the life-course? Will their lives in adulthood be defined by negative relationships with family members and intimate partners, unemployment, substance abuse, conflict with others in prison, and early mortality? These questions are addressed in this book by analyzing data on a cohort of over 500 youth who participated in interviews for the assessment of psychopathy traits and who have been followed for several decades into adulthood. Because the goal of the book is to reach a broader audience, statistical analyses are supplemented with case studies illustrative of the underlying quantitative data.

What is the rationale for dedicating an entire book to psychopathy traits in adolescence? In forensic psychology, psychopathy is considered one of the most important individual-level risk factors for future offending (Hart, 1998). Psychopathy is routinely assessed among adjudicated adults and youth, both on its own and as part of broader risk assessment protocols (e.g., Viljoen et al., 2010). Psychopathy is commonly considered in criminal legal system decisions regarding sentencing, level of security, eligibility for parole, and release conditions (Hart, 2016). There is considerable controversy, however, about whether psychopathy *should* be considered in certain criminal legal system decisions, especially those involving capital cases in which the death penalty is on the table (DeMatteo et al., 2020).

It is important to study psychopathy traits in adolescence because early identification provides opportunities for intervention. In this book, I will describe how the notion of psychopathy as untreatable is another myth perpetuated by pseudoscience and popular culture. Since psychopathy is often assessed in criminal legal system proceedings, it is critical to have an understanding, not just of when it matters, but also when it does not. The goal of this book is not to tout psychopathy as the most important factor in adolescent development. Instead, the goal is to use data to identify whether, and in what ways, psychopathy traits in adolescence matter for adult development.

What makes this book different from the dozens of other academic books on psychopathy that have been overlooked in favor of podcasts and YouTube videos? This book is not merely a review of psychopathy literature. Chapters 3–10 present new data on psychopathy traits in adolescence and their relationship to various outcomes in adulthood. My goal is to balance the need for discussions about psychopathy that are based on empirical evidence rather than populist beliefs and sensationalism with my ability to draw upon my experiences interviewing incarcerated youth. I focus on youth psychopathy traits because this is my area of expertise, and my research thus far contradicts popular assumptions about the stability of psychopathy, its treatability, and deterministic interpretations. This book addresses a call from Hervey Cleckley, one of the pioneers of psychopathy research, to study the impact of psychopathy traits, not just on offending, but on social and health outcomes as well.

If the assessment of psychopathy stigmatizes youth and results in particularly punitive sentences, including decisions in the United States regarding the death penalty, then why study psychopathy? My perspective is that these negative labels reflect problems with *people* and *systems* rather than inherent flaws in the psychopathy construct. As will be demonstrated in this book, psychopathy traits in adolescence are associated with more serious patterns of offending over the life-course, including higher likelihoods of chronic offending, violent offending, and lengthier periods of time spent incarcerated. Psychopathy traits in adolescence are also associated with a variety of negative social and health outcomes in early adulthood, including weaker social bonds, a higher degree of conflict in prison, substance use issues, and even early mortality. To overlook the effect of psychopathy traits on social and health outcomes because of how a small group of researchers, politicians, and policymakers have co-opted the term for ideological purposes or to further specific policy agendas ignores the reality that there are people whose psychopathy traits are harmful to themselves and others. Acknowledging this does not preclude the possibility of change. Instead, it highlights the potential benefit of early, humanistic intervention and treatment strategies to help reduce the likelihood of offending and negative social and health outcomes.

Acknowledging the importance of psychopathy is not an endorsement of determinism. Too often, assumptions have been made that youth with psychopathy traits are destined for negative outcomes, especially serious offending. John Dilulio (1995), an American political scientist at Princeton University, asserted that the next decade would see an unprecedented increase in hundreds of thousands of youth "superpredators" who were characterized by psychopathy traits. Even experts with years of training assessing psychopathy shared Dilulio prediction (e.g., Lykken, 1995). Although the anticipated new wave of "superpredators" was proven false (Payne & Piquero, 2020), assumptions that these young people were destined to offend at a high rate in adulthood (Dilulio, 1995) had enormously detrimental consequences for how such youth were responded to by the criminal legal system and discussed in the media. For example, the wrongfully convicted boys known as the Central Park Five were viewed as prototypical superpredators and were described using various racist dog whistles used to marginalize Black youth (Hinton, 2019). It is critical that discussions of psychopathy avoid reigniting these sorts of false beliefs.

The goal of this book is to increase understanding of psychopathy while providing a path for identifying treatment and intervention strategies that can lead to positive adult outcomes. I have interviewed some youth with psychopathy traits who I think will remain a danger to the public throughout their life-course. However, I have also interviewed some youth with psychopathy traits who, in adulthood, demonstrated potential for rehabilitation. In either scenario, the goal should be to prioritize prevention and intervention strategies that reduce the likelihood of further harm.

Acknowledgments

The data analyzed in this book would not have been possible without the efforts of more than 100 student volunteers and Research Assistants who contributed to data collection, coding, and cleaning over a 25-year period. The data also would not have been possible without the assistance of funding from the Social Sciences and Humanities Research Council of Canada. I am grateful to Emily Watton and Anna Hubbard from Cambridge University Press for their patience and support throughout this project. I wrote this book with students in mind. Several students provided valuable feedback on earlier drafts of this book. Thanks to Kathleen Moody (Simon Fraser University) for feedback on clarifying the distinction between psychopathy, antisocial personality disorder, and sociopathy. Thanks to Sidra Capriolo (University of Alabama) for thoughtful advice on clarifying language and concepts for a broader audience and for recommendations on how to integrate themes from past chapters into future ones.

Most importantly, I want to thank all the participants from the ISVYOS who generously shared their stories with our research team.

Abbreviations

CORNET	Corrections Network
CRNA	Community Risk Needs Assessment
DSM	*Diagnostic and Statistical Manual of Mental Disorders*
HROIP	High Risk Offender Intervention Program
ISVYOS	Incarcerated Serious and Violent Young Offender Study
PCL-R	Psychopathy Checklist – Revised
PCL:YV	Psychopathy Checklist: Youth Version
RNR	Risk–Need–Responsivity Model
SNA	Social Network Analysis
YCJA	Youth Criminal Justice Act
YOA	Young Offenders Act
YPI	Youth Psychopathic Traits Inventory

Structure of the Book

Each chapter in this book can stand alone, but the book is meant to be read cover-to-cover. Results from one chapter often inform later chapters. The purpose of the first two chapters is to help make sense of some key themes within the psychopathy literature. Understanding the empirical analyses in this book requires a shared understanding of what psychopathy means, or at least what I mean when I discuss psychopathy. Chapter 1 traces the origins of psychopathy research and reviews different definitions of psychopathy. The goal in this chapter is to familiarize readers with what psychopathy means to different groups, including what I mean when I describe people with psychopathy traits. Chapter 2 provides an overview of key debates within the psychopathy literature and addresses some of the myths of psychopathy that have been perpetuated by pop culture sources.

Chapters 3–10 constitute the empirical core of this book. Chapter 3 describes the data used, including how psychopathy was measured and what I looked for during interviews to assess for psychopathy traits among youth. Chapter 4 examines the reliability and validity of the PCL:YV in the current data source. This step is necessary to build trust among readers that this measure of psychopathy is reliable and valid. Chapters 5 and 6 examine the relationship between psychopathy traits in adolescence and outcomes in adulthood, including offending outcomes, social functioning, and health. Chapters 7 and 8 examine the intersection between psychopathy traits, social/health outcomes, and future involvement in offending. Chapters 9 and 10 address key policy questions. Chapter 9 examines whether the relationship between psychopathy traits and offending has changed across generations and whether this has implications for court-ordered risk assessment tools. Chapter 10 examines whether people with psychopathy traits respond to periods of incarceration with reduced rates of offending.

Chapter 11 concludes the book by synthesizing the findings and highlighting themes that this book failed to address but that are nonetheless important to the psychopathy research. I discuss limitations of the analyses presented in the book, including the fact that analyses were not preregistered, and what to do about these limitations in future work. Overall, I hope this book will help those interested in psychopathy, especially undergraduate and graduate students, understand what psychopathy is, what it is not, when it matters, and when it does not.

CHAPTER 1

The Elusive Definition of Psychopathy

Popular culture descriptions of psychopathy appeal to a wide audience. Journalist and filmmaker Jon Ronson's TED Talk on psychopathy has 24 million views as of January 2025 (TED, 2012, August 12). I often show this TED Talk to students to illustrate what popular culture gets wrong about psychopathy. In his review written in *The British Journal of Psychiatry*, Dr. Peter Tyrer (2012) described Ronson's book, which formed the basis of the TED Talk, as trivializing and stigmatizing psychopathy "in the search for cheap laughs and better sales" (p. 167). Several subject-matter experts who were interviewed for the book indicated that Ronson used exaggerated or fictional accounts of their interviews (Society for the Scientific Study of Psychopathy, 2012).

Why is such an inaccurate source on psychopathy so widely viewed? Learning about psychopathy through mediums like TED Talks, True Crime podcasts, and YouTube tutorial videos is appealing because academic writing tends to be inaccessible. Academic reference books and peer-reviewed papers on psychopathy are literally inaccessible because many are behind expensive paywalls. These sources are also figuratively inaccessible because their use of jargon and technical language makes them difficult to understand. Readers who are new to psychopathy research often need to refer to multiple other sources to gain the background knowledge necessary to understand a single paper. It is also easy to come across two different papers with contradictory views on psychopathy. Although it is not problematic to have different perspectives on psychopathy, readers too often are left in the dark as to why these contradictory perspectives exist and whether one is more accurate than the other.

The fact that interested audiences are so often left in the dark with respect to the academic literature on psychopathy is disappointing because of how prominent the concept has become in criminal legal system decision-making. Dr. John Monahan, a pioneer in forensic psychology and risk assessment, noted on the cover of *The Handbook of Psychopathy* that psychopathy is "the most important forensic concept of the early 21st century" (Monahan, 2006). Part of the importance of psychopathy is based on its association with offending. The strength of this association resembles the impact of a wide range of proven interventions, such as the relationships between tutoring and academic achievement, reduced class sizes and academic achievement, and heart surgery and reductions in mortality (Hart, 1998). In North America, the criminal behaviour of people with psychopathy traits contributes to billions of dollars in financial costs (Gatner et al., 2023). Whether rightly or wrongly, psychopathy has a major impact on decisions in the criminal legal system. To evaluate whether this influence is appropriate first requires an understanding of how psychopathy is defined.

Chapter Goals

Those interested in learning about psychopathy often face two unenviable options. The first is to read expensive, technical, inaccessible, and at times contradictory academic literature. The second option is to access popular culture sources that are often misinformed about the academic literature on psychopathy and, whether purposefully or by mistake, give an inaccurate description of what subject-matter experts mean when discussing psychopathy. My goal in writing this book is to make psychopathy research accessible without sacrificing the accuracy of the content. Readers will not receive a watered-down version of the science behind psychopathy. When technical language is unavoidable, I use case studies that illustrate complex concepts.

Making psychopathy research accessible begins with establishing a shared understanding of the construct. This chapter focuses on a very basic yet important question: What is psychopathy? Answering this question can be challenging because there is no universal definition. Thus, to have a comprehensive understanding of different perspectives, this chapter traces 200 years of discussions on psychopathy and explains how and why different definitions have emerged. A clear understanding of psychopathy is important because, in practice, the stakes associated with misattributing a person's behaviour to psychopathy are high. The criminal legal system regularly assesses psychopathy to make decisions about a person's future, including their freedom. Psychopathy has important real-world implications.

Due to its association with offending, psychopathy is regularly assessed to assist with decisions about sentence length, probation conditions, candidacy for treatment programs, parole decisions, jury deliberations, and, in some jurisdictions, the death penalty. To be clear, I am not advocating that psychopathy *should* play a role in all of these decisions. My point is that, whether right or wrong, the criminal legal system uses information about psychopathy to make decisions with far-reaching consequences. At a minimum, clear-sighted decision-making requires an understanding of what psychopathy is (and what it is not). I begin with a discussion of why definitions of psychopathy matter.

Definitions Matter

Researchers studying cancer are often interested in whether and to what extent cancer contributes to early mortality. However, fibromyalgia, anemia, pleurisy, and other illnesses have signs and symptoms that overlap with cancer and also increase the risk of mortality. The American Cancer Society (2025) has therefore taken care to develop clear definitions of various cancers. Clearly defining cancer allows doctors and clinicians to distinguish cancer from other diseases, which in turn allows researchers to have a shared understanding of cancer and make more precise conclusions about the specific contribution of cancer to mortality.

It is difficult to make precise conclusions about the contribution of psychopathy to offending if a shared understanding of psychopathy is lacking. There are major differences between how psychopathy is described in the literature produced by subject-matter experts[1] and how it is described in popular culture. Even within the academic literature, there are some key differences in how psychopathy is defined. As mentioned by Dr. Robert Hare, the lead developer of the Psychopathy Checklist (PCL), even more troubling is the fact that subject-matter experts do not bother to provide their definition of psychopathy before describing the relationship between psychopathy and negative outcomes like violent crime (Hare, 2022).

The goal of this book, and this chapter in particular, is to help reduce confusion about the meaning of psychopathy. As a starting point, here is how I define psychopathy:

---

[1] By subject-matter experts, I am referring to those who publish peer-reviewed papers on psychopathy or who are responsible for assessing psychopathy as part of clinical practice (e.g., forensic psychologists).

- Psychopathy is a multidimensional syndrome, which means that it consists of the convergence of observable and subjective traits from different personality domains (Monroe & Anderson, 2015).
- The personality traits that comprise psychopathy mainly come from interpersonal, affective, and behavioural domains of functioning.
- Core interpersonal traits are those that describe people as, for example, self-centred, entitled, and manipulative.
- Core affective traits are those that describe people as, for example, detached, callous-unemotional, and unempathic.
- Core behavioural traits are those that describe people as, for example, having poor behavioural control, a lack of reliability, and a tendency to be sensation seeking.
- These core traits are found in both youth and adults, but the expression of these traits may differ across developmental stages. This concept is referred to as heterotypic continuity.
- Psychopathy is maladaptive, meaning that the personality traits cause functional impairment in day-to-day life (e.g., negative relationships with others).
- Psychopathy is dimensional (e.g., a sliding scale representing the degree of psychopathy traits) rather than categorical (e.g., a clear demarcation between psychopath and nonpsychopath).
- The personality traits that define psychopathy tend to be relatively stable over time and across different social contexts.
- Stability in one time period (or context) does not guarantee stability in another time period (or context).
- Involvement in criminal behaviour is not a psychopathy trait.

Other descriptions of psychopathy also exist, and at least some subject-matter experts will disagree in whole or in part with how I have described psychopathy (see Debate #2 in Chapter 2). In Chapter 4, I review whether the traits I identified as core to psychopathy hold up to empirical analysis. It is not necessary for readers to adopt my definition as their own. However, providing this working definition of psychopathy is critical for developing a shared understanding of what I mean when I use the term throughout the book. In the following subsection, I explain why a shared understanding is important.

Using Definitions to Develop a Shared Understanding of Psychopathy

In the first half of the twentieth century, Austrian philosopher Ludwig Wittgenstein designed his "Beetle in a Box" thought experiment to illustrate the importance of definitions (see Wittgenstein, 1993). Wittgenstein described a scenario with a group of people, each having their own private box that contains a "beetle." Each person is only aware of what a "beetle" is by inspecting their own box. Nobody in the group can see inside the box of the other group members. The box could contain anything, including the same thing, something different, or even nothing at all. The term "beetle" simply represents whatever happens to be in a particular box at a particular time. Each person can freely discuss the characteristics of their beetle, but it is impossible to verify what is actually inside another person's box. The purpose of Wittgenstein's experiment is to illustrate that the meaning of a word can be understood by how it is used. It does not matter if each person has a different "beetle" in their box as long as each person can communicate what this beetle means to them. Similarly, it does not necessarily matter if subject-matter experts define "psychopathy" differently as long as each communicates what psychopathy means to them. Words earn their meaning through communities where there are shared rules about how to use language. These shared rules and public descriptions mean that even in the absence of a formal definition, a word like psychopathy can still have meaning, and correct and incorrect usages of the word can be identified.

Wittgenstein wanted to illustrate how people may experience pain (i.e., "the beetle") in vastly different ways. Being open and publicly describing one's pain helps create a shared understanding. At issue in the academic literature is the tendency for definitions and descriptions of psychopathy to be private. The private nature of psychopathy definitions has contributed to a lack of shared language. The lack of a shared language occurs even among practitioners responsible for assessing psychopathy (Shipley & Arrigo, 2001). The lack of a shared language for psychopathy is especially true when comparing academic and public communities.

By Wittgenstein's definition, subject-matter expert definitions of psychopathy are not public. The academic literature on psychopathy is quite literally private, given that much of this literature is published in journals behind expensive paywalls. It is critical for subject-matter experts to be more public with their research on psychopathy, given how impactful expert opinions can be in changing public perceptions and attitudes (Pornpitakpan, 2004). The academic literature on psychopathy is also figuratively private because it uses inaccessible jargon and other dense language that is confusing to most readers, especially those who are looking to introduce themselves to psychopathy research. The private nature of academic research on psychopathy is unfortunate because there is a clear public interest in the topic. This is not a new issue; Cleckley (1976), one of the key figures in contributing to contemporary descriptions of psychopathy, noted that a major barrier to effectively addressing psychopathy traits was the general public's lack of knowledge (p. 31).

Despite public interest, only 15 percent of laypeople report learning about psychopathy through academic sources (Ostapchuk, 2018). This is unfortunate given that experimental research shows that exposing laypersons to clear descriptions of psychopathy can help debunk myths that create stigma about psychopathy as a mental health disorder (Ostapchuk, 2018). People are far more likely to report that their understanding of psychopathy is based on intuition or popular culture sources. Journalist and filmmaker Jon Ronson's TED Talk on psychopathy has over 24 million views on YouTube. Ronson's description of psychopathy is accessible and, to some, entertaining (TED, 2012, August 12). Although I take issue with Ronson's depiction of the academic literature on psychopathy, he at least satisfies Wittgenstein's emphasis on making his definition of psychopathy public. I can point out the aspects of Ronson's depiction of psychopathy that I disagree with. The academic literature's failure to publicly express its views on psychopathy means that audiences are unable to identify instances in which Ronson's description of psychopathy conflicts with academic descriptions of psychopathy. As will become clearer in Chapter 2, Ronson's description of psychopathy is, at best, an inaccurate representation of the academic literature. At worst, Ronson's TED Talk is disingenuous storytelling. Subject-matter experts must accept responsibility here. Audiences who are new to the concept of psychopathy cannot be expected to identify incorrect descriptions of academic definitions of psychopathy. Such an expectation is especially unreasonable when academic descriptions of psychopathy remain both literally and figuratively private.

To reiterate, making academic research on psychopathy more public and less private and more accessible and less inaccurate does not require the development of a universally agreed-upon definition of psychopathy. In fact, universal definitions of a phenomenon can be problematic. As Wittgenstein noted, absolute or fixed definitions give the impression that "some thing" is "one thing." Psychopathy is polysemous; it refers to different ideas both within and outside of academic and clinical settings. Moreover, descriptions of psychopathy evolve over time. If good science is self-correcting, then revisiting descriptions and revising measures of psychopathy in light of new information should be encouraged (Skeem & Cooke, 2010). Subject-matter experts can be more public about their work by writing for *The Conversation* and other outlets designed to communicate scientific research. TEDx Talks, media interviews, and using social media are a few examples of how to improve knowledge mobilization.

Academic Pessimism Regarding Psychopathy

The failure of subject-matter experts to communicate the meaning of psychopathy has also led to skepticism in some academic circles regarding the existence or meaningfulness of psychopathy and the methodological rigor of psychopathy research (Maruna, 2025). Subject-matter experts too often have made flippant claims about psychopathy, including that it factors into all crime (DeLisi, 2016) and that it is untreatable (Harris & Rice, 2017). Such claims have been glommed onto by other academics who do not read the psychopathy literature more fully or seemingly ignore other psychopathy research if it does not fit their desired narrative. In this case, the desired narrative is to depict psychopathy research as biased and lacking in rigour. For example, some writers have overlooked a substantial body of recent research showing that psychopathy traits can change over time (e.g., Hawes et al., 2014; McCuish & Lussier, 2021) and instead concluded that mainstream psychopathy research denies the possibility of change among people with psychopathy traits (American Society of Criminology, 2024; Larsen, 2025; Maruna, 2025).

If the meaning of psychopathy cannot be communicated clearly, why should anyone believe that it exists? Edwin Sutherland, whose training was in sociology and who became one of the pioneers of criminology, rightfully criticized psychiatrists for discussing psychopathy without addressing how to measure the construct in a reliable way (Sutherland, 1949). Similarly, given the lack of reliable and valid measures Tennenbaum (1977) questioned the value of constructs like psychopathy to the study of criminal behaviour. From Sutherland's perspective, the definition of psychopathy seemed to vary from one psychiatrist to the next and was, in effect, used as a multipurpose tool that allowed a person's difficult behaviour to suddenly be understood and explained. In effect, resembling Wittgenstein's beetle in a box experiment, each psychiatrist was confined to looking inside their own psychopathy box without considering how others described psychopathy.

Sutherland and Tennenbaum's criticisms had a lasting impact on sociologists' and criminologists' perspectives on psychopathy.[2] For example, at

---

[2] The issue is not that Sutherland and Tennenbaum were wrong about the lack of reliable measures of psychopathy. The issue is that psychologists eventually addressed these criticisms, a fact that seems to be overlooked by commentators some who adopt a narrow reading of the psychopathy literature.

the 2023 American Society of Criminology Conference in Philadelphia Pennsylvania, the largest criminology conference in the world, then-President Dr. Shadd Maruna delivered his Presidential Address to conference attendees (see American Society of Criminology, 2024[3]). As part of this address, Dr. Maruna posited that psychopathy was essentially a disorder "invented in the 1990s in academia" by a group of Canadians on the fringes of forensic psychology who brought this "bizarre idea" into mainstream psychology. Dr. Maruna's framing of psychopathy as a Canadian idea that exists on the fringes of psychology contrasts with the fact that there are dozens of translations of psychopathy measures that are used throughout the world (Hoff et al., 2014). As illustrated in the following sections, at odds with Maruna's claim that psychopathy was "invented in the 1990s in academia" (American Society of Criminology, 2024) is the fact that descriptions of psychopathy date back thousands of years.

Early Descriptions of Psychopathy

Descriptions of psychopathy traits emerged centuries before the term "psychopathy" entered the daily language of forensic psychologists. For example, Theophrastus (371–287 BCE), a student of Aristotle, described the "unscrupulous man" as manipulative and unrepentant. Yildrim (2015) provides an excellent historical tracing of psychopathy's conceptual origins. Psychopathy traits have been described in Shakespeare plays (e.g., Aaron the Moor in Titus Andronicus). The idea of psychopathy traits is not just a Western phenomenon. The Yoruba people in Nigeria use the term "Arana Kan" to describe someone who is malicious, bullheaded, and defies others. The term "kulangeta" is used by Yupik-speaking Inuit Peoples to describe people who persistently lie, steal, cheat, and know that what they are doing is wrong but simply do not bother to change (see Kiehl, 2015). The term "psychopathy" may have been "invented" by researchers, but that does not make the traits that underscore the psychopathy construct any less real.

French psychologist Philippe Pinel (1745–1826) is credited with providing one of the first formal attempts to describe psychopathy. Pinel used the term *manie sans délire* to describe people whose problem behaviour (*manie*) occurred without (*sans*) the presence of delusions (*délire*). Pinel used this term to describe people who were aware that they were engaging

---

[3] The Presidential Address is available on YouTube (www.youtube.com/watch?v=VR9cJMgstb8) and discussions of psychopathy, including the idea that it was "invented," begin around 26:45.

in harmful behaviour but simply did not care. This contrasted with much of the prior work in psychiatry that aimed to identify disorders in which people were either entirely unaware of their behaviour or unaware that their behaviour was wrong or causing harm. American psychiatrist Benjamin Rush (1812) suggested that because people were aware of, but ultimately morally unconcerned by, their own behaviour, it was of religious and legal importance to have psychiatry assist in the treatment of psychopathy (see Millon et al., 1998). Psychiatrists like Pinel and Rush viewed people with psychopathy traits as morally ambiguous (e.g., lacking remorse). Pinel and Rush believed that people were born with these traits and, in the absence of intervention, would remain indifferent regarding the impact of their behaviour.

British psychiatrist J. C. Prichard had a much different perspective than Pinel and Rush. He believed that people with psychopathy traits enjoyed harmful behaviour and therefore described the psychopath as morally deplorable. Whereas Pinel and Rush called for medical intervention rather than incarceration, Prichard called for severe social and legal punishment (see Toch, 1998). This description of Prichard's perspective is not intended as an endorsement. Rather, it illustrates the type of unsubstantiated claim about psychopathy from certain psychiatrists that Sutherland later criticized.

German scholar Julius Koch (1892) was perhaps the first to use the term psychopathy ("psychopathische"). He used this term to describe the "suffering soul." Critical to informing contemporary definitions of psychopathy was Koch's emphasis that psychopathy traits were stable over the life-course and consistent across social situations. Ultimately, descriptions of psychopathy traits by Koch, Prichard, Rush, and Pinel received criticism for being overly broad. Under these descriptions, essentially any deviation from reason or morality was viewed as an indicator of psychopathy (Ellard, 1988).

The path from Pinel to contemporary descriptions of psychopathy that inform twenty-first century research hardly followed a straight line. Whereas psychiatrists like Pinel and Koch emphasized personality dimensions of psychopathy, psychiatrists of the early twentieth century tended to use the construct of psychopathy as an amorphous placeholder for classifying abnormal behaviour, especially sexual offences (Lussier et al., 2021; Veal & Ogloff, 2022). In contrast to twenty-first century research, which often uses psychopathy to understand criminal behaviour, twentieth-century research tended to use atypical criminal behaviours to describe psychopathy. In this earlier era, it was not the personality traits of the patient that led to a psychopathy diagnosis, but rather the nature of the behaviour that was perpetrated. In the early twentieth century, certain psychiatrists and political figures used this view of psychopathy to justify eugenics, including the forced sterilization of patients treated for psychopathy (Rafter, 1997). German psychiatrist Richard von Krafft-Ebing (1904) described people with psychopathy traits as "morally depraved" and "savages." He felt that the answer to psychopathy was social condemnation, ostracism, and long-term incarceration (see Arrigo & Shipley, 2001; Toch, 1998). The tendency for the True Crime genre of the twenty-first century to describe psychopathy in the same way that it was described during the eugenics movement of the twentieth century is a major reason for my pushback against popular culture's representation of the academic literature on psychopathy.[4]

By the mid-twentieth century, perspectives on psychopathy shifted away from punishment and condemnation and back toward a focus on treatment. Although this may sound like a progressive approach, treatment strategies of this era were far from humane (see Chapter 2). Although there was more of a focus on treatment, psychiatrists continued to get things backward by focusing on the crime committed to make a diagnosis of psychopathy. For example, Sexual Psychopath Laws were created in the mid-twentieth century to give courts the power to label a person a psychopath if their offence was of a sexual nature (Karpman, 1948). Koch's emphasis that psychopathy was defined by personality traits was not reflected in these laws. Similarly, Pinel's emphasis on how people with psychopathy traits were aware of their behaviour was forgotten and replaced with the view that the sexual psychopath had little or no control over their behaviour (Roth, 1952).

Psychiatrists tended to ascribe the psychopathy label to people whose behaviour did not fit within social convention. Sociologists were especially critical of psychiatry's tendency to pathologize any sign of perceived dysfunction, including homosexuality, hysteria, divorce, and both over- or under-participation in social affairs (Becker, 1963). Psychiatrists were often concerned with less severe forms of social deviancy because cases of extreme violence or perversion were thought to be preceded by these less serious behaviours. Unfortunately, psychiatrists overlooked an obvious but critical question. Specifically, how often do people involved in minor forms of perceived social deviancy go on to perpetrate acts of extreme

---

[4] For example, the True Crime television show *Signs of a Psychopath* retrospectively examines people involved in heinous crimes and, based solely on the nature of those crimes, makes assumptions that the perpetrator must therefore be a psychopath.

violence? This issue, referred to as a false positive error, pervaded psychiatry and psychology research for decades. In reality, people involved in minor forms of social deviance rarely escalated to more harmful behaviours.

In sum, although nineteenth-century descriptions of psychopathy focused on personality traits, the early ideas of Pinel and Koch were co-opted in the early twentieth century. Psychopathy became a device used by psychiatrists to label certain unwanted or atypical behaviours. It took nearly half a century to realign the focus of psychopathy research with its conceptual roots.

The DSM and Its Failed Attempt to Clarify Psychopathy as a Mental Disorder

To address concerns about broad, vague, and subjective descriptions of mental disorders, the American Psychiatric Association created the *Diagnostic and Statistical Manual of Mental Disorders* (DSM). The DSM is referred to as "the bible of US psychiatry" (Pickersgill, 2012, p. 544) and includes sections on how to use the manual, diagnostic criteria for different conditions, and on emerging measures and models, including attention to how cultural differences might impact assessment. The first version of the DSM was developed in 1952, and although it was not developed specifically to resolve issues with inconsistencies in the description of psychopathy, one of its goals was to reduce conceptual drift. Specifically, it was recognized that how psychopathy was described by Pinel and Koch differed from how psychiatrists later applied the concept (e.g., creation of Sexual Psychopathy Laws) as a catch-all category for socially undesirable or aberrant behaviour (Karpman, 1951).

Psychopathy, Sociopathy, and Antisocial Personality Disorder in the DSM

I am about to describe a relatively confusing history of how the terms psychopathy, sociopathy, and antisocial personality disorder have been used. To reduce confusion, it may be helpful to keep in mind that these three terms,[5] at least in my view, do not represent three different disorders. Over the history of the DSM, three different terms have been used, all of which were intended to describe the same disorder characterized by maladaptive personality traits. Where the terms differ is with respect to

---

[5] To add to the confusion, the term dissocial personality disorder is also used as an alternative term to psychopathy (Arrigo & Shipley, 2001).

(1) the level of detail with which they describe personality traits and (2) the importance given to criminal behaviour as a defining feature of the disorder. This reflects a problem, not just with the DSM, but with a failure by subject-matter experts to address confusion about psychopathy, sociopathy, and antisocial personality disorder. This inconsistency has created confusion not only among jurors and other laypeople but even among subject-matter experts. For example, professionals tasked with assessing psychopathy have reported experiencing challenges in their forensic practices due to changing definitions and opinions on psychopathy (Arrigo & Shipley, 2001).

The DSM-I and DSM-II used the term sociopathic personality disturbance to reflect Dr. Hervey Cleckley's (1941, 1976) description of psychopathy in his groundbreaking book, *The Mask of Sanity*.[6] Cleckley's book was a response to vague descriptions of psychopathy that dominated the first half of the twentieth century. Cleckley's book aligned with the DSM's overarching goal of formalizing the definition of disorders like psychopathy. In line with Pinel and Koch, instead of defining psychopathy by the presence of abnormal criminal behaviour, Cleckley's description focused on maladaptive personality traits, such as callous disregard for others. It is not entirely clear why the DSM borrowed so heavily from Cleckley's description of psychopathy yet decided to use an entirely different term in sociopathic personality disturbance. One possibility is that the DSM-I and DSM-II emphasized that sociopathic personality disturbance included persistent involvement in antisocial behaviour. Thus, sociopathic personality disturbance included descriptions of psychopathic personality traits but also included the consequences of these traits.

In the 1970s, the American Psychiatric Association initiated a major overhaul of the DSM. This overhaul included removing all references to sociopathy as a clinical construct. The DSM-III replaced sociopathic personality disturbance with antisocial personality disorder. The change in name, despite an effort to capture the same concept, is similar to how Coca-Cola replaced "old Coke" with a slightly sweeter version of "new Coke" in 1985 (only to return to "Classic Coke" shortly thereafter). Antisocial personality disorder was meant to reflect the same construct as psychopathy/sociopathic personality disturbance. However, in the eyes of

---

[6] What Cleckley means by a mask of sanity can be inferred from the epigraph of his book, which reads "non teneas aururm totum quod splendet ut aururm." This quote is attributed to French theologian and poet Alanus de Insulis (Alain de Lille) and translates to "do not hold everything as gold that shines like gold" (Israel, 1997). *The mask of sanity* was meant to describe individuals who are able to feign or conceal their true feelings.

many researchers, antisocial personality disorder failed to capture Cleckley's focus on personality traits.

Dr. Lee Robins spearheaded the transition from sociopathic personality disturbance to antisocial personality disorder. Part of the goal of the DSM-III was to develop more objective methods of measuring disorders. Although this goal was reasonable in principle, Robins' efforts to make the assessment of psychopathy more reliable resulted in stripping away the consideration of personality traits, which were previously considered core components of psychopathy. For example, Cleckley's description of psychopathy emphasized that traits such as a lack of remorse were key indicators of the construct. Such traits were accounted for in DSM-I and DSM-II descriptions of sociopathic personality disturbance. Robins believed that it would be difficult for psychiatrists from different jurisdictions to reliably assess emotional traits like remorse. Therefore, such traits were removed from the criteria for antisocial personality disorder. Robins believed that histories of antisocial and criminal behaviour could be assessed more objectively and reliably, and thus such behaviours were prioritized in the definition of antisocial personality disorder/psychopathy. Before being quick to judge Robins' decision, keep in mind the state of psychology and psychiatry at the time. Critics like Sutherland questioned the subjective decision-making of psychiatrists. Robins' revisions addressed concerns about vague and broad descriptions of disorders by moving the measurement of antisocial personality disorder/psychopathy toward more objective criteria.

Antisocial personality disorder, which remains in the most recent version of the DSM (DSM-5), in essence reflects a watered-down version of psychopathy. Criteria for antisocial personality disorder are as follows (see DSM-5 for precise descriptors):

- The individual must be at least 18 years of age at the time of assessment.
- Evidence of at least three forms of antisocial or criminal behaviour occurring since age 15, including participation in illegal acts, aggressive behaviour, irresponsible behaviour, and lack of remorse.
- Evidence of at least three forms of antisocial or criminal behaviour prior to age 15, including frequent bullying, frequent fighting, cruelty to animals, cruelty to people, and sexual behaviour problems.
- Behaviours are not occurring during expressions of symptoms of schizophrenia.

Measuring antisocial personality disorder using indicators proclaimed to be more objective came at a cost. Similar to the difference between a cold and pneumonia, the measurement criteria for antisocial personality disorder (a cold) are effectively a watered-down version of psychopathy (pneumonia). Only about one in three people who meet the criteria for antisocial personality disorder also score high on contemporary measures of psychopathy (e.g., PCL-R).[7]

Researcher Opposition to Antisocial Personality Disorder

Several subject-matter experts disagreed with Robins' decision to emphasize behavioural characteristics of psychopathy in the DSM's description of antisocial personality disorder. Shipley and Arrigo (2001) questioned how the DSM could claim that antisocial personality disorder adequately reflected the psychopathy construct when most of the core personality traits that define psychopathy were ignored by the DSM criteria. Millon (1981) argued that the criteria for antisocial personality disorder were overly inclusive. Too many people would be identified as having antisocial personality disorder/psychopathy. For example, Michael, discussed in the Preface of this book, represents the type of person who might be classified as a psychopath if the focus were mainly on behavioural characteristics. Millon felt that ignoring personality characteristics meant that antisocial personality disorder criteria failed to clarify *why* criminal behaviours were being perpetrated in the first place and thus would not be helpful for guiding treatment. Similarly, Gacono and Hutton (1994) acknowledged that the unique traits of psychopathy that were important for understanding the development of criminal behaviour had been excluded from the DSM's description of antisocial personality disorder.

Hart and Hare (1997) raised concerns that DSM-III criteria for antisocial personality disorder were not selected based on empirical evidence of their ability to predict future criminal behaviour. There was also no empirical basis for the decision to require at least three behavioural indicators and to distinguish between indicators occurring before vs. after age 15. Why three behavioural indicators and not four? Why age 15 and not age 14? In effect, psychopathy's rebranding from sociopathic personality disturbance to antisocial personality disorder was not driven by science[8] but by a desire for

---

[7] More recent versions of the DSM have revised the criteria for antisocial personality disorder in ways that bring it closer to contemporary clinical descriptions of psychopathy (Lynam & Vachon, 2012), but these criteria still are less exhaustive than those used in contemporary measures of psychopathy.

[8] It was not as if Robins demonstrated that the criteria outlined in the DSM-III for antisocial personality disorder were the best way to measure psychopathy. This shift was a matter of

simplicity. The behavioural criteria for antisocial personality disorder also exhibit substantial redundancy. For example, engaging in sexually coercive behaviour before age 15 could also be viewed as a form of criminal behaviour, a form of bullying, and a form of cruelty to others.

Reviewing the DSM's Contribution to Psychopathy Descriptions

To summarize, in theory, sociopathic personality disturbance and antisocial personality disorder are not different constructs. Nor are they, in theory, different from psychopathy. At different times, the DSM has used sociopathic personality disturbance and antisocial personality disorder as clinical concepts meant to represent psychopathy. Different names for the same thing.

Reference to sociopathic personality disturbance essentially has been extinguished from academic research on psychopathy for nearly half a century. Reference to sociopathy is found almost exclusively in popular culture, where it is used as a tool to identify people who persistently engage in antisocial behaviour. Unfortunately, such usages have misled audiences into believing that sociopathy is a clinical term with contemporary importance and distinct from psychopathy. For example, in the BBC television series *Sherlock Holmes*, the titular character claims that they are not a "psychopath" but rather a "high functioning sociopath" and that it is important to "know the difference." The difference, in the mind of Sherlock and others,[9] is that psychopathy has a genetic cause, whereas sociopathy has an environmental cause. In reality, contemporary academic literature rarely references sociopathy and certainly does not contrast psychopathy with sociopathy. Despite the persistence of discussions of sociopathy, even in science-promoting blogs (Jewell & Raypole, 2024), reference to sociopathy has disappeared from the DSM. The term has also disappeared from the research agendas of subject-matter experts. For example, the term psychopathy appeared in the 2024 American Psychology-Law Society Annual Conference Program on 90 occasions.

---

professional networking and politics. Robins was in the inner circle of Robert Spitzer, the psychiatrist tasked with revamping the DSM-III.

[9] Other ways in which popular culture has distinguished psychopathy from sociopathy are by describing psychopathy as more manipulative and intelligent and sociopathy as more unpredictable and unrestrained (e.g., "@drjaleelmohammed" of TikTok). Although people like "@mindfoodsteph" on TikTok might be holding a copy of the DSM-V while making these claims, those who actually read the DSM-V will not come across this distinction.

Sociopathy/sociopathic personality disturbance was not mentioned once. In the academic literature, research on sociopathic personality disturbance has effectively gone by the wayside.

In addition to sociopathy, antisocial personality disorder is commonly used to refer to psychopathy. After stripping away references to personality trait indicators of psychopathy, antisocial personality disorder, as originally defined in the DSM-III, effectively described people who were chronically involved in antisocial behaviour. The DSM-III intended for antisocial personality disorder to reflect psychopathy, just not the personality-based version of psychopathy described by Cleckley and others. Lynam and Vachon (2012) argued that the DSM missed an opportunity to unify the constructs of psychopathy and antisocial personality disorder by allowing the description of these two constructs to drift apart.

In sum, antisocial personality disorder was, in theory, intended to represent psychopathy. However, the criteria used to measure antisocial personality disorder provide such limited coverage of psychopathy traits that, in practice, it makes very little sense to consider psychopathy and antisocial personality disorder as two names for the same thing. It is noteworthy that subject-matter experts with different perspectives on core traits of psychopathy nevertheless agree that DSM-based definitions of antisocial personality disorder have conceptually drifted substantially from definitions of psychopathy (Haslam, 2003; Lynam & Vachon, 2012; Millon, 1981).

Contemporary Descriptions of Psychopathy

With the DSM's use of antisocial personality disorder only scratching the surface of psychopathy traits,[10] subject-matter experts have developed their own descriptions and measures of psychopathy. Virtually all contemporary descriptions of psychopathy were heavily influenced by Cleckley's book, *The Mask of Sanity*. In this section, I begin by describing Cleckley's version of psychopathy. I explain how Cleckleyan psychopathy remains one of the dominant contemporary perspectives on psychopathy. I also discuss three other perspectives that, although clearly influenced by Cleckley, also have

---

[10] Excluded from this discussion is the relatively recent development in the DSM-V of using limited prosocial emotions as a specifier attached to the diagnostic criteria for conduct disorder. This represents another way of capturing the construct of psychopathy under a different name. However, there are concerns that this approach, like antisocial personality disorder, may overestimate the prevalence of psychopathy (Colins et al., 2020).

unique characteristics that have resulted in distinct contributions to how psychopathy is measured and researched in the twenty-first century.

The Mask of Sanity as a Foundation for Contemporary Research on Psychopathy

In his book, Cleckley used a series of case studies from his experience working with psychiatric patients to emphasize four main characteristics of psychopathy. These characteristics are central in virtually all contemporary descriptions of psychopathy.[11] First, psychopathy manifests in a wide range of social domains, including interactions at school, work, with family, friends, and intimate partners. The assessment of psychopathy, therefore, should not be restricted to a person's criminal interactions. Second, psychopathy requires an examination of a person's thoughts, feelings, attitudes, and behaviours. This implies that interviews are essential for assessing a person's emotions and views toward people. This second characteristic of psychopathy was disregarded by Robins when developing the criteria for antisocial personality disorder. Third, psychopathy is a multidimensional construct. This means that psychopathy is the manifestation of multiple traits from different domains of personality functioning that come together to form the overarching construct. Fourth, because psychopathy includes subjective indicators of personality traits,[12] nuanced and comprehensive measures were needed. Cleckley (1976, pp. 28–29) was clear that the measurement of psychopathy was complex and required consideration of traits from multiple domains.

Cleckley did not address his own call to develop nuanced measures of psychopathy. However, he left a detailed map for others to follow.[13] Through case studies of his former patients, Cleckley identified 16 traits spanning interpersonal, affective, and behavioural domains of functioning. Interpersonally, Cleckley defined psychopathy by manipulative, superficially

---

[11] Not everything Cleckley wrote is endorsed in contemporary descriptions of psychopathy. For example, Cleckley suggested that intelligence, low levels of anxiety, fearlessness, and boldness were core features of psychopathy. The relevance of these traits has been, and continues to be, the subject of much debate.

[12] By subjective, I mean that such traits require some inference to assess. For example, a lack of empathy cannot be observed directly, but it can be inferred either from statements from the person being assessed or by their responses and attitudes toward scenarios.

[13] It is important to distinguish between how psychopathy is described and how it is measured. As Cooke et al. (2022) explained, a measure of psychopathy is like a map used to navigate the terrain. The map is not a perfect reflection of the terrain; however, some maps are more detailed and more closely capture the nuances of the terrain than others (Cooke et al., 2022).

charming, and manipulative traits. Affectively, Cleckley viewed a lack of remorse, empathy, and connectivity to others as the prototypical features of psychopathy. Affective traits included a lack of emotional depth beyond the superficial, figuratively implying that psychopathy includes an ability to hear, but not feel, the music (i.e., semantic aphasia). Behaviourally, he described psychopathy as involving socially disruptive and antisocial behaviour. Although some of Cleckley's patients were involved in criminal behaviour, evidence of prior involvement in criminal behaviour was not viewed as essential to the assessment of psychopathy (Arrigo & Shipley, 2001).

It was not until several decades after Cleckley's description of psychopathy that researchers attempted to systematically measure Cleckley's version of psychopathy. Robert Hare and David Cox (1978) initiated the formal measurement of Cleckley's definition of psychopathy by developing a "7-point scale of psychopathy, the conceptual framework for the ratings being typified best by Cleckley's (1976) *The Mask of Sanity*" (Hare, 1980, p. 111; emphasis in original). This preliminary scale marked the starting point for the development of the PCL, and then, after a period of refinement, the Psychopathy Checklist – Revised (PCL-R; Hare, 2003). The PCL-R consists of 20 items, each scored on a three-point scale, that measure deficits in interpersonal, affective, behavioural, and antisocial domains of functioning. These items are rated by experts who have been trained in the assessment of psychopathy. Although the PCL-R is the most widely-used measure of psychopathy and often described as the gold standard, it is important not to conflate the PCL-R *with* psychopathy. As Gatner (2019) pointed out, "a PCL-R score is not psychopathy any more than an intelligence test score is intelligence itself" (p. 5). The most common criticism of PCL measures (there is also a screening version and a youth version) is their inclusion of items reflecting involvement in criminal behaviour, which marks a drift from Cleckley's description of psychopathy (Skeem & Cooke, 2010). Hare has responded to these criticisms on multiple occasions (see Chapter 2), and has argued (Hare, 2022) that the field should not be too quick to universally accept Cleckley's definition of psychopathy. Just as a single measure of psychopathy should not be confused *with* psychopathy, Cleckley's description of psychopathy should not be regarded as the universal truth about psychopathy.

Although not accepted as a universal definition, Cleckley's description of psychopathy, in addition to influencing the development of PCL measures, has helped form the basis of three additional major perspectives on the definition of psychopathy. Table 1.1 summarizes the extent to which these perspectives converge and diverge on key points. If there was

Table 1.1 Contemporary descriptions of psychopathy

Definition	Key measure	View of successful psychopathy	Structure of psychopathy	Criminal behaviour as indicator of psychopathy	Key traits
Cleckley	PCL Family (Expert Rating)	Possibly	Multidimensional; additive	Possibly	Affective personality traits[†]
Comprehensive Assessment of Psychopathic Personality (CAPP)	CAPP Interview (Expert Rating); CAPP Self-Report	No	Multidimensional; additive	No	Self-centred, manipulative, unempathic[††]
Triarchic model	Psychopathic Personality Inventory – Revised (PPI-R), Triarchic Psychopathy Measure (Tri-PM) (Self-Report)	Yes. Boldness provides a mask of sanity	Sometimes treated as multidimensional; Orthogonal	No	Boldness, meanness, disinhibition[†††]
Extreme version of general personality	Elemental Psychopathy Assessment (Self-Report)	Possibly	Multidimensional; additive	No	Unspecified

Notes. [†] Cleckley (1976); [††] Hoff et al. (2012); [†††] Patrick (2010a).

any doubt as to Cleckley's contribution to contemporary descriptions of psychopathy, Westen and Weinberger (2004) summarized his work as follows (p. 599):

> Virtually all current research on psychopathy presupposes the observations of a brilliant clinical observer [Cleckley, 1941/1976] whose clinical immersion among psychopaths over 60 years ago still provides the foundation for the measure [the PCL-R] considered the gold standard in psychopathy research.

The Triarchic Model of Psychopathy

The triarchic model of psychopathy was developed based on a review of theoretical and clinical descriptions of psychopathy, including Cleckley's work, as well as empirical research on psychopathy. This model proposes three dimensions of psychopathy: boldness, meanness, and disinhibition (Patrick, 2010b). Meanness and disinhibition reflect the affective and behavioural traits of psychopathy described by Cleckley. Two features of the triarchic model distinguish it from other contemporary descriptions of psychopathy. I discuss these in greater detail in Chapter 2. First, the triarchic model is distinct because of its emphasis on boldness as a defining feature. Boldness refers to the processes that allow a person to be manipulative or dominant over others or deceive others without any anxiety or nervousness (Patrick, 2022). Patrick (2010a, 2018) argued that boldness allows individuals to adopt the "mask of sanity" described by Cleckley. Dr. Scott Lilienfeld and others have suggested that boldness reflects Cleckleyan psychopathy descriptions of fearlessness that allow someone to lie without anxiety (Lilienfeld et al., 2016).

A second way in which the triarchic model is distinct from other descriptions of psychopathy is its suggestion that psychopathy can be an adaptive construct. This means that psychopathy may contribute to positive social and life outcomes, including associations with prosocial peers, higher levels of resiliency, and fewer internalizing problems like depression (see Dotterer et al., 2017). Patrick et al. (2012) specifically focused on the role of boldness as an adaptive trait that allowed people to act without fear. Most other descriptions, by contrast, emphasize that psychopathy is a maladaptive personality disorder that influences negative life outcomes.

Measures of psychopathy based on the triarchic model include the PPI-R (Lilienfeld & Widows, 2005) and the Tri-PM; (Patrick et al., 2009). Unlike the PCL-R, which requires a trained professional to conduct an interview and score the instrument, the PPI-R and Tri-PM are self-report instruments completed via a pencil-and-paper survey. Respondents rate a series of statements on a Likert scale (e.g., from "strongly disagree" to "strongly agree"). Research on the PCL generally reports positive correlations between interpersonal, affective, and behavioural traits (McCuish et al., 2018b) whereas research on triarchic-based measures indicate that boldness is orthogonal to meanness and disinhibition. The term orthogonal means that boldness is not correlated with meanness or disinhibition (Gatner et al., 2016; Lilienfeld et al., 2018a; Patrick, 2018; Patrick et al., 2009). It remains unclear whether this result reflects the uniqueness of the triarchic model itself or limitations inherent to self-report methods of assessing psychopathy.

Whereas the self-report nature of the PPI-R is a potential weakness, a strength of this instrument is that it was developed using a bottom-up approach. By contrast, the PCL-R and Psychopathy Checklist: Youth Version (PCL:YV) were developed using a top-down approach, in which traits were selected based on Cleckley's description of psychopathy and then validated based on the 20 items included. A bottom-up approach is where psychopathy traits are selected from a large list of possible traits. These traits are then included as items in a measurement tool. The measurement tool is further refined through statistical analysis, where items are culled or modified to improve reliability and validity (Livesley, 2007). A bottom-up approach tends to be more inclusive, thus reducing the likelihood that important traits were excluded from the measure. A bottom-up approach ensures that measures are data-driven and not only informed by clinical experience.

The Comprehensive Assessment of Psychopathic Personality

Unlike the triarchic model's suggestion that psychopathy traits are adaptive, the CAPP model (Cooke et al., 2004) was developed under the assumption that psychopathy reflects maladaptive personality traits. To avoid overreliance on Cleckleyan descriptions, the CAPP was developed through a systematic review of the academic literature. Whereas the PCL-R includes just 20 items, the CAPP model includes 33 items, referred to as symptoms. A unique feature of the CAPP is that it was developed and refined through interviews with subject-matter experts (Cooke et al., 2004, 2012). The validation of the CAPP conceptual model included prototypicality analysis, in which subject-matter experts reviewed individual symptoms of psychopathy included in the CAPP and specified the extent to which each symptom was emblematic of psychopathy. Thus, like the triarchic model, the CAPP model can be considered a bottom-up approach. The CAPP developers believed that it was better to identify through statistical analysis whether certain symptoms should be excluded from the construct (Cooke et al., 2012). This meant that the developers favored including symptoms even if they potentially were not central to psychopathy. To this point, all 33 symptoms have been retained in the CAPP conceptual model.

The symptoms of psychopathy identified in the CAPP conceptual model are described using a lexical approach. A lexical approach assumes that the meaning of psychopathy is encoded in natural language. Contrary to Maruna's assertion that psychopathy traits were "invented in the 1990s" (American Society of Criminology, 2024), the CAPP developers argued that since psychopathy traits have been observed for thousands of years, they should be describable using natural language rather than terms-of-art or scientific jargon (Cooke et al., 2012). This view of psychopathy aligns with Wittgenstein's (1993) argument that definitions are crafted through the contexts in which they are used in everyday life.

The 33 symptoms identified by the CAPP developers (Cooke et al., 2004) were conceptually allocated into 6 domains. The Attachment domain reflects a failure to form caring, close, and stable emotional bonds with others. The Behavioural domain involves problems developing adaptive strategies to deal with life tasks in a systematic, consistent, planned manner; instead, behaviour is impulsive and disruptive. The Cognitive domain describes rigid thought patterns, negative attitudes toward others, and poor concentration and planning. The Dominance domain focuses on problems in relationships, including a manipulative, insincere, controlling, and garrulous interpersonal style. The Emotion domain depicts an inability to fully experience and regulate certain emotions and issues with the appropriateness of affective responses. The Self domain reflects an unrealistic, incomplete, and egocentric self-identity in which people have an inflated perception of social roles and relations with others.

The CAPP-Institutional Rating Scale (CAPP-IRS) formalizes the measurement of the CAPP conceptual model (Cooke et al., 2012). Like the PCL, the CAPP-IRS is an expert-rating tool in which a trained assessor conducts an interview and subsequently rates symptoms. Unlike the PCL-R and PCL:YV, the CAPP-IRS avoids giving attention to a person's criminal history as part of the assessment of psychopathy. The CAPP-IRS developers thus prioritized the measurement of maladaptive personality traits associated with psychopathy. Even the Behavioural domain of the

CAPP-IRS avoids requiring raters to assess criminal conduct to complete ratings. Consistent with this focus, the absence of behavioural anchors in the CAPP-IRS ensures that the assessment emphasizes personality traits. For example, raters do not need to confirm specific behavioural anchors (e.g., "shouting at an intimate partner") to assess the severity of a symptom (e.g., "uncaring").

My experience implementing the CAPP-IRS (e.g., Dawson et al., 2012; McCuish et al., 2019) is that, as its name suggests, it is far more comprehensive than PCL-based measures of psychopathy. This benefit must be balanced against the longer administration time. I also feel that it took me longer to develop confidence in using the CAPP-IRS compared to the PCL:YV. This is not because the CAPP-IRS manual is less clear, nor do I believe that my training was insufficient. There is simply much more to consider when administering the CAPP-IRS. I certainly prefer both instruments to self-report measures. With incarcerated youth populations, I regularly witnessed participants struggling to understand interview questions. Semi-structured interviews allow for clarifying questions, something that is not possible with self-report survey measures.

Psychopathy Traits as Extreme Versions of Broader Personality

The CAPP defines psychopathy as a combination of maladaptive personality traits *specific* to psychopathy. A simpler perspective is that the personality traits that comprise psychopathy are not necessarily unique to psychopathy. Instead, the traits that comprise psychopathy reflect extreme versions of general personality traits. Describing psychopathy as an extreme expression of personality traits differs from perspectives that describe psychopathy as a personality disorder. Having a personality disorder implies some form of dysfunction or maladaptive consequence (e.g., involvement in criminal behaviour, negative social relationships). In contrast, having extreme personality traits does not necessarily imply dysfunction. For example, being extremely introverted is not necessarily maladaptive if steps are taken to be engaged socially when needed. Thus, the triarchic model views psychopathy as adaptive; the CAPP model views psychopathy as maladaptive; and the perspective that psychopathy merely reflects extreme versions of general personality is somewhat neutral on the matter. It is noteworthy that these three perspectives have such unique views despite all being influenced by Cleckley. This reiterates Wittgenstein's (1993) point about the importance of being public rather than private about definitions. One could claim that inside their box is not a beetle but "Cleckleyan psychopathy." However, failure to expand upon what "Cleckleyan psychopathy" means could result in assumptions of a shared understanding of psychopathy when, in reality, there are important differences.

There are several conceptual models that describe different dimensions of human personality. The five-factor model is especially prominent (see Miller, 2012, for a review). This model is commonly referred to as the "Big Five." The five-factor model specifies a hierarchical organization of personality traits from five domains: Extraversion, agreeableness, conscientiousness, neuroticism, and openness to experience. The acronyms "CANOE" and "OCEAN" are helpful devices for remembering these five traits. Extraversion describes the tendency to be assertive and sociable rather than quiet and reserved. Agreeableness describes a preference for being cooperative rather than combative. Conscientiousness describes the ability to approach tasks systematically and without distraction. Neuroticism refers to unstable and negative emotions rather than emotional stability. Openness to experience refers to a sensitivity to others and a willingness to try new things (Miller, 2012).

Widiger and Lynam (1998) outlined how psychopathy fits within the five-factor model. Again, it is the *extreme* expression of personality traits that relates to psychopathy. From the Extraversion factor, traits resembling psychopathy included an absence of warm and positive emotions. Another trait from the Extraversion factor, sensation-seeking, is present in extreme form for people with psychopathy traits. From the Agreeableness factor, traits relevant to psychopathy include the absence of modesty, care for others, and earnestness. From the Conscientiousness factor, a lack of discipline, goal-directed behaviour, and diligence are consistent with psychopathy. From the Neuroticism factor, traits include high levels of impulsivity and anger, along with a lack of depression. The fifth factor, Openness to Experience, was considered to lack any indicators of personality traits relevant to psychopathy (Lynam & Miller, 2015).

The Elemental Psychopathy Assessment (EPA; Lynam et al., 2011) was developed as a self-report questionnaire that reflects maladaptive versions of five-factor model traits. The EPA items measure interpersonal antagonism, emotional (in)stability, disinhibition, and narcissism dimensions of psychopathy. The EPA overlaps not just with the five-factor model but also with Cleckley's description of interpersonal, affective, and behavioural domains of dysfunction (Patrick et al., 2009; Sellbom et al., 2019). To combat concerns about self-report measures, the EPA includes two validity scales. One scale tests for inattention to survey questions (e.g., "I try to eat something almost every day"). The other scale assesses social desirability bias. Social desirability bias reflects a person's efforts to portray themselves in an overly positive light (e.g., "I have never in my life been angry at another person"). Like the CAPP conceptual model and the associated CAPP-IRS measure of psychopathy, the EPA favors an over-inclusive strategy by incorporating a broad range of personality traits to help identify and eliminate traits that are not central to psychopathy.

Chapter Summary

Although psychopathy is considered one of the most important concepts in forensic psychology and the criminal legal system (Monahan, 2006), the academic literature on psychopathy is relatively inaccessible to readers without prior background knowledge. This is unfortunate given the clear public interest in psychopathy research. This interest has been satiated by resources that are more easily accessible, including popular psychology books, TED Talks, and True Crime podcasts. Unfortunately, these resources tend to be wildly inaccurate and there is empirical evidence that they fail to advance the general public's understanding of psychopathy (Keesler & DeMatteo, 2017; Ostapchuk, 2018). I wrote this chapter with the goal of building toward a shared understanding of the history of psychopathy as a disorder. There is not too much of a divide between Pinel's concept of *manie sans délire* in the early nineteenth century and perspective on psychopathy in the twenty-first century. However, in the period between Pinel and contemporary research, there has been substantial variation in how psychopathy has been described. Some descriptions, especially in the early twentieth century, were influenced by positive attitudes toward the eugenics movement. Such descriptions were rightfully attacked by criminologists and sociologists (e.g., Sutherland, 1949; Tennenbaum, 1977). Although psychopathy research has evolved, the views of some criminologists have not necessarily been updated, leading to skepticism about the meaningfulness of psychopathy and the rigor of psychopathy research (American Society of Criminology, 2024; Maruna, 2025).

The DSM has contributed to confusion, not just among general audiences, but also among some subject-matter experts, about what psychopathy is and whether it is the same as antisocial personality disorder or sociopathy (Shipley & Arrigo, 2001). In short, the DSM has used both antisocial personality disorder and sociopathy as terms intended to represent psychopathy. The term sociopathic personality disturbance was replaced in later versions of the DSM by antisocial personality disorder.

The study of sociopathy has all but disappeared from the research agendas of subject-matter experts. Antisocial personality disorder represents a simplified, watered-down version of psychopathy that emphasizes behavioural manifestations of the construct and overlooks key personality traits.

Hervey Cleckley, a pioneer of contemporary psychopathy research, identified interpersonal, affective, and behavioural domains of functioning as central to psychopathy. The PCL-R, sometimes referred to as the gold standard in the assessment of psychopathy (Boduszek & Debowska, 2016), is based on Cleckley's description of psychopathy. Three other contemporary descriptions of psychopathy and their associated measurement tools include the triarchic model (and the PPI-R), the CAPP conceptual model (and the CAPP-IRS), and the view of psychopathy as an extreme manifestation of general personality traits (and the EPA). There is considerable overlap between these descriptions, especially in terms of the identification of interpersonal and affective traits as central features of psychopathy. However, as discussed in the next chapter, this overlap has not prevented plenty of debate within the academic literature on the nature of psychopathy.

CHAPTER 2

Psychopathy Debates, Myths, and Misconceptions

The academic literature on psychopathy can be quite contradictory. For example, if someone reads literature describing the triarchic model, they will likely reach conclusions about psychopathy that differ in important ways from the conclusions that are made by someone who focuses on psychopathy literature describing the Comprehensive Assessment of Psychopathic Personality (CAPP) model. The more someone reads, the more confusing things may seem. Dr. Chris Patrick compiled the *Handbook of Psychopathy*, which includes 31 chapters and over 800 pages (Patrick, 2018). Patrick's (2018) handbook could be read cover to cover and still leave readers uncertain about what constitutes the central personality traits of psychopathy. This is not to imply that individual chapters are unclear, only that there is substantial variation between chapters. In chapter 6 of the handbook, a lack of behavioural constraint is identified as central to psychopathy (Nelson & Foell, 2018). In chapter 7 of the handbook, affective dysfunction is described as the hallmark of psychopathy (Viding & Kimonis, 2018). In chapter 8 of the handbook, boldness is identified as the defining feature of psychopathy (Lilienfeld et al., 2018a). This is not a criticism of individual works, but it is important to acknowledge that, clearly, there is a lack of consensus about the defining features of psychopathy (Lilienfeld et al., 2012; Skeem & Cooke, 2010).

Chapter Goals

This chapter will not proclaim to uncover the "true" definition of psychopathy. Instead, I emphasize that different perspectives on psychopathy exist and explain how they differ. I focus on five debates in the academic literature on psychopathy. There are certainly more than five debates, but these five are especially helpful for clarifying why different perspectives on the definition of psychopathy exist. The point of discussing these debates is not to determine a winner but, instead, to illustrate where the different perspectives on psychopathy stand. The lens through which psychopathy is studied plays a critical role in what a given research community believes. For example, proponents of the triarchic model tend to study psychopathy by administering self-report surveys to college students. Proponents of the Psychopathy Checklist (PCL) tend to study psychopathy by conducting interviews with people who are incarcerated. Accordingly, not only is psychopathy being measured differently, but it is also studied within very different populations. It is no surprise that debates arise.

Debate #1: Is Criminal Behaviour a Trait or Consequence of Psychopathy?

Cleckleyan, triarchic, CAPP, and general personality models place limited to no emphasis on criminal behaviour as a characteristic of psychopathy. However, it is necessary to examine a person's history of antisocial behaviour and criminal legal system involvement when considering the *Diagnostic and Statistical Manual of Mental Disorders* (DSM) definition of antisocial personality disorder or when assessing psychopathy using instruments like the Psychopathy Checklist – Revised (PCL-R) and Psychopathy Checklist: Youth Version (PCL:YV). The inclusion of criminal behaviour items in the PCL-R, the most widely used measure of psychopathy, has led to substantial debate about whether criminal behaviour should be considered a psychopathy trait or instead a consequence of psychopathy traits. The height of this debate came in 2010, when Drs. Jennifer Skeem and David Cooke published a paper in *Psychological Assessment* questioning whether criminal behaviour was a central component of psychopathy. Drs. Robert Hare and Craig Neumann wrote a response defending the PCL-R.

The PCL Is Oversaturated with Criminal Behaviour Items

Skeem and Cooke (2010) argued that the PCL-R was oversaturated with items tapping into involvement in criminal behaviour. Five of the PCL-R's 20 items (see Hare, 2003) are represented under its Antisocial factor; 3 of these items require directly measuring criminal behaviour (juvenile delinquency, revocation of conditional release, and criminal versatility) and the other 2 require directly measuring evidence of criminal or antisocial behaviour (poor behavioural controls, early behavioural problems). Skeem and Cooke argued that if psychopathy is a personality disorder, then the measurement of psychopathy should focus on personality traits. Further, one of the most common reasons to measure psychopathy is to assist in establishing the likelihood of recidivism (Viljoen et al., 2010). Concerns about circular logic enter the debate if criminal behaviour is used to measure psychopathy, which then, in turn, is used to predict criminal behaviour. This is described as a tautological issue in which behaviour is used to predict behaviour.

Criminal Behaviour Is Not Emphasized in the PCL

Hare and Neumann (2010) argued that although criminal behaviour could be an indicator of psychopathy, the PCL-R did not actually place much emphasis on criminal behaviour. However, Neumann et al. (2015) later suggested that "antisociality is a core component of the psychopathy construct" (p. 678) and argued that any description or measure of psychopathy is incomplete if it does not include antisocial behaviour. Hare (2022) clarified that antisociality is different from criminality. He argued that antisociality is central to the PCL scales and to psychopathy, but that criminality and criminal behaviour are not. In some ways, this is true. PCL items focusing on indicators of antisociality, like poor anger control, are not necessarily measuring involvement in crime.

Although Hare (2022) argued that criminality is not central to the PCL scales, a closer look at the PCL-R manual indicates that raters are required to give substantial attention to a person's involvement in criminal behaviour. For example, one item from the PCL-R, revocation of conditional release, is entirely based on the extent to which an individual violates court orders. Another item is based on "serious criminal behaviour" and another based on "criminal versatility" (Hare, 2003). In Chapter 1, I introduced the concept of a behavioural anchor. The CAPP conceptual model of psychopathy emphasized that anchors are not specific symptoms/traits, but rather cues that can be used to help determine whether a specific symptom is present (Cooke et al., 2004). With the PCL scales, behavioural anchors appear to be direct measures of items that are meant to reflect antisociality. For example, the item measuring revocation of conditional release is likely meant to capture a person's criminogenic attitude, unwillingness to follow rules, and incorrigibility. However, instead of measuring personality traits emblematic of such attitudes, behavioural anchors (i.e., revocation of conditional release) were used to directly tap into such attitudes.

Summary of Debate #1

Involvement in criminal behaviour is emphasized as part of ratings on the PCL measurement tools. Three items require direct measurement of criminal behaviour. Other items *could*, but do not *necessarily*, get scored by referring to a person's involvement in criminal behaviour. The emphasis on criminal behaviour differs from other measurement tools such as the CAPP-Institutional Rating Scale (IRS) and the Psychopathic Personality Inventory – Revised (PPI-R). This reflects the view from the CAPP conceptual model and triarchic model that people with psychopathy traits are at a higher risk for criminal behaviour, but that criminal behaviour is not a direct indicator of psychopathy. This debate is directly addressed in Chapter 4, where I statistically examine whether criminal behaviour provides meaningful information about a person's level of psychopathy.

Debate #2: What Is the Structure of Psychopathy?

In this section, I review debate regarding the structure of psychopathy and whether/how different traits come together to form the psychopathy construct. Table 2.1 summarizes some key terms, listed in alphabetical order, that are used throughout this section. Following Lilienfeld et al.'s (2019) description of the literature, I highlight four perspectives on the structure of psychopathy: psychopathy as a taxonic syndrome, psychopathy as a classical syndrome, psychopathy as an emergent interpersonal syndrome, and psychopathy as a network syndrome. A syndrome implies that psychopathy represents a constellation of different traits (Lilienfeld, 2013). These four perspectives differ in their views on how psychopathy traits come together. Understanding the structure of psychopathy has important implications, particularly for identifying the causes of psychopathy and informing treatment strategies. If all psychopathy traits have a common cause, then that common cause should be treated. If psychopathy traits are uncorrelated and share distinct causes, then unique treatment strategies may be needed to address or prevent specific clusters of traits from emerging (see Lilienfeld, 2013; Lilienfeld et al., 2018a, 2019).

Understanding different perspectives on the structure of psychopathy requires clarifying what it means to describe psychopathy as a latent construct and as a multidimensional construct. A latent construct represents something that cannot be measured through direct observation. The term comes from the Latin "lateo," which means "to lie hidden" (Krabbe, 2017). Most people have a pretty good idea of what aggression is. However, aggression is not something that is directly observed. We do not see "aggression," but we do see specific actions and behaviours (e.g., yelling, punching, and kicking) that we label as aggressive. Thus, people can vary in the quantity and type of their aggression, but measuring

Table 2.1 *Key terminology when discussing the structure of psychopathy*

Term	Description	Key reading
Additive construct	Contrast with configural construct. All traits of psychopathy are correlated and thus can be summed together to reflect the overarching latent trait.	Lilienfeld et al. (2019). Personality disorders as emergent interpersonal syndromes: Psychopathic personality as a case example. *Journal of Personality Disorders, 33*(5), 577–622.
Classical syndrome	Contrast with emergent interpersonal and network syndromes. Individual psychopathy traits are caused by the overarching latent construct of psychopathy; these traits cluster together (i.e., are correlated). Views psychopathy as an additive construct.	Lilienfeld (2013). Is psychopathy a syndrome? Commentary on Marcus, Fulton, and Edens. *Personality Disorders: Theory, Research, and Treatment, 4*, 85–86.
Configural construct	Contrast with additive construct. Psychopathy is a multidimensional construct comprised of traits from interpersonal, affective, and behavioural dimensions. These dimensions are not necessarily correlated; psychopathy may be greater than the sum of its parts. Interactions with domains should be examined.	See additive construct reading.
Dimensional	People differ in their level of psychopathy traits, rather than there being qualitatively distinct groups where psychopathy traits are either fully present or fully absent.	Guay et al. (2007). A taxometric analysis of the latent structure of psychopathy: Evidence for dimensionality. *Journal of Abnormal Psychology, 116*(4), 701.
Emergent interpersonal syndrome	Contrast with classical and network syndrome perspectives. Based on the idea of a formative construct, where individual personality traits, when coming together, cause the construct of psychopathy.	See additive construct reading.
Formative construct	Contrast with reflective construct. When individual traits come together, they form a broader construct. The items of the PCL define (or cause) the construct measured.	Slaney et al. (2011). Is my test valid? Guidelines for the practicing psychologist for evaluating the psychometric properties of measures. *International Journal of Forensic Mental Health, 10*(4), 261–283.

Table 2.1 (*cont.*)

Term	Description	Key reading
Latent trait	Operationalizing a particular construct through the collection of different items.	Johnstone and Cooke (2004). Psychopathic-like traits in childhood: Conceptual and measurement concerns. *Behavioral Sciences & the Law*, 22(1), 103–125.
Multidimensional	Psychopathy is defined by multiple traits from different domains of personality functioning (e.g., interpersonal, affective, and behavioural).	Lilienfeld (2018). The multidimensional nature of psychopathy: Five recommendations for research. *Journal of Psychopathology and Behavioral Assessment*, 40, 79–85.
Network syndrome	Contrast with classical and emergent interpersonal syndromes. Endorses the idea that traits may cause each other as opposed to being caused by (or causing) a latent trait.	Verschuere et al. (2018). What features of psychopathy might be central? A network analysis of the Psychopathy Checklist-Revised (PCL-R) in three large samples. *Journal of Abnormal Psychology*, 127, 51–65.
Reflective construct	Contrast with formative construct. Individual traits come together because they reflect a common cause. Psychopathy causes the items of the PCL.	See formative construct reading.
Syndrome	From the Greek "to run together"; refers to the intersection of multiple traits from different domains of functioning. Whether these traits correlate with each other is debatable (e.g., classical syndrome versus emergent interpersonal syndrome).	See multidimensional reading.
Taxonic syndrome	The antithesis of a dimensional viewpoint; the idea that there are naturally occurring groups that can be classified as distinct entities.	See dimensional reading.

aggression requires examining behaviours and attitudes. Similarly, the notion of psychopathy as a latent construct means that psychopathy is not directly observed, but the traits that define psychopathy can be directly observed and measured.

A multidimensional construct implies that psychopathy reflects the intersection of multiple traits from different domains. From a general personality perspective, traits that comprise psychopathy are not unique to psychopathy. For example, self-centredness is a trait of psychopathy but also of narcissistic personality disorder. What distinguishes narcissistic personality disorder from psychopathy is with respect to which other traits co-occur with self-centredness. Psychopathy reflects a constellation of interpersonal, affective, and behavioural traits that occur together. Narcissistic personality disorder reflects the intersection of interpersonal and affective traits, but some of these traits, such as social vulnerability, are not the same traits observed in psychopathy. Narcissistic personality disorder also does not include many of the defining behavioural features of psychopathy (Miller et al., 2010). Conceptualizing psychopathy as a multidimensional disorder implies that instruments must measure the full breadth of psychopathy traits and avoid including foil traits irrelevant to psychopathy, so as to not misattribute other disorders (e.g., narcissistic personality disorder, borderline personality disorder) as psychopathy.

Psychopathy as a Taxonic Syndrome

Like other perspectives, the taxonic syndrome perspective describes psychopathy as a multidimensional latent construct. The distinguishing feature of the taxonic syndrome perspective is its claim that there are discrete groups of people who are qualitatively distinct from others. A taxon represents a discrete category in which there is a clear standard for who meets this category (e.g., fits inside the box) and who does not meet this category (e.g., fits outside this box). For example, everyone who is healthy has approximately the same temperature, and everyone who has the flu has approximately the same temperature. There is a clear gulf between the two groups. There is no grey area. From a taxonic syndrome perspective, there is a clear distinction between "psychopaths" and "nonpsychopaths." Taxonic syndrome perspectives are reflected in how research on the PCL-R in the 1980s and 1990s tended to classify anyone with a score of 30 or higher as a psychopath and anyone with a score lower than 30 as a nonpsychopath. However, empirical research provides little evidence that psychopathy is a discrete category (Guay et al., 2007, 2018; Walters et al.,

2007). Individuals vary in the degree of psychopathy traits, rather than fitting into sharply demarcated groups.

Referring to psychopaths as a distinct category of people is an example of William James' Psychologist's Fallacy (see Ashworth, 2009). The Psychologists' Fallacy describes how subjective experiences are mistaken for the true nature of a phenomenon. In the context of the assessment of psychopathy, interacting with someone with psychopathy traits can *feel* like talking to an entirely different type of person (Lilienfeld et al., 2018a). These traits may shape one's impression of someone, but this does not imply that psychopathy is a taxon. Instead, this unique impression may give credence to the idea of psychopathy as a folk concept that captures a recognizable character archetype (Lilienfeld et al., 2019). I am certainly not being critical of anyone who feels that their conversation with a person with psychopathy traits felt fundamentally different from conversations with other people. I have had this experience myself, and I discuss some of these conversations in Chapter 3. But, this experience does not make it a reality that people with psychopathy traits are a fundamentally distinct group of people. Conceptualizing psychopathy as a folk concept does not deny the existence of psychopathy traits. Rather, it highlights that psychopathy may not define a unique category of person, but instead reflects the distinctive impression that such individuals create, a sense that this is someone to guard against (Lilienfeld et al., 2018a).

Psychopathy as a Classical Syndrome

Unlike the taxonic syndrome perspective that psychopathy reflects a discrete class of people, the classical syndrome views psychopathy as a dimensional construct. A dimensional view should not be conflated with descriptions of psychopathy as multidimensional (i.e., co-occurrence of multiple traits). Dimensionality contrasts the idea that people are qualitatively distinct groups where psychopathy traits are either fully present or fully absent. The classical syndrome perspective also makes explicit hypotheses about how the traits comprising the latent construct of psychopathy come together. Specifically, psychopathy traits are described as existing causally downstream from the underlying psychopathy construct. From this perspective, psychopathy is a reflective construct because traits "reflect" the underlying latent construct (Krabbe, 2017). A key principle of the classical syndrome perspective is that, because traits share a common cause, they are highly correlated. The traits are therefore "additive," and so it is valid to represent the psychopathy construct by adding up scores on individual items. A key implication of viewing psychopathy as a classical syndrome is that treating the underlying disorder will address all individual psychopathy traits.

The CAPP conceptual model aligns with the classical syndrome perspective. Several studies have found support for the classical syndrome perspective using confirmatory factor analysis[1] (Jones et al., 2006). Critics of the classical syndrome note that methods examining correlations between items may be biased toward finding support for the classical syndrome (Lilienfeld et al., 2019). For perspectives on psychopathy like the triarchic model (Chapter 1) that view different dimensions of psychopathy as orthogonal (i.e., uncorrelated), methods like confirmatory factor analysis may be inappropriate because they tend to rule out traits that are uncorrelated.

Psychopathy as an Emergent Interpersonal Syndrome

Like the classical syndrome perspective, the emergent interpersonal syndrome perspective views psychopathy as a dimensional latent construct. The classical syndrome describes psychopathy as a reflective construct where psychopathy causes individual traits (i.e., top-down). In contrast, the emergent interpersonal syndrome perspective describes psychopathy as a formative construct where individual traits cause the construct of psychopathy (i.e., bottom-up; see Slaney et al., 2011). The classical syndrome perspective describes psychopathy as an additive construct where traits from different domains can be summed together. The emergent interpersonal syndrome perspective describes psychopathy as a configural construct, meaning that the different traits that comprise interpersonal, affective, and behavioural domains of functioning are not necessarily correlated (Lilienfeld et al., 2019). The PPI-R was developed to reflect the triarchic model of psychopathy. Research on the PPI-R indicated that boldness is not correlated with disinhibition (Lilienfeld et al., 2018a). Researchers should thus examine the interaction between domains as opposed to simply summing up domain scores (Lilienfeld et al., 2018a). To give a crude example, imagine that 90 percent of people who are interpersonally dominant, charismatic, and manipulative tend to also be

---

[1] Confirmatory factor analysis is discussed in greater detail in Chapter 4. In brief, confirmatory factor analysis is used to evaluate whether a measure of psychopathy is consistent with theoretical or clinical understandings of psychopathy. If Cleckley defined psychopathy by interpersonal, affective, and behavioural features, then does an instrument meant to measure Cleckleyan psychopathy (e.g., the PCL-R) have items that systematically cluster/correlate into interpersonal, affective, and behavioural dimensions?

warm, empathetic, and expressive. Thus, positive correlations between these two trait domains are common. However, the psychopathy "sweet spot" occurs when these traits diverge, thus representing atypical cases in which someone is extraverted and charming but also low in empathy, warmth, and caring (Lilienfeld et al., 2019).

Psychopathy as a Network Syndrome

Like the classical syndrome and emergent interpersonal syndrome perspectives, the network syndrome perspective views psychopathy as a dimensional construct. However, the network perspective is neutral with respect to whether psychopathy is a latent construct. The network syndrome perspective (e.g., Crego & Widiger, 2015) eschews both reflective and figurative construct descriptions of psychopathy. Instead, it considers the possibility that individual traits share bi-directional associations with other traits (e.g., a trait like lack of remorse may influence a trait like failure to accept responsibility and vice versa; see Lilienfeld et al., 2019). From a network modeling perspective, the centrality of a trait in relation to the overarching psychopathy network is determined by the strength of its associations with other traits, rather than by assuming a single overarching latent construct (Cramer et al., 2010).

Whereas the structure of psychopathy typically has been examined in terms of how many different factors (e.g., interpersonal, affective, and behavioural) underlie a particular measure and the relationship between factors (e.g., correlated per the CAPP or orthogonal per the triarchic model), network modeling is useful for determining which specific traits best represent psychopathy (Verschuere et al., 2018; Verschuere & Te Kaat 2020). The network syndrome perspective is relatively new and has received less empirical attention. However, psychopathology network modeling, discussed in Chapter 4, appears well-suited for examining whether psychopathy represents extreme manifestations of general personality traits.

Debate #3: Is There a Successful Version of Psychopathy?

The term successful psychopathy is typically used to describe people with psychopathy traits who experience socioeconomic success and/or commit crimes without being detected and punished (Persson & Lilienfeld, 2019). In theory, successful psychopathy describes people who, despite being unqualified, are able to work their way up the corporate ladder through charm and manipulation, including taking advantage of an intimate partner's financial generosity and then discarding them when they are no longer of value for improving social mobility. If successful psychopathy exists, people described by this term will not be found in jail cells but rather in boardrooms, country clubs, and other status-enhancing contexts.

Some argue that successful psychopathy is a contemporary phenomenon (Irtelli & Vincenti, 2017). This argument is based on the idea that modern profit-obsessed work environments, such as those depicted in films such as *Wall Street* and *The Wolf of Wall Street*, have created the "successful psychopath." I disagree with this assessment. In Chapter 1, I described the early twentieth-century tendency to use psychopathy as an amoebic placeholder for classifying abnormal behaviour, especially sexual behaviour. I believe the same mistake is being made in the early twenty-first century. People who behave selfishly for financial gain are often labeled as successful psychopaths despite lacking many of the hallmark traits of psychopathy. Such behaviour is a problem, but it is not necessarily attributable to psychopathy.

Whether the concept of successful psychopathy is endorsed seems to depend on whether psychopathy is viewed as an emergent interpersonal syndrome, in which traits can be adaptive, or a classical syndrome in which psychopathy traits are viewed as maladaptive. Those who describe psychopathy as an emergent interpersonal syndrome also tend to consider boldness central to psychopathy (Lilienfeld et al., 2019). Boldness is viewed as the essential characteristic of successful psychopathy. Boldness provides the adaptive ability to be charismatic, daring, and influence others without anxiety. In turn, these traits promote socioeconomic success, including employment in high-earning professions, a positive social reputation, and connection to prestigious people. From a classical syndrome perspective, since psychopathy is maladaptive, the idea of successful psychopathy is an oxymoron. Psychopathy cannot be successful if it causes social dysfunction. In addition to the idea of successful psychopathy hinging on whether psychopathy is viewed as adaptive or maladaptive, the endorsement of ideas about successful psychopathy also hinges on how success is defined.

Does Successful Psychopathy Depend on the Meaning of Success?

Some scholars have used Cleckley's (1976) book, *The Mask of Sanity,* as evidence of the notion of successful psychopathy (e.g., Ullrich et al., 2008). To me, this is a misreading of Cleckley's work. Cleckley's case studies describe people whose short-term financial gains are regularly interrupted by violence, the breakdown of relationships, hospitalization, and incarceration. As noted by Lynam and Miller (2015), Cleckley (1976) acknowledged that what would be considered successful psychopathy represents an incomplete manifestation of the disorder. Cleckley's description of patients in professional careers like "businessman," "scientist," and "physician" all appear within the section of his book describing "incomplete manifestations or suggestions of the disorder." Lilienfeld et al. (2018b) referred to Cleckley's writings as describing "a veneer of seemingly healthy functioning that disguises a severe affective and behavioral abnormality" (p. 516). I agree with this assessment, but I would add that this implies that there is no such thing as successful psychopathy by any true meaning of the term "success." We would have to define success very narrowly and superficially if we considered success to include relationships that were based on lies and careers that were unearned or formed through intimidation and bullying.

From my view of success, a person's lack of emotional depth, a core feature of psychopathy, cannot be considered socially adaptive, at least not in the long run. Yes, a lack of emotional depth may facilitate deception or acting without consideration of consequences, but this is hardly "success." A lack of emotional depth may help someone fire thousands of people to increase their own financial stability. However, should positive outcomes earned by stepping on the heads of others be viewed as an example of success? A person's high socioeconomic status should not be used as an indicator of success if such achievements are offset by the cost of being unhappy, emotionally distant, and without meaningful relationships. If success is intended to improve well-being, psychopathy should not be considered successful, given the myriad of social and health problems experienced by people with psychopathy traits (Beaver et al., 2014) and those who come into contact with them (Leedom, 2017).

Boldness and Research Samples

In my view, boldness without interpersonal and affective deficits is inherently positive. However, it is also my view that boldness without interpersonal and affective deficits is not reflective of psychopathy. Some studies make conclusions about psychopathy while examining boldness alone, without the co-occurrence of interpersonal and affective deficits (Lilienfeld et al., 2018a). The disagreement between researchers is not so much about whether boldness can influence success; it seems quite clear that it does. The tension comes from whether boldness on its own should be used to make broader conclusions about psychopathy and its relation to success. Any perspective that views psychopathy as a multidimensional construct must reject as empirical evidence of successful psychopathy those studies that only look at the relationship between boldness and success. Boldness alone would be, as Cleckley put it (1976), an incomplete example of the manifestation of psychopathy.

It may not be a coincidence that subject-matter experts who endorse notions of successful psychopathy tend to conduct research in the general population (e.g., college students) rather than in prisons. Psychopathy traits are rarely observed at high levels among the general population (Skeem & Mulvey, 2001). One of the pitfalls of viewing psychopathy as a dimensional construct is that it allows researchers to claim that they are studying psychopathy even though very few people in their sample have a high number of psychopathy traits.[2] My concern is that studying psychopathy in the general population results in psychopathy test scores that may reflect only high levels of boldness and not high levels of interpersonal/affective traits. Thus, increases in psychopathy test scores may be correlated with successful life outcomes, but these test scores do not capture psychopathy. On the other hand, it is possible that my pessimism toward the idea of successful psychopathy stems from my experience interviewing people in prison who were caught for their offences and tended to come from more troubled backgrounds. It is possible that researchers who study psychopathy in prisons fail to find evidence of successful psychopathy because we are examining a population where such success is unlikely to manifest. That said, in a community sample, using a screening version of the PCL-R, Coid et al. (2009) found that higher scores were associated with a lack of social success, including being unhoused, having suicidal thoughts/behaviours, and not working or being economically inactive.

Overall, the mental gymnastics required to produce evidence of successful psychopathy is like calling something chocolate after taking out the

---

[2] For example, researchers could claim that participants with a test score on a self-report measure of psychopathy that was 1 SD above their sample's mean are people with "high" psychopathy traits. The issue here is that the mean level of psychopathy traits is so extremely low that being 1 SD above the mean does not imply that a person scored high on this particular instrument. I could administer a multiple-choice university-level algebra exam to a group of fourth graders. Assuming that everyone fully completed the test, there would be some students who scored 1 SD above the mean. This does not mean they got a high grade; they simply were lucky to have guessed correctly on certain multiple-choice questions.

sugar/sweeteners (interpersonal deficits), the dairy/dairy substitutes (affective deficits), and the cocoa powder (behavioural deficits). Perhaps without these ingredients, you can still technically get to a point where you are allowed to call a product "chocolate" ("psychopathy"), but it would be far removed from the true essence of chocolate.

Debate #4: Can Self-Report Tools Measure Psychopathy Reliably?

Expert rating tools, such as the PCL-R or CAPP-IRS, are completed following a semi-structured interview and review of correctional files and other collateral sources. The reliable use of these measures requires formal training conducted by the developer of the tool or someone with substantial experience implementing the tool. Following training, interrater reliability is assessed by comparing the ratings of two or more assessors who independently rated the same person. Evidence of successful training (and successful reliability of the measurement tool) occurs when there is a high degree of overlap between multiple independent ratings of the same person. Self-report measures of psychopathy, such as the Triarchic Psychopathy Measure (Tri-PM), PPI-R, and Elemental Psychopathy Assessment (EPA), are based on structured surveys in which the participant reads a statement and responds using a Likert scale to signify the degree to which they agree or disagree with the statement. If reading comprehension is an issue, sometimes survey questions will be read aloud to a participant by a Research Assistant.

I have been trained in the use of both the PCL:YV and CAPP-IRS. I also have experience administering self-report measures of psychopathy. I cannot imagine a scenario in which I would prefer to use self-report measures. The training required and the length of time to complete an assessment make expert rating tools more expensive to implement. In my view, the downside of a longer assessment using an expert rating tool is outweighed by the downside of using a self-report tool that poorly measures psychopathy. The primary reason I hold this belief is outlined in the next section.

Self-Report Measures and the Inopportunity for Clarification

If psychopathy traits influence poor insight into one's own problems (e.g., a failure to recognize sensation-seeking or impulsive behaviour; a failure to recognize the consequences of interpersonal conflict), then perhaps measuring psychopathy in ways that exclusively rely on personal insight may be inappropriate.³ With self-report surveys, core psychopathy traits are especially susceptible to issues with reliable measurement. For example, empathy is susceptible to both intentional (e.g., lying about having empathy) and unintentional (e.g., poor insight into one's lack of empathy) response distortion (Gatner, 2019). Expert rating tools at least allow interviewers to ask follow-up questions and clarify participants' experience of emotions to elicit more nuanced detail. Expert rating tools also provide opportunities for clarifying questions in instances where a young person may misunderstand a question. For example, I regularly administered a survey that asked incarcerated youth whether they were able to "work out when other people were scared." The question was meant to examine the ability of youth to have insight into the emotions of others. It was not uncommon for youth to interpret "work out" as "hitting the gym." Without a Research Assistant to provide clarification, the reliability of this item would be compromised.

Some researchers have used parent- or teacher-reports to assess psychopathy. However, these measures appear somewhat unreliable given that there is a lack of convergence between parent and teacher reports on the same youth (Milledge et al., 2019). Parents, in particular, may be reluctant to acknowledge that their child lacks empathy or may have their own difficulties with insight into their child's behaviour and emotions (Kiehl, 2015). In general, administering two different self-report measures of psychopathy to the same participant can yield quite different results.

Concerns about the reliability of assessing psychopathy boil down to an issue of method-mode mismatch (Hart & Cook, 2012) and face validity. Face validity refers to whether an instrument is relevant to the construct it intends to measure (Holden & Jackson, 1985). Inherent to psychopathy is a tendency to lie and deceive, which challenges the face validity of self-report measures. It may not be the best idea to use self-report measures in which answers go unchecked and are not referenced against alternative sources of information. Lying certainly can also occur in an interview as part of the completion of expert-rating tools, but again, with an interview, there is an opportunity to ask clarifying questions and develop rapport (see Chapter 3). Even if an instrument includes a measure of social desirability

---

³ Some researchers have concluded that PCL-measured psychopathy is not associated with empathy deficits (Larsen et al., 2024). Another possible conclusion is that it is difficult to identify empathy deficits in people with psychopathy traits when relying on self-report measures of empathy. People with psychopathy traits may have less insight into whether their emotions have any sort of functional impairment. Another issue is that such studies tend to be underpowered and thus not suited to detecting even medium-to-large effects (Verschuere et al., 2021).

bias, such scales are not designed to detect subtle forms of manipulation (Lilienfeld & Fowler, 2006). As further evidence of method-mode mismatch, self-report instruments are typically completed in under an hour and therefore risk being influenced by the participant's mood state. Expert rating scales typically involve multiple interviews with the participant and incorporate file-based information that covers a broader range of the participant's life-course (Dawson et al., 2012).

The Prominence of Boldness in Self-Report Measures

When it comes to debate regarding the importance of boldness to the construct of psychopathy, the side of the debate that a subject-matter expert leans toward seems to depend on their preferred method for measuring psychopathy. Those who use expert rating tools seem to reject boldness as a central feature of psychopathy (Gatner et al., 2016). Those who use self-report measurement tools like the EPA or Tri-PM fall on the other side of this debate. Thinking back to the discussion of response distortion, self-report measures may give the false impression that boldness is a central feature of psychopathy. Whether through dishonesty or lack of insight, people with psychopathy traits may be more likely to misrepresent themselves as being bold. If people with psychopathy traits tend to be deceitful, grandiose, braggarts, and lack insight, then they may also overestimate their social status. This, in turn, may explain why research on boldness tends to report evidence of successful psychopathy (see Gatner et al., 2016, for a similar argument). People who endorse items on a survey that are meant to capture boldness may not reflect true low levels of anxiety and fearlessness, bur rather a tendency to lie and/or boast about accomplishments, feats, and masculinity.

Issues with Expert-Rating Measures (and the Experts Who Use Them)

Using expert-rating measures does not guarantee that psychopathy is measured reliably. Field reliability involves evaluating whether psychopathy is assessed accurately in nonresearch settings where there is no guarantee of confidentiality. This includes legal settings where psychopathy is measured for the purpose of completing risk assessment instruments to inform a judge about a person's likelihood of reoffending. One way to assess field reliability is by comparing multiple assessments of the same people over time. Among a small sample ($n = 27$), Sturup et al. (2014) found that there was quite a bit of variability in the scores on individual items from the first assessment to later assessments. Sturup et al. (2014) viewed this as evidence against the reliability of the PCL-R. An alternative interpretation is that scores on certain PCL-R items may legitimately change over time, reflecting the malleability of psychopathy traits (McCuish & Lussier, 2018). For example, a change in the callous-unemotional item of the PCL-R may reflect a response to treatment received while incarcerated.

Murrie et al. (2008) examined field reliability by looking at whether expert witnesses retained by defense counsel and those retained by the prosecution differed in their ratings of the same defendant. Murrie et al. reported that experts for the prosecution tended to score the PCL-R higher compared to experts retained by the defense. There appears to be some partisan bias in how the PCL-R is scored in legal settings. That said, several other studies report that the field reliability of expert rating tools resembles the reliability of those tools in research settings (Ismail & Looman, 2018; Olver et al., 2020). Divergent findings could reflect research design differences across studies. For example, higher field test reliability may be observed in legal systems that are less adversarial or in jurisdictions where expert witnesses receive better training or are more qualified to act as an expert and assess psychopathy.

Debate #5: Do People with Psychopathy Traits Change?

The debate about whether people with psychopathy traits change can be divided into two parts: (1) does treating people with psychopathy traits reduce their likelihood of reoffending, and (2) do psychopathy traits themselves actually change? Regarding the overarching notion of treatment and change, some subject-matter experts have questioned whether it was ethical to treat psychopathy because of the potential for people with psychopathy traits to learn how to feign remorse[4] or disrupt the treatment progress for others within a program (Slovenko, 2006). In developing his sociological theory of psychopathy, Dr. Harrison Gough suggested that "treatment cannot be imposed upon the psychopath" (Gough, 1948, p. 361). As pointed out by Salekin et al. (2010), (1) such ideas are mostly antiquated and not based on empirical evidence, and (2) people with psychopathy traits are not the only group who feign treatment progress and cause disruptions in treatment programs.

---

[4] This relates to instances in which the person receiving treatment learns to parrot the words of their treatment provider and understands what to say in court to get a reduced sentence.

Although the idea that people with psychopathy traits cannot be treated may be a hallmark of popular culture depictions of psychopathy (Ronson, 2011), Cleckley (1976) was optimistic about the possibility of treatment. An entire chapter of his book[5] called for improvements in the quality of mental health care to enhance treatment programs for people with psychopathy traits. Cleckley (1976) lamented the quality of programs designed to reduce reoffending and was pessimistic about whether people with psychopathy traits would respond positively to such programs (p. 439). However, he also felt that people with psychopathy traits would be responsive to methods that were "safer as well as more rational and humane" (p. 506) and praised certain institutions for recognizing and making genuine efforts to treat people with psychopathy traits (p. 36). Cleckley (1976) made it clear that "the chief aim of the present work is to help, in however small a way, to bring patients of this sort into clearer focus so that psychiatric efforts to deal with their problems can eventually be implemented" (p. 41).

Before discussing recent research on the treatment of people with psychopathy traits and changes in psychopathy traits themselves, I address where initial pessimism came from with respect to the value of treating people with psychopathy traits.

Psychopathy and Therapeutic Pessimism

Pessimism regarding the ability of people with psychopathy traits to benefit from treatment is mainly due to a single study. The Oak Ridge Study was initiated in the 1960s by Canadian psychiatrist Elliot Barker as an experimental intervention program. Patients, including teenagers, were held at the Penetanguishene Mental Health Centre in the Canadian province of Ontario. The program required "patients" to sleep together in a large, brightly-lit room while they underwent experimental treatments, including receiving doses of lysergic acid diethylamide (LSD). Patients were sometimes stripped naked and forced to eat from wall-mounted feeding tubes meant to represent a woman's breast. The Fifth Estate, a television program produced by the Canadian Broadcasting Corporation, provides a stark description of patients' experiences, including sexual abuse and military-inspired torture techniques (Burgess, 2021). The program ended in 1975[6] after an incident in which 26 patients were simultaneously administered doses of LSD (Bruineman, 2021).

---

[5] Albeit the 67th chapter in his book ... don't worry, they're short.
[6] Other sources suggest the program did not end until 1983.

Surprisingly, some Canadian researchers spoke positively about the Oak Ridge Study. Dr. Marnie Rice and her colleagues (1992, p. 69) described the study as follows:

> A seeming rape is attempted in order to impregnate the patient with ideas that may prevent a further, more subtle, and more menacing rape: the rape that the illness perpetrates upon the patient, and the rape that a sick society maintains upon a few of its sicker members.

Essentially, Dr. Rice suggested that violating patients' rights was justified because of the potential for those patients to violate the rights of others. Decades later, Harris and Rice (2017) used data from the Oak Ridge Study to examine recidivism outcomes. They reported that patients reoffended at a high rate and therefore psychopathy should be considered untreatable. This idiosyncratic, experimental, and, in my view,[7] unethical, degrading, and inhumane program has done a lot of heavy lifting for proponents of the perspective that people with psychopathy are not responsive to treatment. The Oak Ridge Study was exactly the type of program that Cleckley (1976) criticized when describing why many existing programs were ineffective in addressing psychopathy traits. Cleckley was not suggesting that people with psychopathy traits could not change; rather, he argued that the type of experimental nonsense practiced in the Oak Ridge Study was not going to be helpful.

One of the biggest misperceptions of the Oak Ridge Study was the notion that it was reserved for people with psychopathy traits. Long after the Oak Ridge Study ended, researchers coded the files of patients using the PCL-R. These studies revealed that only a small number of patients actually presented with psychopathy traits. Harris et al. (1993) noted that most patients were diagnosed with either schizophrenia or psychosis (also see Harris & Rice, 2017). Psychopathy rarely overlaps with such disorders (Lykken, 2018). People were coerced into the Oak Ridge Study when judges and psychiatrists did not have answers for their behaviour. This again reflects the centuries-old problem of misusing the term psychopathy to label people whose behaviour was confounding. Nevertheless, some researchers continued to cite findings from the Oak Ridge Study when making their conclusion that people with psychopathy traits respond poorly to treatment (Hare & Neumann, 2010).

---

[7] I am not the only one who holds this view. In 2021, the Ontario Superior Court ruled that patients of the Oak Ridge Study were to be awarded $10,000,000 for the physical and psychological turmoil that was experienced (Bruineman, 2021).

Psychopathy and Change in Risk Following Treatment

When it comes to more recent empirical literature, a tentative conclusion is that people with psychopathy traits are less likely to participate in treatment, attend consistently, and follow program requirements/guidelines (e.g., Olver, 2022; Olver & Wong, 2009; Sewall & Olver, 2019; Wilkinson et al., 2016).[8] However, people with psychopathy traits who successfully complete treatment appear to be as likely to desist from offending as people without psychopathy traits who complete treatment. Salekin et al.'s (2010) review of treatment studies indicated treatment success for both youth and adults with psychopathy traits but with more evidence of success for youth. Polashek and Daly (2013) noted that people with psychopathy traits who enter into treatment can experience reductions in dynamic risk factors, which may in turn influence desistance from offending.

The Mendota Juvenile Treatment Center developed a program that emphasized improving interpersonal interactions and social skills, developing positive attachments, and committing to prosocial activities. The program also aimed for a high ratio of staff to youth. Compared to youth with psychopathy traits who experienced treatment as usual, youth with psychopathy traits who were placed in this specialized program were less likely to recidivate in the future (see Caldwell et al., 2006, 2007). Similar findings have been reported for adults (Olver et al., 2013; Wong et al., 2012). In sum, people with psychopathy traits who successfully complete treatment are at a lower risk for reoffending compared to people with psychopathy traits who do not receive/complete treatment. This conclusion is tentative because randomized controlled trials have not yet been conducted. Chapter 10 provides a more exhaustive accounting of treatment strategies for people with psychopathy traits.

Psychopathy and the Assumption of Trait Stability

Initial assumptions about the stability of psychopathy traits were influenced less by empirical research and more by the observation that psychopathy traits do not develop *de novo* in adulthood. Virtually all incarcerated adults who score high on the PCL-R make it clear that their

---

[8] There is less evidence of a responsivity to treatment issue if the treatment program is multimodal (i.e., focusing on multiple issues) and intensive (i.e., many sessions). Focusing on prevention (rather than intervention) and ensuring that treatment is individualized also appear to help improve the beneficial impact of treatment (De Brito et al., 2021).

psychopathy traits emerged early in the life-course. This information was often (wrongfully) used to conclude that children and youth who show signs of psychopathy traits will continue to do so over the life-course. Concluding from adult retrospective reports that psychopathy is stable over the life-course is a methodological mistake referred to as Robins' paradox. Robins (1978) observed that virtually all adults involved in serious or violent criminal behaviour were antisocial as children. However, when using prospective longitudinal data, which involves following participants forward as opposed to asking participants to look backward (retrospective), Robins found that most children involved in antisocial behaviour do not become involved in criminal behaviour in adulthood. In other words, relying on retrospective accounts from adults leads to overestimations of the stability of antisocial behaviour. It is possible that the same phenomenon occurs with psychopathy.

The idea that psychopathy traits do not change often was merely assumed rather than empirically tested. For example, Kent Kiehl (2015) wrote in his book *The Psychopathy Whisperer* that "a considerable amount of research suggests that the affective and interpersonal traits of psychopathy are relatively stable from adolescence to adulthood" (p. 192). At the time, there was no research with sufficient methodological rigour to support such a conclusion. For quite some time, research on the stability of psychopathy lacked the appropriate type of research design to make reliable conclusions about psychopathy. Cross-sectional research only measures psychopathy at a single point in time, and stability cannot be inferred from a single measurement.

Using Longitudinal Research to Directly Measure Change or Stability in Psychopathy Traits

Being introverted may not be "curable" (Kagan & Snidman, 2009), but this does not mean that introverted traits cannot change (Cain, 2013). Similarly, just because psychopathy is comprises personality traits, and just because personality traits are not viewed as "curable" (Granneman, 2020; Kagan & Snidman, 2009), does not mean that psychopathy traits are fixed.

For quite some time, the only longitudinal studies that included repeat measures of psychopathy between adolescence and adulthood relied on community samples. For a variety of logistical reasons (see Chapter 3), it is easier to conduct longitudinal research within community samples compared to samples of people in prison. However, as mentioned in

Chapter 1, psychopathy traits are rare in the general population. So, when studying the stability of psychopathy in community samples, about 100 participants are needed before coming across one with clinically meaningful levels of psychopathy traits (Skeem & Mulvey, 2001). It is hard to study the stability of psychopathy among populations where psychopathy is unlikely to be found in the first place.

Community studies tend to report moderate to high correlations between psychopathy test scores at different time periods (Lynam et al., 2007). These correlations are sometimes interpreted as evidence that people with psychopathy traits in adolescence are likely to continue exhibiting these traits in adulthood. However, it is possible that the reported stability of psychopathy test scores comes from the fact that people who score low on a measure of psychopathy at one period of time tend to score low at another period of time. Researchers in these community studies (e.g., Forsman et al., 2008; Hemphälä et al., 2015; Lynam et al., 2007) often failed to clarify whether stability came from low scores remaining low or whether stability was also due to high scores remaining high. If psychopathy traits are not present in adolescence, it is unlikely that they will emerge in adulthood (Lynam, 1998). Therefore, moderate to high correlations between psychopathy scores over time may primarily reflect the stability of low scores rather than the persistence of high psychopathy traits. In other words, what is stable is not necessarily the presence of psychopathy traits; rather, what is stable is the absence of psychopathy traits.

Cauffman et al. (2016) examined the stability of psychopathy traits in a sample where such traits were far more common. Using longitudinal data on 202 incarcerated youth in the United States who were followed into adulthood, Cauffman et al. (2016) found that having a high PCL:YV score in adolescence by no means guaranteed having a high PCL-R score in adulthood. In the same study, Cauffman et al. (2016) also examined repeated measures of the PCL-R and found greater evidence of stability among adults. This aligns with research on general personality traits that finds greater stability of personality as people move through adulthood (Caspi & Roberts, 2001). Overall, psychopathy traits may be less stable during the transition from adolescence to adulthood but exhibit greater stability from the start of adulthood onward.

Cauffman's findings on youth have been replicated in various examinations of data from the Pathways to Desistance Study. The Pathways to Desistance Study is one of the most detailed and impressive longitudinal studies ever conducted in the field of criminology. The study involved repeated interviews over an 84-month period with 1,354 youth who experienced incarceration in either Phoenix, Arizona, or Philadelphia, Pennsylvania. Participants received multiple assessments of psychopathy using the Youth Psychopathic Traits Inventory (YPI), which is a self-report measure of psychopathy (Andershed et al., 2002). I developed a formula for measuring individual-level change in psychopathy traits and applied this formula to the Pathways to Desistance Study sample (see McCuish & Lussier, 2021).[9] This formula uses the reliable change index to examine whether within-individual change that results in rank-order change in test scores is meaningful. The reliable change index requires evidence that change is beyond what might be anticipated by measurement error. Across six year-over-year comparisons, we found that nearly 70 percent of the sample experienced at least one instance of a relative decrease in YPI test scores. Among the three subscales of the YPI, the grandiose-manipulative subscale was most likely to demonstrate change over time. This subscale reflects the Interpersonal factor from the PCL:YV.

The observation of instability in psychopathy traits could be because we used a self-report instrument, which may be a less reliable approach to measuring psychopathy. We observed a change in psychopathy *test scores* rather than a change in psychopathy itself. It is possible, especially in the case of self-report measures like the YPI, that changes in test scores across time reflect limitations in measurement accuracy, as opposed to psychopathy traits truly changing. At the very least, whether due to actual change or difficulty with reliable measurement, the findings mean that it is important that the criminal legal system be careful in assuming that psychopathy traits of youth persist over the life-course. Kiehl (2015) claimed that "we are moving rapidly toward

---

[9] Researchers are interested in three types of change: raw score change, rank order change, and relative change. Raw score change reflects, for example, an instance where "Dan's" score on the YPI at wave 2 was 30 points lower compared to their score at wave 1. The problem with examining raw score change alone is the potential for change to be normative in a sample. What if most people experienced a 30-point change in test score? Did Dan really change, or at least change meaningfully? Rank order change reflects whether the raw score change resulted in Dan changing places with other members of a sample on a ranking of highest to lowest scores on the YPI. At wave 1, Dan may have ranked 10th among 100 total participants. At wave 2, Dan may have ranked 40th. Is changing rank-order with 30 people meaningful? Relative change examines whether Dan's raw score change resulted in a rank order change in psychopathy. Individuals who experience relative stability either do not experience a meaningful change in test score, or they do, but not in a way that also results in a meaningful rank order change. A key question is with respect to what constitutes meaningful change.

being able to identify children who are at the highest risk for developing lifelong personality disorders" (p. 192). This perspective may require updating, given research from Cauffman et al. (2016) and findings from the Pathways to Desistance Study.

Myths and Misconceptions about Psychopathy Perpetuated by Popular Culture

Debates in the academic literature stem from relatively small differences of opinion. Differences are much more substantial with respect to how psychopathy is described within the academic literature versus how it is portrayed in popular culture, including television, movies, newspaper/magazine editorials, and new forms of media (e.g., podcasts, TikTok). Differences between the academic literature and popular culture in terms of how they describe psychopathy are not inherently problematic because popular culture is not necessarily trying to inform about psychopathy. If the purpose of popular culture depictions of psychopathy is entertainment, this could contribute to stigma, but there is also some onus on the person consuming this content to think critically about whether popular culture reflects reality. Differences become problematic when popular culture misrepresents the academic literature on psychopathy while simultaneously claiming to provide audiences with accurate information about it (Ronson, 2011).

My issue is not with popular culture describing psychopathy inaccurately. My issue is with popular culture describing the academic literature on psychopathy inaccurately, yet giving their audience the impression that they are accurately describing how psychopathy is defined and discussed in the academic literature. Again, subject-matter experts must accept some responsibility for inaccurate descriptions of their work. If we want our work to be described accurately, we should stop leaving so much room for confusion.

Ludwig Wittgenstein (1993) wrote that "the truth cannot force its way in when something else is occupying its place" (p. 119). In this case, the "truth" represents how psychopathy is described in the academic literature, and the "something else" represents popular culture portrayals of psychopathy that occupy the minds of many and have created misunderstanding about psychopathy as a personality disorder. It should thus be the goal of subject-matter experts to dismantle inaccurate portrayals of psychopathy so that rigorous research occupies its rightful place.

Do Popular Culture Resources Improve Knowledge?

Keesler and DeMatteo (2017) surveyed the general public to understand whether exposure to popular culture portrayals of psychopathy improved a person's understanding of the academic literature's description of psychopathy. People who spent more time watching popular culture depictions of psychopathy were more confident in their understanding of psychopathy. However, Keesler and DeMatteo found no correlation between exposure to media depictions of psychopathy and a person's ability to identify traits that subject-matter experts consider characteristic of psychopathy. In line with the Dunning-Kruger effect,[10] people who had more exposure to media depictions of psychopathy *believed* that they possessed more knowledge about psychopathy. However, they were no better at identifying psychopathy traits than people with less exposure to media depictions of psychopathy. The film and TV industry is not responsible for educating the public about psychopathy. Keesler and DeMatteo's (2017) study illustrates that subject-matter experts need to be more public-facing and more accessible when it comes to their research on psychopathy. In general, journalists tend to pose their questions about psychopathy to people who do not have any expertise in assessing or conducting research on psychopathy traits (Wahl et al., 2002). Experimental studies indicate that people who are educated about psychopathy by subject-matter experts are better able to detect myths and misinformation regarding psychopathy (Ostapchuk, 2018).

Table 2.2 summarizes some of the ways in which popular culture portrayals of psychopathy diverge from how psychopathy is described in academic literature. I elaborate on these sources of confusion in the sections that follow.

Overestimating the Prevalence of Psychopathy

Empirical studies estimate that approximately 1–2 percent of the general population presents with high psychopathy traits (Coid et al., 2009; Sanz-García et al., 2021; Skeem & Mulvey, 2001). Laypeople tend to overestimate the prevalence of psychopathy in the general population by a factor of 10 (i.e., 10–20 percent; Ostapchuk, 2018). The general public may get the impression that psychopathy is more prevalent because, for over

---

[10] The Dunning–Kruger effect describes situations in which people with limited knowledge on a particular subject overestimate their understanding of this subject.

Table 2.2 *Clarifying points of confusion regarding psychopathy*

Popular culture myth	Reality
Psychopathy is pervasive.	Psychopathy reflects approximately 1 percent of the general population.
Psychopathy is the same as psychosis.	Unlike psychosis, psychopathy is unrelated to hallucinations and delusional patterns of thinking.
The assessment of psychopathy is relatively straightforward and is based on the presence or absence of particular traits.	The term "checklist" comes from a measure of psychopathy named the Psychopathy Checklist. However, this measure of psychopathy is more complex than simply 'checking off' which traits are present or absent.
Psychopathy explains the most heinous types of offences.	First, most people with psychopathy traits are not involved in extreme violence like sexual homicide. Second, when it comes to extremely violent offences, other traits like sexual sadism, which are not germane to psychopathy, may better explain such crimes.
The psychopath is often portrayed as an evil genius or mastermind.	If anything, there is a small negative correlation between psychopathy and intelligence.

100 years, trusted sources keep telling them that this is the case. In the late nineteenth century, the *Macon Telegraph* suggested that anyone discovered to be a "psychopath" should be hanged immediately (Keesler & DeMatteo, 2017). *The Philadelphia Inquirer* suggested that more than 10 percent of soldiers would return from World War I (WWI) as psychopaths. Television shows like *Peaky Blinders* helped to perpetuate this myth. In the 1950s, Robert Lindner, author of *Rebel Without a Cause: A Hypnoanalysis of a Criminal Psychopath*, explained juvenile delinquency as an outbreak of mass psychopathy. Norman Mailer described the hipster as a "philosophical psychopath" for having the courage of nonconformity (Seabrook, 2008). One of the most egregious instances of overestimating the prevalence of psychopathy was perpetrated by John Dilulio. Dilulio, an American political scientist working at Princeton University, asserted that the next decade would witness an unprecedented increase of hundreds of thousands of youth "superpredators" who were characterized by psychopathy traits (Dilulio, 1995). This assertion was proven false (Payne & Piquero, 2020).

Part of the reason for overestimating the prevalence of psychopathy is that seemingly every podcast or docuseries in the True Crime genre will describe anyone involved in extreme violence as a "psychopath." Interviews with laypeople indicate that a fictional serial killer (e.g., Dexter Morgan of *Dexter*) is the most likely person to come to mind when hearing the term psychopathy (Ostapchuk, 2018). In many cases, these fictional serial killers are poor representations of the psychopathy construct. The term psychopathy "has been tainted by its long and seamy relationship with criminality and popular culture, which began with true-crime pulps and continues today in TV shows like CBS' *Criminal Minds* and in the work of authors like Thomas Harris and Patricia Cornwell" (Seabrook, 2008). The availability heuristic concept describes how people believe that an event is more likely to occur if examples of that event readily come to mind. If sources on crime most commonly consumed by the general public regularly label people as psychopaths, it is reasonable to presume that the public will overestimate the prevalence of psychopathy.

Empirical research on the prevalence of psychopathy in the general population is complicated by several issues. First, if psychopathy is treated as dimensional rather than categorical, then it is difficult to estimate its prevalence; there is no clear threshold to claim that psychopathy is present or absent. Second, setting aside the issue of psychopathy as dimensional versus taxonic, clearly, psychopathy traits are relatively rare. Accordingly, large samples are needed for studies of the general population to include enough persons with clinically meaningful levels of psychopathy traits. For example, Berluti et al. (2025) examined Tri-PM scores among 289 persons recruited using online survey software. If clinically meaningful levels of psychopathy are present in 1–2 percent of the population, then only about five people in this study would meet this threshold. Berluti et al. (2025) reported a mean score on the Tri-PM of 57.89 ($SD = 17.46$) and that test scores were normally distributed.[11] The 58 Tri-PM items are scored 0–3, and test scores range from 0–174. Thus, on average, participants indicated that each item was not true for them. Given the standard deviation (SD), about 95 percent of participants scored less than 95 on the Tri-PM, meaning that about 95 percent of participants did not average a "2"

---

[11] A red flag that readers can look for when interpreting studies of community samples is whether authors report the mean score and SD on the measure of psychopathy. Studies that do not do this may be trying to mask the fact that few participants in their sample actually scored high on such measures.

(e.g., responded "somewhat true").[12] The third issue is that when the prevalence of psychopathy traits is rare, studies of community samples that report evidence of an association between psychopathy and offending or other negative outcomes (e.g., Berluti et al., 2025) may in fact simply be observing a relationship between nonpsychopathy and nonnegative outcomes. This issue reflects one where researchers fail to examine calibration of instruments; do high scores predict negative outcomes just as well as low scores predict positive outcomes (see Helmus & Babchishin, 2017)?

Conflating Psychopathy with Other Disorders

Another source of confusion comes from conflating psychopathy and psychosis. Perhaps because of their similar spelling, there is a tendency for the media to use these terms interchangeably (Wahl, 1995). Unlike psychosis, psychopathy is unrelated to hallucinations and delusional patterns of thinking. Pinel was clear about this over 200 years ago with his term *manie sans délire*. Unlike psychosis, psychopathy traits do not impair a person's awareness of their behaviour. For example, in Canada, people with psychosis can be found not criminally responsible for their behaviour if they were unaware of what they were doing, or at the very least, were not aware that what they were doing was wrong. In the Oak Ridge Study, people with psychosis were colloquially referred to as psychopaths, thereby perpetuating the belief that psychopathy is associated with delusional behaviour. In contrast, people with psychopathy traits may have a poor moral understanding of their behaviour, but they are nevertheless aware that certain behaviours contravene criminal laws (Berryessa, 2016). Psychosis can be considered a foil trait of psychopathy. A foil trait refers to a trait that is the antithesis of psychopathy (Cooke et al., 2012).

Jon Ronson explains that his book, *The Psychopathy Test* is about madness. For about 20 pages of his book, beginning on page 66,

---

[12] Proponents of the use of self-report measures of psychopathy in community samples may argue that if their instruments are normally distributed, this indicates that they have a sufficient proportion of their sample with meaningful levels of psychopathy. This would be a mistake. The normal distribution of *test scores* is not the same as the normal distribution of *psychopathy traits*. As indicated by expert rating scales like the PCL-R and PCL:YV, traits that are scored a "1" (i.e., possibly applies) do not provide evidence of psychopathy (would equal an average score of 20 on the PCL:YV, which would not be considered evidence of psychopathy). The problem is that some researchers use moderate evidence of the presence of a trait as clear evidence of psychopathy. This conflicts with the perspective that psychopathy traits are stable across time and social contexts. It may be more appropriate to think of psychopathy as a half-normal distribution, where 80 percent of the population presents with no psychopathy traits and then among the other 20 percent of the population, traits are normally distributed (see Coid et al., 2009).

Ronson (2011) confuses schizophrenia and other psychotic disorders with psychopathy. He suggests that symptoms of schizophrenia are evidence of psychopathy and that people with such symptoms are at a high risk for violence. Similarly, Joaquin Phoenix's depiction of Arthur Fleck in *Joker* (Phillips, 2019) has been referred to as an example of psychopathy (Rose, 2019). Yet, Arthur Fleck is shown to lose his sanity through delusions, hallucinations, and a lack of control over his behaviour. Both Ronson's book and *Joker* contradict early descriptions of psychopathy as mania without delusion. They also contradict contemporary descriptions of psychopathy that emphasize that people with psychopathy traits remain aware of their behaviour. As others have explained (e.g., Skryabin, 2021), the chimera of co-occurring symptoms of different mental disorders (e.g., psychopathy and schizophrenia) amalgamated into a single character like Arthur Fleck is unlikely in the real world. However, characters like the Joker are repeatedly described as both psychopathic and schizophrenic (Forsman, 2024). When Ronson gives the impression that psychopathy resembles madness, not only is the public misled about psychopathy, but schizophrenia is further stigmatized by wrongly implying that it is associated with a high risk for violent behaviour.[13]

Assessing Psychopathy versus "Spotting" Psychopathy

The purpose of assessing psychopathy is sometimes misunderstood in popular psychology books. For example, Jon Ronson described being disappointed when the man whom he was interviewing provided evidence against the presence of psychopathy. Ronson, a journalist and television writer, appeared frustrated that he did not have a more sensational story to share. In contrast, in both academic and clinical settings, the goal of assessing psychopathy is not to find psychopathy. Ruling out psychopathy traits is just as important as identifying them. I have been involved in the assessment of dozens of youth who perpetrated homicide offences but who also reported strong ties to family members, remorse for their behaviour, and a desire to live a more prosocial life. They also struggled with experiences of trauma and abuse, heroin addiction, gang involvement, and a host of other risk factors. Assessing psychopathy helps to confirm when

---

[13] Douglas et al.'s (2009) meta-analysis indicated that the relationship between psychosis and risk for violence is highly variable depending on how this relationship is examined (e.g., community samples or incarcerated samples, type of comparison group). Overall, they concluded that psychosis on its own was not sufficient to indicate a high risk for violence and that the impact of psychosis on risk for violence was far weaker than the impact of psychopathy on risk for violence.

psychopathy is not a risk factor. This distinction is necessary to develop accurate case management plans aimed at preventing violence (Wong et al., 2012).

The complexity involved in assessing psychopathy is often underestimated. Popular True Crime Podcasts like *Criminal* and *True Crime Psychology and Personality: Narcissism, Psychopathy, and the Minds of Dangerous Criminals* advertise themselves as able to answer questions such as "how do you spot a sociopath?" Ironically, these podcasts also claim to be about "science" and "psychology" rather than the sensationalizing of violent offences. However, there is no science of "spotting psychopathy." Dozens of YouTube videos commonly imply that psychopathy is something that can be spotted by knowing what to look for in short interactions with other people. As a reminder, psychopathy traits are personality traits that are stable over time and social context; they cannot be reliably inferred from a single interaction.

Ronson (2011) believed that taking Dr. Robert Hare's training course on the PCL-R would allow him to spot psychopaths by interpreting body language and patterns of speech. The academic literature may have contributed to this misunderstanding. Calling the most well-known measure of psychopathy a checklist (i.e., the Psychopathy Checklist; Cunha et al., 2020) can give the impression that the assessment of psychopathy is as straightforward as ticking items off a shopping list. Kiehl (2015) noted that popular culture depictions of psychopathy tend to rely on a single behaviour or trait to extrapolate the presence of psychopathy. For example, Ronson suggested that psychopathy could be identified through a process of reducing people to their "maddest edges" and their most extreme behaviour. Even though Ronson claimed that he completed PCL training, the manuals for expert rating tools like the PCL explicitly explain that traits (e.g., a lack of empathy) qualify as evidence of psychopathy only if they manifest across multiple life domains (e.g., at work, with family, and with friends) and across time (Forth et al., 2003; Hare, 2003).

Psychopathy and Unrelated Traits

People with psychopathy traits do not necessarily engage in heinous or violent crimes. However, there is a tendency for popular culture to either (a) focus exclusively on people with psychopathy traits who are involved in serial killing and other serious crimes (e.g., Ted Bundy) or (b) assume that if a heinous crime was committed, it must have been committed by a person with psychopathy traits. The True Crime television show *Signs of a*

Psychopath retrospectively examines people involved in heinous crimes and, on the basis of involvement in such crimes, makes assumptions that the perpetrator must be a psychopath.

I have interviewed many youth who score high on the PCL:YV and the CAPP-IRS but whose offence history consists of, comparatively speaking, relatively mundane offences like motor vehicle theft, minor assault, and failing to abide by probation conditions. True Crime podcasts seem disinterested in telling the stories of such youth. As a consequence, the public's exposure to psychopathy tends to come from sensationalized cases, such as those involving sexual sadism. It is certainly true that perpetrators of sexually sadistic acts tend to score high on measures of psychopathy (Mokros et al., 2011). However, sadism is neither necessary nor sufficient to score high on a measure of psychopathy. The tendency for True Crime podcasts and other mediums to discuss sexual sadism and psychopathy simultaneously can give the impression that sexual sadism is pathognomonic of psychopathy. Pathognomonic refers to a feature so definitive of a disorder or disease that its presence guarantees a diagnosis. The tendency of popular culture to only discuss psychopathy in the context of bizarre, violent, or sadistic behaviours has created the impression that such characteristics are guaranteed signs of psychopathy (Edens et al., 2013a; Helfgott, 2013; Keesler & DeMatteo, 2017).

Another example of popular culture misrepresenting pathognomonic features of psychopathy is with respect to intelligence. This misrepresentation is so pervasive that it has been labeled the "Hannibal Lecter Myth" (DeLisi et al., 2010; Kavish et al., 2018) . The Hannibal Lecter Myth refers to how Anthony Hopkins' portrayal of psychopathy in *Silence of the Lambs* created the impression that all people with psychopathy traits are criminal masterminds. On the contrary, empirical studies indicate that higher levels of psychopathy traits are negatively associated with intelligence quotient (IQ; Johansson & Kerr, 2005; Walsh et al., 2004). This does not mean it is impossible for high psychopathy traits and high IQ to converge. My colleague Stephanie Dawson and I observed this convergence in our interviews with two incarcerated youth involved in extremely serious and violent crimes (see Dawson et al., 2012). However, the pairing of psychopathy and high IQ appears to be the exception rather than the rule. Inundating the public with stories of Ted Bundy and Hannibal Lecter types has created the perception that high intelligence, necrophilia, physical strength, attractiveness, and serial killing are common among people with psychopathy traits.

Chapter Summary

Debates within the academic literature remain ongoing. What is relatively settled is that that popular culture depictions of psychopathy poorly reflect this literature. Learning about psychopathy from the media fails to improve a person's comprehension of what constitutes psychopathy traits (Keesler & DeMatteo, 2017). Misunderstandings of psychopathy traits seems to be perpetuated by popular culture's conflation of psychopathy and psychotic disorders like schizophrenia. In television and film, the term psychopath is used generically to describe anyone whose behaviour is especially sinister, vile, or abnormal. These portrayals misrepresent how psychopathy is described in the academic literature.

The public's fascination with psychopathy has influenced blogs, YouTube videos, and TED Talks that try to communicate to the public how to "spot" psychopathy. Journalist Jon Ronson has lectured millions of people on how to spot psychopathy by examining a person's maddest edges, even though the actual assessment of psychopathy is far more complex and reliant on evidence of consistent traits and attitudes across multiple social contexts. Even accurate depictions of psychopathy, such as in reviews of infamous serial killers like Ted Bundy and Clifford Olson, can create misunderstanding. These cases involved offenders with additional traits unrelated to psychopathy, such as intelligence, sexual sadism, necrophilia, and pedophilia, that influenced the nature of their crimes.

In the academic literature, debates about psychopathy include discussions around whether it is best conceptualized as categorical (taxonic) or dimensional. A categorical viewpoint essentially suggests that psychopathy traits are either entirely absent or entirely present. A dimensional perspective recognizes that there is greater variability and gradations of severity. Although some argue that among people with psychopathy traits there exists a group who can be considered "successful psychopaths," others contend that psychopathy traits are inherently maladaptive and thus do not promote life success. Much of this debate hinges on how success is defined. Should wealth without happiness be considered success? In addition to definitional debates, the academic literature is fragmented regarding how to measure psychopathy. This disagreement boils down to two main issues: (1) whether criminal behaviour should be considered in the measurement of psychopathy and (2) whether self-report measures of psychopathy are a reliable alternative to expert rating tools that require structured interviews and collateral information.

CHAPTER 3

The Incarcerated Serious and Violent Young Offender Study

Chapter 1 clarified how the academic literature describes psychopathy. It is one thing to think about psychopathy as a concept. It is another thing to actually measure this concept. It took several decades to move from Cleckley's description of psychopathy to the measurement of psychopathy via the Psychopathy Checklist – Revised (PCL-R). Similarly, it is one thing to develop theories about why psychopathy poses a risk for criminal behaviour. It is another thing to statistically examine the relationship between psychopathy and criminal behaviour. The first step in moving from concepts and theories to empirical analysis is data collection. The statistical analyses performed in this book are based on data from the Incarcerated Serious and Violent Young Offender Study (ISVYOS). The ISVYOS was initiated in 1998 by Professor Raymond Corrado, who at the time worked at Simon Fraser University in British Columbia, Canada. I began working on this project in 2008 and became Principal Investigator in 2016.

Chapter Goals

The goal of this chapter is to give readers insight into how psychopathy data were collected as part of the ISVYOS. The importance of data collection cannot be overstated. Data collection allows for the testing of concepts and theories in the academic literature as well as the ability to empirically debunk myths and misconceptions about psychopathy that have been perpetuated by popular culture. Just because data are available, and are analyzed, does not mean that they are valuable. Analyzing unreliable data is worse than having no data. In the absence of data, we must acknowledge the uncertainty of our theories. Worse, if our conclusions about theories are based on unreliable data, we may develop a false sense of confidence about the accuracy of our findings. The Oak Ridge Study, which examined people thought to have psychopathy traits before there was ever a reliable measure of psychopathy, gave some academics the impression that psychopathy was untreatable (Harris & Rice, 2017). The example of using unreliable data in the Oak Ridge Study to make conclusions about psychopathy is emblematic of why research in the social sciences is facing a replication crisis (Lilienfeld & Strother, 2020).

Careful data collection is also beneficial for developing research ideas. As a graduate student Research Assistant for the ISVYOS, I conducted interviews with over 300 youth who were incarcerated. Data collection has an intraocular effect. Research ideas hit you square between the eyes. Basically, I spent so much time collecting data that research ideas were impossible to miss. For example, by interviewing and reading the criminal record of one of the leaders of a street gang in the Metro Vancouver area, I observed that he had committed two homicides, 10 years apart. These two homicides involved many of the same people. Some co-offenders from the first homicide were co-offenders in the second homicide. Other co-offenders from the first homicide were victims in the second homicide. Mapping criminal networks is a well-established field of research (Bouchard, 2020). However, at the time, I knew nothing of this field. Through the process of data collection, my exposure to information on co-offending led me to ask questions about how gang leaders recruit co-offenders. This question led to a series of conference presentations and eventual publication of a paper on searching for a suitable co-offender (McCuish et al., 2015). Chapters 6–8 use this knowledge to examine the criminogenic social networks of people with psychopathy traits.

More closely related to the topic of psychopathy, my experience interviewing youth with psychopathy traits led me to question a prominent theory in criminology. Drs. John Laub and Robert Sampson developed a theory of desistance from criminal behaviour known as the age-graded theory of informal social control (e.g., Laub & Sampson, 2003). This theory is sometimes colloquially referred to as "turning point theory" and describes how life events like marriage, employment, and parenthood are a normative part of the life-course and facilitate desistance from criminal behaviour. I began to question this theory because of my experience interviewing youth with psychopathy traits. Recall descriptions of psychopathy from Chapter 1. Psychopathy traits include a disdain and callous disregard for others, a disinterest in work, a preference to manipulate and bully, and a willingness to lie even in situations with seemingly little benefit. Why would I expect employment, marriage, and parenthood to have a positive impact on desistance from criminal behaviour? My interest in looking at psychopathy and desistance from criminal behaviour influenced the basis of my PhD dissertation, four journal articles, and now this book. While the intraocular effect of my time as a Research Assistant helped me develop ideas, it is necessary to push beyond assuming that Drs. Laub and Sampson were wrong about turning points happening for everyone. I needed to collect, analyze, and present data, regardless of whether they supported my assumption. Hence, the focus of this book is on understanding what happens in adulthood for youth with psychopathy traits.

Another way to build trust in research is through preregistration (Benning & Smith, 2023). Preregistration was not appropriate for this book because, although I present new analyses, the analyses are based on existing data that have been examined in various ways (see McCuish et al., 2021 for an overview). To help improve transparency, I followed Benning and Smith's guidelines for postregistration. This includes uploading code to my GitHub page (https://github.com/EvanMcCuish). In Chapter 11, I discuss what can be done in the future to improve the reliability and transparency of research.

The first section of this chapter describes ISVYOS data collection procedures. The second section describes some of my experiences and lessons learned when interviewing youth for the purpose of measuring psychopathy. Although this section is based on personal anecdotes rather than the science of interviewing (see, for example, the work of Dr. Elizabeth Loftus), I argue that it can nevertheless provide graduate students and others with helpful insights into the process and challenges associated with the assessment of psychopathy.

ISVYOS Research Design

To investigate whether youth psychopathy traits impact life-course development, I focus on 535 participants from the ISVYOS who received an assessment on the Psychopathy Checklist: Youth Version (PCL:YV; Forth et al., 2003). All participants were interviewed in youth custody facilities in the Province of British Columbia, Canada, between 1998 and 2011. Bureaucratic red tape can make custody centres a difficult place for researchers to access (Fox et al., 2011). The ISVYOS was fortunate to have the backing of key politicians and criminal legal system personnel who were aware of the absence of research on incarcerated youth, especially in Canada. The Ministry of Children and Family Development, which is responsible for the care of all incarcerated youth in British Columbia, granted consent to the ISVYOS research team to invite youth across all custody facilities in the province to participate in the study. Custody staff allowed the ISVYOS research team to interview all youth, regardless of their security risk, mental health status, or offence history. For example, I regularly interviewed youth during periods of their separate confinement following fights in custody. Thus, ISVYOS Research Assistants were not prohibited from interviewing youth with potential behavioural problems. I would also note that placement in separate confinement did not necessarily mean that a young person had behavioural problems. Fights in custody could occur for a variety of reasons, including self-defence.

Various government agencies in Canada were motivated to support the ISVYOS because, especially in the 1990s, little was known about the backgrounds and prior experiences of incarcerated youth. Canadian researchers and politicians were comfortable acknowledging the limitations of their knowledge and therefore approached youth justice theory and policy more cautiously. In contrast, American researchers and politicians had strong opinions regarding the future of youth crime in the United States. For example, John Dilulio's superpredator theory claimed that there was a new "breed" of tens of thousands of morally impoverished youth superpredators who wandered the streets indiscriminately engaging in extreme violence against strangers (see Bennett et al., 1996; Dilulio, 1995). Dilulio's discussion of the youth superpredator as callous, manipulative, erratic, and impulsive resembled contemporary descriptions of psychopathy. Dilulio had no research to support his claims. Nevertheless, these claims influenced some policymakers' belief that long-term prison sentences were needed to deter youth from involvement in violent offending (Becker, 2001). Recall Michael's case description in the Preface. Michael was involved in two homicides separated by about 10 years. To Dilulio, this could have served as the quintessential example of his superpredator theory. However, neither of Michael's offences was a random attack against strangers. His offences were not motivated by the types of callous, manipulative, erratic, and impulsive personality traits that Dilulio warned about. Data on youth like Michael were not available to provide an evidence-based assessment of Dilulio's superpredator theory. It was through the ISVYOS that the British Columbia Ministry of Children and Family Development hoped to develop a more evidence-driven understanding of incarcerated youth.[1]

---

[1] For readers interested in the broader findings from the ISVYOS, in 2021, I wrote a book with my colleagues, Patrick Lussier and Raymond Corrado, that described the ISVYOS in detail (McCuish

Sample

ISVYOS participants lived throughout the province of British Columbia, which covers nearly 950,000 km² (approximately 1.5 times the size of Texas). Most of the sample resided in Metro Vancouver, which is located in the southern part of British Columbia, has a population of just over 2.5 million people, and covers about 2,800 km². At the time of data collection, youth in British Columbia were incarcerated at a rate ranging between approximately 40–80 per 100,000 (Statistics Canada, 2024a). During a similar period, youth in the United States were incarcerated at a rate ranging between 196 and 355 (OJJDP, 2019). The ISVYOS sample thus likely differs from incarcerated youth in the United States. In the United States, youth can be incarcerated for status offences and other minor offences. In Canada, status offences were abolished in 1984, and since 2003, youth cannot be incarcerated for minor offences unless they also have a history of repeat offending. Nearly 50 percent of ISVYOS participants reported that they were incarcerated due to their involvement in a violent offence (e.g., assault, homicide, sexual assault, uttering threats). Between ages 12–17, 70 percent of the sample incurred at least one conviction for a violent offence.

Throughout the book, I refer to the 535 ISVYOS participants who received an interview and rating on the PCL:YV as the PCL:YV Cohort. The PCL:YV Cohort averaged nearly 100 more days spent incarcerated between ages 12–17 compared to the rest of the sample. Part of this discrepancy could reflect Research Assistants' tendency to recruit people involved in more serious offences to complete the PCL:YV interview. A simpler explanation is that youth who spent more time in custody had more opportunity to participate in the ISVYOS, and this is why they are overrepresented in the PCL:YV cohort.

The PCL:YV Cohort includes 433 boys, 98 girls, and 4 participants who lacked information regarding gender due to an unwillingness to report.[2] The average age of the sample at the most recent wave of data collection used was 32.92 (standard deviation (SD) = 4.72). In terms of ethnicity, most participants self-reported as White (59.5 percent). Indigenous People represent only about 6 percent of the population of

---

et al., 2021). We also published a journal article describing how to access the data (see McCuish et al., 2022).

[2] None of the youth who received a PCL:YV assessment self-identified as transgender or another non-binary descriptor. It is also possible that non-binary youth were more likely to elect not to self-report their gender.

British Columbia. However, in line with official statistics in BC Corrections, Indigenous youth represented 25.6 percent of the PCL:YV Cohort. The remainder of the sample with data on ethnicity self-reported as Asian, Black, Hispanic, or another minority group (e.g., Southeast Asian). Due to the rarity with which participants self-reported identifying with these other ethnic groups, analyses that controlled for ethnicity combined such participants into a single group reflecting non-Indigenous minority status (15.0 percent of the sample). Participants were born between 1979 and 1998. Having participants born in different decades allows for the examination of questions regarding whether it is "who a person is" (e.g., the presence of psychopathy traits) or "when a person is" (e.g., the era in which they come of age) that most strongly impacts adult outcomes (see Chapter 9). Participants were recruited between 1998 and 2011. During this period, Canada's youth criminal legal system transitioned from the *Young Offenders Act* to the *Youth Criminal Justice Act*. Having one cohort who experienced the Young Offenders Act ($n = 351$) and one cohort who experienced the Youth Criminal Justice Act ($n = 184$) allows for the examination of whether the influence of youth psychopathy traits on adult outcomes was mitigated or exacerbated by exposure to a particular youth criminal legal system (see Chapter 9).

Procedures

The ISVYOS employed dozens of undergraduate and graduate student Research Assistants, including myself, to administer structured and semi-structured interviews to incarcerated youth. Research Assistants attended custody centre units to recruit participants. Approximately eight residents were housed in each unit. Each resident typically had their own room, especially during the tail-end of data collection. Most residents congregated in the unit's common area and would be in the middle of watching TV or playing chess or cards when Research Assistants arrived at the unit. Research Assistants only approached youth during their recreational time to avoid interrupting valuable programs/services. Residents were asked if they would like to participate in a research project for Simon Fraser University. Ensuring that participants understood that Research Assistants worked for the university was important because residents tended to distrust anyone who worked for the youth criminal legal system or social services. Youth who agreed to participate were interviewed in a private room to help maintain confidentiality. Prior to receiving an interview for the purpose of completing the PCL:YV, all participants completed a structured intake interview.[3] The amount of time required to complete the intake interview depended on the participant's cognitive abilities, attention span, and motivation. It was advantageous to complete the interview over at least two sittings to avoid participant fatigue. The interview addressed, among other themes, substance use, schooling, aggression and criminal behaviour, family background, perceptions of the criminal legal system, and self-identity and mental health. When relevant, several of these factors were controlled for in the statistical analyses presented in this book.

I started working on the ISVYOS in 2007. By 2011, I was primarily interested in what happened to the participants I interviewed. I read the works of several pioneers in longitudinal research in criminology, including Drs. Sheldon and Eleanor Glueck, David Farrington, Terrie Moffitt, Rolf Loeber, Robert Sampson, and John Laub. A central component of the research of these scholars was the examination of whether and how youth change as they enter adulthood. Unfortunately, practical and ethical challenges prevented the ISVYOS from following up with participants in adulthood. However, British Columbia Corrections uses a program called the Corrections Network (CORNET). CORNET is a client management software program used to record information about all people, including ISVYOS participants, adjudicated by the criminal legal system in British Columbia.

Using official data is a common practice in criminology. However, administrative data sources are typically limited, especially in the United States, where they include official measures of offending but little additional information useful for understanding criminal legal system involvement. The use of administrative data to facilitate multivariable longitudinal research is not new, but this work is primarily in fields like epidemiology (Drefahl et al., 2020; Wall-Wieler et al., 2017; Zylbersztejn et al., 2018). CORNET is different from population registry data in countries like Denmark or Sweden, as it is limited only to people under BC Corrections supervision. However, it is still impressive and far more detailed when compared to administrative sources in the United States.

---

[3] The intake interview included an English translation of the MASPAQ (Manuel sur des mesures de l'adaptation sociale et personnelle pour les adolescents Québécois) that was originally developed by Drs. Le Blanc, Frechette, and McDuff (1991). The intake interview also included the Massachusetts Youth Screening Instrument-2 and Schneider's (1990) Good Citizen Scale. For additional details, see McCuish et al. (2022) and the ISVYOS Codebook, which is publicly available on the ResearchGate webpage. I can also accommodate requests for copies of the intake interview.

Information stored on CORNET includes (1) official involvement in the criminal legal system, (2) health information, (3) involvement in treatment/intervention programs, (4) housing status, and (5) community- and institutional-based risk assessment tools. Table 3.1 summarizes the information available on CORNET, the source of the information, and how the information was used to create a longitudinal dataset. For this book, I focused on sources of CORNET data that provided information regarding offending, social, and health outcomes. Detailed descriptions of these outcomes, including how they were measured, are presented in their respective chapters.

Control Variables

Chapters 4–10 represent the empirical chapters of this book. When appropriate, all analyses of the relationship between psychopathy and different outcomes (e.g., crime, social environment, and health) account for various control variables measured during self-report interviews in adolescence, that fit one of seven themes: (1) demographic characteristics, (2) difficult family environment, (3) substance use, (4) self-identity, (5) victimization, (6) school behaviours and experiences, and (7) residential mobility. Certain chapters included additional control variables, and these are discussed in the relevant chapter.

In terms of the variables included in each of these themes, demographic characteristics include ethnicity and gender. A difficult family environment was measured via the sum of six items in which participants were asked to report whether biological parents or siblings had trouble with alcohol or drugs, had experienced physical or sexual abuse, had a criminal record, or had a mental illness. Substance use was measured as a versatility scale defined by the sum of participants' reports of whether they had used any of the following illicit substances: alcohol, marijuana, hallucinogens (e.g., acid, mushrooms), ecstasy, heroin, cocaine, crack cocaine, crystal methamphetamine, and the abuse of prescription pills. Self-identity was measured using Schneider's Good Citizen Scale, which consists of 15 traits coded on a 1–7 scale (see, e.g., Schneider & Ervin, 1990). For example, participants were presented with two opposing traits (e.g., Bad/Good) and asked which one they felt better represented themselves. Certain items were reverse-coded so that higher scores indicated a positive self-identity. Victimization was measured by participants' self-reports of whether they experienced physical abuse. Schooling was measured via participants' self-reports of whether they were attending school prior to incarceration.

Table 3.1 *Non-exhaustive description of information included within CORNET administrative data*

Type of data	Information included	Source of information	Longitudinal component
Official offending	Charges, convictions, admissions/releases from custody, court location, custody location, each time participant appears in court, type(s) of sanction, length of sanction(s). Specifies transfers to different institutions and the probation office responsible for supervision.	Court records provided by JUSTIN, a system used in the province of British Columbia for managing court appearances/case flow, etc.	Dates (YYYY/MM/DD) for all entries.
Risk assessment tools	The Community Risk-Needs Assessment (youth and adult versions), the Institutional Risk Assessment (youth and adult), the Structured Assessment of Violence Risk in Youth (Borum et al., 2002), and various sexual offending and intimate partner violence risk assessment tools.	Probation officers, institutional social workers, correctional officers, and institutional and community case managers. Practitioners, interview participants, and collaterals.	Completion date (YYYY/MM/DD) included for all risk assessment tools; does not necessarily correspond with date information acquired.
Tombstone data	Height and weight of participants. Home address, emergency contacts, and a list of people approved to visit in custody.	Completed by institutional correctional officers at each admission to custody.	Dates (YYYY/MM/DD) for each updated entry.

Table 3.1 (*cont.*)

Type of data	Information included	Source of information	Longitudinal component
Client logs (community)	Presentence reports detailing the participant's substance use history, mental health, family history, etc. Case management plans detailing participant's strengths/weaknesses, goals for intervention, and improvements. Identifies when a participant moved outside the province or died. Identifies who the person interacts with positively/negatively.	Case managers and probation officers interviewing participants and collateral contacts. Also includes the practitioner's observations of participant behaviour and attitudes.	The time (date, hour, and minute) for each entry. Includes contact while incarcerated or under some form of community supervision.
Client logs (prison)	Behaviour in the institution, including institutional charges for misbehaviour, who the participant associates with, attitude toward staff, and other residents. Identifies who the person interacts with positively/negatively. Injury forms (e.g., nature of injury and how it happened).	Correctional officers, institutional probation officers, and youth social workers. Includes collateral contacts from lawyers, family members, and intimate partners.	The time (date, hour, and minute) for each entry. Completed daily when the participant is incarcerated.
Institutional alerts	Names of people the participant is to have no contact with (e.g., participant assaulted another person; a person assaulted participant; participant co-offended with this person).	Correctional officers, intel from police, institutional and community probation officers, and case managers. No-contact orders.	Dates (YYYY/MM/DD) for each unique alert. Reflects the date alert added and not necessarily the date of the incident.

Finaly, residential mobility was measured via participants' self-report of whether they had left their primary residence before age 12 to go and live somewhere else.

Measuring Psychopathy

All 535 participants received a rating on the PCL:YV. The PCL:YV is the instrument most commonly used by forensic clinicians to measure youth psychopathy traits (Viljoen et al., 2010). Dr. Adelle Forth and her colleagues, Dr. Robert Hare and Dr. David Kosson, developed the PCL:YV to reflect the same factor structure associated with the PCL-R (Forth et al., 2003). The PCL:YV includes four domains of functioning: interpersonal (e.g., impression management, manipulation), affective (e.g., shallow affect, lack of remorse, lack of empathy), behavioural (e.g., stimulation seeking, parasitic orientation), and antisocial (e.g., early behaviour problems, poor anger control) domains of functioning. In PCL:YV language, these domains are referred to as factors. Based on prior research examining the structure of the PCL:YV, 18 of the 20 items of the PCL:YV load onto Interpersonal ($k = 4$), Affective ($k = 4$), Lifestyle ($k = 5$), and Antisocial ($k = 5$) factors. The remaining two items did not suitably fit any of the four factors. Debate continues about whether this four-factor model should be retained or whether it is more appropriate to use a three-factor model that excludes the Antisocial factor on the basis that criminal behaviour is a consequence and not a trait of psychopathy. I directly address this debate in Chapter 4.

To develop the PCL:YV, each of the 20 items of the PCL-R was adapted or redefined to be developmentally appropriate for youth. The logic of these adaptations is based on the concept of heterotypic continuity, which means that the same trait will manifest in different ways over the life-course. For example, the PCL-R item *many short-term marital relationships* is not applicable for youth and so the PCL:YV's equivalent item reflects *unstable interpersonal relationships*. Similarly, the PCL-R and PCL:YV include items with identical names, but assessing these items requires different interview questions and scoring criteria. For example, a parasitic orientation is an item that is assessed on both instruments. For adults, being dependent on parents for financial support is often an indicator of a parasitic lifestyle. For youth, dependence on parents is not parasitic but rather part of normative development. Thus, more extreme behaviour (e.g., refusal to help parents around the house, bullying siblings for money) is required to be evidence of a parasitic orientation in adolescence.

The 20 items of the PCL:YV are scored using a combination of file-based information from collateral sources (e.g., parents, probation officers, psychologists, social workers) and a semi-structured interview lasting approximately 60–90 minutes. Details regarding the interview and how items are assessed are discussed in the next section of this chapter. Items are rated on a 0–2 scale (0 = *item does not apply*; 1 = *item applies somewhat*; 2 = *item definitely applies*). Ratings are determined by assessing the extent to which an item is stable across developmental history and social context. For example, to score high on the PCL:YV item reflecting a lack of remorse, a person must lack remorse in their negative interactions across a range of relationships and social domains (e.g., family, friends, employers, co-workers) over time. ISVYOS raters, therefore, considered file and interview information from the full life-course.

ISVYOS participants averaged a score of 21.77 on the PCL:YV ($SD = 6.76$). Said differently, across the 20 items, participants averaged a score of just slightly over one, indicating that the item "somewhat applies." Although research has generally moved away from taxonomic descriptions of psychopathy (see Chapter 2), a score of 30 or greater traditionally has indicated "high" psychopathy traits. About 15 percent of the sample scored 30 or more. In the Pathways to Desistance Study, which consisted of incarcerated boys and girls in the United States, the average score on the PCL:YV was 15.89 ($SD = 7.68$). The nearly six-point higher average in the ISVYOS sample highlights the relative severity of incarcerated samples in Canada compared to the United States. I return to this point in Chapters 9 and 10.

Alternative Measures of Psychopathy

The academic literature's tendency to frequently measure psychopathy using PCL measures has created concern that the measure has become conflated with the construct. The PCL:YV is just one approach to measuring psychopathy. As part of assessing the validity of the PCL:YV, it is important to examine its convergence with other measures of psychopathy. For example, a strong correlation between the PCL:YV and the Comprehensive Assessment of Psychopathic Personality – Institutional Rating Scale (CAPP-IRS) could imply that two instruments with different perspectives on the core traits of psychopathy nevertheless identify the same people with psychopathy traits. Conversely, A weak correlation between the PCL:YV and CAPP-IRS could imply (a) that conclusions about psychopathy differ depending on the measure used or (b) one measure more accurately measures psychopathy traits. In Chapter 4, I examine the relationship between the PCL:YV and two other measures of psychopathy: the CAPP-IRS and the Millon Adolescent Clinical Inventory Psychopathy Content Scale. These two measures are discussed in more detail later in the chapter.

As discussed in Chapter 1, the CAPP is a conceptual description of psychopathy that was developed using a lexical approach. The CAPP was designed to address the perception that the PCL was overreliant on indicators of criminal behaviour in the measurement of psychopathy (Cooke et al., 2004, 2012). The CAPP model includes 33 symptoms allocated into 6 conceptual domains: attachment, behavioural, cognitive, dominance, emotion, and self. The CAPP-IRS interview is used to rate the 33 symptoms on a 7-point scale, where 0 equates to *not present* and 6 equates to *very severe*. The interview is structured from less to more personal questions, which helps with rapport-building. Like the PCL:YV, only ISVYOS participants who completed the intake interview were eligible for a subsequent interview to score the CAPP-IRS. Institutional file records were consulted in preparation for the interview and to assist with ratings. Training on the CAPP-IRS included defining and explaining the meaning of symptoms, explaining the meaning and purpose of different interview questions, and reviewing and discussing video recordings of interviews conducted for the assessment of psychopathy. Typically, interviews lasted two to three hours and were completed over multiple days.

The Millon Adolescent Clinical Inventory (MACI) is based on Theodore Millon's theoretical perspective of personality (Millon & Davis, 1993). One component of the MACI is the Psychopathy Content Scale. The Psychopathy Content Scale includes 20 true or false items. Higher scores indicate a greater degree of psychopathy traits. Unlike the PCL:YV and CAPP-IRS, the Psychopathy Content Scale is a self-report instrument. The Psychopathy Content Scale reflects the description of psychopathy as extreme manifestations of normative personality traits. This differs from the PCL:YV, which includes items that do not tap into general personality traits (e.g., criminal versatility, severity of offending, history of early antisocial behaviour). Utilizing the MACI to investigate the positioning of psychopathy within a broader structure of personality and affective disorders is particularly informative given Millon and Davis' (1993) emphasis on the interconnectedness of psychopathological disorders. There is evidence that the MACI Psychopathy Content Scale correlates with PCL:YV test scores and is informative of violent reoffending (Amato et al., 2008; Murrie & Cornell, 2000; Murrie et al., 2004).

Assessing Psychopathy among Incarcerated Youth: Lessons Learned through Interviews

If youth cannot be interviewed effectively, then the answer to the question of whether the PCL:YV can reliably measure psychopathy is a resounding "no." For a decade (1998–2011), the ISVYOS trained more than a dozen Research Assistants to interview youth for the purpose of assessing psychopathy. Popular culture writers like Jon Ronson have depicted the measurement of psychopathy as something that is done relatively arbitrarily. Unlike Ronson's (2011) claims, my PCL:YV and CAPP-IRS training did not teach me to "spot" a "psychopath." In fact, the training I received from Dr. Stephen Hart (one of the developers of the CAPP-IRS and the PCL:SV) reinforced the idea that the assessment of psychopathy was complex and required strong interview skills[4] to probe the depth and robustness of personality traits across social contexts.

I was fortunate to learn many lessons from interviewing over 300 incarcerated youth. This section addresses what I looked for (and what I did not look for) when interviewing participants for the purpose of scoring PCL:YV items. I focus on the PCL:YV given that the analyses presented in this book are based on this instrument. I describe the measurement approach for 13 of the 20 PCL:YV items. These items are contained in the Interpersonal, Affective, and Lifestyle factors. The remaining items are mainly from the Antisocial factor and are primarily scored by reviewing file information. Thus, interview skills for rating these items are not as important. To communicate information on these traits, I use interview data from five ISVYOS participants. The circumstances of these cases are summarized in Table 3.2. Although I use these examples to help illustrate how psychopathy traits manifest for youth, it is important to remember that a single example does not mean that a person will score a "2" on the

---

[4] I have discussed some of these skills and strategies (e.g., interview preparation, developing rapport, dealing with lying during the interview, adapting interview strategies to be developmentally appropriate for youth) in other publications (e.g., McCuish et al., 2019, 2021). In these publications I focused on general interviewing strategies, including how to build rapport, engage in active listening, and ask questions appropriate for the developmental stage of incarcerated youth. I also recommend that readers who are interested in the assessment of psychopathy in clinical and forensic contexts consider additional sources that address some of the unique legal requirements that are not applicable to my experience within a research context (e.g., Cooke & Logan, 2018; Gacono, 2000; Kosson et al., 2016).

Table 3.2 *Ratings for case studies from the ISVYOS*

	Jacob	Owen	Justin	Albert	David
Demographics					
Gender	Male	Male	Male	Male	Male
Age	17	18	17	17	16
Ethnicity	White	White	White	Indigenous	White
Offending history					
Youth convictions	5	1	2	13	17
Age at first conviction	17	17	15	12	13
Violent offender	Yes	Yes	Yes	Yes	Yes
PCL:YV					
PCL:YV total score	33	35	31	36	29
Interpersonal factor	8	8	7	8	3
Affective factor	7	8	8	8	8
Lifestyle factor	6	8	7	9	7
Antisocial factor	8	7	5	7	9
CAPP-IRS[†]					
CAPP-IRS total score	145	161	162	181	132
Attachment domain	4.00	5.75	5.75	5.75	4.25
Behaviour domain	4.33	5.00	3.83	5.83	4.83
Cognitive domain	4.20	3.60	5.00	5.40	3.80
Dominance domain	5.00	4.83	4.67	5.83	2.50
Emotion domain	4.20	4.80	4.40	4.80	4.80
Self domain	4.43	5.29	5.86	5.29	4.00

† For CAPP-IRS domain scores, the average symptom score is shown rather than total score to account for differences in the number of symptoms within each domain.
Notes. The average CAPP-IRS score for the male subsample from the ISVYOS was 69.83 (SD = 36.53). The average PCL:YV score was 22.73 (SD = 7.28).

corresponding item. This is meant to be illustrative and is not a substitute for formal training on the PCL:YV.

Assessing psychopathy is not just about finding psychopathy traits; it is also about ruling them out. I describe interview strategies for the accurate assessment of psychopathy among incarcerated youth. This means determining how to ask questions in a manner that is sensitive to this particular developmental stage and population (e.g., limited language skills). It also means that asking follow-up questions is important to differentiate, for example, youth who truly lack remorse from youth who have difficulty finding the words to express what remorse means to them and how they show it.

Manifestations of Psychopathy Traits from the Interpersonal Factor

PCL:YV items from the Interpersonal factor include impression management, grandiose sense of self-worth, pathological lying, and manipulation for personal gain. Broadly speaking, interpersonal traits refer to a desire to control, dominate, and manipulate others. Tactics for carrying out such desires can vary (e.g., physical or mental abuse), and youth who score high on the Interpersonal factor will use these tactics across criminal and non-criminal interactions with family, friends, teachers, employers, peers, and others.

Impression Management

Impression management reflects an insincere presentation. Youth will make a concerted effort to present themselves in an overly positive light. This can come across as superficially charming. Engaging in impression management does not necessarily imply success in influencing someone's impression. In my experience, ISVYOS participants were quite transparent in their attempts to manage my impression of them. For example, when interviewing boys who reported they had a girlfriend, they would often talk about how they were always very polite and respectful toward their girlfriend's parents. When asked why, they explained that they wanted to give their girlfriend's parents the impression that they were "a nice guy." They hoped this image would afford them some leeway when it came to being out past curfew. Impression management may also manifest through long-winded answers to simple questions or the unnecessary and repeated use of jargon and other technical language. Justin reported that he liked to study niche topics so that he could make others feel inferior for not having the same level of knowledge. He quoted Mark Twain and then extended a phonily sympathetic hand toward me, and said, condescendingly, "I'm sorry, that might be too esoteric a reference for you."[5] In effect, Justin liked to illustrate his superior intelligence (i.e., impression management) while also trying to control the conversation by focusing on topics that

---

[5] Quotes are not always direct. I relied on handwritten interview notes, which captures the sentiment but not necessarily the precise words of the participant. I also changed specific words that might

only he understood. When Cleckley (1976) described Max as his prototypical case of someone with psychopathy traits, interestingly, Max used a superficial knowledge of Shakespeare for the same purposes that Justin used Twain: "He liked to rattle off his little round of fragmentary quotations, the connections and connotations of which he realized only in the most superficial sense" (p. 58).

Adults tend to underreport their negative behaviour in interviews (Book et al., 2006). In contrast, youth may attempt to engage in impression management by bragging about or exaggerating their antisocial behaviour or defiance of authority (Harter, 1990).[6] In the context of custody facilities, "the heavy" is a slang term that refers to the person on a unit who tends to exert control over other residents. This can include determining who does certain chores, how much "rent" (e.g., canteen items) a person must pay to live hassle-free on the unit, who is allowed to be admitted to the unit, and who should be removed. The heavy may issue an "eviction notice" via letter or by initiating a fight. Often, the heavy will have someone else do their fighting for them. They may be described by staff as "setting up fights." Some youth may try to portray themselves as the heavy as a means of impression management (i.e., projecting toughness). Consulting file information can be helpful to verify whether a participant's claims were supported by notes and observations from correctional staff.

It is also important to consider impression management outside the custody context. Owen and Jacob claimed that they were well-known in their respective cities for their ability to fight. David noted "I hate the law, I'm an outlaw" and suggested that "residents who talk to staff are a rat, kinda a bitch. Kids who hang around staff just don't want to get beat up." Owen repeatedly discussed his ability to manipulate sexual partners and get others to pay for items such as food and bus tickets. Owen's descriptions of events conflicted with file information indicating that he was often ostracized by peers and not well-liked. Jacob bragged about making thousands of dollars a day selling drugs, renting limos, and partying in strip clubs. Jacob talked about threatening the boyfriend of his female friend by waiting for the boyfriend to return home to find Jacob sitting at a table with a gun resting on the tabletop and pointed toward the boyfriend.

---

reveal the identity of a participant. This means changing names, locations, referencing their mother rather than their father, etc.

[6] The tendency to exaggerate antisocial behaviour and associated lifestyle may be more likely during interviews conducted for research purposes as opposed to court-ordered psychological assessments, where there may be consequences associated with acknowledging involvement in antisocial behaviour.

During the period in question, Jacob was in his mid-teens and was living in a group home. His self-presentation appeared aimed at conveying that he was living up to his father's reputation as a member of a well-known gang. However, per collateral sources in the community, he did not live the type of lifestyle he described.

Grandiose Sense of Self-worth

Grandiosity reflects a person's tendency to believe that they are better than others. They may brag excessively. Their perception of their abilities can enhance their sense of entitlement and belief that they are deserving of special privileges or rights. Youth who are grandiose may try to dominate conversations and appear overconfident and unfazed about the future. Their effort to control conversations is related to their desire to focus on themselves. This is different from controlling conversation to avoid negative topics, which more closely aligns with impression management.

Assessing grandiosity requires encouraging youth to talk about how they view themselves. This can be challenging because youth may have difficulty developing insight into who they are or may have difficulty putting their insights into words due to limited language development compared to adults. This challenge can be especially common in custody settings where there is a higher prevalence of learning disorders (Quinn et al., 2005). One way to acquire information about a youth's sense of self is by asking them about how they compare to others. However, asking adolescents to talk about how they are different from an undefined group of others (e.g., "Do you think you are different from most people?") may be too abstract. Participants often replied by saying "I don't know," "Nothing," or "How am I supposed to know what other people are like?" Relationships with peers and experiences in school are particularly important at this developmental stage. Asking youth to compare themselves to their friends can provide a useful reference point for revealing self-perceptions. For example, when asked about his friend group, Justin commented, "My friends are merely a fragment of myself, like a Venn diagram with me in the center." Justin, who dropped out of school, had this to say about the education system:

> There is a problem with the school system, which is why I dropped out. The work is made for kids who don't know anything so I'm not going to do it. ... Teachers are condescending, so I don't like them. The education system sucks. Kids at school are arrogant and immature. These people seem

to go out of their way to avoid truths and avoid bettering themselves through intelligence.

Some youth with psychopathy traits can initially give the impression that they care for others. Follow-up questions are necessary to gain insight into the origins of this concern. In some cases, follow-up questions can reveal underlying grandiosity. For example, when Justin discussed his girlfriend, he recalled an incident where she was almost seriously hurt. When asked to elaborate on why he felt worried about his girlfriend, Justin revealed that he cared about his girlfriend because he viewed her as a positive extension of himself. Justin did not care about his partner's well-being. He cared about his girlfriend the way some people care about their car. They might be worried about their car door being scratched in a parking lot, but they do not actually care about the well-being of the car, they care about how damage to their car impacts themselves. When asked what he liked about his girlfriend, Justin mentioned that she "didn't vocalize much." He noted that she "took it all in" and liked what she saw in him. In effect, Justin liked her because she was quiet, listened to him, and did not threaten his sense of superiority. People with psychopathy traits thus may be more prone to view others as trophies or status symbols. Justin's comments about women reinforced the likelihood that he cared little about the well-being of his partner: "I don't respect my mom because of her lack of motivation and effort, and she is too emotional during arguments.... Females are bat shit crazy, cheating sluts [they] are there for sex and to clean up after me."

Pathological Lying

Pathological lying refers to an individual's tendency to lie pervasively across a variety of social situations. Impression management, discussed earlier in this chapter, is a form of deceit that involves curating others' perceptions of oneself. In the case of traits like impression management or manipulation for personal gain, there is some tangible benefit or strategic purpose. Pathological lying, however, refers to the frequency and persistence of deceit, including the tendency to lie even without any clear benefit, and showing little concern if caught in a lie. When caught in a lie, the person may choose to continue to lie based on their belief that they can talk their way out of being caught. For example, when asked about his current offence, Albert reported that he was convicted of a homicide. I mentioned to Albert that his correctional file indicated that he was convicted of a sexual offence. Albert calmly doubled down on his lie. He described a scenario in which he killed someone for kidnapping his brother. He explained that the file that I reviewed was wrong, that a clerical error had been made, and that he had never appeared in court to face charges for a sexual offence. Albert further noted that his lawyer was in the process of having the sexual offence conviction removed from his correctional file and that I should contact his lawyer to verify the information. Although I did not contact his lawyer, none of what Albert said was supported. There were countless documents in his file indicating his involvement in a serious sexual offence.

In my experience, pathological lying was not difficult to detect because ISVYOS participants were not especially skilled in their ability to lie. This aligns with Dr. Robin-Ann Cogburn's PhD dissertation research. Cogburn (1993) found that people with psychopathy traits are not superior in their ability to deceive others. Certainly, people with psychopathy traits lie more frequently and with less concern than the average person, but in contrast to the Hannibal Lecter myth discussed in Chapter 2, their ability to "successfully" lie is not better than average. Although lying is not necessarily difficult to detect, a bigger challenge is the fact that persistent lying can negatively impact the reliability of an interview. There are several strategies to avoid or address potential deceit during an interview.

Building rapport is helpful for preventing dishonest interview responses. Rapport develops by showing participants that you sincerely care about their story and that you can be trusted. Before and during the interview, I explained to participants that I was in a nonjudgmental role. This helped encourage openness and minimize deceitfulness.

If it is believed that a participant is not telling the truth, to maintain rapport, as long as the lie does not harm the reliability of the interview, it may be best to just ignore it. In instances where a participant might be lying and further clarification is needed, a method of challenging information without damaging rapport is referred to as the Columbo approach.[7] This approach involves reacting to the youth's deceptive answers with confusion. I might state, "I am confused. You just said that prior to your incarceration you were going to school, but in your file your probation officer noted that you had been expelled. Could you help me understand what is going on here?" Instead of creating confrontation, this places the participant in an authority position where they assist the

---

[7] This approach is named after the iconic, bumbling television series detective whose disheveled appearance and non-threatening questions helped elicit honest answers. The television show *Poker Face* represents a modern take on *Columbo*.

confused interviewer in understanding contradictory information. This helps with rapport because it puts the interviewer and participant on the same side. Higher-intensity challenges (e.g., accusation of lying or turning the interview into an interrogation) may harm the reliability of the remainder of the interview.

Manipulation for Personal Gain

Manipulation for personal gain reflects an individual's tendency to lie specifically to gain an advantage. Manipulation can also occur without lying, such as by exploiting others. More often, misrepresentation or cheating are used as tools through which individuals attempt to deceive others for personal benefit. Youth with a tendency to manipulate will view their relationships through the lens of what the other person can offer them. Attempts to manipulate extend across a variety of social contexts and often are not particularly elaborate. In fact, given the lack of evidence of an association between psychopathy and higher IQ, it should not be surprising that although people with psychopathy traits may be more prone to engaging in manipulative behaviour, they are not more likely to be successful in such attempts.

Justin was up-front about being manipulative toward others:

> [I am] able to be whoever I want to project, like the arrogant, condescending know-it-all. I can mold my personality and get people's reactions…. I like testing the waters before I reveal who I really am. I'll act calm and knowledgeable; I'll show the rest of me later on.

Justin's tendency to manipulate was reflected in his interpersonal exchanges:

> I don't see the point of making a deal if I am not going to benefit… I'm very particular about grammar, I have arguments with friends over sentence structure, I often get kicked out of chat rooms for commenting on people's grammar.

Not all youth are as forthcoming as Justin. Albert was adamant that he did not try to manipulate others. However, he was described by custody staff as "sneaky" and "polite when he wants something." Albert would subtly victimize others by coercing younger or weaker inmates to fight one another so that he would not get in trouble for fighting. This tactic of setting up others to get in fights was repeatedly discussed by Cleckley (1976) in his review of experiences treating people with psychopathy traits.

Manifestations of Psychopathy Traits from the Affective Factor

PCL:YV items from the Affective factor include lack of remorse, shallow affect, callous/lack of empathy, and failure to accept responsibility. Shallow affect and callous/lack of empathy represent lovelessness/coldness, whereas lack of remorse and failure to accept responsibility represent guiltlessness (Patrick, 2010a). Youth scoring high on the Affective factor rarely speak positively about family and friends. They may express a disinterest in forming close bonds with others. Although they may not prefer to be alone, they generally do not report much happiness spending time with others. They may actively harm those in their social circle. Youth with psychopathy traits who have harmed others will have difficulty understanding how their behaviour was harmful. They may express an "I'm-not-them, I-don't-know" attitude when asked about the feelings of others. They will fail to act in a manner expected, such as by helping friends or family in need.

Strong interview skills are needed to discern whether a lack of attachment to family is related to psychopathy traits or to environmental circumstances. Adverse childhood experiences perpetrated by family members (e.g., Baglivio et al., 2015), placement in foster care (Yang et al., 2017), and the incarceration of a parent (e.g., Rodriguez et al., 2009) are common in the backgrounds of incarcerated youth. If an ISVYOS participant indicated that they did not feel attached to their family, it was important to ask follow-up questions to establish whether the lack of bonds was related to psychopathy traits or represented an understandable defence mechanism in response to abusive experiences at home. If youth indicated that they were uncommitted to family members or did not actively do things to help family, follow-up questions were important to gain insight into whether the participant's family was not a positive part of their life.

Lack of Remorse

This item describes youth who do not regret harmful actions. Youth may suggest that they have nothing to be sorry about. The PCL:YV item measuring failure to accept responsibility refers to a refusal to accept responsibility for negative behaviour. People who lack remorse may technically accept responsibility for their behaviour but will also show a lack of concern for the consequences. Some apologies may be superficial and done so primarily for the purpose of reducing punishment. Youth who spend substantial time in court or who understand how the criminal legal system functions may be aware that demonstrations of remorse can act as a mitigating factor that lessens the severity of their sentence. Follow-up questions can help identify why youth feel bad about their behaviour. Youth indicating that they regret the offence or feel sorry for the victim should be asked to explain why they regret the offence or how their behaviour may have affected the victim. Youth who lack remorse may be unable to express or explain how their behaviour affected their victim and may instead only acknowledge that they regret their offence because of the consequences to themselves. Owen claimed to be sorry for his offence, but when asked to explain why he felt sorry, he stated:

> I haven't done a lot that requires me to be sorry for. I don't know, largely I regret it [the offence] for myself, and then for my family. The last thing I need is to be depicted as a bad person.

David noted that he regretted assaulting a taxi driver, but later acknowledged that the reason he regretted it was because "I got charged with it. Wasn't something I wanted to happen, but it had to happen." David said that it "had to happen" because he did not have cab fare. In other cases, youth are more direct about not having remorse. Regarding his index offence (a violent crime), Justin mentioned that he could have felt remorse, but doing so would accomplish nothing, as the action had already been carried out, and expressions of remorse would be patronizing.

Shallow Affect

Shallow affect refers to youth with limited expressions of emotion. Their emotions may lack depth or meaning, and relationships with others may seem superficial. For example, Justin reported that his friendships were based on his desire to "do different things" rather than on connecting with others. Youth may describe emotions but demonstrate difficulty explaining what emotions feel like and what precipitates a particular emotion. There may be a discordance between the nature of an experience and the emotional tone in which the experience is described. Although Jacob suggested he was generally happy, when asked to specify what he liked about his life, Jacob noted that "you haven't felt empowered until you have held a gun to someone's head."[8] Follow-up questions regarding Justin's relationship with family members and friends indicated that his lack of

---

[8] Emotions (e.g., happiness) that are expressed in response to antisocial behaviour or to the hurt experienced by others are not considered examples of positive affect.

emotional investment in relationships was unrelated to trauma, generalized across a variety of different types of relationships, and applied to various social contexts:

> I am detached enough from my father to not care about his absence. It is hard to listen to my mom. I think is a respect thing. Most of my friends are from school. They are temporary and can be replaced. I don't feel loyalty to anyone. Very early in life I decided that everyone was an idiot. At around 13 I isolated myself from everyone.

Callous/Lack of Empathy

The callousness component of this item refers to a willingness to harm others and a disregard for the impact that this behaviour has on others. A lack of empathy refers to the inability to understand how another person might feel. Youth who score high on this item do not feel the emotional pain of others and have difficulty considering (or fail to consider) the experience of victims. Callousness may be demonstrated through violence that goes beyond what is necessary in the commission of an offence (e.g., continuing an assault after robbing someone of their wallet).

Owen indicated that he did things to help his sister because of their "family bond." Yet, when asked to provide examples, he laughed and said, "I've probably tried to beat her up more than anyone." Owen acknowledged that he looked for a girlfriend when he was stuck in a rut and that the relationship was just to "kill time." Owen indicated that his lack of regard for the well-being of others extended across a wide range of relationships:

> I don't like to have lots of friends because it is too hard to please everyone.... I'm only friends with people who don't expect me to do things.... My girlfriend never really expects me to take her anywhere, and I don't really want to take her anywhere.... I had the decency to go on a break with my girlfriend before hooking up with another girl.... I just told her I wanted to go on a break, she was upset, but at the same time I was going to jail ... it was a bit selfish [laughing]. When my mom criticizes me, I call her fat. I'm not going to cry about it.... Most people think I am an asshole. I like to bully in a roundabout way. I like to push people's buttons to try and get them to react, to get them angry.

Failure to Accept Responsibility

This item describes youth who are unwilling to accept the consequences of their behaviour. They show little interest in change and disvalue the opinion of others. Youth will minimize, justify, or blame others for their negative behaviour. Justin suggested that all of his misbehaviour was a product of growing up without a father. Yet, as readers may recall from previous sections, Justin cared very little about his father and other family members. Justin was compelled (not through psychosis) to go through with his current offence because he needed to commit "mental suicide." He argued that he had to hit rock bottom to change, and therefore his offence was justified as it would improve his life. Justin talked about having an overactive imagination as a child. He would often make up fantasy worlds and then use these fantasies to justify his behaviour. Justin blamed others for labeling him as a genius because this placed too much pressure on him to succeed.

One way that youth in custody displace blame is through how they allocate responsibility for their offences and other problematic behaviour. Owen stated that "I'm less responsible than my co-accused, it was his idea all along. I was in the wrong place at the wrong time." This statement contradicted Owen's earlier claim in the interview, in which he described enjoying the planning that went into the commission of his offence. Justin justified the selection of the victim in his index offence on the basis that she was "unremarkable" and therefore did not deserve to be spared from harm.

Manifestations of Psychopathy Traits from the Lifestyle Factor

PCL:YV items from the Lifestyle factor include stimulation-seeking, parasitic orientation, lack of goals, impulsivity, and irresponsibility. Youth who score high on the Lifestyle factor typically show a disinterest in attending school.[9] These youth prefer to live day to day rather than follow a schedule or develop a routine. When they do have meetings or a set schedule, they are frequently late or absent. They engage in reckless behaviour that puts themselves and others at risk. This can include using a variety of drugs and seeking out dangerous, adrenaline-inducing activities. During the interview, youth who score high on the Lifestyle factor may persistently fiddle with their hands or other objects. They may pace the room, constantly adjust clothing, require frequent breaks, and fail to listen to questions. File information may reveal frequent removals from classrooms/treatment

---

[9] There are a variety of reasons why youth might be disinterested in attending school (e.g., experiencing bullying). Follow-up questions are necessary to help identify the source of the disinterest in school attendance.

programs due to misbehaviour. Their school records may indicate a history of behavioural management plans. Traits within the Lifestyle factor overlap with attention-deficit/hyperactivity disorder (ADHD) and other behavioural disorders. It is important to keep in mind that high scores on the Lifestyle factor alone are not sufficient for scoring high on the PCL:YV. For example, ISVYOS participants averaged a score of 21.77 on the PCL:YV. The maximum score on the Lifestyle factor is 10.

Stimulation-Seeking

Stimulation seeking reflects a persistent interest in taking risks, engaging in novel experiences, and seeking excitement. This can manifest in experimenting with illicit substances and engaging in dangerous behaviour such as driving recklessly. Routine activities (e.g., chores) tend to go unfinished due to boredom. As mentioned, youth like Justin appreciate friends for the opportunity to engage in different activities as opposed to developing emotional connections. Sensation seeking can be observed in the interview through antagonistic behaviour from youth who want to elicit a strong reaction from the interviewer.[10]

The interview is not necessarily the most stimulating experience, which may lead to challenging behaviour. Albert was unable to sit still. He fidgeted with his hands, sometimes requiring a deck of cards to keep busy. He contorted his face with his fingers. He rocked a wobbly table back and forth. I suggested that we fix the table. Albert agreed that the table should be fixed, but declined to help me. As part of compensation for participating in the interview, Albert was provided with juice and chips. He ate the bag of chips in seconds, ripped the juice box into small pieces, and chewed on the straw and chip bag. Another youth I interviewed played with his juice box to such an extent that the ink from the juice box rubbed off onto his hands. As always, it is important to consider that (a) the interview represents only one context for observing behaviour and (b) fidgety or restless behaviour alone is hardly sufficient evidence of psychopathy.

---

[10] Some participants asked intrusive questions (e.g., "How much money do you make?"). In isolation, such questions could reflect curiosity. If such questions persisted despite attempts to refocus the participant, it may be because the participant wanted to gain information to use against the interviewer (e.g., "I bet I make more money than you"). Control over the interview can be maintained by playing to the egocentricity of youth. To keep the interview on track, I would mention that I am really interested in the youth's opinion and that the interview is supposed to be all about them.

Parasitic Orientation

Individuals with a parasitic orientation exploit others, but unlike the item from the Interpersonal factor that taps into manipulation for personal gain, a parasitic orientation is more active. Individuals will avoid employment/school, will not help with chores, and overly rely on others by presenting themselves as incapable or deserving of sympathy. It is important to distinguish parasitic orientation from the kinds of reliance on others that are normative for youth. For example, parasitic orientation may be evident among adults who rely on family members for financial support and housing, but this is normative during adolescence and thus would not be considered evidence of parasitic orientation. Instead, youth may bully peers for money or coerce younger or smaller peers to do things on their behalf. Youth with a parasitic orientation may be described by parents, teachers, or custody staff as needy, demanding, and high-maintenance. Cleckley (1976) described such patients as perpetually asking for favours. Youth who reflect this trait will constantly question direction from others, be slow to follow rules, and spend excessive time attempting to bargain or negotiate.

Lacks Goals

Youth who lack goals will mention that they prefer to live day to day and do not like thinking about the future. Youth who score low on this item have realistic goals, know what is required to accomplish them, and typically take steps toward their goals. Youth who score high on this item may describe a goal but have no realistic path or plan to achieve it. One youth discussed his desire to be a doctor despite dropping out of school in grade 9 and having been given a prison sentence of 25 years for first-degree murder. David expressed a desire to stop using crack cocaine and indicated that he was going to attend treatment upon release. Instead of directly challenging David, which could damage rapport, I asked simple follow-up questions about his relationship with his girlfriend. David noted that he was excited to see her upon release. This provided an indication that David did not intend to proceed directly to the inpatient treatment program that he discussed previously. In talking about his girlfriend, David noted that she was in jail and that their activities as a couple included "selling and smoking drugs and going to the beach a couple times." In other words, although David expressed a desire to attend treatment, he showed little interest in taking the steps necessary to ensure this happened. In effect, unlike more normative adolescent behaviours that result from a lack of planning (e.g., failing to do homework, missing curfew), David failed to plan major aspects of his life, such as enrolling in school and attending substance use counseling.

Impulsivity

Impulsive youth lack self-control, which means they tend to prefer immediate gratification, lack foresight, and rarely, if ever, engage in self-reflection (Gottfredson & Hirschi, 1990). Youth who are impulsive fail to consider the consequences of their behaviour and also tend to denigrate people who value behavioural control. Incarcerated youth whom I interviewed often referred to those willing to delay gratification as soft or perceived them to be "rats" who could not be trusted. It is important to reiterate the dysfunctional component of this psychopathy trait. It is not just that youth are impulsive; it is that this impulsivity leads to difficulties in everyday life. Many presentence reports or psychiatric evaluations include tests relating to a youth's ability to maintain attention, and these test scores can provide valuable insight into impulsive traits. Compared to adults, poor organization is a relatively normative feature of adolescence. Interviews with youth should explore the extent to which impulsivity causes functional impairment. As mentioned, David's index offence involved assaulting a cab driver after getting into a taxi without any money. When asked about whether he considered the consequences of being unable to pay, David proudly stated that he chose not to think of the consequences of his actions.

Irresponsibility

Irresponsibility describes youth who fail to meet reasonable expectations. They often engage in reckless behaviour that puts the safety of others in jeopardy. Being organized is part of demonstrating responsibility. Youth who are irresponsible will not follow rules, especially when on probation or when expected to fulfill community service hours or other court-ordered obligations. The structured nature of custody may give the impression that interviewees are more organized than reality. For ISVYOS participants, points for cleanliness and organization were earned as part of an institution's token economy system.[11] Thus, youth had external motivations

---

[11] Under a token economy system, positive behaviour is rewarded through additional privileges (e.g., later bedtime) and financial incentives.

for being tidy. However, they may brag about being irresponsible when in the community. Although Albert asserted that he was highly organized while in custody, when asked about what he liked to do in his spare time in the community, he stated:

> In my own time I like to do stupid shit, go around and steal things. Instead of going to school I would just stay home or wander the streets.... I once wrote a complaint form [in custody] but was too lazy to hand it in.... I clean in here only because it is mandatory.

Chapter Summary

Quality data are necessary to test research questions about psychopathy. Sometimes, this is needed to push back against speculative narratives, such as Dilulio's conception of the youth superpredator, which seemed to be driven by political ideology rather than evidence. Quality data are also essential for reliably testing the validity of different theoretical perspectives regarding psychopathy, including determining its core traits and its relationship with offending. Having reliable measures of psychopathy begins with careful research design. The analyses in this book use data from the ISVYOS. The ISVYOS was initiated in 1998, and data collection continued until 2025. The ISVYOS was one of the first large-scale studies to measure psychopathy traits among youth. In fact, data collected from this study were used to help create the PCL:YV manual developed by Dr. Adelle Forth and her colleagues.

This book focuses on 535 incarcerated youth who received an interview and rating on the PCL:YV. The purpose of this book is to address whether having psychopathy traits in adolescence influences life-course development. These 535 youth are now adults, and through a correctional software program, the ISVYOS research team collected data on various crime, social, and health outcomes in adulthood. We also collected data on psychopathy using additional measures, including the CAPP-IRS and MACI Psychopathy Content Scale. The relationship between these different measures of psychopathy is described in greater detail in Chapter 4.

Collecting reliable data on psychopathy is challenging. Substantial thought must go into the practice of assessing psychopathy. Although many popular culture resources may lead readers to believe that the assessment of psychopathy is straightforward, in reality, it is complex and requires strong interview skills to probe the depth and robustness of personality traits across social contexts. Psychopathy is not something you "spot," such as by reading body language or interpreting vocabulary choices. The assessment of psychopathy is not as simple as going through a checklist of whether traits are present or absent. The assessment of psychopathy does not begin with an assumption that psychopathy traits are present, seeking only evidence to support that assumption. The goal of assessment is to identify whether and to what extent psychopathy traits are present. Assessing interpersonal, affective, and behavioural traits of psychopathy requires developing rapport with the participant, engaging in active listening to ask appropriate follow-up questions, and understanding nuanced differences in psychopathy traits, including how such traits may be expressed in adolescence versus normative youth personality development.

CHAPTER 4

The Reliability and Validity of Psychopathy Measures

In his book *The Mask of Sanity*, Dr. Hervey Cleckley (1976) drew upon his clinical experience to describe how psychopathy traits manifested across a variety of individual case studies. However, to move beyond anecdotal evidence and establish systematic standards, clinical descriptions need to be translated into measurable tools. The Psychopathy Checklist: Youth Version (PCL:YV), which is the instrument of focus in this book, is just one of more than a dozen measures of psychopathy. There are two main reasons that multiple measures of psychopathy exist. First, measures of psychopathy are typically guided by clinical descriptions of psychopathy, but as indicated in Chapter 2, clinicians can have quite distinct ways of describing psychopathy. For example, the triarchic model describes boldness as a core trait of psychopathy. Accordingly, if the goal is to develop an instrument that reflects the triarchic model of psychopathy, such as the Psychopathy Personality Inventory – Revised (PPI-R), it is necessary to include survey items that capture the concept of boldness. Other measures, like the PCL:YV, were influenced by Dr. Cleckley's description of psychopathy, which the developers of the PCL:YV believed placed very little emphasis on boldness and therefore did not include items that tapped into this trait. Thus, the PCL:YV would not be the ideal instrument if researchers were interested in measuring the triarchic model.

A second major reason that multiple instruments exist is that psychopathy traits are not measured in a test tube.[1] Two instruments influenced by the same clinical description of psychopathy may vary in the degree to

---

[1] In Chapter 3, I mentioned that ISVYOS participants averaged a score of 21.76 on the PCL:YV. The most accurate conclusion I can make about this average score is that it is wrong. Across 535 participants who received ratings on 20 items (10,700 decisions), it seems likely that for at least one of these ratings, a youth who received, for example, a score of "1" on a particular item should have been scored a "2." Researchers must consider how pervasive such errors are; this is something that can be empirically examined as part of the assessment of a measurement tool's reliability and validity.

which they capture this description accurately. There may also be multiple interpretations of the same theoretical description of psychopathy, leading to different measurement strategies. Both the Psychopathy Checklist – Revised (PCL-R) and the Comprehensive Assessment of Psychopathic Personality – Institutional Rating Scale (CAPP-IRS) are influenced by Cleckley's description of psychopathy. Thus, they attempt to measure the same construct. However, the CAPP-IRS was developed in part because the authors of this tool believed that the Psychopathy Checklist – Revised (PCL-R) included too few items relating to personality traits (Cooke et al., 2004). Measures like the Psychopathic Personality Inventory – Revised (PPI-R) and Triarchic Psychopathy Measure (Tri-PM) were developed based on the opinion that Cleckley considered boldness a key indicator of psychopathy. Measures like the PCL-R and CAPP-IRS were also based on Cleckley's description of psychopathy, but the developers of these instruments interpreted Cleckley's description of psychopathy differently and thus did not prioritize the inclusion of items measuring boldness.

Chapter Goals and Analyses

Chapters 5–10 of this book focus on the predictive validity of psychopathy: do psychopathy traits in adolescence increase the likelihood of negative outcomes in adulthood? However, to start this book by answering such questions would be to put the cart before the horse. It is necessary to first evaluate whether the PCL:YV was measured reliably and validly for the ISVYOS sample. For example, it does not matter if a measure of psychopathy predicts reoffending if it is not reliable or valid. This might mean that the measure used can help in understanding offending, but if the measure is not reliable or valid, it cannot contribute to understanding psychopathy's influence on offending. The goal of this book is not to prove that psychopathy influences negative outcomes. The goal is to measure psychopathy accurately so that we can better understand evidence for and against the influence of psychopathy in adolescence on various offending, social, and health outcomes in adulthood.

Despite what Jon Ronson, True Crime Podcasts, and TikTok influencers want their viewers to believe, measuring psychopathy is not an easy task; it is not something that can just be "spotted." Moving from clinical or theoretical descriptions of psychopathy (i.e., conceptualization) to an approach for measuring psychopathy (i.e., operationalization) is difficult. Assessing the reliability and validity of an instrument helps to evaluate whether the task was completed successfully. In this chapter, I assess the reliability and validity of the PCL:YV among 535 Incarcerated Serious and Violent Young Offender Study (ISVYOS) participants.

Reliability was assessed via indicators of interrater reliability and internal consistency of the PCL:YV. Validity was assessed in two ways: construct validity and convergent validity. Construct validity was evaluated using confirmatory factor analysis, item response theory, and psychopathology network modeling, allowing for an examination of the structure of psychopathy at the factor and item level. Convergent validity was examined by looking at the correlation between the PCL:YV and two other measures of psychopathy: the CAPP-IRS and the Millon Adolescent Clinical Inventory (MACI) Psychopathy Content Scale.

PCL:YV Reliability

A measure is reliable if it produces the same result each time it is applied. Two types of reliability examined in this chapter are interrater reliability and internal consistency. Interrater reliability refers to the extent to which independent raters assign the same test score for the same person. Poor interrater reliability indicates potential issues with training or knowledge of psychopathy on the part of the rater or with specific administrative issues with the instrument. For example, imagine a scenario in court where two expert witness psychologists, one for the defence and one for the prosecution, reach markedly different conclusions about a youth's PCL:YV score. Assuming both were adequately trained and behaved ethically, the different scores could reflect administrative challenges in measuring PCL:YV items consistently (e.g., vague criteria or guidelines in the PCL:YV manual for scoring particular items). Internal consistency refers to the degree of convergence between individual PCL:YV items. In other words, do items on an instrument correlate with one another in the expected manner?

Interrater Reliability

Twenty-eight ISVYOS Research Assistants received training on the PCL:YV. All Research Assistants had prior experience administering the structured intake interview to ISVYOS participants. Training was primarily conducted by Dr. Stephen Hart, who assisted in the development of the PCL-R, led the development of the Psychopathy Checklist: Screening Version (PCL:SV), and co-authored the CAPP. Training sessions focused on defining items from the PCL:YV, explaining the purpose of different interview questions, and reviewing and discussing video recordings of interviews conducted for the assessment of psychopathy. Research Assistants were also trained to review file-based information (e.g., index offence, family history, and performance in school) to better understand the participant's background, contextualize participant responses, and assist with the scoring of PCL:YV items.

Interrater reliability was evaluated by assigning six Research Assistants to three pairs. Each pair interviewed and rated 10 different participants. Both raters were present for the interview. For each pair, one rater led the interview with the first participant, and the other rater led the interview with the next participant. The degree of agreement in PCL:YV ratings was calculated between raters. Each member of the pair was blind to the other member's ratings. Both raters also separately reviewed file-based information as part of scoring procedures. As part of her PhD thesis in the Department of Psychology at Simon Fraser University, Dr. Gina Vincent (2002) calculated intraclass correlation coefficient values to inspect the extent of interrater reliability across the ISVYOS Research Assistants who participated in the interrater reliability evaluation. The intraclass correlation coefficient indicates the proportion of observed variance in PCL:YV test scores that is due to true variability between participants rather than variability between raters. Possible values range from −1.00 to 2.00. Intraclass correlation coefficient values closer to 1.00 indicate a higher level of agreement between raters. Dr. Vincent reported that interrater reliability for the PCL:YV was excellent (0.92) among ISVYOS Research Assistants. This indicates that independent raters, blind to each other's scores, generally scored the same participant in a consistent manner. Thus, the ISVYOS avoided issues with the PCL:YV producing inconsistent results as an indicator of psychopathy traits.

Internal Consistency

Even though interrater reliability was high, it is possible that Research Assistants were all trained in the wrong way, which could lead to systematically under- or overestimating scores on certain items of the PCL:YV. Internal consistency refers to whether items designed to measure different aspects of a construct reliably measure that construct (Vogt, 2007). Internal consistency provides evidence that items were scored accurately by indicating whether items within a scale correlate in the anticipated direction. If a particular item was systematically underestimated, it would have a weaker than anticipated correlation with other items, leading to lower levels of internal consistency. Cronbach's alpha provides information on internal consistency by determining the correlation between items on a scale. Cronbach's alpha values of greater than 0.70 are considered acceptable as they indicate that at least 50 percent of variance in the construct is accounted for by items in the scale (0.70 × 0.70 = 49 percent). Cronbach's alpha for the 20 items of the PCL:YV equaled 0.81, meaning that the measure had good internal consistency.[2]

PCL:YV Validity

Reliability indicates whether a measure is stable or consistent in its application. Evidence of reliability does not mean that the PCL:YV accurately measures psychopathy. Reliability just indicates that the PCL:YV consistently measures *something*. Assessments of validity help indicate whether the PCL:YV is assessing clinical descriptions of psychopathy. In this section, I examine construct validity and convergent validity. Construct validity refers to whether the PCL:YV is measuring psychopathy as intended, in this case, as a reflection of Interpersonal, Affective, Lifestyle, and Antisocial deficits. Convergent validity refers to whether the PCL:YV is positively correlated with other measures of psychopathy, in this case, the CAPP-IRS and MACI Psychopathy Content Scale. I use three different techniques to assess construct validity: confirmatory factor analysis, item response theory, and network analysis. PCL:YV items are outlined in Table 4.1.

Confirmatory Factor Analysis of the PCL:YV

Confirmatory factor analysis is a classical test theory technique[3] that allows for an inspection of whether the factor structure of the PCL:YV aligns with theoretical expectations and prior research. For example, confirmatory factor analysis can help examine whether the four-factor model proposed

---

[2] Cronbach's alpha is the more well-known indicator of internal consistency, but it is meant for scales constructed via interval-level items and tends to underestimate the reliability of scales like the PCL:YV that are based on ordinal items. Polychoric ordinal alpha is a more appropriate indicator of internal consistency when a scale is comprised of items with a limited range (Gadermann et al., 2012). In this case, the polychoric ordinal alpha value for PCL:YV total scores was 0.84.

[3] Classical test theory techniques assume that a person's score on the PCL:YV reflects (1) a person's true score on psychopathy as a latent trait and (2) error on the PCL:YV rating. With just a single measurement, it is not possible to distinguish the extent to which a person's score on the PCL:YV is their true score vs. error (e.g., inaccurate measurement).

Table 4.1 *Description of PCL:YV items*

	CFA figure label	Network figure label	Mean	SD
Interpersonal factor				
Impression management	x1	Int1	0.73	0.73
Grandiose sense of self-worth	x2	Int2	0.79	0.76
Pathological lying	x3	Int3	0.60	0.69
Manipulation for personal gain	x4	Int4	1.05	0.74
Affective factor				
Lack of remorse	x5	Aff5	1.34	0.68
Shallow affect	x6	Aff6	0.84	0.74
Callous or lacking empathy	x7	Aff7	1.16	0.72
Failure to accept responsibility	x8	Aff8	1.20	0.74
Lifestyle factor				
Stimulation seeking	x9	L9	1.26	0.67
Parasitic orientation	x10	L10	0.63	0.67
Lacks goals	x11	L11	0.86	0.74
Impulsivity	x12	L12	1.19	0.67
Irresponsibility	x13	L13	1.21	0.66
Antisocial factor				
Poor anger control	x14	Anti14	1.42	0.67
Early behavioural problems	x15	Anti15	1.09	0.78
Serious criminal behaviour	x16	Anti16	1.75	0.45
Revocation of conditional release	x17	Anti17	1.43	0.75
Criminal versatility	x18	Anti18	1.52	0.71
Unclassified PCL:YV Items				
Impersonal sexual behaviour	x19	Unc19	0.89	0.82
Unstable interpersonal relationships	x20	Unc20	0.75	0.78

Notes. Each item ranges from 0 to 2. Labels reflect how the item is indicated in figures for the confirmatory factor analyses and network analyses. CFA = confirmatory factor analysis; SD = standard deviation.

by Hare and colleagues (e.g., Hare & Neumann, 2010; Neumann et al., 2015) better reflects the structure of the PCL:YV among ISVYOS participants compared to the three-factor model proposed by Cooke and Michie (2001) that excludes the Antisocial factor. One challenge in examining whether the factor structure of the PCL:YV aligns with prior research is that the PCL literature has identified over a dozen ways in which this model can be represented (Cooke et al., 2007; Jones et al., 2006). Even within the same model (e.g., four-factor model), there are differences of opinion regarding how to measure this model. Said differently, for researchers examining the structure of the PCL:YV using confirmatory factor analysis, it can be hard to know which factor structure they are expected to confirm.

For parsimony, I test and compare the fit of three models: a four-factor hierarchical model, a four-factor correlated model, and a three-factor hierarchical model. A correlated three-factor model was not tested because it is mathematically equivalent to the hierarchical three-factor model.[4] Correlated models and hierarchical models differ in terms of the hypothesized structure of a latent construct (i.e., a construct that cannot be directly observed but can be captured via observable indicators; see Chapter 2). Correlated factor models specify statistical associations between factors. For example, in a correlated four-factor model, a positive correlation is hypothesized to exist between the Interpersonal and Affective factors. Hierarchical models assume that the correlation between factors is spurious (i.e., not real). The correlation is considered spurious because the association between factors is accounted for by a common cause, in this case, the latent trait of psychopathy. Unlike hierarchical models, correlated models do not specify an overarching disorder that produces specific psychopathy traits. Instead, correlated models *can be* consistent with the hypothesis that psychopathy occurs when traits from different personality domains co-occur. This distinction between hierarchical models and correlated models is similar to the distinction between reflective (hierarchical) constructs and formative (correlated) constructs discussed in Chapter 2 (see Table 2.1).

Comparing the fit of the four-factor correlated model to the fit of the four-factor hierarchical model was necessary to investigate different theoretical perspectives on the structure of psychopathy (see Debate #2 from Chapter 2 for a refresher). If psychopathy traits are extreme manifestations

---

[4] A Psychopathy Checklist (PCL) three-factor correlated model has three correlations among the factors, and the hierarchical model also has three loadings on the superordinate psychopathy factor. In contrast, the PCL four-factor correlated model has six correlations among the factors, whereas the hierarchical model has only four loadings on the superordinate psychopathy factor. I did not include the use of testlets originally specified by Cooke and Michie (2001) in their three-factor model. Testlets can be used in instances where researchers believe that a pair of items was scored using the same or similar information, thereby inflating their correlation beyond what is accounted for by the latent factor. In my view (also see Skeem et al., 2003), if this were to occur, it suggests an issue with how items were scored by users of the PCL or an issue with the PCL manual. In essence, testlets may reflect an issue with training and not with theories about the factor structure of psychopathy.

of general personality traits, a correlated model *may* more accurately reflect the structure of psychopathy. This does not imply the absence of a latent construct, as each factor is itself a latent indicator (e.g., the Interpersonal factor is a latent construct). Keep in mind that confirmatory factor analysis is not the appropriate method to test the perspective that psychopathy is an emergent interpersonal syndrome because this perspective considers the possibility that certain psychopathy traits (e.g., affective traits) are uncorrelated or even negatively correlated with other psychopathy traits (e.g., interpersonal traits). This possibility is not captured in confirmatory factor analysis, which emphasizes positive intercorrelations across items.

Analyses in this section addressed three questions: (1) Is there evidence for the construct validity of the PCL:YV? (2) Does a correlated or hierarchical model better describe the structure of the PCL:YV data? (3) Is the PCL:YV underpinned by three or four factors?

Confirmatory factor analyses were performed to assess and compare the fit of the correlated and hierarchical four-factor models (Figures 4.1 and 4.2) and the hierarchical three-factor model (Figure 4.3). Goodness-of-fit statistics for each model are shown in Table 4.2. Based on these fit statistics, each of the three models examined was a good fit to the data. However, it is possible that some good-fitting models fit better than other good-fitting models. I used the DIFFTEST option in the statistical software program Mplus (Muthén & Muthén, 2011) to compare the four-factor hierarchical model that is nested within the four-factor correlated model. A nested model uses all the same variables and cases as another model but specifies at least one additional parameter to be estimated. In this case, the hierarchical model (see Figure 4.3) adds additional paths from each factor to the latent construct of psychopathy. These paths are excluded from the correlated model in Figure 4.2. The DIFFTEST was significant, which implies that the four-factor correlated model is a better fit to the data compared to the four-factor hierarchical model.

The DIFFTEST function in Mplus cannot be used to directly compare the correlated four-factor model to the hierarchical three-factor model because they do not include the same variables. Specifically, the hierarchical three-factor model excludes items from the Antisocial factor. However, with respect to fit indices, the Standardized Root Mean Square Residual[5] was lower for the three-factor model, and the Comparative Fit Index values

---

[5] Root Mean Square Residual is more commonly reported, but the Standardized Root Mean Square Residual is similar and more appropriate in this context because it is better suited to the ordinal nature of PCL:YV items (see Shi et al., 2020).

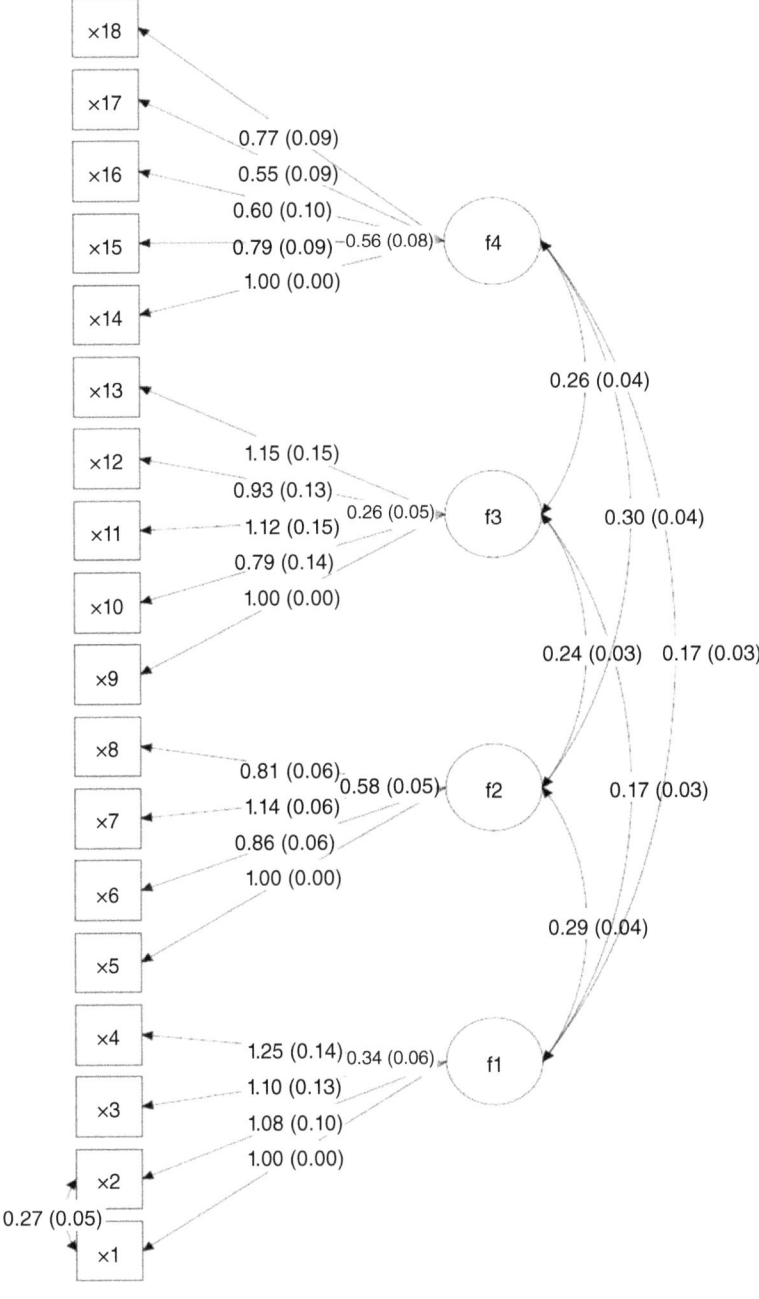

Figure 4.1 PCL:YV correlated four-factor model.
Notes. See Table 4.1 for corresponding items (e.g., x1 = impression management). f1 = Interpersonal factor; f2 = Affective factor; f3 = Lifestyle factor; f4 = Antisocial factor.

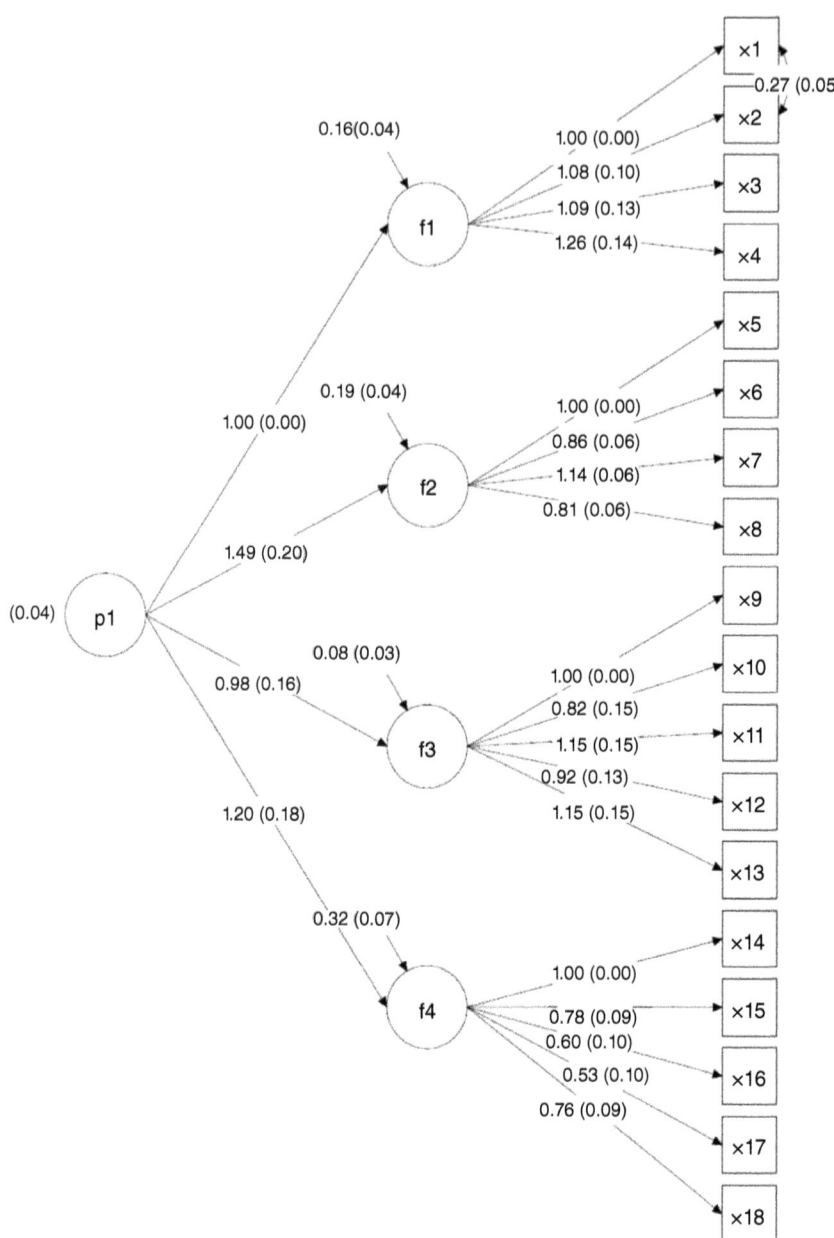

Figure 4.2 PCL:YV hierarchical four-factor model.
Notes. See Table 4.1 for corresponding items (e.g., x1 = impression management). f1 = Interpersonal factor; f2 = Affective factor; f3 = Lifestyle factor; f4 = Antisocial factor. p1 represents psychopathy as a superordinate factor and is what makes this a hierarchical model that is distinct from the correlated model in Figure 4.1.

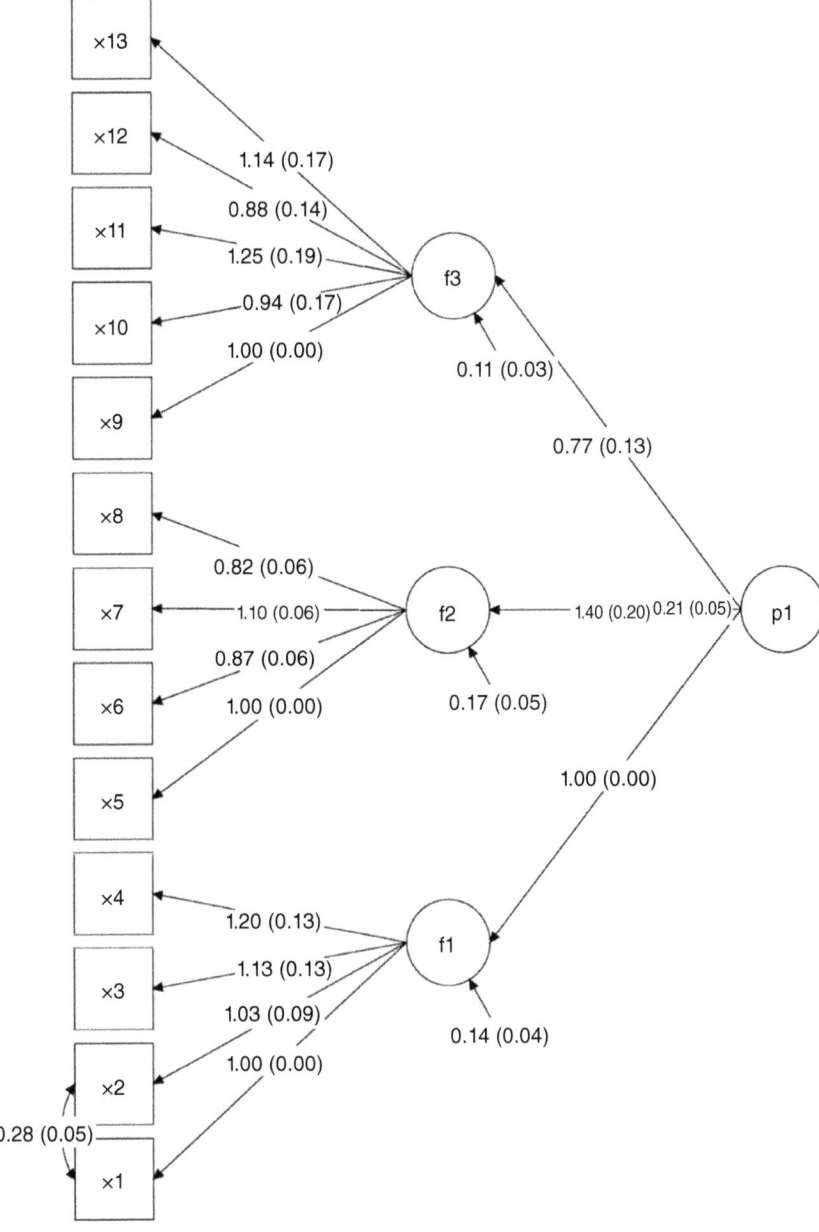

Figure 4.3   PCL:YV hierarchical three-factor model.
Notes. See Table 4.1 for corresponding items (e.g., x1 = impression management). f1 = Interpersonal factor; f2 = Affective factor; f3 = Lifestyle factor; f4 = Antisocial factor. p1 represents psychopathy as a superordinate factor.

Table 4.2 *Fit Indices for different confirmatory factor analysis models*

Model	χ^2 (df), p	SRMR	CFI	RMSEA (90% CI)
Hierarchical four-factor	449.04 (131), $p < 0.001$	0.073	0.885	0.067 (0.061–0.074)
Correlated four-factor	421.24 (129), $p < 0.001$	0.070	0.895	0.065 (0.058–0.072)
Hierarchical three-factor	253.69 (62), $p < 0.001$	0.064	0.913	0.076 (0.066–0.086)
Modified model[†]	χ^2 (df), p	SRMR	CFI	RMSEA (90% CI)
Hierarchical four-factor	421.74 (130), $p < 0.001$	0.071	0.895	0.065 (0.058–0.072)
Correlated four-factor	393.05 (128), $p < 0.001$	0.068	0.904	0.062 (0.055–0.069)
Hierarchical three-factor	221.48 (61), $p < 0.001$	0.060	0.927	0.070 (0.060–0.080)

[†] Each modified model included the addition of a single path of error covariation between two items from the Interpersonal factor (impression management and grandiose sense of self-worth).

Notes. SRMR = Standardized Root Mean Square Residual; CFI = Comparative Fit Index; RMSEA = Root Mean Square Error of Approximation. CFI $\geq$ 0.90, SRMR $\leq$ 0.08, and a RMSEA $\leq$ 0.08 were considered as indicating adequate fit (Hu & Bentler, 1999). CFI assesses the improvement in the fit of a model over that of a baseline model with no relationship among the model variables (Kline, 2010). SRMR is a measure of the mean absolute correlation residual, and RMSEA indicates "badness of fit."

were higher for the three-factor model. This implies that a three-factor model is a better fit to the data.

Confirmatory factor analysis is exactly how its name sounds; it is used to confirm (or fail to confirm) the fit of a predetermined factor structure. But what if, for example, the predetermined factor structure of a correlated four-factor model could be improved? Modification indices provide information about whether adjusting the parameters of a model would improve model fit. Consistent with other studies using confirmatory factor analysis to examine the structure of PCL instruments (Jones et al., 2006), modification indices showed that all three models would be improved by accounting for error covariation between the first two items on the Interpersonal factor (impression management and grandiose sense of self-worth). This finding is intuitive. Being grandiose (e.g., persistent bragging) may serve as a tool for managing impressions. Thus, there is some conceptual overlap that may lead to conflation of the two items. After including this modification, as shown at the bottom of Table 4.2, fit indices for the hierarchical three-factor model remained superior to those for the four-factor correlated model.[6]

The main takeaway from these analyses is that although there was support for each of the four-factor correlated model, four-factor hierarchical model, and three-factor hierarchical model, the inclusion of an Antisocial factor did not meaningfully improve model fit. A hierarchical three-factor model, therefore, appeared to fit the data best. I would caution against making conclusions about whether psychopathy is a reflective (hierarchical) construct or a formative (correlated) construct because the hierarchical three-factor model is statistically equivalent to a correlated three-factor model (see footnote 4).

Item Response Theory Analysis of the PCL:YV

Confirmatory factor analysis is not informative of how much individual items contribute to understanding psychopathy. For example, is a lack of remorse or a tendency to be sensation seeking more informative of psychopathy? Item response theory can be used to address such questions. Item response theory was traditionally used in education research to identify which questions on a test were most informative of a person's abilities or knowledge. Some questions might be answered correctly by most testtakers and therefore are less informative of overall knowledge. Other questions might only be answered correctly by people with a particularly high intelligence quotient (IQ) or aptitude for that subject.

The logic of item response theory can be extended to psychopathy research by examining, for example, whether callous-unemotional traits are (1) typical among people with higher levels of the latent trait of psychopathy and (2) atypical among people with lower levels of the latent trait of psychopathy. Item response theory can be used to learn about how much information a particular item provides regarding a person's total score on the PCL:YV. Item response theory also indicates how likely it is for a person to score high on a particular item given their overall score on the PCL:YV.

With the PCL:YV, it is common to sum together its 20 items, each of which ranges from 0 to 2, to get a total test score with possible values

---

[6] The Standardized Root Mean Square Residual decreases in value with additional paths (i.e., increasing degrees of freedom; see Taasoobshirazi & Wang, 2016). The fact that the value was smaller in the three-factor model, despite having fewer degrees of freedom, supports the retention of a hierarchical three-factor model over the correlated four-factor model.

ranging from 0 to 40. This is referred to as an additive scale and assumes that each item carries the same weight; each item contributes equally to a person's level of psychopathy. A score of "2" on lack of remorse contributes the same amount of information to a person's total PCL:YV score as a score of "2" on sensation seeking. But what if a lack of remorse is a more important indicator of psychopathy than sensation seeking? An additive scale cannot make such distinctions. It may be the case that traits like a lack of empathy, manipulativeness, and a lack of remorse only manifest at high levels of the latent trait of psychopathy. Identifying traits that tend to occur only when overall levels of psychopathy are high has clinical significance (Cooke & Michie, 1997).

The literature on item response theory is careful to distinguish between the level of a test score and the level of a latent trait. Ideally, a person's test score on the PCL:YV wouldl perfectly reflect the level of psychopathy as a latent trait. However, if certain items from the PCL:YV poorly reflect the latent trait of psychopathy, then low/high scores on the PCL:YV will fail to discriminate between youth with low/high levels of the latent trait of psychopathy. This would be especially concerning because (a) the PCL:YV is regularly used in legal settings (Viljoen et al., 2010), (b) scores on the PCL:YV are used to make statements about levels of psychopathy, and (c) when such scores are communicated in legal and mental health settings, it can have an impact on a young person's freedom (Dillard et al., 2013).

Dr. Siny Tsang's research used item response theory to examine the importance of psychopathy items among incarcerated youth who received ratings on the PCL:YV. Items from the Antisocial factor had the lowest discriminatory power. This means that such items (e.g., versatility of criminal behaviour) were similarly likely to be rated as "definitely applies" (i.e., a "2") across people with low, medium, and high scores on the PCL:YV (Tsang et al., 2015). This finding is intuitive considering that Dr. Tsang's sample consisted of incarcerated youth. Virtually all incarcerated youth have histories of criminal behaviour, and thus criminal behaviour is certain to be present regardless of a person's level of psychopathy traits. Not all incarcerated youth have psychopathy traits; the average score on the PCL:YV for Dr. Tsang's samples (which included the Pathways to Desistance Study) was around 15. It follows that criminal behaviour items poorly discriminate between incarcerated youth with higher vs. lower PCL:YV total scores. Item response theory is therefore useful for addressing debates regarding the inclusion of criminal behaviour in the measurement of psychopathy. However, it is also possible that the importance of criminal behaviour to psychopathy would be higher in samples of youth

Table 4.3 *Estimated PCL:YV item parameters*

	α	SEα	b_1	SEb_1	b_2	SEb_2
Impression management	0.859	0.127	−0.301	0.102	1.840	0.136
Grandiose sense of self-worth	1.08	0.136	−0.440	0.109	1.660	0.137
Pathological lying	0.928	0.132	0.051	0.103	2.327	0.152
Manipulation for personal gain	1.182	0.143	−1.410	0.132	1.102	0.125
Lack of remorse	**1.548**	0.178	−2.765	0.208	0.227	0.124
Shallow affect	**1.268**	0.143	−0.678	0.117	1.751	0.149
Callous or lacking empathy	**2.005**	0.222	−2.335	0.212	0.964	0.153
Failure to accept responsibility	1.127	0.132	−1.771	0.139	0.583	0.112
Stimulation seeking	0.689	0.114	−2.090	0.145	0.504	0.098
Parasitic orientation	0.605	0.122	−0.133	0.097	2.231	0.148
Lacks goals	0.930	0.113	−0.703	0.107	1.526	0.127
Impulsivity	0.646	0.107	−1.887	0.136	0.741	0.100
Irresponsibility	0.883	0.117	−2.161	0.152	0.745	0.108
Poor anger control	1.132	0.149	−2.619	0.180	−0.129	0.109
Early behavioural problems	0.791	0.114	−1.179	0.116	0.665	0.106
Serious criminal behaviour	**0.521**	0.134	−5.719	0.713	−1.159	0.109
Revocation of conditional release	**0.465**	0.13	−1.755	0.129	−0.346	0.096
Criminal versatility	0.675	0.126	−2.079	0.137	−0.673	0.101
Impersonal sexual behaviour	**0.593**	0.119	−0.499	0.100	0.977	0.106
Unstable interpersonal relationships	0.766	0.114	−0.224	0.104	1.461	0.124

Notes. The three most discriminating and three least discriminating items are in bold. α = slope parameter; b_1 and b_2 = category threshold parameters; SE = standard error.

from the community (for similar logic, see Cooke & Michie, 1997). Additional research using nonoffending sample is needed; unfortunately, this cannot be addressed with the ISVYOS data.

I used item response theory, performed using Mplus statistical software, to analyze the 20 items of the PCL:YV.[7] Key output from this analysis is reported in Table 4.3. There are two key terms that must be understood to interpret the findings. First is the term discrimination. In Table 4.3, items that discriminate most precisely are identified by larger values of "*a*." Discrimination refers to how well a specific trait of psychopathy

---

[7] Item response theory assumes that a scale is unidimensional. However, this assumption is rarely met in analyses of scales measuring personality data. The confirmatory factor analyses conducted above indicated that ISVYOS PCL:YV data were not unidimensional. However, a principal component analysis with polychoric correlations of the 20 items showed nearly a 3:1 ratio of eigenvalues between a one-factor solution and a two-factor solution. Additionally, fit statistics for the one-factor solution imply an adequate model (RMSEA = 0.079, SRMR = 0.088, and CFI = 0.810).

discriminates between different levels of psychopathy. With respect to the PCL:YV, discrimination indicates the probability that an item was given a specific score across the range of psychopathic trait levels. For example, studies that ask subject-matter experts to rate the importance of psychopathy traits routinely identify a lack of empathy as prototypical of psychopathy (i.e., a core trait; Hoff et al., 2012). Thus, it would be anticipated that people with a high overall score on the PCL:YV would be likely to be rated as a "2" on the item assessing empathy. As indicated in Table 4.3, based on the item response theory analysis, lack of remorse, shallow affect, and callous or lacking empathy were the three PCL:YV items with the highest discriminating values. For reference, Dr. Frank Baker, who helped pioneer research using item response theory, noted that values of "a" less than 0.65 indicate inadequate discriminating power, $a > 1.34$ is considered a "high" discrimination parameter, and $a > 1.69$ is considered "very high" (Baker, 2001). Note that the literature extending item response theory to psychopathy has set somewhat lower benchmarks, where values greater than 1.0 indicate good discriminative validity (Bolt et al., 2004; Dillard et al., 2013).

The second key term that must be defined to interpret Table 4.3 is threshold. Discrimination works by using information from an item to determine how informative that item is of the latent trait. Threshold parameters use information from the overall latent trait to determine how informative the latent trait score would be of a particular item. Specifically, a threshold parameter indicates how much of an increase in the latent trait would be needed to move from one response option of an item to the next response option for that item (e.g., to move from a "1" on a given PCL:YV item to a "2" on that same item). In effect, the threshold parameter indicates item difficulty. Items that are more difficult tend to be endorsed only at high levels of the latent trait. In Table 4.3, the b_1 and b_2 values are between-category threshold parameters that depict the likelihood of a higher rating given a participant's level of the latent psychopathy trait. Lower values indicate that high scores are common even for people with low levels of psychopathy. In the context of the PCL:YV, b_1 indicates the threshold between response choices "0" (item does not apply) and "1" (item applies somewhat), and b_2 indicates the threshold between response choices "1" and "2" (item definitely applies). As indicated in Table 4.3, especially high levels of psychopathy are needed before receiving a "2" on items measuring pathological lying and parasitic orientation. In contrast, even people with low levels of psychopathy tended to receive a "2" on items measuring serious criminal behaviour and criminal versatility.

Journey to the Core: Using Item Response Theory to Identify Psychopathy's Most Important Traits

Like the movie *Memento*, I'm going to start at the end and track backwards. I identified 13 PCL:YV items that were the most important indicators of psychopathy. Throughout this book, I will refer to these 13 items collectively as the core traits of psychopathy as defined by the PCL:YV. The 13 items are shown in Figure 4.4 and include: impression management, grandiosity, pathological lying, manipulation for personal gain, lack of remorse, shallow affect, callous/lack of empathy, failure to accept responsibility, lack of goals, irresponsibility, poor anger control, early behavioural problems, unstable interpersonal relationships. The main conclusion from this process is that all eight Interpersonal and Affective items provided meaningful information. This is consistent with Tsang and colleagues' (2015) conclusion that items from the Interpersonal and Affective factors are at the core of psychopathy.

I did not arrive at these items by accident, nor did I select these items by my own choosing. I'll retrace my steps. The steps I followed were guided by Dr. Alexander Eichenbaum's process for determining items that provide meaningful information about a latent trait (see Eichenbaum et al., 2019, 2021).

The first step in this process was to determine whether there were any PCL:YV items that had weak discriminatory power. Looking at Table 4.3, four items had discrimination values of less than 0.65 (parasitic orientation, serious criminal behaviour, revocation of conditional release, impersonal sexual behaviour). Based on Baker's (2001) criteria, these items did not provide meaningful information about the latent trait of psychopathy. These items were thus discarded in the search for the core traits of psychopathy.

The second step was to examine expected response functions for the 16 remaining items. Expected response functions determine how effective an item is in distinguishing trait levels (Bolt, 2017).[8] One indicator that an item functions well is when the peak of the curve for a lesser response option (e.g., a "0" on the PCL:YV item) consistently remains beneath the response curve for a greater response option (e.g., a "2" on the PCL:YV item) across all levels of the latent trait. What this means is that people who score a "0" on a particular item basically never have a higher PCL:YV

---

[8] Information characteristic curves are another common way of inspecting item functioning. However, expected response functions are easier to interpret because they include only a single line that indicates the expected item score as a function of theta (see Bolt et al., 2004, for further reading).

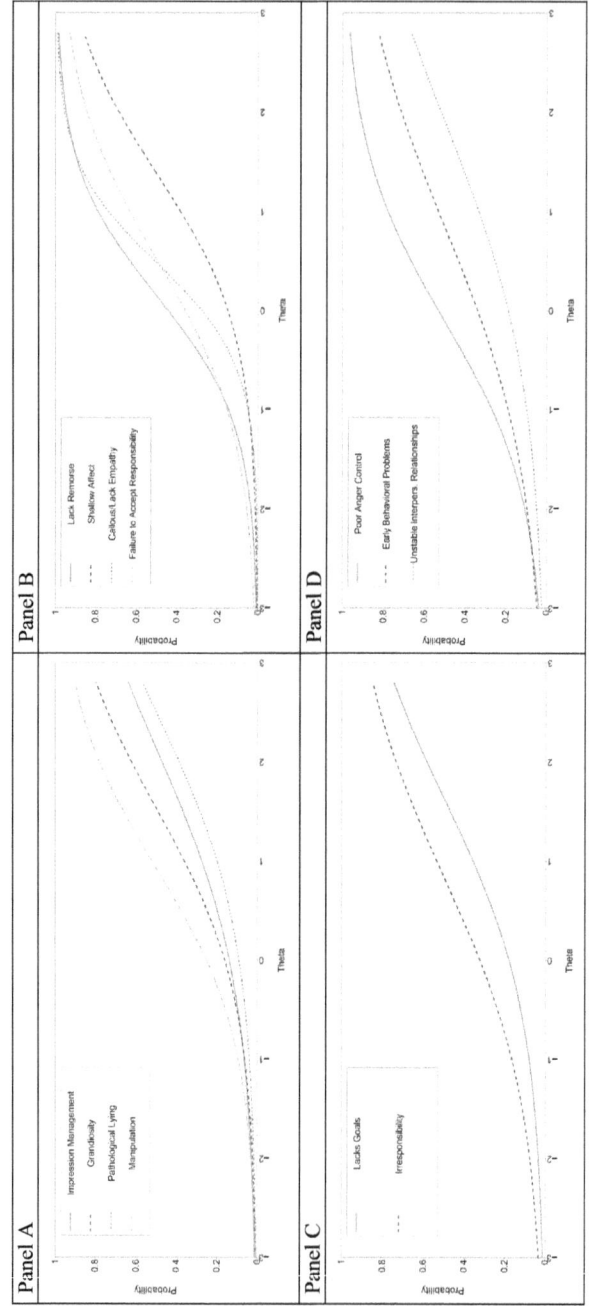

Figure 4.4 Expected response functions indicating the probability of scoring a "2" on the given PCL:YV item. *Notes.* Only items that meet the criteria for providing meaningful information are shown.

total score compared to people who scored "2" on that same item. For the remaining 16 items, all met this criterion.

Finally, the third step involved examining information functions to determine any instances of a flat information curve. A flat line would indicate that minimal information was learned about the probability of item endorsement across different levels of the latent trait. Someone might have higher levels of psychopathy, but this did not necessarily indicate a higher score on the item in question. The items measuring stimulation seeking, impulsivity, and revocation of conditional release all displayed especially flat information curves. These items were thus excluded from the search for the core traits of psychopathy.

To review, I considered a PCL:YV item to provide meaningful information about the latent construct of psychopathy if it had at least adequate discriminating power, its expected response functions indicated theoretically anticipated distributions of item scores as a function of theta (i.e., as the latent trait of psychopathy increased, so did the probability of an increase in item score), and it provided meaningful information across different levels of the latent trait.

I use Figure 4.4 to help visualize why these 13 items were considered to contribute meaningful information about psychopathy. Each item gets a line indicating the expected response function for participants who scored a "2" on a particular item. Items are divided across panels according to their respective factor. Panel D also includes the unclassified item "unstable interpersonal relationships." The x-axis shows the level of the latent trait of psychopathy. The y-axis shows the probability of scoring a "2" on the item in question, given a person's level of the latent trait. Ideally, we want to see a sharp increase in the probability of scoring a "2" as theta (x-axis) increases. When sharp increases occur, the line in question forms an "S" shape to indicate that more meaningful information is provided. The item measuring lack of remorse (Panel B) is a clear example of this "S" shape. Not surprisingly, this item also had a very high discriminating (α) value (see Table 4.3).

What Do Core Traits Tell Us about the Nature of Psychopathy?

There are some important implications that come with the identification of these 13 core PCL:YV items. In line with Cooke and Michie (1997), compared to items from the Lifestyle and Antisocial factors, items from the Interpersonal and Affective factors tended to occur at higher levels of the latent trait of psychopathy. This may imply a stronger socioeconomic and familial influence on Lifestyle and Antisocial items compared to Interpersonal and Affective items. This aligns with research that describes Lifestyle and Antisocial factors as reflecting social deviance. Although purely speculative and only mentioned here for the purpose of encouraging future research, traits that are not core to psychopathy may have a clearer environmental basis. This does not imply that core traits are definitively biological in their origin.

Overall, the findings support the notion that the PCL:YV contains items that help discriminate between youth with high levels of the latent trait of psychopathy and youth with low levels of the latent trait of psychopathy. Of note, the correlation between PCL:YV total scores and a summed scale of these 13 core items is 0.943. The correlation between scores on the three-factor model and this scale of 13 core items is 0.945. This indicates that, at least with the ISVYOS dataset, researchers could focus only on these 13 core items without losing much information about psychopathy. Consequently, the process of measuring psychopathy could be simplified, thereby reducing the amount of time required to complete an assessment. This also means that the relationship between PCL:YV test scores and external outcomes (e.g., offending, informal social control) is likely to be similar regardless of how PCL:YV test scores are represented in statistical models. In effect, focusing on these 13 items may not improve our understanding of the relationship between psychopathy and offending, but it does indicate the potential to measure psychopathy more efficiently while maintaining the same level of predictive validity. This possibility was directly addressed in Chapter 5.

Network Analysis of the PCL:YV

From a psychopathology network theory perspective, psychopathy comprises a system of intercorrelated traits. The idea is that traits may influence each other. This differs from, for example, the idea of a reflective construct in which a latent construct causes individual traits. In psychopathology network analysis, nodes represent specific traits (e.g., PCL:YV items) and edges represent the degree of association between traits. Unlike item response theory, where the importance of a PCL:YV item is interpreted according to its association with the underlying latent trait, network analysis identifies the importance of a particular PCL:YV item based on its connectivity to other items. Network analysis can complement item response theory by providing further evidence of the importance of a particular item to psychopathy.

Network analysis uses different indices to help identify which nodes are most well-connected to other nodes in the network. In psychopathology

PCL:YV Validity

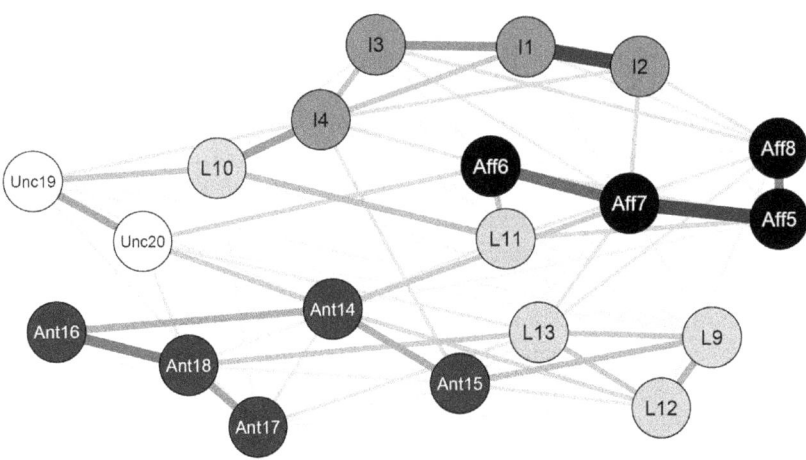

Figure 4.5 Graphical LASSO network graph of the PCL:YV.
Notes. See Table 4.1 for the meaning of node labels. Nodes represent the 20 items of the PCL:YV and the edges represent the partial correlations between items. Interpersonal factor = nodes I1–I4; Affective factor = nodes Aff5–Aff8; Lifestyle factor = nodes L9–L13; Antisocial factor = nodes Ant14–Ant18. Unclassified items = Unc19 and Unc20. Thicker edges denote stronger associations. All edges reflect positive correlation coefficients.

network modeling, one of the most commonly examined indices is strength centrality.[9] Strength centrality refers to the sum of the weights of all edges connected to a node. In this case, edge weights reflect the size of the correlation between nodes. Negative correlations subtract from the level of strength centrality. In past research on adults, items from the Affective factor of the PCL have stood out as most central, and items from the Antisocial factor that measure prior criminal behaviour have stood out as least central (Preszler et al., 2018; Verschuere et al., 2018).

The network of 20 PCL:YV items is shown in Figure 4.5. The edges between nodes indicate the correlation between two PCL:YV items while conditioning on all other items.[10] All edges were positive. In line with the

---

[9] Betweenness centrality describes the number of instances in which a node falls on the shortest path (i.e., shortest edge) between two other nodes. Removal of nodes high in betweenness centrality would create a sparser network by removing indirect connections between other nodes. Closeness centrality refers to the average distance of a particular node from all other nodes in the network; shorter edges represent greater closeness. Nodes higher in closeness centrality might help clarify how symptoms from different factors/domains come together to form the underlying construct. Because items high/low in strength centrality tended to be the items also high/low in closeness/betweenness centrality, I only discuss strength centrality. For further discussion regarding centrality indices in psychopathology network modeling, see Opsahl et al. (2010) and Borsboom and Cramer (2013).

[10] The network was produced using the qgraph package (Epskamp et al., 2012) in R. The qgraph package includes the EBICglasso function to estimate network structure. This package uses the

confirmatory factor analysis presented earlier in the chapter, there was clear clustering of items into their respective Interpersonal (top), Affective (right), Lifestyle (bottom), and Antisocial (left) factors. The strongest edgeweight was between "lack of remorse" (Aff5) and "callous/lack of empathy" (Aff7).

The five PCL:YV items with the highest strength centrality included Aff5, Aff7, "Early Behavioural Problems" (Ant14), "Impression Management" (I1), and "Manipulation for Personal Gain" (I4). These items were all identified in the item response theory analysis as providing meaningful information psychopathy. The five PCL:YV items with the lowest strength centrality included "Serious Criminal Behaviour" (Ant16), "Revocation of Conditional Release" (Ant17), "Parasitic Orientation" (L10), "Impulsivity" (L12), and "Impersonal Sexual Behaviour" (Unc19). These items were identified in the item response theory analysis as providing limited information about the construct of psychopathy.

Bootstrapping analyses (see footnote 10) were used to examine whether strength centrality values significantly differed across nodes. The darkshaded rectangles in Figure 4.6 indicate significant differences in strength centrality between the item on the x-axis and the corresponding item on the y-axis. The strength centrality value for Aff7 is significantly higher compared to all but one (Ant14) item from the PCL:YV. Items I4 and Ant14 also stand out as having strength centrality values significantly higher than the majority of PCL:YV items. In contrast, the strength centrality value for Ant16 is significantly lower compared to the majority of PCL:YV items. Once again, this may reflect the nature of the ISVYOS sample; most participants had histories of criminal behaviour, but most participants also did not have high scores on the PCL:YV.

---

graphical least absolute shrinkage and selection operator (LASSO) function to produce a Gaussian graphical model that errs on the side of avoiding false positives by removing true edges rather than potentially including spurious ones (Epskamp & Fried, 2018). This approach involved penalizing the model so that small correlations were reduced to zero (i.e., indicating no edge between nodes). Comparisons of the size of strength centrality values across nodes were performed using the bootnet package (version 1.1.0; Epskamp & Fried, 2018). Like prior network studies (e.g., Verschuere et al., 2018), these analyses were generated using 2,500 bootstrap samples and included (a) the casedropping subset bootstrap, which examines the stability of centrality indices over random subsamples of progressively smaller sample size; (b) the correlation stability (CS) coefficient, which represents the maximum proportion of the sample that can be dropped while maintaining a 0.95 probability that the correlation between the baseline centrality index and bootstrapped subsamples is 0.70 or higher; and (c) the bootstrapped difference test, which evaluates whether two nodes significantly differ on a given measure of centrality. The CS-coefficient for strength centrality was 0.59, which means that differences between nodes according to strength centrality can be interpreted reliably (Epskamp et al., 2017).

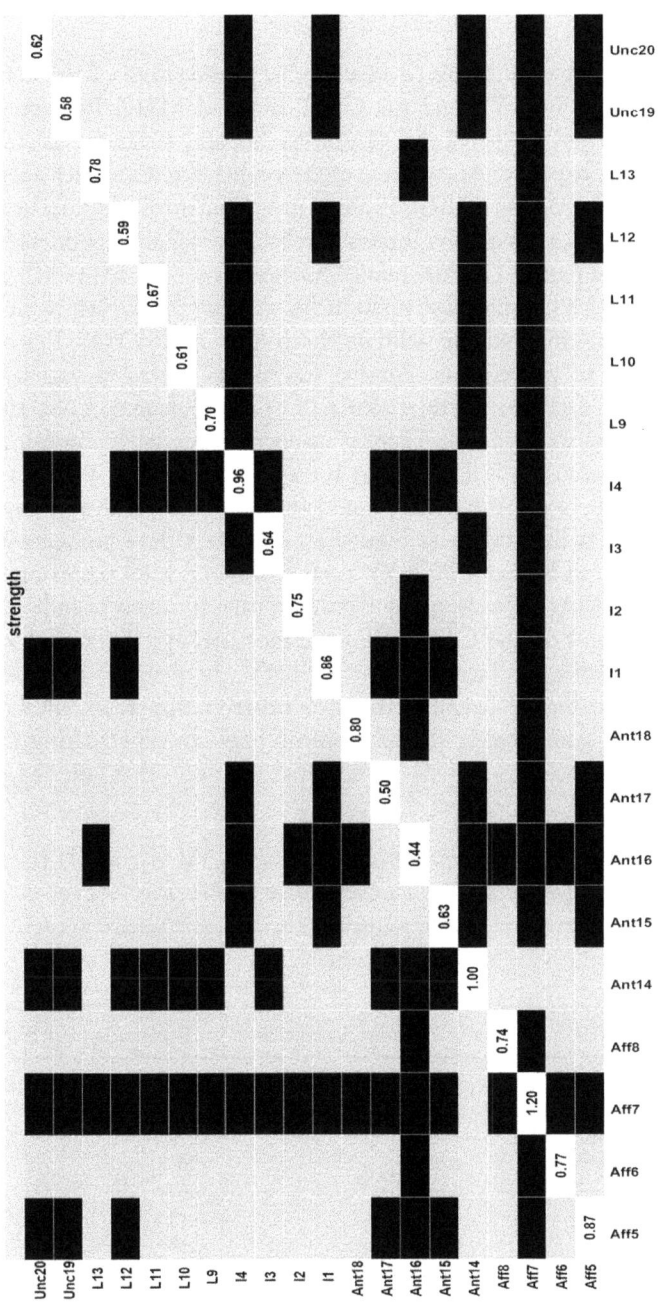

Figure 4.6 Bootstrapped differences in strength centrality across the 20 PCL:YV items.

Note. Grey boxes indicate nonsignificant differences, black boxes indicate significant differences in strength centrality between items. Strength centrality value is plotted on the diagonal. Labels are shown in alphabetical order. See Table 4.1 for the item that each label refers to.

Convergent Validity

Convergent validity was examined through an investigation of the correlation between the PCL:YV and the CAPP-IRS and MACI Psychopathy Content Scale. The CAPP-IRS and MACI Psychopathy Content Scale were summarized in Chapter 3. As evidence of their reliability, Cronbach's alpha values for CAPP-IRS and MACI Psychopathy Content Scale total scores were 0.93 and 0.72, respectively. Interrater reliability was also conducted for the CAPP-IRS as part of Dr. Amanda McCormick's (2007, 2015) MA and PhD theses (Dr. McCormick also hired me to work on this project, which is how I ended up in graduate school). Each pair of ISVYOS Research Assistants rated 10 participants. For the CAPP-IRS, intraclass correlation coefficients were excellent for total scores (0.91) and adequate to excellent for domain scores (0.69–0.86). There is no interrater reliability assessment for the MACI because it is a self-report survey.

Correlations between the PCL:YV and these other measures of psychopathy are shown in Table 4.4. Figure 4.7 visualizes the significant and positive association between PCL:YV total scores and total scores on the CAPP-IRS and MACI Psychopathy Content Scale. In terms of individual factors, total scores on the CAPP-IRS were most strongly associated with scores on the Affective factor of the PCL:YV. In general, correlation coefficients were higher between the two expert rating tools (PCL:YV and CAPP-IRS) compared to the relationship between expert rating tools and self-report measures. It is interesting to note that the MACI

Table 4.4 *Convergent validity between the PCL:YV and the MACI Psychopathy Content Scale and CAPP-IRS*

	MACI Psychopathy Content Scale Total Scores	CAPP-IRS Total Scores
	r (Correlation Coefficient)	r (Correlation Coefficient)
PCL:YV Total Scores	0.311***	0.798***
PCL:YV Four-Factor Model	0.308***	0.784***
PCL:YV Three-Factor Model	0.231**	0.794***
Interpersonal factor	−0.009	0.655***
Affective factor	0.203*	0.659***
Lifestyle factor	0.336***	0.550***
Antisocial factor	0.415***	0.386***

* $p < 0.05$; ** $p < 0.01$; $p < 0.001$.

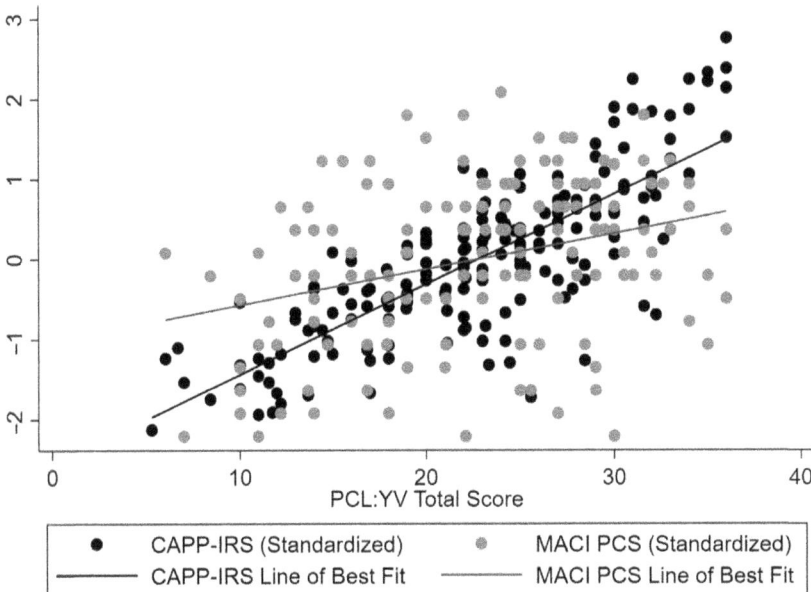

Figure 4.7 Correlation between PCL:YV total scores and other measures of psychopathy. *Notes.* CAPP-IRS and MACI Psychopathy Content Scale (PCS) scores were standardized to facilitate comparison. The steeper slope for the CAPP-IRS line of best fit compared to the MACI Psychopathy Content Scale line of best fit implies that the CAPP-IRS has a stronger correlation with the PCL:YV.

Psychopathy Content Scale was most strongly correlated with the Antisocial factor of the PCL:YV. According to the item response theory and network analyses in this chapter, items from the Antisocial factor, especially "*Serious Criminal Behaviour*" and "*Revocation of Conditional Release*," were consistently among the least relevant to psychopathy in this sample. Thus, the correlation between the MACI Psychopathy Content Scale and the PCL:YV was not especially strong, and was primarily due to the MACI's association with items that were least relevant to psychopathy. As highlighted in the item response theory and network analysis, items from the Interpersonal factor were particularly core traits of PCL:YV-measured psychopathy. Yet, scores on the Interpersonal factor and MACI Psychopathy Content Scale total scores were not significantly correlated. This was not unique to the PCL:YV. MACI Psychopathy Content Scale total scores were not significantly correlated with the Dominance and Self domains of the CAPP-IRS. It is possible that the MCAI Psychopathy Content Scale, which relies on participant self-reported responses to questions with dichotomous (i.e., True/False) answers, is not a particularly useful measure of psychopathy.

Chapter Summary

The remaining chapters in this book focus on whether PCL:YV scores are informative of offending, social, and health outcomes. A goal of this chapter was to give readers confidence that the results in the upcoming chapters are based on reliable and valid information about psychopathy. As indicated in this chapter, items on the PCL:YV tended to correlate with each other (internal consistency) and ISVYOS Research Assistants tended to independently give the same participant a similar score on the PCL:YV (interrater reliability). In terms of construct validity, the PCL:YV factor structure aligned with past theoretical and empirical research. The best-fitting factor structure was a hierarchical three-factor model. This model is distinct from a hierarchical four-factor model in that items from the Antisocial factor are excluded. This model is also unique from a correlated four-factor model because hierarchical models specify psychopathy as a superordinate factor that accounts for the association between the Interpersonal, Affective, and Lifestyle factors. Although a hierarchical three-factor model best fit the data, both the correlated and hierarchical four-factor models were also a good fit to the data.

Item response theory analysis and network analysis provided evidence that several of the items from the Antisocial factor did not contribute meaningful information to the measurement of psychopathy. Items like "revocation of conditional release" were common for high and low scorers on the PCL:YV and weakly correlated with other PCL:YV items. Items from the Interpersonal and Affective factors were identified as core traits of PCL-based psychopathy. These findings may be sample-specific. Histories of antisocial behaviour are not just common in incarcerated samples; such histories are required to be included in this population. It therefore follows that indicators of antisocial and criminal behaviour poorly index psychopathy traits, since youth without psychopathy traits nevertheless had at least some history of antisocial behaviour. These findings may also be specific to the PCL:YV and thus future research should perform similar analyses using other reliable measures of psychopathy.

In Chapter 1, I provided a description of what I felt to be certain core traits of psychopathy. Core interpersonal traits are those that describe people as, for example, self-centered, entitled, and manipulative. Based on the item response theory analysis, core interpersonal traits, as measured by the PCL:YV, included impression management, grandiosity, pathological lying, and manipulation. Grandiosity and impression management share some overlap with self-centeredness and manipulation and pathological lying overlaps with my description of manipulative traits of psychopathy. I noted in Chapter 1 that core affective traits are those that describe people as, for example, detached, callous-unemotional, and unempathic. Based on the item response theory analysis, core affective traits, as measured by the PCL:YV, included lack of remorse, shallow affect, callous/lack of empathy, failure to accept responsibility. Being detached describes people who are emotionally distant from others, which overlaps with someone with shallow affect. Being callous-unemotional and unempathic clearly overlaps with lack of remorse and callous/lack of empathy items from the PCL:YV. Failing to accept responsibility was not accounted for in my description of psychopathy. I noted in Chapter 1 that core behavioural traits are those that describe people as, for example, having poor behavioural control, a lack of reliability, and a tendency to be sensation seeking. Based on the item response theory analysis, core behavioural traits, as measured by the PCL:YV, include those who lack goals, have poor anger control, and histories of early behavioural problems. Poor anger control and sensation seeking overlap with poor behavioural control. Missing from my original description of psychopathy was an emphasis on people who fail to behave in reliable ways.

CHAPTER 5

Psychopathy Traits in Adolescence and Persistent Offending through Adulthood

Recidivism refers to whether people already in conflict with the law reoffend over a set follow-up period (e.g., five years after release from prison). Over 100 studies have examined the relationship between psychopathy traits and recidivism. Several meta-analyses and narrative reviews have summarized these studies. The general conclusion is that most research examines recidivism over short-term (e.g., three-to-five-year) periods and finds a significant association between psychopathy traits and recidivism (Blais et al., 2014; Edens et al., 2007; Hart, 1998; Leistico et al., 2008). With over 100 studies, what is left to be said about the relationship between psychopathy and offending? To start, contemporary research on psychopathy is primarily conducted by those working in the fields of forensic psychology or correctional psychology. When examining the relationship between psychopathy and offending, these fields primarily focus on implications for risk assessment. Risk assessment is meant to help communicate to the criminal legal system a person's probability of recidivism. Communicating a person's likelihood of recidivism can also involve case formulation. Case formulation involves describing whether certain types of crimes are more likely, the context in which such crimes are likely to occur, and strategies for managing risk (Ogonah et al., 2023). Psychopathy measures are not risk assessment tools, but they are often used as part of the process of completing a risk assessment, engaging in case formulation (i.e., determining how to manage risk), and guiding the intensity of the intervention strategy (Guy et al., 2010).

I understand why forensic psychology and correctional psychology place so much emphasis on studying recidivism, given that this is of major interest to court and corrections officials. However, studying the relationship between psychopathy and *recidivism* is a very limited approach for learning about the relationship between psychopathy and *offending*. Recidivism only identifies whether an event happens. Recidivism is not informative of factors like the frequency, timing/duration, and severity of offending. Recidivism is, therefore, a very limited measure of offending and is not ideal for evaluating the predictive validity of psychopathy. Take, for example, three people who are followed for five years following release from custody. The first person does not reoffend, the second reoffends once, and the third reoffends seven times. In recidivism studies, the first person is placed into the nonrecidivist category, and the other two people are described as recidivists. This illustrates a failure to address within-group heterogeneity. We have two recidivists with very different patterns of reoffending. Is someone who commits one new offence more similar to someone who commits seven new offences than they are to someone who does not reoffend? Studies in criminology on desistance say no. Desistance from criminal behaviour is described as a process that includes recidivism (Bushway et al., 2001). In fact, some desistance studies may identify the first two people as desisters and the third person as following a pattern of persistence. In other words, recidivism carries different meanings when comparing forensic psychology to criminology. I am not suggesting that we abandon research on recidivism, only that research on psychopathy and reoffending has good reasons to look beyond recidivism outcomes.

One way to look beyond single-item indicators of reoffending is by learning from the criminal career paradigm (Blumstein et al., 1988). The criminal career paradigm may seem confusingly named because it is not about people who offend to earn a living (i.e., career criminals), nor is it only about people who offend over long stretches of time. The criminal career paradigm is about acknowledging heterogeneity in patterns of offending and attempting to understand this heterogeneity through different offending parameters, including the timing, frequency, severity, and duration of offending over the life-course (Blumstein et al., 1988). Criminal career research is often interested in identifying and describing chronic offending. Early studies on chronic offending conducted in the United States identified that about 7–8 percent of all offenders accounted for more than 50 percent of all offences (Wolfgang et al., 1972). A large amount of research since this time has explored different ways of measuring chronic offending (for a review, see chapter 2 of McCuish et al., 2021). The idea underlying this research is that recidivists vary in their level of offending and therefore should not be treated as a homogenous group with a similar likelihood of reoffending. This is what much of the risk assessment literature and psychopathy research does. However, it does not have to be this way. Chronic or persistent offending helps capture multiple dimensions of offending by looking at both its *frequency* and its *duration*.

I think that forensic psychology and correctional psychology have much to learn from criminology with respect to measuring reoffending. Similarly, criminology has much to learn from forensic psychology and correctional psychology regarding the measurement of risk factors. For example, Drs. Robert Sampson and John Laub analyzed data on several hundred youth followed into later stages of adulthood and concluded that "differences in adult criminal trajectories cannot be predicted from childhood ... based on theoretical risk factors at the individual level" (Sampson & Laub, 2003, p. 588). I think this conclusion might come as a surprise to researchers in forensic and correctional psychology. It becomes less surprising when looking at (a) which risk factors Sampson and Laub (2003) examined and (b) how these risk factors were measured. Specifically, these authors relied on single-item indicators of relatively common childhood experiences (e.g., temper tantrums) that were dichotomized as present/absent. They then declared that nothing from childhood/adolescence could help predict persistent offending. One factor commonly overlooked by many criminologists is psychopathy. Part of the reason that psychopathy is overlooked by criminology may relate to the tendency of sociologists and criminologists to hold beliefs about psychopathy that are not informed by research developments over the last 20–30 years (Maruna, 2025).

In sum, forensic psychology and correctional psychology tend to rely on single-item indicators of reoffending (i.e., recidivism) when examining the predictive validity of complex, multidimensional disorders like psychopathy. Similarly, criminologists often rely on single-item indicators of risk factors (e.g., presence of temper tantrums) when examining the prediction of complex, multidimensional indicators of offending such as persistent offending, which captures both frequency and duration of offending. This chapter brings together the detailed approach criminology uses to measure offending over the life-course with the careful attention given to the measurement of psychopathy in forensic and correctional psychology.

Chapter Goals and Analyses

Although a number of studies report a relationship between psychopathy traits and reoffending (Corrado et al., 2004; DeLisi et al., 2014a,b; Dyck et al., 2013; Flexon & Meldrum, 2013; Gretton et al., 2004; Hare, 1996, 2001; Kennealy et al., 2010; Piquero et al., 2012; Ribeiro da Silva et al., 2012; Salekin, 2008; Schmidt et al., 2011; Vachon et al., 2012; Vaughn & DeLisi, 2008; Vaughn et al., 2008; Vincent et al., 2008), questions about this relationship are hardly settled. Observations that the relationship between the Psychopathy Checklist (PCL) and offending is primarily due to scores on the Lifestyle/Antisocial factors (commonly referred to as the social deviance component of psychopathy; for example, see Kennealy et al., 2010). This has resulted in some questioning whether it is even necessary to assess psychopathy, given its core interpersonal and affective traits appear unrelated to recidivism (e.g., Walters, 2004).

Similar to Walters, Larsen (2025) recently suggested that psychopathy is either uninformative or only weakly informative of offending and therefore psychopathy assessments should be abandoned. Larsen's summary of the extant literature was characterized by several mistakes. The following are some of his conclusions and why they are mistaken:

1. Psychopathy is not informative of recidivism
    a. Larsen reached this conclusion based on studies that combined false positives (i.e., where someone had high psychopathy traits but did not recidivate) and false negatives (i.e., where someone without high psychopathy traits did recidivate). False negatives should only be considered if psychopathy is viewed as the sole explanation for recidivism. This is certainly not the case, as evidenced by the fact that risk assessments regularly focus on psychopathy as one of many important risk factors. Larsen also failed to acknowledge that the statement "people with psychopathy traits are very likely to recidivate" is perfectly compatible with the statement "people with psychopathy traits are only moderately more likely to recidivate compared to others in prison."
    b. Larsen's argument that psychopathy assessment should be abandoned was premised on the idea of biases in legal decision-making. Although I do not contest that such biases exist, these biases reflect issues with adversarial legal contexts, not with psychopathy as a construct.
2. Psychopathy is not informative of "high risk" or "dangerous" statuses (not my terms)
    a. Larsen inappropriately relied on studies of psychopathy and recidivism to make conclusions about whether psychopathy is evidence of dangerousness. Recidivism captures very broad patterns of reoffending, ranging from sexual homicide to staying out past curfew while on probation. Recidivism was never

intended to be an indicator of dangerousness because recidivism primarily includes people involved in non-serious offences.

b. Base rates of recidivism are high in populations that tend to offend at a high rate (including the ISVYOS sample). When base rates of recidivism are high, false positives will be common. Thus, Larsen's criticism of the usefulness of psychopathy is misguided because the problem lies primarily with research designs not meant to address questions about dangerousness.

The main contribution of this chapter is to examine the relationship between psychopathy traits in adolescence and persistent offending over a 20-year period into adulthood. These analyses allowed for the measurement of repeated recidivism captured through participants' thirties and forties. This helped avoid issues with short-term follow-up periods that cannot fully capture patterns of persistent offending. This chapter also examines the relationship between psychopathy and specific single-item indicators of recidivism, including homicide offences and sexual offences, which may be more appropriate for evaluating whether people with psychopathy traits should be considered "dangerous." Contrary to Walters' perspective, at the case-study level, core affective and interpersonal symptoms, in the absence of extreme behavioural impulsivity, have been viewed as central to explaining involvement in especially violent offences such as rape and homicide (Chan et al., 2010; Dawson et al., 2012; Myers et al., 2010). In sum, the relevance of psychopathy to criminal behaviour may depend on how criminal behaviour is measured.

There are several studies that use item response theory and psychopathology network modeling to identify core traits of psychopathy. There are also several studies on the relationship between psychopathy and persistent offending. These two research areas are rarely integrated. This chapter builds from the item response theory analyses in Chapter 4 by examining whether core psychopathy traits as measured via the Psychopathy Checklist: Youth Version (PCL:YV) are informative of persistent offending. This approach helps directly address concerns that the predictive validity of PCL instruments is driven primarily by items from the Lifestyle and Antisocial factors, which are considered least reflective of psychopathy (Walters, 2004).

Measuring Persistent Offending

I use the term persistent offending to describe high-rate patterns of offending that continue across the life-course. Interest in chronic offending was popularized by Marvin Wolfgang and colleagues' (1972) research on 10,000 youth from the Philadelphia Birth Cohort study. This cohort included boys born in 1945 who were followed into adulthood. Wolfgang et al.'s findings highlighted that there was heterogeneity *among* individuals involved in crime and not just heterogeneity *between* individuals who were arrested and those who were not. About 6 percent of the sample were responsible for just over 50 percent of all arrests for the entire cohort. For example, if there were 5,000 arrests among the 10,000 youth, this 6 percent (600 people) were responsible for 2,500 of these arrests. This 6 percent of the sample had a minimum of five arrests each. Accordingly, chronic offending came to be defined as people who had committed at least five offences. Criminologists have had mixed perspectives on what to do about chronic offending. Some suggested that chronic offending was evidence of the need for early, humanistic, and empirically-driven intervention strategies (e.g., social assistance, psychoeducation; Farrington & Welsh, 2008). Others considered whether incarcerating people for lengthy periods based on expectations about what they would do in the future (i.e., selective incapacitation) was more appropriate (Greenwood & Abrahamse, 1982). The latter led to, for example, failed three strike policies in the United States, whereas the former has had success through programs like Stop Now and Plan, which emphasize heuristic cognitive-behavioural interventions (see Augimeri et al., 2018).

Over time, concerns were raised about the definition of chronic offending. First, the definition was specific to boys from the Philadelphia Birth Cohort. Five arrests may represent a relatively exclusive group in community samples, but what about incarcerated youth? Those with five prior arrests included a much larger group than 6 percent. For context, between ages 12 and 17, more than 80 percent of the Incarcerated Serious and Violent Young Offender Study (ISVYOS) PCL:YV Cohort incurred at least five convictions. Thus, this first issue reflected concerns about the generalizability of Wolfgang et al.'s (1972) definition of chronic offending. A second issue was that this definition of chronic offending lacked a time component. Two individuals may have been arrested five times, but one of these individuals may have accumulated five arrests in one year, and the other person was arrested once every year for five years. Arguably, these represent different offending patterns. One of the selling points of the concept of chronic offending is that it helps address within-group heterogeneity by not treating all recidivists as the same. Measuring chronic offending based solely on the frequency of offending ignores an important time component that also can help account for heterogeneity in offending patterns. Overall, these two concerns reflected the need to develop a measure of offending persistence that captures involvement in higher rates of offending that continue across the life-course.

Developing Theories and Methods for Measuring Persistent Offending

In the 1990s, two touchstone papers were published that dramatically reconceptualized the study of offending persistence. First, Dr. Terrie Moffitt outlined her dual taxonomy theory in which she identified two meta-trajectories. The first, described as an adolescence limited pattern, represented about 90–95 percent of the population. For this meta-trajectory, offending emerged in mid-adolescence and ended by late adolescence. Offending stopped because youth were able to bridge the maturity gap between physical maturity and social maturity. Entering adulthood provided opportunities for autonomy and independence that did not involve engaging in crime (e.g., going to university, getting a job, and being in a relationship). The second meta-trajectory, described as a life-course persistent pattern, represented about 5–10 percent of the population. For this group, offending emerged early in the life-course due to the intersection of neuropsychological deficits like psychopathy and a difficult familial environment. The early initiation of antisocial behaviour was associated with an escalation in the severity and persistence of this type of behaviour through adulthood. Offending continued through adulthood because of either (a) a resistance to the beneficial effects of being employed and being married or (b) a tendency to self-select into relationships that would not deter antisocial behaviour (e.g., choosing a partner who also engaged in crime). Thus, Dr. Moffitt helped develop a theory for why offending occurred early, happened often, and continued over time.

The second touchstone paper was written by Drs. Daniel Nagin and Kenneth Land (1993). They developed a statistical technique, referred to as semi-parametric group-based modeling, that allowed researchers to examine within a sample the frequency of offending at each year of age, referred to as an offending trajectory. This analysis uses a grouping method to identify the number of aggregate trajectories that fit a sample best. Figure 5.1 provides an example of trajectory modeling using ISVYOS data (also see McCuish et al., 2021). Reconviction rates across each wave (year of age) are shown across each trajectory group. Two trajectories, representing approximately 30 percent of the sample, indicate patterns of offending persistence across 20 years of data. Thus, Nagin and Land's analysis, colloquially referred to as trajectory modeling, helped to identify patterns of offending persistence.

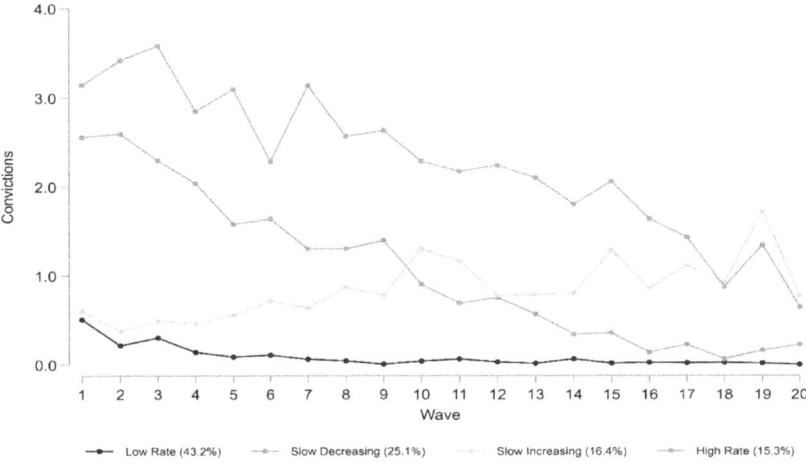

Figure 5.1 Example of the output from semi-parametric group-based modeling.

There are some well-justified criticisms of how this method has been used and interpreted by researchers. Just like criticisms of the taxonic syndrome perspective on psychopathy, these trajectories should not be interpreted as naturally occurring phenomena (see Skardhamar, 2010, for details). Instead, trajectories should be viewed as statistical approximations of the reality of offending patterns as an unknown continuous distribution (e.g., dimensional rather than taxonic). It would therefore be a mistake to review Figure 5.1 and conclude, for example, that there are precisely four distinct offending trajectories. Instead, for this sample, four trajectories appeared to be the number that best balanced fit and parsimony. The best-fitting model would be one where a trajectory was modeled for each individual, but this is exceedingly complex. Issues with trajectory modeling are not so much with the method itself but with how users of this method present and describe their data. Trajectory modeling is useful for making sense of complex patterns and creating more homogeneous (i.e., similar) groups from more heterogenous (i.e., diverse) data.

Moffitt's (1993) dual taxonomy provided a theoretical starting point for why a risk factor like psychopathy might be associated with persistent offending over the life-course. Nagin and Land's (1993) trajectory modeling approach provided a methodological starting point for modeling patterns of offending over the life-course. Together, these approaches offer a foundation for studying the relationship between psychopathy and persistent offending.

Refining Methods for Measuring Persistent Offending

Semiparametric group-based modeling is one method of representing trajectories. I have routinely used this analysis in my own research. However, this method has limitations. For example, selecting the number of trajectory groups that best represent a sample can be more art than science. The user must write code telling a software program how many trajectories to produce. Many model fit indices are provided in trajectory modeling to help make decisions about the number of trajectory groups to retain. Sometimes, different indices give different recommendations about the number of trajectories to retain. Some users may prefer to rely on the model fit indicator that recommends a more parsimonious solution (i.e., fewer trajectories). Some users may believe that a greater number of trajectories should be retained to improve the probability of correctly assigning a given person to the right trajectory. There is also inherent imprecision in group assignment, as each participant is assigned to a trajectory regardless of how well that aggregate trajectory reflects their pattern of offending. When different model fit indices point to different decisions, the user is forced to prioritize one index over the other. Different users may have different priorities (e.g., parsimony vs. fit), leading to different decisions about the number of trajectory groups to retain, even within the same dataset.

Instead of using semi-parametric group-based modeling, I model offending trajectories using generalized estimating equations. This analysis allows for the examination of between-group differences in levels of offending over time while accounting for the fact that a person's past offending is correlated with their future offending. For the generalized estimating equation models presented in this book (also see Chapters 8 and 9), each wave of data, represented by a person's year of age, indicated the probability of whether a participant incurred a conviction during that particular wave.[1] I also look at the same question, but examine the probability of whether a participant was incarcerated for at least one month. Instead of probabilistic outcomes, I typically would look at the number of convictions and the number of days incarcerated at each year of

---

[1] The intracluster correlation was modeled as an identity matrix. I specified a first-order autoregressive working correlation matrix that assumes convictions occurring/incarceration nearer in time are more strongly correlated than convictions/incarceration occurring further apart in time (Twisk, 2013). This analytic strategy facilitates modeling between-group differences in offending over time and accounts for the clustering of convictions within individuals (Hardin & Hilbe, 2007). Robust standard errors were specified in case of correlation matrix misspecification.

age. However, probabilistic outcomes are more intuitive. The substantive interpretations of the findings remain the same regardless of whether looking at convictions/incarceration as a rate or as a dichotomous (yes/no) outcome. Examining the probability of conviction at each year of age differs substantially from typical recidivism studies in which only one instance of recidivism is examined across the whole study period. Generalized estimating equations allow for the modeling of repeated recidivism across multiple waves of data.

The Importance of Understanding Persistent Offending

Persistent offending causes substantial physical and emotional harm to victims. People involved in persistent offending also face their own challenges, including being at a high risk for serious victimization that requires hospitalization (e.g., Ryu & McCuish, 2022) and even early mortality (Pauls, 2019). I see the study of persistent offending as important, not because it helps to identify who should be incarcerated for long periods of time, but because understanding the development of persistent offending may allow for proactive steps to be taken to initiate treatment. It is important to develop evidence-based humanistic interventions that address characteristics in childhood/adolescence, including extreme forms of marginalization, which are associated with an increased risk of persistent offending. Such characteristics of children and youth should not be used to justify deterrence, punishment, and selective incapacitation because there is substantial evidence that a change in patterns of offending does occur over the life-course (Laub & Sampson, 2003).

The availability and use of intervention and prevention programs are often limited by budgetary considerations. Policymakers may be hesitant to invest in proactive programs aimed at preventing persistent offending given that the benefits are not realized for several decades. If someone is 5 years old, it will take 20+ years to identify whether they are associated with a pattern of persistent offending. Policymakers may prefer to communicate to the public the immediate benefits of programs on crime prevention and community safety. To offer policymakers insight into the benefits of proactive intervention strategies, it is important to communicate the cost savings that come from preventing persistent offending over the life-course (see Table 5.1 for a summary of estimated costs).

In a study of youth involved in the criminal legal system in Toronto, Day and Koegl (2019) reported that the cost associated with chronic offending was more than $16,000,000 (CAD) per person. This included

Table 5.1 The costs of persistent offending

Study	Location	Definition of persistent offending	Measurement Period	Factors in cost assessment	Cost of chronic offending per person
Cohen and Piquero (2009)	Philadelphia, PA, USA	6% of boys are responsible for 50+% of all crime (averaging 68 total arrests)	Ages 8–26	Costs of detected and undetected crimes, victim costs, criminal legal system costs, and lost opportunity costs	$2,600,000 (USD)
Piquero et al. (2013)	London, England	Conviction trajectories. Persistent offending trajectory averaged 21.13 convictions	Ages 10–50	Security expenditures and insurance administration, consequences of crime, and response to crime	$95,241 (USD)
Allard et al. (2020)	Queensland, Australia	Arrest trajectories. Persistent trajectory averaged approximately 75 arrests	Ages 10–31	Criminal legal system costs, social and economic costs	$118,375 (AUD)
Day and Koegl (2019)	Toronto, Canada	Conviction trajectories. Persistent trajectory averaged 28.47 convictions	Ages 12–26	Victim costs, correctional costs, procedural justice costs, and costs of undetected crimes	$16,954,604 (CAD)

Notes. Average cost in Allard et al. (2020) is based on average after combining Indigenous and Nonindigenous estimates.

costs to victims, costs to corrections (e.g., housing of inmates), and other criminal legal system costs, such as financing police investigations and court costs. In Australia, a single youth involved in persistent offending costs police and correctional services approximately $58,000 (AUD). For police alone, investigating serious offences like homicide costs approximately $140,000 (AUD) per case (Allard et al., 2020). Studies in England estimated that a single chronic offender would cost each United Kingdom citizen approximately $1,000 (USD) over that citizen's lifetime (Piquero et al., 2013). Studies in the United States reported that the average chronic offender incurred costs totaling $2,500,000 (USD) (Cohen & Piquero, 2009; Cohen et al., 2010). Overall, although the costs of chronic/persistent offending vary quite widely depending on the jurisdiction and the types of costs considered (e.g., police, corrections, courts, public health, and social welfare), even the more conservative estimates are substantial. The financial incentive associated with the prevention of a single chronic offender[2] is estimated to be in the millions of dollars (Cohen & Piquero, 2009).

Psychopathy and Persistent Offending

I do not dispute that psychopathy statistically predicts recidivism. The issue I raise is whether focusing on recidivism maximizes the value of psychopathy when it comes to better understanding the development of criminal behaviour. It is a simple numbers game. Among incarcerated populations, the prevalence of recidivism is higher (Bushway & Denver, 2025) compared to estimates of the prevalence of psychopathy. In the ISVYOS PCL:YV Cohort, only about 20 percent of the sample received a score of at least 30 on the PCL:YV. In contrast, 80 percent of the sample recidivated between ages 18 and 23. This means that even if every person with a high score on the PCL:YV recidivated, about 75 percent of recidivists remain who did not score high on the PCL:YV. This is a lot of recidivism left unexplained[3] and underscores that psychopathy is not a sufficient explanation for general offending. The difference between the prevalence of psychopathy and the prevalence of recidivism is why Larsen (2025) mistakenly concluded that psychopathy was weakly related to

---

[2] This can also be considered the prevention of serious offending, given that chronic offenders account for the majority of serious offences as well (e.g., Kempf-Leonard et al., 2001).
[3] This point is somewhat simplified, given that PCL:YV scores should be treated as dimensional rather than as simply high/not high, but the general point stands that recidivism is far more common than the prevalence of clinically meaningful psychopathy traits.

offending. Beyond psychopathy, there are many other risk factors that influence general recidivism. Researchers should therefore think more theoretically about psychopathy's influence on other offending outcomes.

Psychopathy may be more suited to the explanation of rarer offending outcomes like persistent offending. This perspective is not new (Moffitt, 1993). In fact, some theorized that the reason that there is a similar prevalence of people high in psychopathy traits and people associated with chronic offending is because the two groups comprised the same people (DeLisi & Piquero, 2011; Vaughn & DeLisi, 2008). There is a strong theoretical foundation for why people with psychopathy traits are disproportionately represented among those who engage in persistent offending.

Integrating Psychopathy within Situational Action Theory

Wikström and Treiber's (2009) situational action theory conceptualizes offending as the result of three characteristics: (1) a person's propensity to engage in criminal behaviour, (2) the absence of deterrent factors, and (3) situational context. Figure 5.2 provides a conceptual overview of how different psychopathy traits (see Cooke et al., 2004; Forth et al., 2003; Hare, 2003) correspond with each of these three characteristics and may, in turn, influence persistent offending over the life-course.

Criminal propensity is defined as a trait or set of traits that emerge early in the life-course and remain relatively stable over time (Nagin & Paternoster, 2000). Criminal propensity is thought to account for why some people offend at a high rate over the life-course (e.g., Moffitt, 1993). Psychopathy often has been identified as an important indicator of criminal propensity. Certain psychopathy traits may directly increase the propensity for criminal behaviour given their association with aggression, a sense of entitlement, and positive attitudes toward criminal behaviour (Salekin, 2016). A sense of entitlement and intolerance toward others reflects the moralistic component of propensity described by Wikström and Treiber (2009). Impulsive, disruptive, reckless, and aggressive traits of psychopathy overlap with the low self-control component of propensity described by Wikström and Treiber (2009).

In theory, psychopathy traits also influence criminal behaviour indirectly by negating deterrent factors. For example, Wikström and Treiber (2009) noted that a key component of deterrence involves recognizing the likelihood of detection for a specific crime. Behavioural traits of psychopathy, such as impulsivity, a sense of invulnerability, and sensation seeking, may lead people to overlook cues that would normally increase someone's

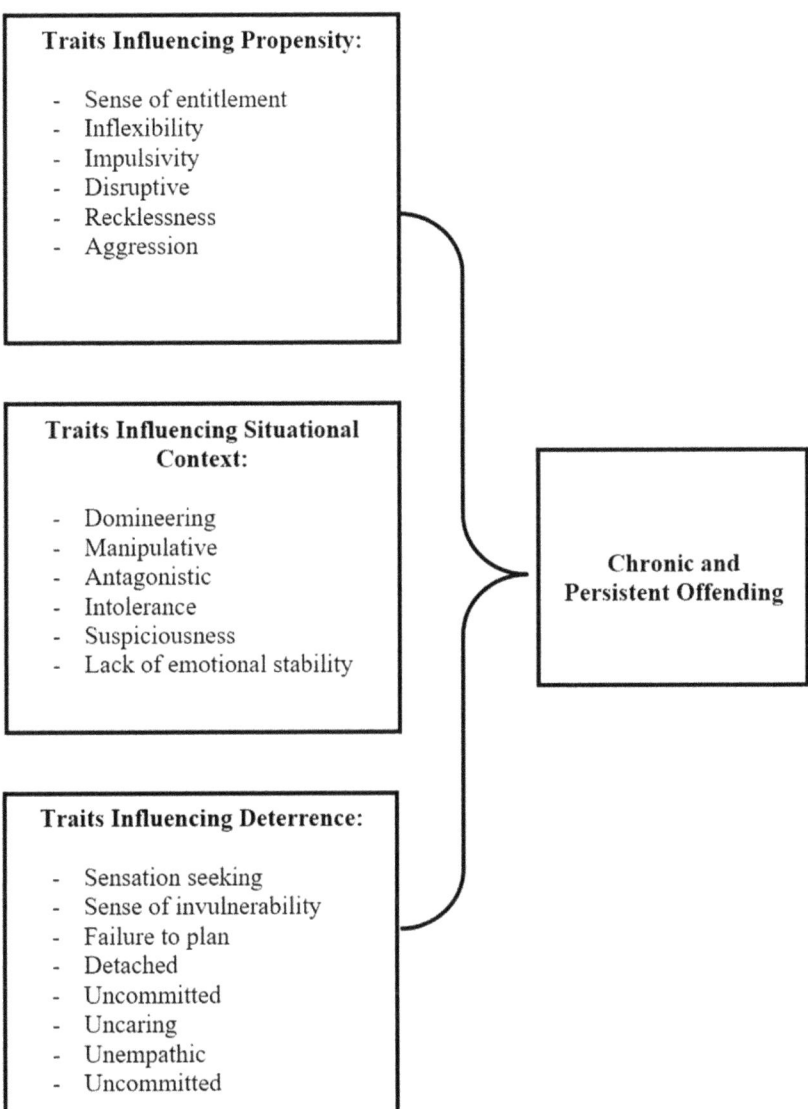

Figure 5.2 Conceptual description of the causal influence of psychopathy traits on offending.

perception of the likelihood of getting caught (Altikriti et al., 2021). Such traits may increase the likelihood of acting on opportunities for criminal behaviour that would otherwise be passed up due to the risk of getting caught. Additionally, affective traits imply a lack of concern for the pain to others and the immorality of criminal behaviour. There is therefore no "braking mechanism" to deter acting upon opportunities for criminal behaviour.

With respect to psychopathy and the situational context component of Wikström and Treiber's (2009) theory, an interpersonal style characterized by domineering, manipulative, and antagonistic traits may place individuals in constant conflict with others, creating conditions conducive to offending. Further, psychopathy traits include inflexible belief systems and a quick temper. Thus, even minor negative interactions may escalate to criminal behaviour. For example, instrumental aggression refers to unprovoked acts, often against strangers, and committed for a specific goal (e.g., robbery). Reactive aggression refers to impulsive, emotional responses to perceived threats or disagreements and is often directed at a stranger. People with psychopathy traits are more likely to engage in instrumental aggression compared to other people. However, this does not imply that they are therefore not reactively aggressive. In fact, Dr. Julie Blais' meta-analysis of 53 studies showed that there is limited evidence that psychopathy is more related to instrumental aggression than reactive aggression (Blais et al., 2014). What may distinguish people with psychopathy traits is their higher likelihood of engaging in both forms of aggression, suggesting that they encounter more situations conducive to offending compared to others.

The Measurement of Offending Persistence Using ISVYOS Data

Measuring offending persistence requires longitudinal data where measures of offending are taken at each year of age. Such data were collected by the ISVYOS research team. The Ministry of Children and Family Development and British Columbia Corrections provided us with access to the Corrections Network (CORNET) software program.[4] CORNET includes data on all individuals involved in the criminal legal system in the

---

[4] CORNET only provided information about criminal legal system involvement within British Columbia. Thus, the study did not have data on participants who became involved in the criminal legal system of another jurisdiction. For reference, British Columbia is 587,031 square miles, making it twice the size of Texas. This means that individuals typically had to relocate a substantial distance before falling outside the jurisdiction of the project. Further, CORNET provided data on instances in which a person was known to have emigrated from the province. CORNET also provided data on mortality. Convictions and time incarcerated after the date of emigration from the province or date of death were coded as missing rather than "zero" to avoid instances of false desistance where individuals were identified as desisters simply because of an inopportunity to offend or to have their offending behaviour recorded.

province of British Columbia. We searched the CORNET files of the PCL:YV Cohort to code, for each participant, the number and type of convictions incurred at each year of age between ages 12 and 40. Data were also used to code the number of days spent incarcerated at each year of age between ages 12 and 40. Age 12 represented the starting point because this is the age of criminal responsibility in Canada. Age 40 reflected the oldest age of ISVYOS participants at the time data were coded. Participants were an average age of 35.69 years (SD = 4.27) when data from CORNET were last collected. Using official indicators of convictions means that offending was likely underestimated for persons who were able to avoid detection. An alternative would be to use self-reported involvement in criminal behaviour, but self-report data are not always more reliable than official measures, especially for repeated measures of offending over the life-course (Kirk, 2006; Lauritsen, 1999).

Convictions and incarceration data were coded as missing for ages where follow-up data were unavailable (e.g., the participant was under age 40; the participant died during the follow-up period). For the analyses in this chapter, I excluded offending information measured between ages 12 and 17 to ensure that the measurement of psychopathy, which occurred while participants were youth, was independent of the measurement of offending. This helps avoid tautological issues in which criminal behaviour items used to measure PCL:YV-defined psychopathy were subsequently predicted by PCL:YV test scores. The distribution of conviction and incarceration events for each year of age is shown in Figure 5.3.

Are Psychopathy Traits in Adolescence Associated with Persistent Offending in Adulthood?

Results from the generalized estimating equation models are based on analyses that accounted for the control variables described in Chapter 3 (e.g., gender, ethnicity, self-identity, family adversity, substance use, residential mobility, and abuse). Unlike traditional studies on psychopathy and offending that examine the odds of recidivism over the entire follow-up period, generalized estimating equations allow me to focus on whether PCL:YV scores are associated with a significantly higher likelihood of conviction or incarceration at each year of age during the follow-up period.

I observed that increases in PCL:YV total scores were associated with significant increases in the likelihood of convictions and the likelihood of incarceration at each year of age during the follow-up period. This illustrates that PCL:YV traits influenced persistent offending. A graphical

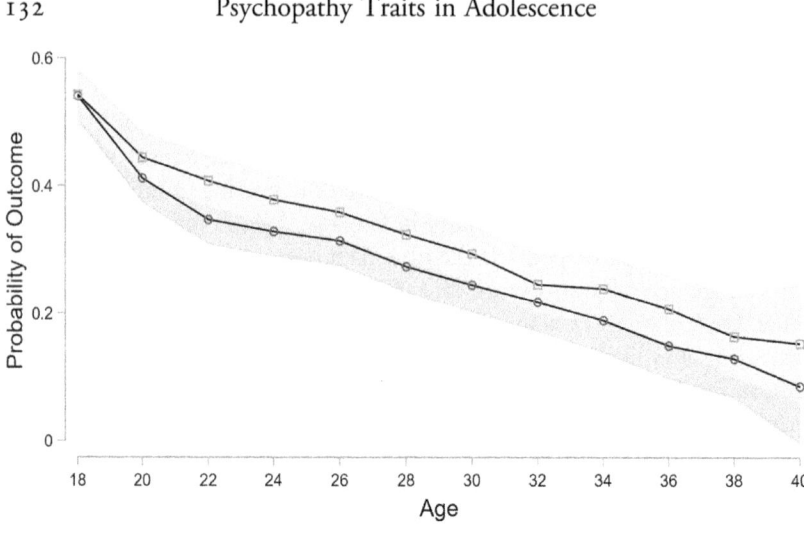

Figure 5.3 Probability of different criminal legal system outcomes at each year of age.
Notes. The shaded area represents the 95 percent confidence interval (CI) of each outcome.

depiction of these findings is shown in Panels A (convictions) and B (incarceration) of Figure 5.4. Throughout the book, I use this same style of figure to visually depict the relationship between independent and dependent variables, which I find more informative and easier to interpret than tables of numbers. The x-axis at the bottom represents levels of the independent variable, in this case, PCL:YV test scores. Technically, PCL:YV scores can range from 0 to 40. I show PCL:YV scores ranging from 5 to 35 because scores outside of this range were extremely rare for ISVYOS participants. The y-axis on the left represents the dependent variable.

In the case of Panel A of Figure 5.4, the dependent variable, convictions, is a dichotomous outcome (i.e., only two possible outcomes; either someone was reconvicted at least once or they were not). The y-axis reflects the probability of the event occurring *at each year of age*. This last point is critical. The analysis does not predict reconviction at any point in time between ages 18 and 40. Instead, it averages probabilities of a reconviction at each year of age from ages 18 and 40. Thus, the analysis indicates the probability of the offending outcome at different levels of PCL:YV total scores. The shaded areas of the graph reflect 95 percent CIs for the probability of reconviction.

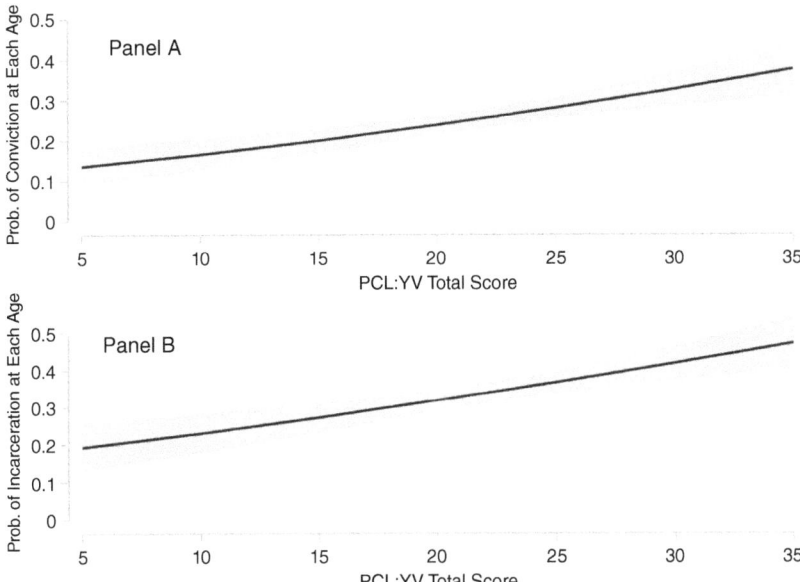

Figure 5.4 The relationship between PCL:YV total scores and the probability of conviction (Panel A) and incarceration (Panel B) at each year of age between ages 18 and 40.

Notes. The probability of incarceration represents the probability of spending at least one month in custody in a given year of age. The shaded area represents 95 percent CI.

Statistical significance does not necessarily translate to importance. Effect sizes indicate the magnitude of the relationship between variables. To describe the impact of high PCL:YV scores on offending, the odds of incurring a conviction at a given year of age were 1.85 times higher for participants with a PCL:YV score of 30 or greater compared to participants with a score of less than 30. Similarly, the odds of being incarcerated at a given year of age were 1.82 times higher for participants with a PCL:YV score of 30 or greater compared to participants with a PCL:YV score of less than 30.

Is the Relationship between Psychopathy and Persistent Offending More Than Just Lifestyle and Antisocial Factors?

Another contentious issue in research on the PCL and offending concerns the Antisocial factor. The Antisocial factor most strongly relates to reoffending. Yet, as indicated in Chapter 4, items from the Antisocial factor are the least informative of psychopathy traits. In other words, what matters most for offending matters least to psychopathy. Should measures of psychopathy include items simply because they help predict reoffending? In my view, no. The goal of measuring psychopathy is not to predict reoffending. If this were the case, it would make sense to include in the measurement of psychopathy as many risk factors as possible, regardless of their alignment with definitions of psychopathy (e.g., gang membership, substance use, peer criminal behaviour, negative family environment). Including these different risk factors might increase the predictive validity of a measure, but many of these risk factors have nothing to do with psychopathy traits. It is therefore important not to place too much emphasis on predictive validity. The primary goal should always be the accurate measurement of psychopathy. If a reliable and valid measure of psychopathy fails to predict reoffending, this still tells us important information about psychopathy (e.g., that psychopathy may be related to more serious forms of offending rather than minor forms of general offending).

I re-ran my analyses in different ways to verify whether the relationship between PCL:YV total scores and offending was driven by scores on the Lifestyle/Antisocial factors. First, I used a three-factor model (validated in Chapter 4) that excludes the Antisocial factor. Increases in three-factor total scores were associated with significant increases in the odds of being convicted at a given year of age during the follow-up period. The same pattern was observed when looking at incarceration. This means that, contrary to what has been said previously about the PCL:YV, the relationship between psychopathy and future offending cannot be attributed to indicators of past criminal behaviour.

As further evidence that core psychopathy traits contribute to criminal behaviour, I created a scale that reflected the sum of the 13 PCL:YV items from the item response theory analysis in Chapter 4 that contributed meaningful information to the latent construct of psychopathy. These items included: impression management, grandiosity, pathological lying, manipulation, lack of remorse, shallow affect, callous/lack of empathy, failure to accept responsibility, lacks goals, irresponsibility, poor anger control, early behavioural problems, and unstable interpersonal relationships. Increases in scores on this scale of core psychopathy traits were associated with significant increases in both a person's probability of conviction and their probability of incarceration at each year of age between ages 18 and 40.

The next set of analyses examined whether specific PCL:YV factors were informative of continued offending in adulthood. For convictions, the

Interpersonal, Lifestyle, and Antisocial factors were each significantly associated with increases in the probability of reconviction in adulthood. For incarceration, all four factors were individually associated with a significantly greater likelihood of spending at least one month incarcerated at each year of age.

Overall, contrary to some prior research, core traits of psychopathy, represented by interpersonal and affective deficits measured in adolescence, were associated with persistent offending throughout the first two decades of adulthood. Although this finding *contrasts* with research indicating that the relationship between psychopathy and offending is driven by criminal/behavioural indicators (Kennealy et al., 2010), it does not necessarily *contradict* these previous findings. By looking at repeated reoffending over several decades, the analyses in this chapter addressed a different question than those of prior research.

Do Youth Psychopathy Traits Predict Offending for Everyone?

There are long-standing concerns about whether risk factors that predict reoffending in the general population will also predict reoffending among underrepresented subgroups from this population (McCuish & Corrado, 2018). Such concerns have extended to research on psychopathy (e.g., McCuish et al., 2018b). Especially in Canada, samples of people involved in crime are often predominantly White and male. It is critical, especially given implications for the criminal legal system, that researchers evaluate the predictive validity of psychopathy for groups who may be under-represented in research samples. The danger is that criminal legal systems that are not attuned to issues of cross-cultural generalizability will make decisions that bring harm to already marginalized groups (see Hart, 2016).

Moderation analyses allow for statistical testing of whether a third variable affects the strength or direction of the relationship between an independent variable like psychopathy and a dependent variable like offending (Baron & Kenny, 1986). In this case, moderation analyses examine whether the influence of psychopathy traits on reoffending varies depending on a person's self-reported gender or ethnic background. With respect to gender, Figure 5.5 illustrates that psychopathy traits are related to reoffending outcomes similarly for both boys and girls. The key detail in Figure 5.5 is the slopes of the two lines for male participants and female participants. These lines essentially run parallel to one another, meaning that for both male and female participants, increases in PCL:YV total scores are associated with increases in the likelihood of conviction/

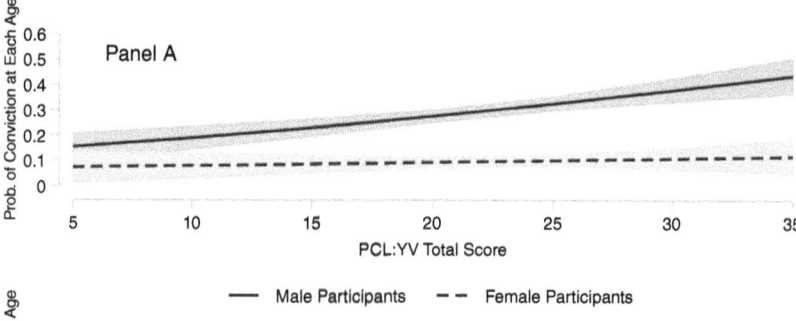
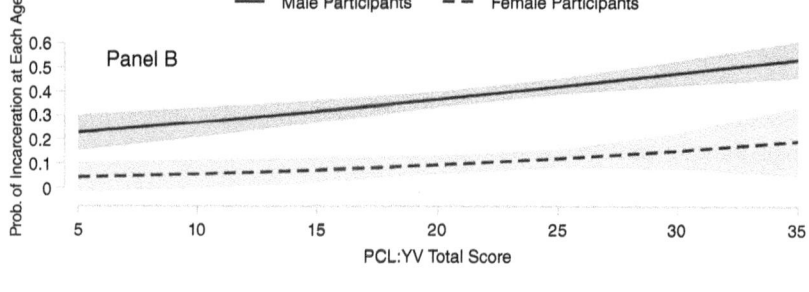

Figure 5.5 The relationship between PCL:YV total score scores and the probability of conviction (Panel A) and incarceration (Panel B) at each year of age between ages 18 and 40 for male and female participants.

Notes. The probability of incarceration represents the probability of spending at least one month in custody in a given year of age. The shaded area represents 95 percent CI.

incarceration. The separation between the two lines simply reflects the fact that male participants, on average, have a higher likelihood of convictions/incarceration at each year of age compared to female participants.

Although this finding supports the predictive validity of the PCL:YV in samples of girls/women, I would not go as far as to say that this means the PCL:YV is a valid measure of psychopathy for girls/women. In Chapter 4, I was unable to test whether the factor structure of the PCL:YV was similar across boys and girls because of the small subsample of girls in the study. Other researchers have noted challenges in reliably assessing psychopathy in female populations because of potential differences in how psychopathy traits are expressed (Forouzan & Cooke, 2005). I did not want to weigh in on this issue because my training focused on the assessment of psychopathy traits among boys.

Similar to gender, questions have been raised about the relationship between psychopathy and offending across ethnicity. Canada has a long and ugly history regarding its treatment of Indigenous People. This history includes influencing the overrepresentation of Indigenous Persons in

Canada's criminal legal system. There are concerns that measures like the PCL:YV contribute to this overrepresentation. In the case of *Ewert v. Canada*, the plaintiff, Jeffrey Ewert, challenged the Correctional Service of Canada's use of the Psychopathy Checklist – Revised (PCL-R) (as well as other instruments). The plaintiff's assertion, supported through expert testimony, was that researchers had failed to establish whether the PCL-R had predictive validity when it came to examining offending outcomes for Indigenous Persons (Hart, 2016). Virtually all studies on the PCL-R and offending outcomes included samples that overwhelmingly comprised White males. Justice Phelan ruled in favour of the plaintiff and specified that the Correctional Service of Canada had violated its principle of evidence-based practice. In the absence of research supporting the PCL-R's reliability and validity with Indigenous offenders, Justice Phelan concluded that the PCL-R should not be used in decisions involving community reentry.

The same type of moderation analysis used to examine the functioning of the PCL:YV across gender was used to examine the functioning of the PCL:YV across ethnicity. As shown in Figure 5.6, regardless of a participant's self-reported ethnicity, increases in PCL:YV scores were similarly associated with increases in the odds of incurring a conviction and being incarcerated. This does not mean that the issue of cross-cultural validity is resolved. Of greatest importance is acknowledging that Indigenous communities may prefer decolonized methods of responding to harmful behaviour that do not include the assessment of psychopathy at all (McGuire, 2022). Addressing the harms of colonization and genocidal practices against Indigenous Peoples[5] does not merely involve evaluating whether psychopathy or some risk assessment tool has predictive validity for this population. Respecting the autonomy and self-determination of Indigenous groups also requires acknowledging that assessing psychopathy may conflict with Indigenous concepts of justice and, therefore, should be avoided regardless of evidence of predictive validity.

Psychopathy Traits and the Perpetration of Harmful Offences

When Dilulio and others warned about youth superpredators, they claimed that youth with psychopathy traits would influence an enormous

---

[5] For example, Canada's history includes forcibly removing Indigenous children from their homes and placing them in residential schools. These schools perpetuated heinous forms of abuse and torture that have had a lasting impact on structural disadvantage among Indigenous Peoples, including poverty, poorer educational and health outcomes, and difficulties with basic rights such as access to water (Ford, 2012). For more details, see Kelm and Smith (2018).

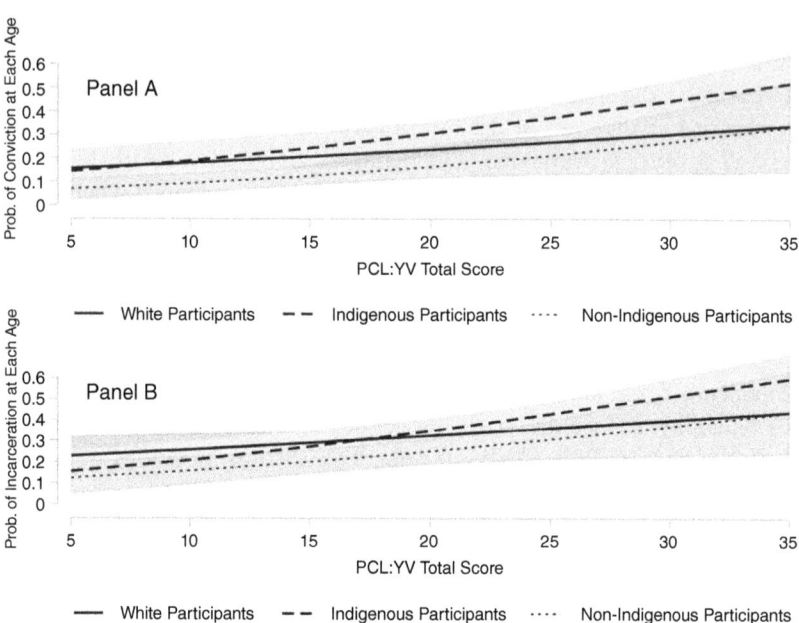

Figure 5.6 The relationship between PCL:YV Total scores and the probability of conviction (Panel A) and incarceration (Panel B) at each year of age between ages 18 and 40 for Indigenous, White, and Nonindigenous participants.

Notes. The probability of incarceration represents probability of spending at least one month in custody in a given year of age. The shaded area represents 95 percent CI. Nonindigenous participants are those who are not Indigenous and not White (e.g., Black, Hispanic).

increase in the homicide rate in the United States. Such claims were purely speculative. If Dilulio was correct, youth with a high PCL:YV score should be disproportionately involved in homicide offences. As a reminder, the PCL:YV Cohort includes 535 youth from the ISVYOS who received a PCL:YV assessment. The PCL:YV Cohort thus includes the full range of possible PCL:YV scores. Within this cohort, 67 participants (3 percent of the sample) were involved in a homicide offence between ages 12 and 40. Homicide offences included first-degree (planned, deliberate) and second-degree (deliberate) murder, but also manslaughter and attempted murder. About 15 percent of the sample scored 30 or higher on the PCL:YV. These percentages overlap, but does this mean that youth involved in homicide offenses are always youth with high scores on the PCL:YV?

Logistic regression is used when the dependent variable in question is a dichotomous outcome (e.g., the only response options are "yes" or "no"). Controlling for demographic characteristics and other risk factors, a logistic regression analysis indicated that, contrary to Dilulio's forecast, PCL:YV test scores did not significantly increase the odds of perpetrating a homicide offence. At the bivariate level, only 12 percent of youth with a score of 30 or more on the PCL:YV were involved in a homicide offence. Said differently, if one assumed that homicide offences were only perpetrated by people with psychopathy traits, nearly 90 percent of the homicides perpetrated by the PCL:YV Cohort would be overlooked. To some, this may be surprising. However, the factors influencing homicide offending are complex (DeLisi et al., 2014; Farrington et al., 2012; Loeber et al., 2005; Loeber & Farrington, 2011). Homicide is a single, rare event, and a lot of randomness can factor into its occurrence. I interviewed several youth for whom, despite having a variety of risk factors, what stood out was the influence of peer pressure. For events that happen repeatedly over the life-course (e.g., persistent offending), randomness is less influential, which may explain the stronger statistical association between psychopathy and persistent offending compared to homicide. For the PCL:YV Cohort, a homicide offence represented a rare, single event that included random chance (e.g., assaults that turned into manslaughter) and may therefore be difficult to predict. Future research in this area may need to consider, for example, evidence of "over-kill" at the crime scene or other modus operandi factors that were not available in the ISVYOS data (Beauregard & Proulx, 2007).

On the other hand, when it came to serious but somewhat more common crime types, such as sex offences (14% of the sample), offences involving a firearm (36% of the sample), and offences resulting in a Federal custody sentence (26% of the sample),[6] logistic regression analyses indicated that PCL:YV total scores significantly increased the odds of each of these offences. Compared to youth with scores of less than 30 on the PCL:YV, youth with a score of 30 or higher on the PCL:YV were 2.69 times more likely to perpetrate a sex offence (95% CI = 1.46–4.96), 1.34 times more likely to perpetrate a firearm offence (95% CI = 0.79–2.26),[7] and 1.82 times more likely to be sentenced to Federal custody (95% CI = 1.06–3.12).

---

[6] A Federal custody sentence refers to a sentence of two years or more in custody.

[7] This CI contains zero, which means the finding is not significant. As a reminder, I use cut scores on the PCL:YV only as a teaching device. There are some things I do in this book that I would not do in a manuscript meant to be submitted to a peer-reviewed journal. What I put stock into is the relationship between PCL:YV total scores and offending outcomes. When treating psychopathy as dimensional and thus looking at total scores, increases in PCL:YV scores are associated with increases in the odds of firearm offending. Interpreting this type of finding is less intuitive because the focus is on the percentage increase in the outcome per one-unit increase in PCL:YV scores as opposed to comparing individuals with high/low test scores.

Psychopathy and the High Risk Offender Intervention Program

Earlier in this chapter, I discussed early intervention and noted that the costs associated with persistent offending were one way to demonstrate to policymakers the importance of early intervention for children and youth with psychopathy traits. In addition to harms to victims, another consequence of failing to intervene early to prevent persistent offending is the cost associated with implementing interventions later in adulthood. The High Risk Offender Intervention Program (HROIP) was initiated in British Columbia by Ronald Hurt. The HROIP functions as a screening program designed to flag adults who appear to be dangerous offenders (a legal designation in Canada that comes with an indeterminate sentence). Such designations imply that more intensive treatment, intervention, or enforcement/punishment may be warranted. The HROIP moves away from the assumption that police and prosecution services are already well-aware of which offenders constitute a danger to the public (Prosecution Service, 2019; Public Safety Canada, 2018). Thus, the HROIP aimed to improve the identification of dangerous offenders being considered for criminal legal system response strategies and is not itself a treatment or intervention program (Public Safety Canada, 2018). The HROIP was designed to improve the process of gathering information when considering whether someone was a dangerous offender (Public Safety Canada, 2018). A swath of information is considered, including police reports, court transcripts, correctional records, and mental health assessments.

Controlling for demographic characteristics and other risk factors, PCL:YV test scores significantly increased the odds of being assigned to the HROIP. A one-unit increase in PCL:YV test scores was associated with an 11 percent increase in the odds of being placed in this program. The odds of assignment to the HROIP were 2.85 times higher for youth who scored at least 30 on the PCL:YV compared to youth who scored less than 30 on the PCL:YV (95 percent CI = 1.31–6.21). Policymakers should consider that failing to help address psychopathy traits early in the life-course cannot simply be offset by avoiding the costs of early intervention. Later in life, the chickens come home to roost, and more reactive criminal legal system programs that also carry financial costs are implemented.

When Do Psychopathy Traits Fail to Predict Persistent Offending?

A false positive refers to instances where a risk factor is present, but the expected outcome does not actually occur. A classic example of a false positive relates to pregnancy tests. Pregnancy tests are designed to detect human chorionic gonadotropin, a hormone that is produced during pregnancy. In other words, human chorionic gonadotropin is an indicator of the likelihood of pregnancy. However, human chorionic gonadotropin can be produced even in the absence of pregnancy, such as in response to the use of certain medications. Thus, a false positive occurs when a pregnancy test detects human chorionic gonadotropin, but there is no actual pregnancy. Similarly, a high PCL:YV test score (taking the place of human chorionic gonadotropin levels) may be an indicator of the likelihood of persistent offending (taking the place of pregnancy). However, a false positive occurs if PCL:YV test scores are high, and so persistent offending is anticipated, and yet persistent offending does not actually occur.

It is important not to mistake statistical significance for a rule of law. A statistically significant relationship does not necessarily mean a strong relationship. At the very least, I want to acknowledge exceptions to the rule and understand why these exceptions occur. Four ISVYOS participants had a PCL:YV score of at least 30, yet had few or no convictions in adulthood. In other words, they were not characterized by a pattern of persistent offending. Why did these false positives occur?

A false positive may occur because a person's PCL:YV test score was inaccurate (e.g., rater error). Perhaps an ISYVOS Research Assistant overestimated someone's true score on the PCL:YV. For example, it is normative for adolescents to have issues with self-control and psychosocial maturity, and some have warned that psychopathy assessments need to carefully distinguish normative from nonnormative adolescent traits (Seagrave & Grisso, 2002). It is possible that ISVYOS Research Assistants scoring the PCL:YV mistakenly used such issues as evidence of psychopathy traits. Perhaps an ISVYOS Research Assistant accurately scored the PCL:YV, and the false positive occurred simply because a PCL:YV test score is an imperfect tool for measuring psychopathy. It is also possible for psychopathy to be measured accurately yet fail to predict persistent offending because not all individuals with psychopathy traits engage in persistent offending (e.g., successful psychopathy). Another possibility is that a participant continued to offend while remaining undetected by the criminal legal system (Gao & Raine, 2010). Finally, as mentioned in Chapter 2, people with psychopathy traits can change. It is possible that a participant's psychopathy traits declined substantially between adolescence and adulthood, thereby reducing the risk of reoffending (McCuish & Lussier, 2018). When data were available, I investigated these possibilities for each of the four false positive

Table 5.2 *Description of false positive cases*

	ISVYOS participant			
	Melissa	Bill	Richard	Rachelle
PCL:YV score	31	30	32	31
Age of onset of criminal cehaviour	Age 14	Age 15	Age 13	Age 14
Convictions (ages 12–17)	11	8	4	11
Convictions (ages 18–23)	0	0	0	1
Convictions (ages 24–29)	0	0	0	7
Convictions (ages 30–35)	0	0	0	0
Days incarcerated (ages 12–17)	362	204	471	433
Days incarcerated (ages 18–23)	0	1	1	7
Days incarcerated (ages 24–29)	0	0	0	57
Days incarcerated (ages 30–35)	0	0	0	0
PCL:YV rating accuracy	Accurate	**Inaccurate**	**Inaccurate**	Accurate
Detection avoidance	Detected	Detected	Detected	**Avoided detection**
Trait changes in adulthood	**Change**	**Change**	No change†	No change

† Although Richard experienced stability in functioning between adolescence and adulthood, this represented stability in other mental health issues, including issues stemming from the consequences of a traumatic brain injury, rather than stability in psychopathy traits.

cases (see Table 5.2). These cases illustrate that there can be a variety of reasons for false positives when examining the relationship between psychopathy and persistent offending.

Melissa

In adolescence, Melissa engaged in violence toward others, manipulated others for money, justified her actions by arguing that she needed drugs, engaged in storytelling, and was noted to have tried to charm and manipulate the Research Assistant interviewing her into bringing cigarettes into the custody center for her. She often intruded on the Research Assistant's space, which is a characteristic of interpersonal dominance. She blamed her mom for her involvement in crime, stole from her mom, ended relationships because she felt bored, and urinated into a cleaning bottle to spray it at others in custody. She was described as solving personal problems in ways that demonstrated a disregard for social rules. In adolescence, she was involved in violent crimes and stalking/harassment. Overall, psychopathy traits were observed across multiple social domains (e.g., with friends, family, strangers, and peers), and there did not appear to be any clear evidence to challenge Melissa's PCL:YV rating.

Keeping in mind that criminologists describe desistance as a process of reducing one's level of offending as opposed to completely abstaining from offending, Melissa appeared to have desisted from criminal behaviour in adulthood. There was also no evidence found in her file to suggest that her probation officer was suspicious of Melissa engaging in criminal behaviour that went undetected by the legal system. Melissa was arrested at ages 25, 27, and 29 for separate assaults. All three assaults were perpetrated against the father of her children. In all three arrests, charges were either not approved or were dropped prior to trial, and thus, she was never convicted. These assaults appeared to be the result of an escalation in mutual conflicts with the father of her children. Melissa was seeking to have the father charged with fraud. Melissa's probation officers rated her as low risk on various risk assessment tools, including the Community Risk Needs Assessment (discussed in Chapter 6).

Melissa's false positive result seemed to stem from genuine changes in psychopathy traits between adolescence and adulthood that subsequently reduced her risk of offending. In contrast to adolescence, in adulthood, Melissa abstained from drugs and alcohol. She cared for her three children, who were in her custody. Although her employment was sporadic, this was likely related to the fact that she was the full-time caregiver for three children, as opposed to disinterest in gaining employment or difficulty meeting job expectations. The level of care she showed toward her children is inconsistent with the presence of psychopathy traits. Although Melissa's adulthood was still characterized by certain challenges, her story is relatively positive compared to other ISVYOS participants.

Bill

The false positive result for Bill may have stemmed from an inaccurate PCL:YV assessment. Bill was a braggadocious youth. He held very positive attitudes toward criminal behaviour and related subcultures. He swore with every sentence, denigrated youth in his unit for being "soft," and his voice rose in excitement when talking about his involvement in criminal behaviour. For example, during his interview,

Bill boasted about the perpetration of brutally violent offences, as well as an assault against a police officer. Bill routinely switched schools or skipped school because he was bored. He also reported that boredom motivated his involvement in criminal behaviour. However, Bill may have given the impression of psychopathy traits rather than actually having psychopathy traits. In contrast to Bill's portrayal of himself, youth custody staff noted that Bill tried to portray himself as more violent and embedded in a life of crime. Probation officers were optimistic about Bill's future. Although Bill claimed to regularly get into fights in custody, there was no record of this in his file. It is possible that such fights went undetected; however, given the collateral information provided by custody staff, it is also possible that Bill wanted to portray himself in a certain light during his interview.

Bill's score may have been more consistent with criminogenic attitudes and low self-control rather than strong features of psychopathy. Criminogenic attitudes are much more amenable to treatment (Walters, 2025). Bill's attitudes and behaviours seemed to reflect a more common characteristic of adolescence known as moral disengagement. Moral disengagement includes a preference for antisocial over prosocial attitudes and an avoidance of internal sanctions (e.g., guilt, threats to self-worth) by rationalizing antisocial behaviour (Bandura et al., 1996). Moral disengagement is correlated with, but not equivalent to, psychopathy traits (McCuish & Gushue, 2022). There is also clear evidence that moral disengagement characteristics tend to be more fleeting than psychopathy traits (McCuish et al., 2020; McCuish & Gushue, 2022). It is possible that with multiple assessments, it would have been clearer that Bill was trying to put on a show rather than genuinely lacking empathy and remorse toward others. The low levels of psychosocial maturity and high levels of moral disengagement that Bill showed in adolescence are known to improve during the transition to early adulthood (McCuish et al., 2020). Although not formally measured, this may have been true for Bill as well.

Bill incurred no new charges as an adult. At age 18, he was held in the sheriff's cells for one day for violating the conditions of his probation for a prior offence committed in adolescence. It did not appear that he was involved in offences that went undetected or unpunished. Practitioners were more concerned about Bill's substance use issues and mental health. On one occasion in adulthood, he attempted suicide. By age 39, it appeared that Bill had not been involved in the criminal legal system for 20 consecutive years.

Richard

Like Bill, Richard's high score on the PCL:YV may have reflected symptoms of mental health problems unrelated to psychopathy. However, unlike Bill, it seems that items on the PCL:YV were scored accurately. The issue is possibly that, in this case, certain PCL:YV items were too broad to clearly distinguish psychopathy from other mental health conditions. A psychological assessment indicated that Richard suffered from a traumatic brain injury. In adolescence, Richard was involved in especially serious offences, including robberies, kidnappings, and arson. There were conflicting reports about his behaviour in custody. Sometimes he was polite and compliant, perhaps reflecting a "mask of sanity," but more often he was loud, disrespectful, and oppositional to staff. Collateral information supported Richard's assertion that he had few friends. While in custody, he attempted suicide and engaged in self-mutilation. On one occasion, he lit a fire in his room, refused to leave, and had to be rescued by staff. In effect, several of the traits that Richard displayed that aligned with PCL:YV items were possibly not features of psychopathy but rather the result of trauma to the brain and poor executive functioning. Richard's behaviour appeared rooted not in a personality disorder but in the effects of a brain injury. This reiterates Cooke et al.'s (2012) point that psychopathy measures are a map; they do not represent the terrain. Scores on a measure should not always be equated with the true disorder.

Although adolescence provided justification for a high score on the PCL:YV, in adulthood, there was little evidence of psychopathy traits. Richard spent just one day in custody at age 20 and then was never again involved in the criminal legal system. There was neither evidence nor suspicion that Richard had been involved in a crime. After one day in adult custody, Richard was transferred to a mental health facility better suited for his needs. His file indicated that he suffered from a severe mental disability (not otherwise specified) and that he was unpredictable. He was noted to have an "odd presentation," and custody staff reported that they had difficulty understanding his thought processes. Staff at the mental health institution noted that Richard was constantly thinking about suicide. This appears to be the reason for his transfer to a mental health facility. The last entry in Richard's file on CORNET came when he was 25-year old. He had written a suicide letter, but it was not possible from the information available to confirm whether he was deceased.

In sum, it seemed that Richard's score on the PCL:YV reflected a combination of symptoms of a traumatic brain injury and other undiagnosed mental health problems. These issues persisted from adolescence to adulthood. In adolescence, these issues contributed to his involvement in serious criminal behaviour. However, in adulthood, these issues seemed to specifically and negatively impact Richard's ability to take on and manage adult roles and responsibilities.

Rachelle

In adolescence, Rachelle engaged in cruelty to animals, fire setting, sexually inappropriate behaviour, aggression toward her younger brother, and intimidating and threatening behaviour toward a wide range of people, including family members, peers, and teachers. She was noted to show poor insight into how these behaviours were harmful. She regularly failed to comply with rules established by her mother, her school, and the criminal legal system. She did not accept responsibility for her crimes. While incarcerated, Rachelle smuggled a knife into her living unit following a family visit. Custody staff suggested that the knife was brought in by a younger sibling. During the same period of time in custody, Rachelle fashioned a bedsheet into a noose and hung it on a wall to serve as a threat to another resident. Mental health professionals suggested that Rachelle was not participating in treatment and appeared unresponsive. Rachelle's mother described Rachelle as desperately needing help and stated that her own attempts to help Rachelle were unsuccessful. Overall, Rachelle's PCL:YV rating appeared reliable.

Rachelle's false positive result appeared related to her ability to avoid detection by the criminal legal system. Rachelle was involved in crime, but the ISVYOS only measured offending in adulthood using official data, so the crimes for which she was not caught and convicted were not recorded. In the rare instances that her crimes were detected by police, she was able to avoid punishment or convince the courts to administer a less punitive sanction. Rachelle's official criminal history in adulthood was more extensive compared to the other three false positive cases discussed so far, but still less extensive than the average ISVYOS participant. Rachelle spent 64 days incarcerated during adulthood and incurred 8 new convictions (i.e., an average of 8 days incarcerated per conviction). For the PCL:YV Cohort as a whole, the average number of days incarcerated per single conviction was 120.53 ($SD = 331.16$). Thus, Rachelle avoided more punitive sanctions.

It was not as if Rachelle was only involved in trivial offences that justified shorter or noncustodial sentences. At age 24, Rachelle was convicted of two counts of drug trafficking and one count of resisting arrest. From then on, although Rachelle was often arrested, she was able to avoid punishment from the courts. At age 28, she was arrested for an assault against an intimate partner and for stealing from them. At age 31, she was involved in a series of thefts. At ages 34, 35, and 37, Rachelle threatened and harassed former partners, but charges were always dropped. All told, in her thirties, Rachelle received charges for a dozen different crimes but avoided conviction in all cases against her. Reports from police and probation officers indicated that Rachelle's involvement in criminal behaviour was much more pervasive. A probation officer noted that another client referred to Rachelle as a notorious drug dealer in the town where she lived. Many of Rachelle's family members were involved in organized crime. Several of the family businesses appeared to be hubs for money laundering, and Rachelle's probation officer believed that even when Rachelle was working legitimately, the business itself remained illegitimate. A police raid on the residence of a family member uncovered large sums of cash that could not be accounted for legally. One of the family businesses included operating an escort agency. Rachelle admitted to her probation officer that she sold drugs to the women working at the agency, which may be evidence of the parasitic orientation feature of psychopathy (Hare, 2003).

Rachelle's psychopathy traits appeared to persist from adolescence into adulthood. While incarcerated, she was noted by custody staff to fake being sick to avoid programs and responsibilities. In response to accusations of stealing from her grandmother, Rachelle reported that her grandmother had dementia and could not be trusted. This did not appear to be true. Probation officers and custody staff described Rachelle as manipulative and presenting as less mature than others her age. Rachelle would remind criminal legal system officials that a family member of hers was a prominent member of the community. Rachelle's probation officer interpreted this as Rachelle insinuating that bad things could happen if the criminal legal system did not treat her favourably. Rachelle told the court that her offences stemmed from a drug addiction. Based on this information, the judge in her case reduced her sentence from custody to house arrest. Several weeks later, Rachelle told her probation officer that she did not actually have a substance use problem. She explained that she only said this to the judge to reduce the severity of her sentence. She suggested to her probation officer that she was addicted to money, not drugs. She claimed that this addiction was due to her former partner giving her thousands of dollars per week. She was now used to living a specific lifestyle and needed to uphold it.[8]

In sum, Rachelle's PCL:YV score appeared to be accurate, with evidence of the continued manifestation of psychopathy traits in adulthood. A different approach to measuring offending (e.g., confidential self-report interviews conducted in adulthood) may have revealed a more persistent pattern of offending (i.e., a true positive result).

Chapter Summary

Research on psychopathy tends to focus on short-term follow-up periods where reoffending is measured as a single-item indicator of recidivism. This is an overly simplistic way of measuring reoffending that fails to account for the heterogeneity of people who can be classified as recidivists. The failure to examine people over longer time periods also means that studies do not distinguish between people who may have offended frequently in a short time frame due to situational factors (e.g., being unhoused) vs. people who persistently offend across long periods of time. Although psychopathy may statistically predict recidivism, there are many other factors associated with reoffending (e.g., substance use, gang involvement, unemployment, peers, structural factors), and recidivism is far more common than psychopathy traits. This means that using psychopathy to explain recidivism will leave much of the variance in recidivism unexplained. Compared to recidivism in the ISVYOS sample, psychopathy traits are far rarer. There is a stronger theoretical rationale to consider psychopathy traits as an important predictor of patterns of persistent offending over the life-course. This rationale was put to the test by examining the relationship between PCL:YV test scores measured in adolescence and repeat convictions and incarceration at each year of age between ages 18 and 40.

Contrary to research critical of the PCL:YV's ability to predict reoffending beyond Lifestyle/Antisocial factors (sometimes referred to as the social deviance component of psychopathy; Kennealy et al., 2010), individually, all four factors of the PCL:YV were informative of repeated convictions and/or repeated incarceration over a long-term follow-up period. The same

---

[8] Rachelle's purported ruse resembles Cleckley's description of how people with psychopathy traits would sometimes feign insanity to avoid criminal responsibility, only to later recant after being institutionalized.

was true when looking at the PCL:YV three factor model and PCL:YV scores that represented the sum of the 13 core items identified by the item response theory analysis in Chapter 4. This difference from past research may reflect my focus on repeat offending over the life-course as opposed to the more typical approach of examining single-item indicators of recidivism. The overarching conclusion is that psychopathy traits earlier in the life-course are informative of persistent offending, and this observation is not confined to the relationship between prior criminal behaviour and future criminal behaviour, which has been an ongoing criticism and concern levied by some against the clinical utility of psychopathy (e.g., Larsen, 2019; Walters, 2004). Psychopathy traits were also informative of single-item indicators of offending that captured more harmful offences, including sexual offending, offending with a firearm, and a court designation as a high risk offender.

Psychopathy traits measured in adolescence via the PCL:YV were associated with persistent offending. Why might this be? It is possible that psychopathy traits in adolescence remained stable over the life-course. Unfortunately, ISVYOS data were insufficient to address questions about the stability of psychopathy traits. However, research elsewhere (e.g., McCuish & Lussier, 2018, 2021) supports the conclusion that psychopathy traits measured between adolescence and adulthood are less stable than previously assumed. If this is true for the ISVYOS sample, why did offending persist decades later? Although PCL:YV test scores in adolescence predicted continued offending for nearly two decades into adulthood, we should not be quick to assume that offending persisted solely because psychopathy traits also persisted. One possibility, which Terrie Moffitt (1993) considered, is the idea that psychopathy traits in adolescence mortgage the future. For example, psychopathy traits may subsequently negatively impact school performance, the development of healthy relationships, and connections to family. In other words, psychopathy creates a negative social environment, and, in turn, this negative environment influences persistent offending. To explore the possibility that the relationship between youth psychopathy traits and chronic and persistent offending in adulthood is mediated or moderated by other outcomes, the next chapter examines whether psychopathy traits in adolescence are related to social and health outcomes in early adulthood.

CHAPTER 6

The Underexplored Costs of Youth Psychopathy Traits

Psychopathy research tends to emerge from the fields of correctional psychology and forensic psychology. Given that these fields often focus on risk assessment, it is not surprising that psychopathy research tends to focus on measuring offending and describing implications for the criminal legal system. This chapter outlines why it is important to also consider other negative outcomes in adulthood, such as social and health consequences, that may be associated with psychopathy traits in adolescence. One reason for overlooking this question is that conducting such research is not straightforward. Prospective longitudinal data are needed to establish the temporal order between psychopathy and the outcome of interest. From a research design perspective, it is critical that psychopathy be measured first; otherwise, it is possible that the negative outcome of interest influenced the development of psychopathy traits and not vice-versa. Another reason for the inattention to negative social and health outcomes is that not all scholars view psychopathy as a maladaptive disorder. For example, those who endorse notions of successful psychopathy view negative social and health outcomes as the antithesis of psychopathy (Patrick, 2010a). From this view, it is axiomatic that psychopathy traits relate to positive outcomes.

If psychopathy is a maladaptive personality disorder defined by traits that cause severe dysfunction, it is important to look beyond criminal behaviour to understand the full scope of this dysfunction. Why assume that traits such as a lack of remorse or care toward others, manipulation, bullying, and lying result in negative interactions with others, where the only outcome is criminal behaviour? It is possible that such traits influence a wide range of social and health costs. This matters independently of research on offending, but criminologists and psychologists should care about the relationship between psychopathy and social/health outcomes because this relationship may help better explain the connection between psychopathy and offending.

Chapter Goals and Analyses

A mediating relationship implies that at least part of the reason youth psychopathy traits influence long-term offending in adulthood is due to the shorter-term influence of psychopathy on social and health outcomes, which in turn also increase the risk for offending. As a starting point, before examining mediating relationships (see Chapter 7), Chapter 6 uses a series of regression analyses to examine the direct relationship between psychopathy traits in adolescence and negative social and health outcomes in adulthood. These outcomes include indicators of informal social control and bonds to others, criminogenic peer networks, substance use, and early mortality. All analyses controlled for risk factors and demographic characteristics described in Chapter 3. The examination of informal social control, criminal social capital, and prison conflict networks used ordinary least squares regression analyses. The examination of substance use issues and mortality used logistic regression analyses, given that both variables were coded as dichotomous outcomes. In the following subsections, I explain how different social and health outcomes in adulthood were measured.

Measurement of Social Outcomes

Informal Social Control

Informal social controls refer to social ties, social roles, and connections to institutions that bond a person to society (Laub & Sampson, 2003). Informal social controls protect against offending by instilling shared prosocial interests and beliefs. Informal social control structures behaviour in ways that reduce opportunities to offend (e.g., time at work). They also provide motivation to refrain from offending to so as to avoid jeopardizing their investment in new social roles and prosocial identities (Laub & Sampson, 2003).

Informal social control was measured using items from the Community Risk Need Assessment (CRNA), a structured assessment tool used as part of the case management practices of probation officers and other professionals working in the criminal legal system in British Columbia. The CRNA was developed by Dr. Bill Glackman, a long-tenured member of Simon Fraser University's School of Criminology. It was designed to reflect the risk-need-responsivity (RNR) model. The RNR model emphasizes matching the level of intervention/service to the specific risk of recidivism and needs of the person. The responsivity component emphasizes matching interventions (and the person providing them) to the background, abilities, and experiences of the person being treated. The CRNA reflects the central eight risk factors of the RNR model (Bonta & Andrews, 2007). These risk factors include indicators of antisocial attitudes and personality traits, crime-involved peers, past criminal behaviour, family and intimate partner issues, education and employment issues, substance use, and unstructured time and activities. The CRNA was intended to be completed every six months to ensure that criminal legal system professionals remained aware of changes in the needs of people under supervision (Gress, 2010).

For the Incarcerated Serious and Violent Young Offender Study (ISVYOS) Psychopathy Checklist: Youth Version (PCL:YV) Cohort, I measured informal social control using participants' first CRNA rating between ages 18 and 23 (M = 18.95; SD = 1.79). This ensured that temporal order was established, as for all participants, the measurement of informal social control occurred after their PCL:YV rating. It was also necessary, given the intention to look at offending outcomes in later chapters, to ensure that informal social control was measured prior to offending. Looking at informal social control in early adulthood provided sufficient time to examine longer-term patterns of offending.

Informal social control is viewed as a cumulative process (Savolainen, 2009). Thus, rather than examining individual items, six items from the CRNA were summed to provide a global rating of a participant's level of informal social control. These items[1] included measures of family relationships, intimate relationships, living arrangements, employment, academic/vocational skills, and financial stability. Family and intimate partner relationships reflect the extent to which parents, siblings, and partners are prosocial vs. antisocial sources of support. Living arrangements reflect stability and security of housing and the extent to which they contribute to investments in the community that strengthen ties to social institutions. The employment item reflects the stability of employment and helpfulness in managing household expenses. Academic and vocational skills reflect the training and educational experiences that create employment opportunities that can enhance positive social networks and foster, in the right circumstances, a stake in conformity. Financial stability reflects, for example, any outstanding debts that the participant may have vs. the ability to make ends meet. Such

---

[1] I have published previous papers where financial stability was excluded from this scale (e.g., McCuish & Lussier, 2025). The reason for this exclusion in previous publications is primarily theoretical; life-course theories did not originally describe financial stability as an indicator of informal social control. I have included financial stability here because it has been used in discussions regarding successful psychopathy.

debts often reflect monies owed to insurance agencies due to motor vehicle offences or street debts (e.g., money owed for drugs).

Items on the informal social control scale are not scored based on answers to a single, specific question. Items are scored holistically on a four-point scale (0–3) using information reported by the participant, collateral contacts (e.g., family members, psychologists, and police), and past reports (e.g., presentence reports and psychological assessments). Normally, the CRNA is scored so that higher scores indicate a higher risk of reoffending. In this case, to align with Laub and Sampson's (2003) discussions of positive sources of informal social control, reverse scoring was used so that higher CRNA scores indicated a greater degree of positive sources of informal social control. The scale has a high degree of reliability (Cronbach's alpha = 0.86).

The CRNA was scored by probation officers. It is possible that participants would be more forthcoming in a confidential interview conducted for research purposes. That said, this type of sample tends to have poor insight into their relationships (Polaschek et al., 2022), and this may be especially true for persons with psychopathy traits (Sellbom et al., 2018). If psychopathy traits influence poor insight into one's own problems (e.g., a failure to recognize sensation-seeking or impulsive behaviour; a failure to recognize the consequences of interpersonal conflict), then perhaps measuring psychopathy in ways that rely on personal insight may not be reliable. The CRNA was completed as part of mandated case management practices and involved drawing upon file information and collateral contacts in addition to the information self-reported by ISVYOS participants (Gress, 2010). Since probation officers coded the CRNA and ISVYOS Research Assistants completed the PCL:YV, I avoided issues with mono-operation bias that have affected research that measures both psychopathy and informal social controls using self-report tools (Burchett et al., 2023). Mono-operation bias refers to situations where the independent variable (e.g., psychopathy) and dependent variable (e.g., employment outcomes) are measured using the same method (e.g., self-report interviews).

Criminogenic Peer Networks in Prison

Another social outcome measured in adulthood reflects the nature of ISVYOS participants' peer social networks while in prison. These networks were measured using social network analysis (SNA). Despite its name, SNA does not refer to social media. SNA represents a set of theories and analytic strategies that help make sense of, for example, a person's social circle, interactions with people within this circle, and the extent to which they are connected to other social circles (Bouchard, 2020). Paying attention to a person's social circle is critical for understanding peer influence on behaviour and how peers' negative behaviours can influence one's own behaviour (Papachristos et al., 2015). There is substantial complexity behind the theories, data collection strategies, and analytic methods associated with SNA. To simplify, I focus on four key concepts: (1) nodes, (2) edges, (3) ego networks, and (4) degree centrality.

Nodes represent the unit of analysis in SNA. A node could be a single person or a single group (e.g., a gang or a terrorist organization). SNA uses sociograms to illustrate patterns of relationships between nodes. In a sociogram, edges represent lines between nodes that illustrate some sort of tie. Edges of different colours or patterns communicate the specific type of tie connecting two nodes. For example, a co-offending relationship represents one type of tie examined in this chapter. Two (or more) people may commit an offence together (e.g., assault against another inmate) or conspire together (e.g., one person distracts prison staff while another steals from the canteen). Edges depict this relationship. When interest is in the network of a specific person, the mapping of their network is referred to as their ego network. Figure 6.1 shows a sociogram of the (hypothetical) co-offending ego network of person "h"; readers will recognize the similarity between this figure and the psychopathology network figure from Chapter 4. In this case, instead of looking at the correlation between different psychopathy traits, each node (circle) represents a single person. Each edge (line) represents whether two people co-offended together. In an ego network, all actors to whom the ego is connected are referred to as alters (Borgatti et al., 2013). The ego network also includes ties among alters, such as instances where a co-offence involved more than two people. This allows for an inspection of the nature of an ego's positioning or embeddedness within their own network and the nature of their interrelationships with other actors (Hanneman & Riddle, 2005). There are different ways to measure network embeddedness.[2] The most straightforward of these is degree centrality. Ego network degree centrality represents the number of ties that an ego has to others in the network.

---

[2] Other metrics for measuring network embeddedness include betweenness centrality, which captures the number of instances where the ego lies between two alters who are not directly connected (e.g., node "h" lies between nodes "i" and "a"; Network density is calculated as the proportion of possible connections that are formed. Higher levels of density indicate greater network cohesiveness; more people are connected. With 11 nodes in the network, each can form 10 possible ties (k = 100). With 21 total ties in the network, the density value equals 0.21.

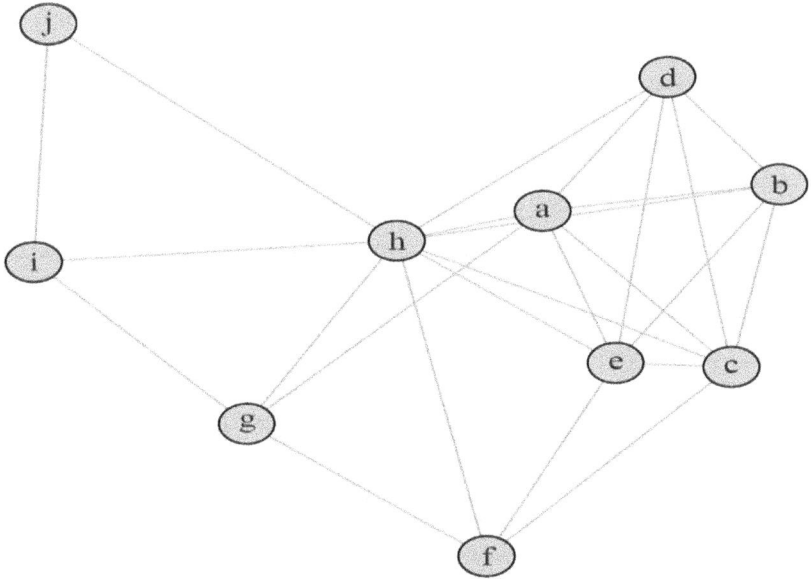

Figure 6.1 Hypothetical ego network of co-offending ties between "h" and their alters on a prison unit.

Notes. Each circle (node) reflects an individual actor in the network, and each edge (line) reflects an instance of co-offending between nodes.

In Figure 6.1, "node h" has nine co-offenders in its ego network. For parsimony, in this chapter, I only focus on degree centrality, as findings were consistent regardless of which network metric was used.

Social network data were collected from each participant's Corrections Network (CORNET) file. When participants were incarcerated, social network data were recorded daily, sometimes every few hours. Research Assistants combed through hundreds of pages of information on each participant to identify ties to other people in prison. This information included presentence reports, client logs documenting behaviour while in custody, and institutional alerts that reported conflicts or past co-offending with others. Each connection to another person (nonstaff) in prison was coded by Research Assistants. Each participant represented an ego, and all people connected to them represented alters. Ties between alters were also coded (e.g., group socializing or group conflicts). For example, if Wyatt, the ego, co-offended with Brandon to commit an assault against Steven, a co-offending tie was coded between Wyatt and Brandon, victimizer ties were coded from Wyatt to Steven and from Brandon to Steven, and victimization ties were coded from Steven to Wyatt and Steven to Brandon.

To give an indication of how many criminogenic ties were formed in prison, an average of approximately eight hours was needed for an ISVYOS Research Assistant to code the ego network of a single participant. Because the coding of ties was so onerous, ego network data extending into adulthood were only available for 182 participants in the PCL:YV Cohort. Similar to the measurement of informal social control, although prison social network data were available for both adolescence and adulthood, to establish temporal order between the PCL:YV and network ties, I focused on prison-based network ties that were formed between ages 18 and 23.

Positive vs. Negative Ties
Not all social ties are equally criminogenic. For example, Wyatt and Brandon were tied together by a co-offence, whereas Wyatt and Steven and Brandon and Steven were tied together through conflict. Criminal social capital refers to the extent to which a person can access opportunities for criminal behaviour through their connections to others (McCarthy & Hagan, 2001). The tie between Wyatt and Brandon describes a positive source of criminal social capital. The second type of tie is negative. For example, Steven may seek retribution against Wyatt. For the analyses in this chapter, prison ties were coded as either positive or negative relationships. Positive relationships included social ties and co-offending ties. Social ties represent a tie to a person known to be involved in criminal behaviour. Co-offending ties include engaging with an alter in a criminal offence or a behaviour that resulted in a charge or official warning in custody (e.g., contraband). Negative relationships included ties based on conflict, including where one party was the clear aggressor (e.g., where an ego victimized an alter or where an alter victimized an ego) or where the conflict was mutual (e.g., shouting at one another on the prison unit, a dispute over a TV remote). Evidence of a clear aggressor allowed for the coding of directed ties that indicate whether the ego perpetrated victimization against others (i.e., a victimizer) or was targeted by others (i.e., victimized).

Measurement of Health Outcomes

Substance Use Issues

The CRNA includes a single item, rated on a 0–3 scale, with higher scores indicating the degree to which substance use negatively impacts a person's ability to abstain from criminal behaviour. Thus, this measure captures not merely the presence of substance use, but the extent to which it is severe enough to interfere with the participant's day-to-day functioning. Only about 2 percent of participants received a "0" indicating that abstinence was a strength in the participant's life and helped prevent them from reengaging in criminal behaviour.

Due to the rarity with which participants scored a "0," the substance use item was recoded so that those who scored "2" or "3" were rated as "high," and those who scored "0" or "1" were rated as "low." Participants who received the highest possible rating were described by their probation officer as, for example, "Binges crack cocaine and blames it on being bored but refuses counseling"; "Unable to see problems and is unreceptive to assistance"; "Refuses counseling"; "Physical and emotional trauma from mother"; "Having a significant drug addiction"; "Offences a direct result of needing money for drugs"; "Not allowed to reside with parents due to severe behavioural and addiction issues"; "No income nor employment. Has been dealing and using crack cocaine since childhood"; "Father overdosed. Brother murdered. Mom addicted to drugs. Drugs, alcoholism, and crime age 10–11"; and "Has been addicted to heroin since age 13. Currently in recovery house. Relationships are stable when not using heroin."

These excerpts help illustrate that physical and mental health are intertwined. Further, the reasons for substance use are not the same for everyone. For some participants, substance use stemmed from trauma. For others, it was related to boredom. For some, the consequence of substance use was involvement in criminal behaviour to get money for drugs. For others, the consequences of their substance use included the breakdown of social relationships. Repeated use of substances such as heroin contributed to debilitating physical health problems. Such patterns of use also produced cascading effects – directly impairing mental health and indirectly worsening it through strain placed on intimate partner and familial relationships.

Early Mortality

Early mortality refers to deaths that occur prior to the average life expectancy in Canada. Given the age of this sample, all deaths reflected instances of early mortality. Each participant's CORNET file was reviewed by ISVYOS Research Assistants to identify evidence of a participant's death. Deaths in the ISVYOS sample were primarily the result of being the victim of a homicide offence or from illicit substance use. Participants were more likely to have their death recorded in CORNET if it was violent or suspicious (e.g., a victim of a homicide) as compared to, for example, a driving accident or disease. Instances of mortality may be underestimated if they did not involve investigation by the criminal legal system or occurred when a participant was not on probation. It is likely that the prevalence of mortality in this sample was underestimated because the ISVYOS did not have access to coroner reports. To address this limitation, ISVYOS Research Assistants relied on newspaper articles and online obituaries and confirmed a death if the name and date of birth matched that of a participant. We also relied on word of mouth (e.g., informed by a probation officer) to help identify additional instances of mortality and details about mortality incidents, including the cause of death. Cause of death information was coded into one of three categories: (1) homicide, (2) overdose, or (3) other (e.g., illnesses such as cancer, suicide, or motor vehicle accidents).

Participants were an average age of about 35 years at the time of the most recent follow-up period. Nearly 10 percent of ISVYOS participants from the PCL:YV Cohort ($n = 48$) were deceased. The average age of mortality was 27.75 years (range = 17–39 years). Although cause of death information was only available for 35 participants, 37 percent of these deaths were due to homicide, and 40 percent were due to an overdose. Participants were targeted in gang-related shootings and were commonly victims of the toxic drug supply crisis in British Columbia. In reading the files of ISVYOS participants, substance use clearly directly (e.g., overdose) or indirectly (violent conflicts, accidents, or health issues) influenced mortality in the majority of cases. There is a widely reported fentanyl crisis in British Columbia (Russell et al., 2024). The issue is not just the potency of fentanyl but also that it is cheaper than heroin. It is not only that heroin is laced with fentanyl, but that fentanyl has become the drug of choice for some people who use drugs (McKnight et al., 2023; Rigg & Kusiak, 2023). Fentanyl misuse was first reported in British Columbia in 2011 (Belzak & Halverson, 2018). However, about 50 of the 151 deaths that occurred among all members of the ISVYOS sample (i.e., not restricted to the PCL:YV Cohort) occurred prior to the first report of fentanyl in the illicit drug supply in British Columbia. The risk of early mortality for the ISVYOS sample, therefore, cannot be attributed solely to the fentanyl crisis. Early mortality among people who experience incarceration has been a persistent issue for decades, long predating the fentanyl crisis. At this stage, it is too early to suggest that experiencing incarceration directly increases the risk of early mortality. Instead, people who are incarcerated are exposed to a constellation of long-standing risk factors – including poverty, trauma histories, substance use disorders, unstable housing, and chronic health issues – that likely contribute to the elevated mortality rates observed in this population.

The Relationship between Psychopathy Traits and Informal Social Control

The transition from adolescence to adulthood provides increased opportunities to begin new roles, earn more responsibility, and gain safeguards (e.g., employment, access to housing, and quality of family, peer, and intimate partner relationships). Collectively, these are referred to as informal social control and are viewed as especially important for reducing involvement in criminal behaviour (Laub & Sampson, 2003). For example, working a full-time job means having a daily routine that reduces opportunities for offending. This job can also lead to increased time spent in the presence of prosocial others who monitor behaviour in ways that reduce the likelihood of offending. Being around prosocial peers can also reshape a person's self-identity toward a more prosocial orientation. Finally, positive employment can lead to emotional investment in the job and its associated roles and responsibilities. People thus may desist from criminal behaviour to avoid jeopardizing their investment in this new social role and contradicting their emerging identity.

For various reasons, people with psychopathy traits may be especially unlikely to experience positive sources of informal social control. This describes the concept of a selection effect, in which a person's background, personality, values, and beliefs inform the type of social environment they are embedded in (Caspi et al., 2005; Caspi & Herbener, 1990; Wright et al., 1999).[3] Affectively, people with psychopathy traits tend to be isolated from others. Some of this isolation is from a lack of direct interaction with others. Another part of this isolation is more metaphorical. People with psychopathy traits can be emotionally disconnected. Thus, people with psychopathy traits may be less likely to have *any* relationships with prosocial others. They may also be less likely to have *positive* relationships with prosocial others, which contributes to unstable or short-lived interpersonal relationships.

Empirical research has rarely examined the relationship between psychopathy and informal social control from a longitudinal perspective. Instead, research on psychopathy and social outcomes has primarily relied on cross-sectional designs, in which people are interviewed at a single point

---

[3] There is an additional concern, which is that, in the rare instances in which positive sources of informal social control are present in the lives of people with psychopathy traits, these sources may not actually matter for reducing their involvement in offending. This view is represented by the concept of treatment effect heterogeneity and is the central focus of Chapter 8.

in time. Although important, cross-sectional research must be interpreted cautiously because it is difficult to establish temporal order between variables. For example, did psychopathy traits lead to poor academic success, or did poor academic success have a cascading impact on psychopathy traits? By relying on longitudinal data, I can establish temporal order between psychopathy traits in adolescence and informal social controls in adulthood. There is a lack of research on whether youth with psychopathy traits self-select into adulthood environments characterized by a lack of positive sources of informal social control.

Another important limitation of previous research on psychopathy and social outcomes is that psychopathy is often measured based on a victim's perception of their partner's personality traits. For example, instead of directly measuring psychopathy, this research assesses relationship quality from the perspective of a victim who believed that they were in a partnership with someone with psychopathy traits. People who have had an intimate partner with psychopathy traits report experiencing a variety of different forms of abuse that have had a lasting impact on their physical and mental health (Forth et al., 2022). Women with partners who have psychopathy traits also tend to have higher average levels of depression and hostility compared to women without such partners (Leedom, 2017). Similar observations have been reported when it comes to people whose friends have psychopathy traits (Ploe et al., 2023).

In addition to harm perpetrated against victims, the assortative mating literature provides a clear theoretical basis for anticipating that psychopathy traits will lead to associations with people who do not promote a positive social environment. In other words, from an assortative mating perspective, people with psychopathy traits are more likely to be in social environments that promote involvement in criminal behaviour. The assortative mating literature hypothesizes that an individual's personality traits influence the nature of adult roles, such as marriage (Krueger et al., 1998). It follows that people with psychopathy traits may be less likely to be involved in relationships with empathetic and caring partners. Instead, people with psychopathy traits may be more likely to be involved in relationships with people who encourage criminal behaviour or engage in criminal behaviour themselves.

Informal social control is more than just relationships. The informal social control scale used in the analyses in this book also included indicators of housing stability, employment, academic/vocational training, and financial stability. When measuring psychopathy via the PCL:YV, some items require accounting directly for a person's employment or school performance. For example, questions about being repeatedly late or absent from school/work are often used to measure a person's score on the irresponsibility item from the Lifestyle factor of the PCL:YV. People with psychopathy traits tend to fail to act in ways that others count on them to. They thus may make poor employees because they lack dependability and accountability (also see Mathieu & Babiak, 2016). People with psychopathy traits tend to lack long-term planning skills that can help motivate delaying gratification and enrolling in academic/vocational training programs (Cooke et al., 2004). In other words, there is reason to believe that psychopathy traits will negatively impact informal social control beyond a person's familial and intimate relationships.

Cross-sectional research using self-report measures has provided evidence that psychopathy traits are negatively associated with career and academic success (Eisenbarth et al., 2022). Former employees of people with psychopathy traits report decreased job satisfaction (Mathieu & Babiak, 2016). If someone with psychopathy traits is in a managerial position, there tends to be higher levels of employee turnover (Kranefeld et al., 2024) and a culture of bullying (Boddy, 2014). However, evidence on whether people with psychopathy traits experience lower levels of job satisfaction is mixed (Kranefeld et al., 2024; Kranefeld & Blickle, 2022). There are at least two possible reasons for discrepancies across studies. One is that some studies emphasize the boldness component of psychopathy and do not require other psychopathy traits to be present when examining the relationship between job satisfaction and boldness (e.g., Lilienfeld et al., 2012; Nai, 2019; Smith & Lilienfeld, 2013). It is thus possible that the positive relationship between psychopathy traits and job satisfaction reflects only a positive association between boldness and job satisfaction. A second reason for the mixed findings could be related to the tendency for studies to focus on samples that underrepresent individuals with clinically meaningful levels of psychopathy traits. Studies of people who are employed tend to find that their samples score quite low on measures of psychopathy, leading to questions about whether what is being measured truly reflects psychopathy. Indeed, this is not surprising. Once again, selection effects seem to matter. If theories are correct that people with psychopathy are less likely to be employed, or less likely to show up to work as scheduled, then such people will not be found in surveys of companies' employees. This is akin to studying the flu among people in the workplace. For one, base rates of the flu are relatively low. For two, people with the flu are likely to be home sick, not at work, and thus not eligible to participate in the survey.

Analyzing the Relationship between PCL:YV Scores and the Informal Social Control Scale

Controlling for various demographic characteristics and other risk factors in adolescence (e.g., family adversity, abuse, and residential mobility; see Chapter 3 for details), I examined the relationship between PCL:YV test scores in adolescence and informal social control in early adulthood. Based on an ordinary least squares regression analysis, increases in PCL:YV total scores were associated with significant decreases in the quality of a person's informal social control (see Figure 6.2). Youth with a high score on the PCL:YV averaged about 1.39 fewer points on the informal social control scale compared to youth who scored less than 30 on the PCL:YV. Importantly, as discussed in the following subsection, high PCL:YV scores in adolescence did not guarantee negative social outcomes in adulthood. It is likely that a variety of factors beyond psychopathy also contribute to a person's lack of informal social control.

Probation officers, who were not aware of the PCL:YV scores of ISVYOS participants, described the social environments of those with high PCL:YV scores in negative terms. Quinn's probation officer described

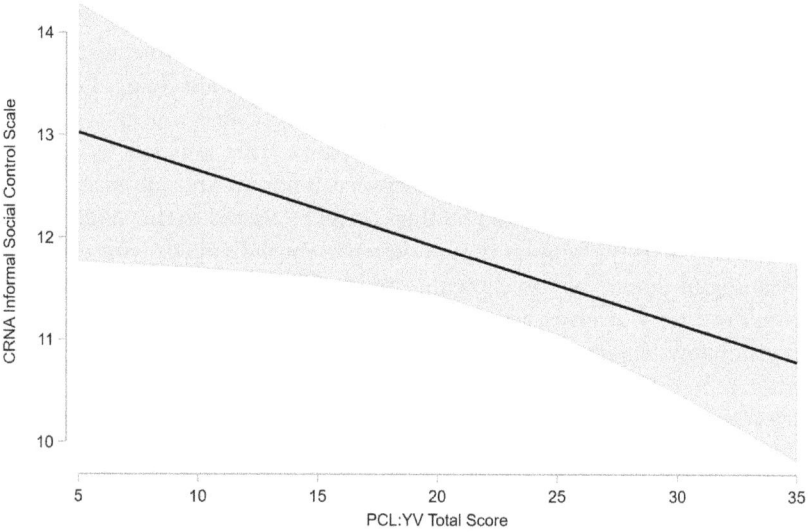

Figure 6.2 The relationship between PCL:YV total scores and a person's CRNA-based informal social control rating in early adulthood.

Notes. The shaded area represents a 95 percent confidence interval (CI).

her as having no ties to family, no employment history, and no vocational skills. Her probation officer noted that she was too volatile and unpredictable to live peacefully with others. Perhaps, in part, because of a lack of a social support system and, in part, because of psychopathy traits that influenced a sensation-seeking pattern of behaviour, Quinn was involved in daily use of crack cocaine. This reveals a complex interplay between personality characteristics, substance use, and informal social control in which the direction of influence is not easily disentangled. During some periods of her life, Quinn's substance use negatively impacted her informal social control. In other periods, the lack of clear bonds to family, unemployment, and precarious housing influenced her continued substance use. In the backdrop, psychopathy traits continued to influence substance use and conflictual relationships with family members.

Mark, who also scored over 30 on the PCL:YV, was told by the courts that he was unable to live with his parents because of his sex offence against his much younger sibling. This impacted both the quality of his relationships with family members and the stability of his living situation. Mark temporarily lived with his girlfriend at her parents' house, where he stayed for free. He had repeated arguments with his girlfriend's parents about his substance use, unwillingness to help with chores, and general negative and hostile behaviour. This pattern of behaviour at his home and his girlfriend's home may be evidence of the continuity of a parasitic orientation. Eventually, Mark was asked to leave his girlfriend's parents' place and sought housing at an emergency shelter. Mark was described as having few friends and was unreceptive to his probation officer's assistance in finding Mark a place to live. There are many similar stories from other ISVYOS participants where there seems to be a clear connection between substance use, negative relationships with family members, and having no fixed address (i.e., an unstable living situation).

For one youth with a high PCL:YV score, contrary to the observed statistical trend, they also scored relatively high on the CRNA informal social control scale (e.g., supportive family). However, during the period in which their CRNA rating was completed, they were also in extremely poor health. The participant eventually died due to illness. It is possible that mistreatment of family members and companions was absent, not because psychopathy traits in adolescence influenced successful social outcomes, but because this particular youth, once they entered adulthood, was in such poor health that they lacked the physical ability to mistreat family members and intimate partners. Another male youth who scored high on the PCL:YV and whose CRNA score indicated positive informal social control may have been successful in manipulating their probation officer. The probation officer suggested that this participant, now an adult, appeared very motivated to change and was receptive to the probation officer's suggestions about developing a more prosocial lifestyle. Yet, the same probation officer noted that their client was secretive about his relationship with family and refused to provide information about where he was living. This type of behaviour can be an indication of gang involvement or that the person is living with people who are also involved in criminal behaviour. It could also indicate an attempt to hide criminal legal system involvement from family members. This participant rarely had a job and relied on crime contacts to make easy money (e.g., selling stolen items on Facebook Marketplace). There appeared to be a discrepancy between what this young adult's life was actually like (i.e., high risk) and how they were scored on the CRNA (i.e., low risk).

Summarizing the Relationship between Psychopathy and Informal Social Control

Overall, psychopathy traits in adolescence were associated with lower levels of positive sources of informal social control in early adulthood. These findings align with research on borderline personality disorder that identified how behavioural instability and impulsivity, self-perceptions, and perceptions of others acted as barriers to building positive social relationships (van Schie et al., 2024). It is important to reiterate that psychopathy is not the only developmental pathway to a difficult future characterized by family conflict, being unhoused and unemployed, and experiencing financial difficulties.

As indicated in the case descriptions discussed in the previous section, even for youth with high psychopathy traits, there were various other factors that contributed to weak sources of informal social control. In ordinary least squares regression, R^2 represents the proportion of variance explained in a dependent variable (e.g., informal social control) that is accounted for by an independent variable (e.g., PCL:YV total scores). In essence, R^2 values indicate how well PCL:YV test scores in adolescence predict CRNA informal social control scale scores in adulthood. PCL:YV test scores accounted for just 2 percent of the variance in the level of informal social control. PCL:YV test scores accounted for more variance compared to other variables, including gender, ethnicity, prior offending, family adversity, and substance use. Nevertheless, the relatively low variance explained serves as a reminder that understanding informal social control in adulthood requires looking beyond a single individual-level characteristic in adolescence like psychopathy. For example, Quinn's and Mark's unstable living situations were likely influenced, in part, by living in Metro Vancouver, which has some of the highest housing costs in the world. Fundamental attribution error describes the tendency to overestimate the importance of individual-level characteristics like psychopathy while ignoring situational factors. Various macro-level circumstances and structural factors should be considered to more fully understand a person's negative social environment.

The Relationship between Psychopathy and Prison Peer Networks

Most criminological theories recognize the importance of peers in shaping the likelihood of involvement in criminal behaviour. For example, differential association theory (Sutherland, 1972) attributes involvement in criminal behaviour almost exclusively to associations with peers involved in delinquency. The social context a person is embedded within is a central pillar of life-course criminology and can act as either a positive or negative turning point (Laub & Sampson, 2003). Traditionally, criminologists have considered "turning points" to be major life events, such as obtaining employment, marrying, or becoming a parent. The peer context, however, was not captured by the measure of informal social control examined in the previous section.

The life-course theory concept of linked lives (Elder, 1994) acknowledges that although people may have free will, their options for behaviour are either constrained or facilitated by their peer networks. Research using data from the ISVYOS showed that gang members were more likely to commit crimes with people who were *not* members of their gang (McCuish et al., 2015). Being in a gang may be viewed by others involved in crime as a positive status symbol. Thus, being in a gang encourages criminal behaviour because many different people view the gang member as a suitable co-offender. Conversely, by invoking their gang's reputation, gang members may find it easier to recruit co-offenders. However, McCuish et al. (2015) also found that when it came to homicide offences, gang members *only* co-offended with other members of their gang. This provides some evidence of how peer groups constrain behaviour. If a person is not part of the gang, they will not be recruited to engage in a homicide offence. This research is part of a broader paradigm in which criminologists examine how a person's social circle exposes them to opportunities to perpetrate or become a victim of violent crime (e.g., Bouchard, 2020; Ryu & McCuish, 2022).

Prisons are a social context that is especially conducive to developing ties to others involved in crime. Since Jeremy Bentham's work in the eighteenth and nineteenth century, prisons have been viewed as places where peers meet and become further entrenched in crime (Geis, 1955). Through social conversations, inmates are presumed to learn from others the skills needed to engage in certain crimes. Meeting peers with pro-crime attitudes may also directly lead to criminal or antisocial behaviour in prison. This may come in the form of joining together (i.e., co-offending) to commit assaults against other inmates or engaging with peers in institutional misconduct (e.g., acquiring and using illicit drugs or alcohol). Engaging in violations of institutional rules while in custody may promote a more general pattern of criminal behaviour upon community reentry.[4]

Several studies have identified prisons as places where inmates build criminal social capital (Bayer et al., 2009; Clemmer, 1950; Damm & Gorinas, 2020; Nguyen, 2020; Nguyen et al., 2017). Criminal social capital includes knowledge passed down from peers to learn skills for committing certain crimes. Criminal social capital also includes developing social relationships and connections with crime-involved individuals, which create opportunities to engage in different types of crime (McCarthy & Hagan, 2001). The ISVYOS did not directly measure skills learned from peers while incarcerated. However, I use prison-based criminogenic social networks to help measure the relational component of criminal social capital. Dr. Krysta Dawson completed her PhD thesis using ISVYOS data and provides an excellent overview of the concept of social capital in criminogenic networks (Dawson, 2021).

SNA can help measure criminal social capital (for details, see Ouellet & Bouchard, 2017) by identifying the size of a person's pool of potential accomplices for certain crimes (McCuish et al., 2015; McGloin & Kirk, 2010; Tremblay, 1993). Prisons are often assumed to be "schools of crime," where connections made in prison can directly facilitate offending through co-offending upon community reentry or indirectly by teaching skills or techniques for committing other crimes (Damm & Gorinas, 2020). SNA can be used to measure the number of positive social ties a person forms with other offenders while incarcerated. Based on the school

---

[4] The idea of prisons as schools of crime is not always empirically supported. For example, in our work examining the impact of incarceration on ISVYOS participants, we found that year-over-year within-individual increases in the amount of time a person spent in custody were associated with year-over-year decreases in the number of convictions incurred (McCuish et al., 2025).

of crime hypothesis, people with more positive social connections in prison are expected to engage in more criminal behaviour following release.

It is fair to wonder what any of this has to do with psychopathy. In my view, there are two clear reasons why psychopathy research should pay attention to the prison context and why SNA is a useful tool for studying this context. First, as indicated in Chapter 5, psychopathy traits in adolescence are associated with significantly longer periods of incarceration. If the school of crime hypothesis is accurate, people with psychopathy traits spend more time "going to school" and thus should be more well-connected to others involved in criminal behaviour. The phrase "birds of a feather flock together" describes the concept of homophily, in which individuals tend to self-select into peer groups resembling themselves. If homophily is observed in prison settings, then people with psychopathy traits may have unique networks that increase their criminal social capital and create additional opportunities for offending.

The second reason to pay attention to the prison context in psychopathy research is because the nature of prison confinement may be conducive to developing conflict with others, which, in turn, influences negative patterns of behaviour and violence that continue into the community. Not all relationships are positive. People with psychopathy traits tend to engage in higher levels of institutional misconduct (Shaffer et al., 2015), which could, in turn, result in prison-based criminogenic networks characterized by frequent conflict with others. SNA does not just involve coding positive ties. Negative or conflictual ties between actors also have important implications for future criminal behaviour (Sierra-Arevalo & Papachristos, 2015). It is possible that psychopathy traits are associated with more conflictual prison-based peer networks, and these negative interactions may extend into the community, contributing to further involvement in violent crime.

Analyzing the Relationship between PCL:YV Scores and Prison Social Networks

Chapter 5 showed that psychopathy traits in adolescence are linked to repeated convictions in adulthood and longer periods of incarceration. By virtue of spending more time in custody, people with psychopathy traits may form larger-than-average prison networks. Such networks may, in turn, help explain the observed association between psychopathy and persistent offending. why psychopathy is associated with persistent offending. The first task is to empirically verify whether people with higher

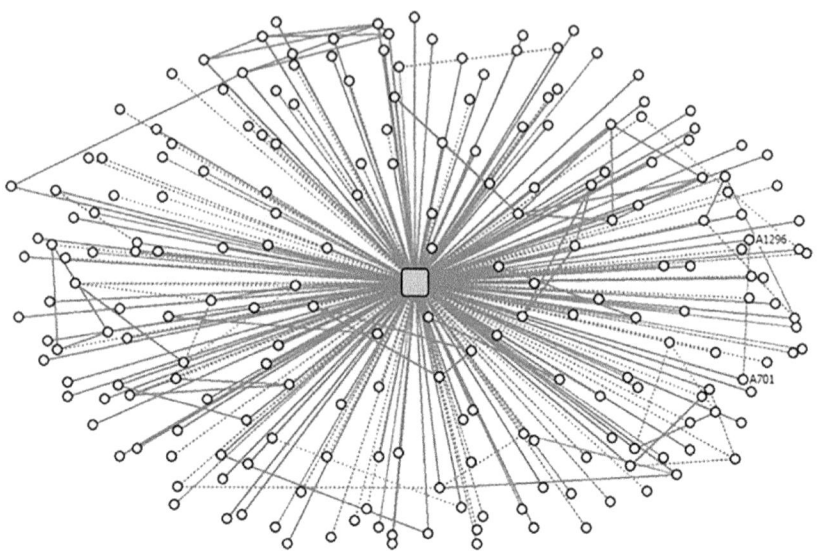

Figure 6.3 The prison-based criminogenic social network of "Chris" measured between ages 18 and 23.

Notes. "Chris" is represented by the square node at the center of the network. Each circle represents another person to whom Chris is connected (i.e., an alter). Solid edges indicate that the tie was positive (i.e., contributed to Chris' criminal social capital). Dotted edges indicate that the tie was negative (i.e., some form of conflict in prison).

PCL:YV scores develop distinct criminogenic prison networks. This chapter addresses that question.

To help understand SNA, Figure 6.3 shows the ego network of a single participant, Chris, who had a high score on the PCL:YV. For Chris and all others from the PCL:YV Cohort, prison-based ego networks were measured between ages 18 and 23. Thus, PCL:YV test scores were measured prior to the measurement of ego networks. In Figure 6.3, Chris is located at the center of the network (grey square node). Each circular node represents a person to whom Chris was connected while in prison.

There are a total of 248 nodes (i.e., alters) and over 550 ties (i.e., edges) in Chris' prison-based ego network. Solid edges between nodes indicate that the tie was positive and, therefore, an indicator of criminal social capital. Positive ties described instances where Chris was noted to have socialized or co-offended with at least one other person in custody. These ties also include connections between alters, such as situations where Chris interacted with two other alters who also interacted with each other during the same event. For example, Steve and Darren smoked marijuana with Chris in Darren's cell, and thus, the tie between Steve and Darren is also coded. There are more than 300 positive ties in Chris' ego network. These types of connections may support Clemmer's (1950) school of crime hypothesis, which posits that prisons create opportunities to learn how to commit crime and to develop relationships with people who also hold criminogenic attitudes.

Although the bulk of Chris' criminogenic ties in prison are positive, his ego network also contains just under 250 negative ties. Negative ties include (1) mutual conflict between people, (2) instances where the ego (e.g., Chris) is victimized by an alter, and (3) instances where the ego victimizes an alter. Positive and negative ties can form during the same event. For example, the bottom of Figure 6.3 shows that Chris had a positive tie with alter "A701" and a negative tie with alter "A1296"; these are not robots nor children of Elon Musk, I just wanted to avoid creating more pseudonyms. The figure also shows that A701 had a negative tie to A1296. Chris and A701 attacked and assaulted A1296 while in their prison cell. This example highlights the complexity of prison-based networks. Chris' positive tie to A701, in a criminal social capital sense of the word, influenced Chris' involvement in a negative interaction with A1296.

Perhaps most noteworthy is the ratio of negative ties due to Chris being victimized by others vs. negative ties due to Chris victimizing others. There were only three instances in which Chris was victimized by alters, yet nearly 40 instances in which Chris victimized alters. Chris regularly physically assaulted, verbally abused, and bullied other people in custody. Bullying, often referred to as "heavying" in prison, included threatening others for extra food or intimidating others into initiating fights in prison. When Chris victimized others, it was often done with the help of other inmates. In fact, approximately 20 *different* alters were involved as co-offenders in Chris' victimization of other inmates.

The case study involving Chris illustrates how someone with a high PCL:YV score developed a prison-based criminogenic network that included substantial levels of criminal social capital as well as numerous negative interactions with peers. Most of these negative interactions involved Chris as the instigator. The empirical question addressed in this chapter is whether Chris' prison network represents the norm or is an exception when it comes to ISVYOS participants with higher scores on the PCL:YV. Thus, I used ordinary least squares regression analyses to examine whether PCL:YV test scores are statistically related to positive and negative criminogenic networks in prison.

Figure 6.4 shows the combined positive tie networks for all 182 members of the PCL:YV Cohort who had their networks coded.

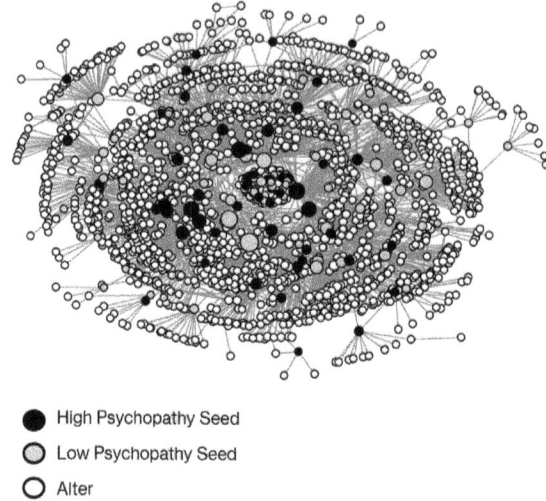

● High Psychopathy Seed
◐ Low Psychopathy Seed
○ Alter

Figure 6.4 Combined ego networks of all positive tie criminogenic peer networks in prison.

Notes. Positive ties indicate instances of criminal social capital in which an ego co-offended or socialized with an alter. Nodes are inflated based on degree centrality. High psychopathy = a score of 30 or greater on the PCL:YV. Low psychopathy = a score of less than 30 on the PCL:YV. Alters reflect ties to people who were not members of the PCL:YV Cohort and thus do not have a PCL:YV rating.

Black nodes identify participants with a PCL:YV score of 30 or greater, and grey nodes identify participants with a PCL:YV score of less than 30. White nodes indicate alters who were not members of the PCL:YV Cohort (e.g., other people whom participants met in prison). Nodes are scaled based on the size of their ego network. What is most noteworthy is the high degree of interconnections throughout the sample. Researchers often think about individual-level factors like psychopathy, substance use, and gang involvement as having an independent impact on criminal behaviour. As shown in Figure 6.4, all 182 ISVYOS participants whose ego networks were coded are just a few handshakes away from one another. They are all part of the same component, meaning that a single participant can reach all other nodes in the network (e.g., by being a friend of a friend; think six degrees of separation).

Figure 6.5 shows the correlation between PCL:YV total scores (x-axis) and positive tie ego network degree centrality (y-axis). There is virtually no relationship observed here. Participants with a PCL:YV test score of 5 (left side of the x-axis) averaged a nearly identical ego network size compared to participants with a test score of 35 (right side of the x-axis). Although Chris' ego network was approximately two standard deviations above the

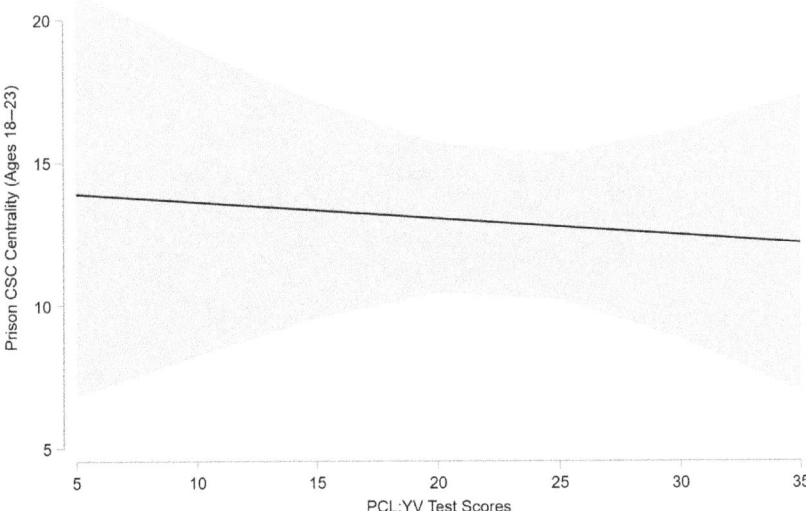

Figure 6.5 Relationship between PCL:YV scores and positive tie degree centrality.
Notes. Positive ties represent different types of prison-based criminal social capital (CSC), including mutual conflict or where one party was the clear aggressor (e.g., where an ego victimized an alter or where an alter victimized an ego). The shaded area represents a 95 percent CI.

ISVYOS sample mean, his ego network appears to be the exception, not the rule, for youth who score high on the PCL:YV. Degree centrality is not the only way to capture the nature of a person's ego network. However, the same conclusion was reached when looking at ego network density and betweenness centrality. PCL:YV scores are not associated with having higher levels of criminal social capital, at least in terms of how it was measured in the ISVYOS data. This was true after controlling for differences in time spent incarcerated.

The combined ego networks defined by negative criminogenic ties in prison are shown in Figure 6.6. Like the network of positive ties, the sample is very interconnected. There are only two components in this network, one of which is a dense network of interconnected conflicts located at the center of the sociogram.

Based on an ordinary least squares regression analysis and controlling for various demographic characteristics and other risk factors, increases in PCL:YV scores were associated with significant increases in negative tie degree centrality (see Figure 6.7). This indicates that psychopathy traits are associated with being embroiled in prison-based conflict with a wide range of people. This raises concerns regarding the safety risks posed by people with psychopathy

The Underexplored Costs of Youth Psychopathy Traits

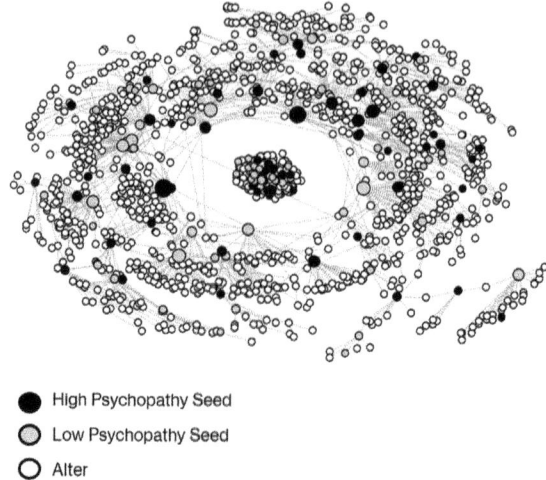

Figure 6.6 Prison-based conflict tie network.

Note. Conflict ties reflect negative interactions, such as where an ego assaulted an alter (i.e., victimization), where an alter assaulted an ego (i.e., victimized), or where mutual conflict occurred. Nodes are inflated based on degree centrality.

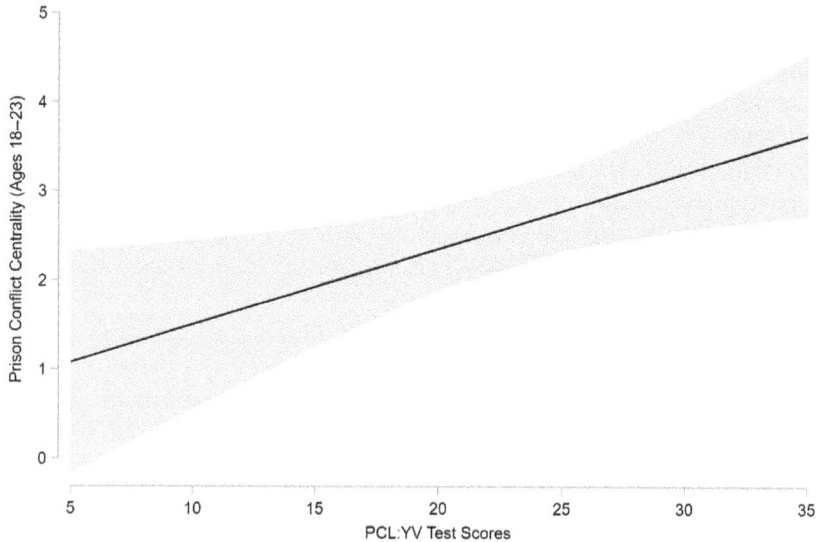

Figure 6.7 Relationship between PCL:YV scores and negative tie degree centrality.

Notes. Negative ties represent different types of prison-based conflict, including mutual conflict or where one party was the clear aggressor (e.g., where an ego victimized an alter or where an alter victimized an ego). The shaded area represents a 95 percent CI.

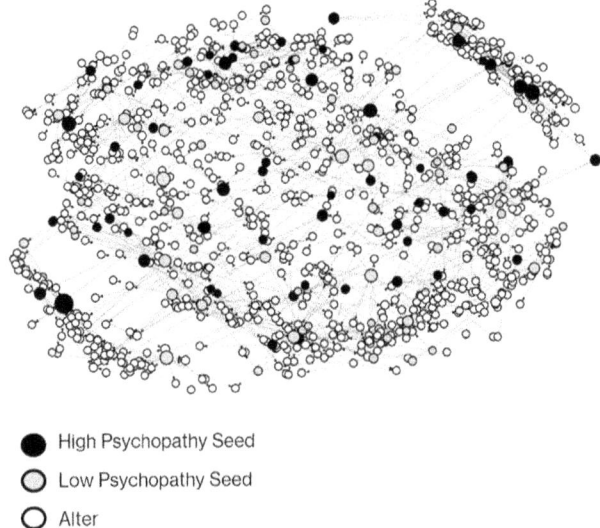

- ● High Psychopathy Seed
- ○ Low Psychopathy Seed
- ○ Alter

Figure 6.8 Combined victimizer ego networks among the ISVYOS PCL:YV Cohort.
Notes. Arrows indicate the direction of victimization. Arrows that extend from a node indicate the aggressor in the conflict. Node size inflated by out-degree centrality (i.e., number of arrows extended out from the node).

traits who are incarcerated. It is not just that people with psychopathy traits have a lot of conflictual relationships; they specifically show a heightened tendency to victimize others. Figure 6.8 shows a directed network depicting instances with a clearly identified aggressor in the conflict. An arrow that extends from a node indicates the perpetrator, while an arrow pointing to a node indicates the victim. Higher PCL:YV scores were associated with increased victimization of others. This means that it is not just that psychopathy influences mutual conflict; psychopathy traits in adolescence were linked to a heightened tendency to victimize others in prison during early adulthood.

Summarizing the Relationship between Psychopathy and Criminogenic Networks

With respect to the positive tie network, criminal social capital gained through connections to peers involved in crime does not appear to explain why people with psychopathy traits have higher rates of offending.[5]

---

[5] Supervising researchers at the beginning of their career and teaching graduate students in quantitative research methods courses, I often hear expressions of disappointment that a relationship is not significant. The goal of research is not to "find significance" or "find a strong

Perhaps this finding should have been anticipated. In the 1960s, sociologist Howard Becker criticized the tendency to rely on a person's perceived psychopathology to explain their involvement in criminal behaviour. Becker (1963) argued that (p. 16):

> We would have to posit a miraculous meeting of individual forms of pathology to account for the complicated forms of collective activity we observe. Because it is hard to cooperate with people whose reality-testing equipment is inadequate, people suffering from psychological difficulties don't fit well into criminal conspiracies.

Based on Becker's perspective, it is possible that people with psychopathy traits do not see a need to build their criminal social capital. They may not need to co-offend with others because they create opportunities to offend independently through repeated attempts to manipulate, antagonize, and bully others. The tendency for people with psychopathy traits to be antagonistic, intolerant, and inflexible toward others (Cooke et al., 2004) implies that they may find it difficult to maintain positive relationships. The failure to observe a large positive tie network for people with high PCL:YV scores may reflect the fact that positive relationships are often a two-way street. Others within the prison environment may learn that a specific person with psychopathy traits is difficult to cooperate with. Therefore, despite spending more time in custody, youth with higher scores on the PCL:YV are not more likely to develop criminal social capital in prison during adulthood.

The negative network findings are consistent with earlier research using ISVYOS data, which found that youth with psychopathy traits were disproportionately involved in institutional misconduct (Shaffer et al., 2015). Prisons are not typically seen as places of rehabilitation (Petrich et al., 2021). There are some exceptions, particularly in youth custody centers in Canada (McCuish et al., 2018a, 2025) and in progressive custody centers in more forward-thinking countries like Norway (Bhuller et al., 2020). Regardless of the custody setting in question, a major concern is whether people with psychopathy traits disrupt positive elements of the prison environment by initiating conflicts with others. Developing patterns of repeated prison-

---

relationship." Rather, the goal is to test our research questions as reliably as possible so that we feel confident in whatever relationship emerges. In this case, I feel confident about how psychopathy was measured. I also feel confident about how criminogenic networks were measured. Part of this confidence comes from the fact that network size is associated with other important outcomes of interest, including offending (see Chapter 7). Thus, I feel confident that, at least based on ISVYOS data, there is a null relationship between PCL:YV scores and the size of a person's criminogenic social network.

based conflict may create learned behaviours and relationship patterns in which conflict is seen as normative. This learned behaviour may carry over into the community, especially if conflicts in prison spill over into the community. Chapter 7 expands on this finding by examining whether the relationship between psychopathy and future offending is explained by negative social ties that emerge while incarcerated.

The Relationship between Psychopathy Traits and Substance Use Issues

Research on people with psychopathy traits has rarely given attention to health outcomes. Part of the difficulty in conducting such research is that the fields of psychopathy research and public health rarely intersect. There is a dearth of datasets that include reliable measures of both psychopathy and health outcomes. This is especially true for data that are longitudinal rather than retrospective. One of the few studies of psychopathy and general health outcomes reported, albeit based on retrospective data, that psychopathy traits increased the likelihood of poorer general health, cancer, diabetes, and high blood pressure (Beaver et al., 2014). Unfortunately, this specific study relied on an ad-hoc self-report measure of psychopathy, referred to as the Add Health psychopathy scale. It is called an ad-hoc scale because the authors simply identified items from a preexisting survey that they felt could indicate psychopathy. This instrument was found to have poor construct validity, meaning it did not correlate with other measures of psychopathy (Jones et al., 2021). The ISVYOS was never designed with the examination of the relationship between psychopathy and health outcomes in mind. Accordingly, data are also somewhat limited. However, the data do allow for an examination of two health outcomes: substance use issues and early mortality.

I focused on substance use issues given early hypotheses about the relationship between psychopathy and living a risky lifestyle (Hare et al., 1988), which can include the use of illicit drugs (Baron, 1999). It would be an oversimplification to suggest that substance abuse occurs only because of sensation seeking tendencies. The previous subsection that discussed the measurement of informal social control illustrated how family dynamics and trauma also impacted substance use. However, in the context of a sample of incarcerated youth, risk-seeking tendencies may be especially relevant to understanding health outcomes in adulthood, including the misuse of illicit substances. Studies on psychopathy traits and substance use in adolescence mostly focus only on callous-unemotional traits. Sakki

176   The Underexplored Costs of Youth Psychopathy Traits

et al.'s (2023) systematic review and meta-analysis of 34 studies revealed a small but significant positive relationship between callous-unemotional traits and substance use. This review also found that longitudinal research was rare. The analyses in this chapter extend prior research by examining the relationship between psychopathy traits in adolescence and substance use issues in adulthood.

Analyzing the Relationship between PCL:YV Scores and Substance Use Issues

Logistic regression analysis was used to examine the relationship between PCL:YV test scores and substance use issues while controlling for demographic characteristics and other risk factors in adolescence. As shown in Figure 6.9, increases in PCL:YV scores were associated with an increased probability of having issues with substance use in adulthood. For youth with a score of 30 or greater on the PCL:YV, the odds of being rated as having issues with substance use in adulthood were approximately 270% higher compared to youth with a score on the PCL:YV lower than 30 (95% CI = 112–653%). At the factor level, each of the Interpersonal, Lifestyle, and

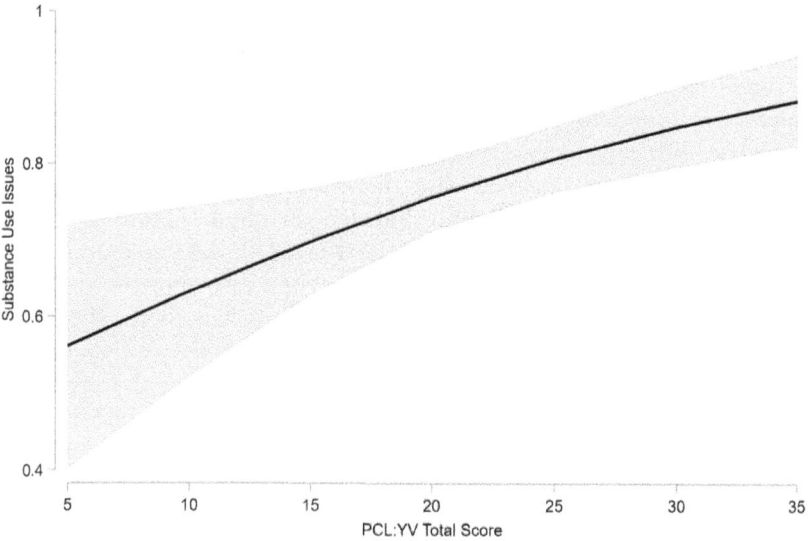

Figure 6.9   The relationship between PCL:YV total scores and a person's CRNA-based substance use rating in early adulthood.

Notes. The shaded area represents 95 percent CI. The y-axis shows the probability of having substance use issues.

Antisocial factors contributed to significantly higher odds of having substance use issues in early adulthood. The Affective factor, which includes callous-unemotional traits that are commonly examined in prior research on substance use (Sakki et al., 2023), was not associated with substance use issues in adulthood.

Summarizing the Relationship between Psychopathy and Criminogenic Networks

The fact that scores on the Interpersonal factor of the PCL:YV independently influenced substance use issues is important because it suggests that substance use is driven by more than just risk-taking tendencies. Johnson and Pandina (1991) reported that youth who experienced interpersonal conflict with family were more likely to use illicit substances as a coping mechanism. Given the level of interpersonal conflict associated with high scores on the Interpersonal factor, substance use may be a frequent coping mechanism for people with psychopathy traits.

As mentioned earlier, it is important to consider that substance use issues are likely influenced by more than just psychopathy traits. Like several other participants with high PCL:YV scores and substance use problems in adulthood, Conor's substance use was not solely influenced by sensation seeking. At a very early age, Conor was exposed to his parents' substance misuse. Conor was eventually placed in foster care because his parents were deemed to be creating unsuitable living conditions. Conor lived with his grandmother for a short time, but his behaviour was too reckless for her, and so he was asked to leave. Although one of Conor's former foster care parents provided him with a job when he became an adult, he regularly failed to show up as scheduled. Instead, he engaged in criminal behaviour in order to afford drugs and other activities associated with a high-risk lifestyle. In Chapter 10, I discuss treatment and intervention strategies for youth with psychopathy traits. Cases like Conor highlight the need to have multifaceted intervention programs, given that psychopathy is a risk factor for substance use issues, and, in turn, these substance use issues, at least for youth like Conor, subsequently contribute to involvement in criminal behaviour.

The Relationship between Psychopathy Traits and Early Mortality

Even if psychopathy researchers are not especially interested in health outcomes, from a research design perspective, they should care deeply about whether psychopathy increases the risk of early mortality. If psychopathy influences early mortality, researchers will likely underestimate the relationship between psychopathy and persistent offending if early mortality is not measured. For example, Chapter 5 examined the relationship between psychopathy traits in adolescence and offending beyond age 30. But what if youth with psychopathy traits were disproportionately more likely to die by age 25? If mortality is not accounted for, these individuals will appear to have desisted from offending. The failure to control for early mortality will inflate the prevalence of false negatives.

From a public health perspective, far more important than the consequences for research design is the fact that early mortality is arguably one of the most severe consequences of psychopathy. Theories that describe why early mortality occurs for offender samples use language that closely overlaps with how psychopathy is described. For example, Tremblay and Paré (2003) theorized three pathways that increase the likelihood of early mortality among people involved in criminal behaviour. First, the occupational-hazard pathway describes how involvement in criminal behaviour directly increases the risk of mortality by exposing the person to dangerous situations (e.g., resistance from victims or retribution). The positive correlation between psychopathy and persistent offending implies that psychopathy traits will indirectly influence early mortality through their effect on offending. Second, the general-hazard pathway describes how people who are involved in criminal behaviour tend to engage in other activities (e.g., substance use and other unhealthy behaviours) that shorten the lifespan. Such activities overlap with psychopathy traits. People with psychopathy traits tend to be sensation seeking, engage in parasitic behaviours, and prefer risk-taking activities. Third, the strain-hazard pathway describes how people involved in crime tend to be exposed to adverse experiences (e.g., physical abuse and neglect) that continue over the life-course and lead directly to early mortality (e.g., suicide) or indirectly through harmful coping mechanisms (e.g., overdose). One major life experience that has been linked to early mortality is incarceration (Butsang et al., 2025). The pains of incarceration create strain by reducing freedom, cutting off ties to family and friends, and creating difficulties in the community through unemployment and lack of access to housing (Kirk & Wakefield, 2018). As illustrated in Chapter 5, PCL:YV scores were associated with longer periods of time incarcerated. Thus, psychopathy traits may also directly or indirectly lead to early mortality through an increased likelihood of adverse life circumstances.

Research on psychopathy and early mortality has mostly focused on adults. This literature has provided evidence that PCL-R scores are associated with an increased risk of mortality. In a study in Finland by Vaurio et al. (2018), adult males scoring 25 or higher on the PCL-R were compared to two groups: (1) adults with scores below 25 on the PCL-R and (2) a sample drawn from Finnish registry data who, presumably, would have scored very low on measures of psychopathy traits (psychopathy was not directly measured in this subgroup). Those with high scores on the PCL-R were found to die at an earlier age compared to the other two groups. They were also more likely to die in violent or unnatural ways. Unnatural causes accounted for 65 percent of deaths in the high psychopathy subsample compared to just 40 percent of deaths in the low psychopathy subsample. For the high psychopathy subsample, these unnatural causes mostly stemmed from motor vehicle accidents, suicide, and homicide (Vaurio et al., 2018). Similar results have been reported when focusing on women in Finland (Vaurio et al., 2022).

I am aware of only one study examining the relationship between psychopathy traits in adolescence and early mortality. Using longitudinal data on formerly incarcerated youth from the United States, Maurer et al. (2024) observed that about 10 percent of their sample were deceased by approximately age 30. Notably, this is nearly identical to the prevalence of early mortality in the ISVYOS, whose members were followed into adulthood for a similar length of time. Maurer et al. (2024) reported that youth who scored higher on the PCL:YV were at an elevated risk of premature mortality. The Interpersonal and Lifestyle factors had the strongest influence on early mortality. Importantly, Maurer et al. (2024) also found that other indicators of adolescent psychopathology, including conduct disorder and attention-deficit/hyperactivity disorder (ADHD), were not associated with early mortality.

Analyzing the Relationship between PCL:YV Scores and Early Mortality

Turning to ISVYOS data, a series of logistic regression analyses examined the relationship between PCL:YV test scores and mortality. Controlling for demographic characteristics and other risk factors in adolescence, increases in PCL:YV test scores were associated with an increased likelihood of early mortality. This relationship is depicted in Figure 6.10. Note the scale of the graph's y-axis. The y-axis only ranges from 0 to 0.40, even though technically the probability of mortality ranges from 0 to 1.00. Mortality was rare for the ISVYOS sample. PCL:YV test scores only

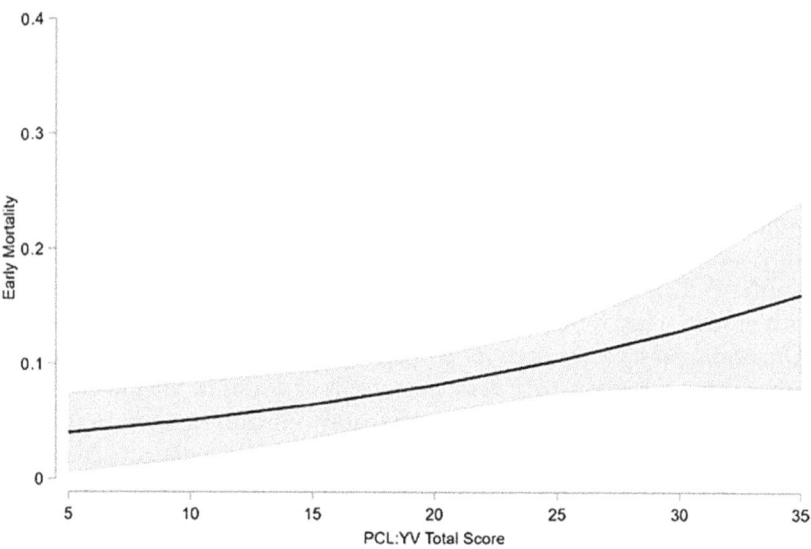

Figure 6.10 The relationship between PCL:YV total scores and the probability of mortality by the end of the study period.
Notes. The shaded area represents 95 percent CI.

modestly increased the probability of early mortality. In fact, and perhaps due, in part, to the rarity of both mortality and high PCL:YV test scores, the odds of early mortality were not significantly greater for those scoring high on the PCL:YV compared to those with a score of less than 30. This is more likely a function of the arbitrariness of 30 as a cut score than a reflection of the irrelevance of PCL:YV scores to mortality. With respect to specific PCL:YV factors, only the Lifestyle and Antisocial factors significantly contributed to the increased risk of early mortality. From Tremblay and Paré's (1993) theoretical perspective, this may relate more directly to the general- and occupational-hazard models in which a risky lifestyle and criminogenic behaviours directly contribute to an increased risk of mortality. In other words, the reason psychopathy traits are statistically related to early mortality may be primarily related to the tendency to engage in risk-taking activities and criminal behaviour as opposed to a direct influence of interpersonal and affective traits on mortality.

With respect to the cause of death, nearly 50 percent of participants who died of a drug overdose had a score of 30 or higher on the PCL:YV. This reinforces findings from the prior section linking psychopathy traits in adolescence to substance use issues in adulthood. By comparison, among participants who died of nonoverdose causes, only 12 percent had a score of 30 or higher on the PCL:YV. The relationship between psychopathy and early mortality appeared to be driven primarily by overdose deaths. The relationship between PCL:YV total scores and drug overdoses could reflect the sensation-seeking tendencies of people with psychopathy traits. In reviewing the case files of ISVYOS participants, those who scored high on the PCL:YV tended to overdose while using their own drugs. However, there were also instances in which participants died as a result of stealing drugs or misusing drugs that were prescribed to others. One participant died as a result of taking methadone that had been prescribed to a family member. Methadone is typically used to treat heroin addiction. There was also evidence of strain-related influences on early mortality. For example, one participant with a score of 36 on the PCL:YV died by suicide while serving a life sentence.

Summarizing the Relationship between Psychopathy and Early Mortality

In Canada, the average mortality rate between ages 15 and 35 is approximately 0.60 per 1,000 (Statistics Canada, 2024b). For the ISVYOS PCL:YV Cohort, about 15 percent of youth who scored high on the PCL:YV experienced a premature death. This equates to an early mortality rate of approximately 15 per 1,000. Given the small sample size, the early mortality rate for youth scoring high on the PCL:YV was approximately 25 times higher than that of the general Canadian population of a similar age. Humanistic intervention strategies aimed at reducing certain traits of psychopathy (e.g., those reflected in the Lifestyle and Antisocial factors of the PCL:YV) are therefore warranted, not just to help reduce risk of reoffending, but to help prevent one's own harm. Although not examined in this chapter, other research has reported that youth coming from difficult life circumstances who also present with callous-unemotional traits are at an especially high risk for suicidal thoughts, behaviours, and attempts (Kemp et al., 2025). Overall, the claim that the assessment of psychopathy should be discontinued entirely (Larsen, 2019) seems questionable, particularly given its role in identifying youth at risk for serious health-related outcomes.

As indicated in Chapter 5, PCL:YV test scores were unrelated to homicide offending. However, they were related to participants' own risk of early mortality. This observation contradicts the excessive focus on psychopathy and serial killing and other forms of homicide that are often emphasized in the True Crime genre.

The Consistency of Findings across Alternative Representation of the PCL:YV

Analyses in Chapter 4 provided evidence that certain PCL:YV items were more informative about the latent construct of psychopathy.[6] I replicated the analyses presented earlier in this chapter, revisiting each social and health outcome but replacing total scores on the PCL:YV with a revised measure defined by the 13 core PCL:YV items as determined by the item response theory analysis. With the exception of mortality, scores on these core items were significantly related to all social and health outcomes examined. The fact that core PCL:YV items were not significantly associated with early mortality reinforces the idea that the relationship between psychopathy and early mortality is primarily driven by heightened involvement in criminal behaviour and a risk-taking lifestyle. These traits did not form the core of PCL:YV-defined psychopathy because the item-response theory analysis found that they contributed little meaningful information to psychopathy test scores.

Chapter Summary

Dr. Dennis Reidy et al. (2015) argued that psychopathy should be treated as a public health issue to enable a more proactive approach to reducing violence, injury, and death. In North America, the economic cost of crime attributable to psychopathy is in the billions of dollars (Gatner et al., 2023). However, it is not just disproportionate involvement in criminal behaviour that matters. As indicated in this chapter, the presence of psychopathy traits early in the life-course has long-term consequences for a person's informal social control, their negative criminogenic peer network in prison, substance use issues, and early mortality. These consequences carry their own economic costs. For example, psychopathy traits in adolescence are associated with social environments defined by financial instability, poor employment and educational/vocational outcomes, and disrupted access to housing. It is important not only to consider the harm that people with psychopathy traits perpetrate against others; they also experience their own forms of harm. Some of this harm may help explain

---

[6] Based on item-response theory analyses, 13 items were identified as contributing meaningful information to the latent construct of psychopathy: impression management, grandiosity, pathological lying, manipulation for personal gain, lack of remorse, shallow affect, callous/lack of empathy, failure to accept responsibility, lacks goals, irresponsibility, poor anger control, early behavioural problems, and unstable interpersonal relationships.

continued involvement in criminal behaviour (see Chapters 7 and 8). Although not directly measured in the ISVYOS data, based on these findings, it is reasonable to assume that youth with psychopathy traits will require social welfare assistance as adults. Thus, in addition to the economic costs associated with crime, psychopathy imposes hidden economic costs through its impact on social well-being and mental and physical health. Importantly, it is not solely economic costs that matter; there are also clear personal and social harms affecting both people with psychopathy traits as well as those within their social networks.

Educating the public about what psychopathy is (and what it is not) and the impact of psychopathy on relationships is important because it may help people take steps to protect themselves from partnering with someone who could cause them harm. There is evidence that people can be educated about psychopathy without the collateral consequence of stigmatizing those with psychopathy traits (Murrie et al., 2005; Ostapchuk, 2018). Framing psychopathy as a public health issue, rather than solely a criminal legal system issue, may also be helpful for developing more proactive approaches to addressing psychopathy traits (Reidy et al., 2015). In contrast, framing psychopathy as something associated with success (see Lilienfeld et al., 2015 for a review) moves in the opposite direction of this policy need. Findings in this chapter are different from findings in studies that use the triarchic model to guide the measurement of psychopathy. Such studies have reported a positive association between boldness traits and general quality of mental and physical health (Rose et al., 2024). One of my concerns is that focusing solely on boldness traits inadequately captures the full construct of psychopathy. Another concern is that the concept of successful psychopathy is often represented as positive outcomes achieved at the expense of others (also see Welsh & Lenzenweger, 2021). People who report achieving financial success through bullying, deceiving, and manipulating others (Babiak & Hare, 2007) should not be considered examples of success.

Framing psychopathy as a public health issue rather than a criminal legal system issue may be helpful for reducing stigma associated with the disorder. The stigma surrounding psychopathy has contributed to a substantial gap in research funding. In Canada, Federal funding for psychopathy-related research is among the lowest compared to the funding for research on other major mental health issues (Gatner et al., 2023). Some policymakers may perceive people with psychopathy traits as undeserving of resources such as treatment. Some mistakenly view psychopathy research as supporting punitive criminal legal system policies and fostering pessimism about treatment (Maruna, 2025). However, these perspectives overlook decades of literature, including Cleckley's (1976) touchstone treatise, which emphasized the need for humanistic treatment of people with psychopathy traits, documented that change in psychopathy traits can occur (Hawes et al., 2014; McCuish & Lussier, 2021), and demonstrated that such change positively impacts a person's informal social control and adult role status (McCuish & Gushue, 2022).

Decisions to assess psychopathy traits have been criticized due to concerns about stigmatization (Larsen, 2019; Petrila & Skeem, 2003). Larsen (2019) suggested that an obvious recommendation was to stop assessing psychopathy because assessment does not help to avoid future negative consequences like recidivism. This would be shortsighted. Findings from this chapter reiterate the importance of people with psychopathy traits being aware of these traits (Shipley & Arrigo, 2001) in order to help prevent negative social and health outcomes, including mortality (also see Maurer et al., 2024; Vaurio et al., 2018, 2022). Experimental studies show that probation officers who are aware that a youth has psychopathy traits do not subsequently recommend more punitive sanctions, nor do they recommend withholding treatment (Murrie et al., 2005). This suggests that at least some professionals within the criminal legal system can engage with youth with psychopathy traits without stigmatizing them. More recent discussions of psychopathy are much more optimistic, or at least are not pessimistic, about the possibility that people with psychopathy traits respond positively to treatment (Polashek & Skeem, 2018; Sewall & Olver, 2019). This marks a departure from conclusions drawn from the Oak Ridge Study and from myths about psychopathy perpetuated by the True Crime genre and other popular culture sources (e.g., Ronson, 2011).

CHAPTER 7

Understanding the Relationship between Psychopathy and Offending

Forensic psychology, correctional psychology, and criminology are probably the three disciplines that produce the bulk of research on psychopathy. If I were to provide a criticism of forensic psychology and correctional psychology, it is that the risk assessment tools they create to predict the likelihood of reoffending are relatively atheoretical. Comparatively less attention is given to *why* psychopathy relates to offending (but see discussions of case formulation; Hart et al., 2011). The lack of attention to theory-building in psychology has been referred to as a "crisis" (Eronen & Bringmann, 2021). Psychopathy is regularly assessed in clinical and forensic settings (e.g., Viljoen et al., 2010) and is commonly included in various risk assessment tools (e.g., Harris et al., 1993; Webster et al., 1997). The inclusion of psychopathy in such tools has been justified on the basis that it statistically predicts recidivism (Blais et al., 2014; Edens et al., 2007; Hart, 1998; Leistico et al., 2008). However, statistical prediction is not informative of the process that connects a putative cause (psychopathy) to an expected outcome (offending; Wikström, 2020). Predicting an outcome is different from explaining an outcome. Although psychologists are often tasked with communicating to courts the scenarios in which someone is more likely to reoffend (Hart et al., 2011), minimal empirical research has been done to understand *why* psychopathy influences offending.

If I were to provide a criticism of criminology, it is that relatively little attention has been given to developing reliable and valid measures of key theoretical constructs. Theories are postulated, but efforts to develop reliable and valid measures of key theoretical constructs are lacking, especially when contrasted with disciplinary standards in psychology for developing measurement tools. As indicated in Chapter 2, psychologists can spend decades debating whether the latent structure of psychopathy is formative or reflective. Criminologists do not seem to have these discussions about their key theoretical constructs of interest. General strain theory, social learning theory, the age-graded theory of informal social control, and the general theory of crime are popular individual-level theories of criminal behaviour. They are taught in virtually every undergraduate criminology theory course. Yet, when the developers of these theories discussed their central constructs of interest (e.g., strain, social learning, informal social control, and low self-control), they did not include a discussion of how these constructs should be measured. Describing a construct is different from explaining its structure and how to measure it.

With the strengths of criminology being the weakness of forensic psychology/correctional psychology and vice versa, this chapter uses criminological theory to better understand the relationship between psychopathy and offending. I draw on state dependence and population heterogeneity meta-theoretical perspectives to provide a framework for thinking about whether different social and health outcomes in early adulthood are mediators of the relationship between psychopathy traits in adolescence and offending throughout adulthood.

A mediator is an intervening variable that comes between an independent variable and a dependent variable (Baron & Kenny, 1986). A mediator helps determine whether an independent variable directly causes a dependent variable (i.e., X $\rightarrow$ Y) or whether an independent variable indirectly causes a dependent variable through its influence on a mediator (i.e., X $\rightarrow$ M $\rightarrow$ Y). Based on the results in Chapter 6, because psychopathy was informative of a person's early adulthood informal social control, negative criminogenic prison networks, and substance use issues, these social and health outcomes potentially mediate the relationship between psychopathy traits in adolescence and continued offending in adulthood. Mediation implies that this relationship is, at least in part, due to (1) the impact of psychopathy traits on early adulthood social and health outcomes (e.g., informal social control, criminogenic networks, substance use) and (2) the subsequent influence of these outcomes on offending.

Chapter Goals and Analyses

The psychopathy literature's almost exclusive focus on statistical prediction has created a disciplinary blind spot when it comes to understanding *why* psychopathy influences offending (Lee & Kim, 2022). Addressing this blind spot is especially important for intervention and risk assessment approaches, which require both an explanation of why psychopathy influences reoffending and the ability to communicate this information to the courts and to develop appropriate treatment plans. For example, some intervention strategies for people with psychopathy traits seek to reduce reoffending by directly treating dynamic risk factors (e.g., personal insight, substance abuse, community support) rather than attempting to change psychopathy traits (Wong et al., 2012). Such strategies rest on the relatively untested assumption that other factors, such as informal social control or patterns of substance use, mediate the relationship between psychopathy and reoffending. Ultimately, the central question concerns identifying the causal mechanisms that link psychopathy to offending. Do psychopathy traits directly lead to crime, or do they exert their influence indirectly by shaping social and health outcomes?

Understanding why psychopathy traits influence involvement in criminal behaviour is an important component of fourth-generation risk assessment protocols (e.g., Douglas et al., 2013). These protocols use case formulation to explain why specific risk factors influence reoffending for a specific person (Hart et al., 2011). For example, it is not enough to identify that substance use influences offending; what matters is understanding whether offending occurs because a person needs money for drugs, because of the pharmacological effects of drugs, or both. Once these causal mechanisms are understood, risk management and other intervention strategies can be more appropriately tailored to prevent reoffending (Viljoen et al., 2019; Viljoen & Vincent, 2020). In effect, evidence-based case formulation and risk management require understanding which risk factors cause offending rather than simply identifying those that statistically predict offending (Gatner et al., 2022; Viljoen & Vincent, 2020). Risk assessment tools that call for case formulation and risk management practices, such as the Historical Clinical Risk Management 20, Version 3 (Douglas et al., 2013), were developed as a response to concerns with unstructured clinical judgement (e.g., relying on clinical experience). Yet, in the absence of research on the causal mechanisms linking psychopathy to offending (Lee & Kim, 2022; Walters & DeLisi, 2015),[1] case formulation and risk management are often guided primarily by clinical experience (e.g., Gatner et al., 2022; Hart et al., 2011; Viljoen et al., 2019; Wong et al., 2012). In other words, case formulation and risk management continue to be influenced by the very kinds of unstructured clinical judgement practices that they were intended to replace.

---

[1] It is more typical for studies to instead treat psychopathy as the mediator in the relationship between, for example, negative childhood experiences and antisocial behaviour (Fowles, 2018).

Given the lack of research examining causal mechanisms that link psychopathy traits to reoffending, Gatner et al. (2022) recommended incorporating criminology theory to guide intervention and case formulation. State dependence and population heterogeneity are two meta-theories that offer different explanations for continued offending over the life-course (Nagin & Paternoster, 2000).[2] State dependence theories use the concept of cumulative disadvantage to explain how negative early developmental experiences impact a person's informal social control and other negative life circumstances, such as substance use issues and conflict in prison. In turn, these environments and circumstances mediate the relationship between early development and continued offending. Population heterogeneity theories use the concept of criminal propensity to explain how stable traits that emerge early in the life-course are a common cause of both a person's negative life circumstances and continued offending (Nagin & Paternoster, 2000). In line with my earlier criticisms of criminological theories, state dependence and population heterogeneity meta-theories do not specify how criminal propensity should be measured. I propose, as have others (e.g., Moffitt, 1993), that clinical descriptions of psychopathy overlap with criminologists' descriptions of propensity.

Comparing the concepts of cumulative disadvantage and criminal propensity can help address the debate regarding whether disrupting the relationship between psychopathy and offending should be approached by intervening directly on psychopathy traits (propensity) or indirectly on criminogenic risk factors that are causally downstream of psychopathy (cumulative disadvantage). This chapter tests these ideas by examining whether psychopathy's relationship with persistent offending is mediated by early adulthood (1) informal social control, (2) substance use issues, and (3) negative criminogenic networks in prison.[3] First, I situate psychopathy within both state dependence (cumulative disadvantage) and population heterogeneity (criminal propensity) frameworks.

---

[2] These two perspectives are not mutually exclusive. For example, a third meta-theory assumes that there are different groups of offenders, some whose offending results from state dependence processes and some whose offending results from population heterogeneity processes (e.g., Moffitt, 1993).

[3] A significant relationship between the independent variable and the mediator is a criterion for mediation analysis. I do not examine whether a positive criminogenic network in prison mediates the relationship between psychopathy and offending because, per Chapter 6, there is no evidence of a relationship between psychopathy traits and the presence of positive criminogenic network ties, and therefore, a key criterion of mediation analysis is missing. I do not examine whether early mortality mediates the relationship between psychopathy and offending. Even though psychopathy increased the likelihood of early mortality, mortality cannot be a mediator because it is not possible to offend following death.

The Psychopathy-Offending Relationship within a Cumulative Disadvantage Framework

Cumulative continuity of disadvantage refers to the process through which adverse life-course experiences in adolescence either erode existing sources of informal social control or hinder their development. Informal social control encompasses a person's social roles (e.g., intimate partner, parent, employee) and the ties formed through bonds to family, friends, neighbours, coworkers, and related institutions (e.g., employer, university; Bellair & Browning, 2010; Caspi & Moffitt, 1995). Informal social controls protect against offending by instilling shared prosocial interests and beliefs. Informal social controls reduce opportunities to offend (e.g., time at work). They also provide a person with the motivation to not offend so as to avoid jeopardizing their investment in new social roles and prosocial identities (Laub & Sampson, 2003).

Criminal legal system involvement has been considered a major contributor to cumulative disadvantage that limits access to informal social control (Nagin & Paternoster, 2000). Employment is considered a key source of informal social control (Laub & Sampson, 2003). Laws requiring criminal record checks during hiring processes may have a cumulative disadvantage effect by decreasing opportunities for employment. In effect, criminal legal system involvement can restrict access to employment opportunities, which are crucial for desistance from criminal behaviour. Accordingly, several researchers have called for laws prohibiting employers from asking about criminal legal system involvement on initial job applications (e.g., Raphael, 2021).

Criminologists are often concerned with how institutions impact cumulative disadvantage. Formal institutions include more than just the criminal legal system. Educational institutions' responses to youth (e.g., suspensions) can have a cascading impact on criminal behaviour by labeling the young person as a delinquent, thereby discouraging prosocial peers from associating with this person. This process is often referred to as the school-to-prison pipeline (Wiley et al., 2020). Despite the emphasis on how formal and informal institutions create cumulative disadvantage, it is also possible that individual-level factors contribute to cumulative disadvantage. For example, a child's inability to regulate their emotions may result in social exclusion and hinder the development of positive social ties that protect against offending. Psychopathy may be a particularly important contributor to cumulative disadvantage because it is associated with poorer outcomes in employment, educational attainment, peer relationships, and intimate partner relationships (Eisenbarth et al., 2022; Forth et al., 2022; Hoffmann & Verona, 2021; Ploe et al., 2023; Seto & Davis, 2021). These points are supported by analyses from Chapter 6.

A cumulative disadvantage perspective, therefore, assumes that the relationship between psychopathy and persistent offending is indirect, operating through the impact of psychopathy on social and health outcomes in adulthood. This assumption remains empirically untested and is addressed in the analyses in this chapter.

The Psychopathy-Offending Relationship within a Criminal Propensity Framework

Criminal propensity is defined as a trait or set of traits that emerge in childhood or early adolescence, remain relatively stable over time, and thus continuously influence the risk of persistent offending over the life-course (Nagin & Paternoster, 2000). Like cumulative disadvantage theories, criminal propensity theories acknowledge that there is a statistical association between factors such as informal social control and offending. However, propensity theories differ in suggesting that this association is spurious once accounting for the impact of criminal propensity. Criminal propensity is considered a common cause of both negative social outcomes (e.g., divorce, unemployment, criminogenic peer networks, and substance use) and offending (Gottfredson & Hirschi, 1990). Individuals who continue offending over the life-course experience negative social and health consequences primarily because of their criminal propensity. Although the criminology literature more typically measures criminal propensity through indicators of low self-control (Nagin & Paternoster, 2000), psychopathy has recently been proposed as a more suitable measure of propensity because it includes, but is not limited to, features of low self-control (DeLisi, 2016; McCuish & Lussier, 2023).

At least conceptually, psychopathy seems to be an appropriate indicator of criminal propensity because it is moderately stable (Lynam, 1998) and is viewed as a direct cause of offending (Gatner et al., 2022). Interpersonal traits are anticipated to influence negative interactions with others, thereby increasing the likelihood of offending and aggressive behaviour (Gatner et al., 2022; Verona et al., 2023). Affective traits are associated with less sensitivity to the well-being of others (Salekin, 2016) and therefore may fail to deter offending. Behavioural traits resemble features of low self-control and antisocial attitudes that are important predictors of reoffending (Gottfredson & Hirschi, 1990). As demonstrated in Chapter 6, psychopathy traits in adolescence also directly influence negative social and health consequences in early adulthood. Looking for short-term personal gain, power, pleasure, and thrills will lead not just to criminal behaviour but also to a lack of investment in jobs and relationships, greater use of illicit substances, and negative interactions in prison. From a criminal propensity perspective, although psychopathy traits influence negative social and health outcomes, these social and health outcomes do not affect the nature of the relationship between psychopathy and offending. Therefore, contrary to expectations from a cumulative disadvantage perspective, interventions focused on improving a person's social and health outcomes would likely not disrupt the relationship between psychopathy and persistent offending.

Measurement and Developing the Mediation Model

With one exception, all measures used in the analyses in this chapter are the same as those discussed in previous chapters, and so I will not repeat their descriptions here. The one exception is the measurement of convictions. Temporal order is a critical aspect of mediation analysis. The outcome variable (Y), which in this chapter is represented by convictions, must come after both the measurement of the predictor (X), which is represented by psychopathy, and the measurement of the mediator (M), which is represented by different social and health outcomes. The mediator must also be measured after the predictor. Whereas Chapter 5 examined convictions starting at age 18, because social and health outcomes were measured in early adulthood, convictions were measured over a three-year period following the measurement of the mediator. On average, the measurement of convictions began at age 21 and continued until age 24. During the follow-up period, participants averaged 4.21 (SD = 5.25) new convictions.

There are four phases to a mediation model. The first is to examine whether there is a relationship between X and Y. As shown in Chapter 5, there is a significant relationship between Psychopathy Checklist: Youth Version (PCL:YV) scores measured in adolescence (X) and repeated convictions in adulthood (Y). The second is to examine whether there is a relationship between X and M. As shown in Chapter 6, there is a significant relationship between PCL:YV scores and each indicator of M (informal social control, negative criminogenic peer social network in prison, and substance use issues). The third step is to examine whether there is a relationship between M and Y. This third step will be addressed in the next sections for each of the three mediators. The fourth step is to

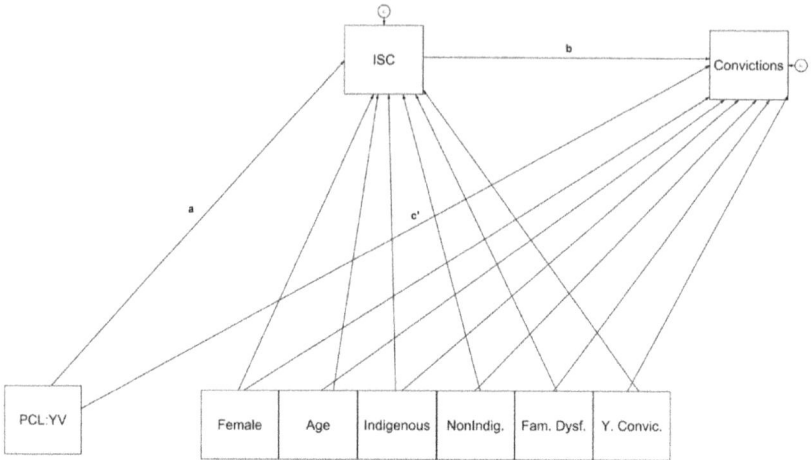

Figure 7.1 Conceptual model examining the mediating impact of informal social control on the relationship between PCL:YV total scores and conviction frequency in adulthood.
Notes. Temporal order was established between PCL:YV total scores, the Community Risk Needs Assessment (CRNA) informal social control scale, and conviction frequency during the three-year follow-up period. PCL:YV = PCL:YV total scores; ISC = CRNA informal social control scale; Convictions = conviction frequency in adulthood; Age = age at CRNA rating; Female = female participant; NonIndig. = NonIndigenous participant; Fam. Dysf = family dysfunction scale; Y. Convic. = number of youth convictions.

put the first three steps together in a single analysis to examine whether the significant relationship between X and Y is reduced after accounting for the relationship between M and Y. Figure 7.1 shows a conceptual model with informal social control as the mediator. The same model was replicated with two different mediators: negative criminogenic peer ties in prison and substance use issues.

There are three possible outcomes of this analysis. First, social/health outcomes have no bearing on the relationship between psychopathy and offending. Second, psychopathy traits directly influence these social/health outcomes, which, in turn, help, but do not fully explain, why people with psychopathy traits have elevated levels of offending. This is referred to as partial mediation. For example, psychopathy traits might influence unemployment in early adulthood, meaning that people with psychopathy traits may have economic difficulties that influence their involvement in crime. However, they may still engage in criminal behaviour for reasons unrelated to economic difficulties. Third, the entire reason why people with psychopathy traits offend at a higher rate is because of psychopathy's influence on these other negative outcomes that, in turn, contribute to offending. This is referred to as full mediation. With full mediation, for example, the only reason people with psychopathy traits continue to offend over the life-course is because of a lack of employment.

The mediation analysis was modeled using the `sem` program for Stata (a statistical software program). The mediation model involved simultaneously (1) estimating the direct effect of total PCL:YV scores on conviction frequency in adulthood (i.e., c' in Figure 7.1), (2) estimating the indirect effect of PCL:YV scores on conviction frequency in adulthood through the mediator (i.e., **a** and **b** in Figure 7.1), and (3) combining the direct and indirect effects to obtain the total effect of PCL:YV scores on conviction frequency in adulthood. Potential issues with reverse causality were avoided because temporal order was established between the PCL:YV (baseline assessment measured in adolescence), each mediator (measured in early adulthood), and conviction frequency in adulthood (measured after the mediator).

Identification of a significant mediating effect requires more than observing a significant coefficient for each link in the mediation chain (i.e., **a** and **b**). The `nlcom` program for Stata was used to produce bias-corrected bootstrapped confidence intervals ($b = 1,000$), which is well-suited for testing indirect effects (Hayes, 2013). In essence, bootstrapping involves repeatedly drawing random subsamples of the original sample and performing the same analysis on these random subsamples. Using random sampling with replacement repeated 1,000 times to estimate the model creates a distribution of indirect effect coefficients. A significant mediating effect occurs if the 95 percent confidence interval (CI) of these 1,000 estimates does not contain zero. In other words, I am not simply looking for a significant mediating effect in a single analysis; I am ensuring that this mediating effect is reliable by performing the same analysis 1,000 times on different subsamples and evaluating the consistency of the observed mediation effect.

The sequential ignorability assumption requires that PCL:YV scores are independent of potential confounds related to the specific mediator and conviction frequency in adulthood. This assumption also requires that the specific mediator being examined is independent of potential confounds related to PCL:YV scores and control variables (Imai et al., 2010). In essence, the sequential ignorability assumption asks whether the analysis omitted variables that could impact the relationship between the predictor and mediator or the predictor and the outcome. Although this assumption is untestable, the *mediation* package (Tingley et al., 2014) in R (version 3.6.1; R Core Team, 2018) was used to estimate the proportion of variance that an unobserved confounder would need to explain in both the mediator and outcome to nullify the mediation effect. This analysis can be used to determine how realistic it would be for an unmeasured variable to negate a mediating effect.

Case Study: Illustrations of Mediation

This is probably the most technical chapter so far (sorry, it gets even more technical in Chapter 10). Such technicalities cannot be avoided if the goal is to truly understand how psychopathy relates to offending. In this section, I use case studies to illustrate how different social and health outcomes in early adulthood may, or may not, mediate the relationship between psychopathy traits and offending. Case studies are anecdotal and meant to communicate concepts. They do not actually prove mediation, partial mediation, or no mediation; they just illustrate these ideas. To protect confidentiality, the case studies presented reflect a simplified view of the realities of case formulation.

Example of Full Mediation

Chris, whose prison-based criminogenic social network was described in Chapter 6 (see Figure 6.3), is an example of how social networks can fully mediate the relationship between psychopathy and reoffending. This observation supports a cumulative disadvantage perspective on offending. Chris' score on the PCL:YV was a full standard deviation higher than the rest of the Incarcerated Serious and Violent Young Offender Study (ISVYOS) sample. Chris' prison-based criminogenic network was also substantially larger compared to other members of the ISVYOS sample. Chris incurred nine convictions during the three-year follow-up period, which was one standard deviation above the mean number of convictions for the ISVYOS sample. Thus, there is a clear relationship between Chris' psychopathy traits (X), the size of his network (M), and his offending during the follow-up period (Y).

Chris' background illustrates how a mediation effect might manifest in practice. While in prison, Chris developed a number of negative ties to peers. One of these negative ties was to an alter named Harold. A mutual conflict occurred between the two while in prison, which eventually spilled over into the community. Chris sought out Harold and perpetrated an assault against him, for which he was charged. It could be argued that Chris' psychopathy traits did not directly influence the assault. Instead,

Chris' psychopathy traits influenced a variety of different negative interactions in prison, some of which eventually led to new offences in the community. This suggests that, rather than intervening solely on psychopathy traits, case management and case formulation strategies should emphasize reducing prison misconduct and reconciling negative relationships formed in prison to avoid spillover into the community. Of course, this is just one example of one offence.[4] To truly observe full mediation would require observing this type of pathway for each of Chris' nine convictions during the follow-up period.

Example of Partial Mediation

Tyler scored above 30 on the PCL:YV and incurred 9 new convictions during the follow-up period, putting him one standard deviation above the sample mean. Tyler also scored low on the CRNA measure of informal social control. In particular, he was rated as having criminogenic family and intimate partner relationships and limited educational and vocational training and skills. Although he was rated as having no issues with the stability of his living situation, he was eventually deported from Canada. Over time, his financial stability weakened because he was involved in a car accident while uninsured and owed over $10,000 to an insurance company. It could be argued that psychopathy traits contributed to these weak sources of informal social control. During the follow-up period, Tyler engaged in a series of robberies, including the unlawful confinement of another person while demanding money. This offence appeared to be directly influenced by his need to repay insurance debts. Thus, there is some evidence that Tyler's weak sources of informal social control, namely financial instability, a lack of positive relationships, and unemployment, contributed to his difficulties in lawfully repaying debts. As a consequence, he engaged in criminal behaviour to make money. Several years later, Tyler perpetrated an assault against his girlfriend that was motivated by jealousy and misogynistic attitudes consistent with psychopathy traits. So, on the one hand, some of Tyler's offences were influenced by weak informal social control, implying mediation. However, there was also evidence of crimes that were directly influenced by psychopathy traits that were unrelated to informal social control.

---

[4] In fact, finding this precise example of the diffusion of prison conflict into the community was extremely difficult. A far more common scenario was where conflict in the community carried over to conflict in custody.

This case study provides evidence of both cumulative disadvantage and criminal propensity mechanisms. From an intervention and case management perspective, Tyler's offending requires addressing both psychopathy traits and deficits in informal social control. Case formulation would involve identifying the scenarios in which Tyler's psychopathy traits (e.g., jealousy, desire for control, and lack of concern about the well-being of others) influenced violent offending, as well as scenarios in which his poor financial management and lack of education and vocational training acted as barriers to desistance from offending. Unlike the example with Chris, whose social network fully explained criminal behaviour, for Tyler, psychopathy traits both directly influence criminal behaviour and indirectly influence it through their impact on his social environment.

Example of No Mediation

Tyler's background also provides an example in which his health outcomes did not influence the relationship between psychopathy and offending. Tyler's CRNA indicated that he had substance use issues in adulthood. These issues appeared to be influenced by several psychopathy traits, including recklessness, sensation seeking, and need for stimulation. However, a close look at Tyler's pattern of offending indicates that his offences were not influenced by substance use. His crimes were primarily motivated by jealousy and misogyny, leading to intimate partner violence. Tyler's property offences were primarily motivated by debt following an uninsured car accident. Thus, although psychopathy traits may have influenced Tyler's substance use, substance use was not a criminogenic risk factor.

This case example aligns with a criminal propensity perspective. The implication is that interventions should primarily target psychopathy traits, which, in turn, may reduce both substance use and offending.

Does Informal Social Control Mediate the Relationship between Psychopathy and Convictions?

Table 7.1 reports path coefficients for a model assessing whether informal social control scale scores mediate the relationship between PCL:YV total scores in adolescence and conviction frequency measured during a three-year follow-up period in adulthood. The first phase of the analytic strategy identified a significant path coefficient between PCL:YV total scores and conviction frequency in adulthood ($b = 0.10$, $p = 0.006$). Per z-scores, a

Table 7.1 *Mediation test of cumulative disadvantage (PCL:YV total scores)*

	b (SE)	95% CI	z-score
Direct effects			
PCL:YV → Informal social control (a)	−0.09 (0.03)**	−0.15; −0.02	−2.64
PCL:YV → Convictions (c′)	0.08 (0.03)*	0.01; 0.14	2.18
Informal social control → Convictions (b)	−0.25 (0.05)***	−0.34; −0.16	−5.51
Indirect effect			
PCL:YV → Informal social control → Convictions (ab)	0.02 (0.01)*	0.004; 04	2.38
Total Effect			
PCL:YV → Convictions (c)	0.10 (0.04)**	0.03; 0.17	2.77
Bootstrapped mediation path (1,000 replications)			
Via informal social control	0.02 (0.01)*	0.01; 0.04	2.48

* $p < 0.05$, ** $p < 0.01$, *** $p < 0.001$.
Notes. The model includes all relationships depicted in Figure 7.1. Letters in brackets indicate the specific path modeled.

one standard deviation increase in PCL:YV total score was associated with a 2.77 standard deviation increase in adult conviction frequency. In other words, approximately every seven-point increase in PCL:YV total scores corresponded to an increase of about 12 new convictions. The addition of a direct effect of PCL:YV total scores on conviction frequency in adulthood was associated with a small increase in explained variance ($f^2 = 0.02$) compared to a baseline model that excluded PCL:YV total scores but included all control variables (e.g., demographic characteristics, family adversity, residential mobility, age at CRNA assessment).

The second phase of the analytic strategy identified a significant negative direct effect of PCL:YV scores in adolescence on informal social control in early adulthood ($b = -0.08$, $p = 0.032$). The CRNA was used to assess the quality of a person's adult informal social control, including family relationships, intimate relationships, living arrangements, employment, academic/vocational skills, and financial stability. The third phase of the analytic strategy identified a significant direct effect of the early adulthood measure of informal social control on future conviction frequency in adulthood ($b = -0.25$, $p < 0.001$). This direct effect was associated with a small change in explained variance ($f^2 = 0.06$). Although the direct effect of PCL:YV scores on conviction frequency remained significant, the standardized path coefficient for the informal social control scale was larger (-5.51) compared to the standardized path coefficient for the PCL:YV (2.18). In other words, although both PCL:YV test scores and informal social control scale scores were influential, informal social control had the stronger impact on convictions. This finding is not surprising given that informal social control was measured in early adulthood and therefore was measured closer to the timing of convictions compared to PCL:YV scores.

The fourth phase of the analytic strategy added a path from PCL:YV scores to early adulthood informal social control. This model revealed a significant indirect effect of psychopathy on conviction frequency in adulthood through the informal social control scale. The inclusion of this mediating pathway significantly improved model fit (LR χ^2 [1] = 6.94, $p = 0.008$) but accounted for only 20 percent of the total effect of PCL:YV scores on conviction frequency. The significant direct effect of PCL:YV scores on conviction frequency in adulthood remained, indicating that only partial mediation occurred. This partial mediation effect implies that the pathway between early psychopathy traits and persistent offending in adulthood is partly explained by the tendency for psychopathy traits to influence a negative social environment in early adulthood.

Does a Negative Criminogenic Network Mediate the Relationship between Psychopathy and Convictions?

For parsimony, I do not repeat the model shown in Table 7.1/Figure 7.1, but the same models were applied to the examination of criminogenic networks. Unsurprisingly, given the findings from the previous section, in the first phase of the mediation model, PCL:YV scores had a significant direct effect on convictions in adulthood. For the second phase, the key question was whether a larger network of negative ties to other people in prison increased the rate of reconvictions. A one-unit increase in the number of negative ties was associated with a 0.63 unit increase in the number of convictions incurred during the follow-up period ($b = 0.628$, $p = 0.001$). Per z-scores, a one standard deviation increase in the number of negative criminogenic prison ties was associated with a 1.83 unit increase in the number of convictions during the follow-up period. The third phase of the analytic strategy added a path from PCL:YV scores to negative criminogenic prison ties. In line with findings from Chapter 6, a one-unit increase in PCL:YV total scores was associated with a significant increase in the number of negative criminogenic prison ties. Although significant, the magnitude of this effect was relatively weak. A one standard deviation increase in PCL:YV total scores was associated with a 0.55 unit increase in the number of negative social ties in prison ($p = 0.011$).

The final step in this mediation analysis assessed whether the addition of a path from PCL:YV scores to negative social ties in prison mediated the relationship between PCL:YV scores and offending. This model revealed a significant indirect effect of psychopathy on conviction frequency in adulthood through the measure of negative social tie degree centrality. The inclusion of this mediating pathway significantly improved model fit (LR χ^2 [1] $= 5.33, p = 0.021$) and accounted for approximately 50 percent of the total effect of PCL:YV scores on conviction frequency. The significant direct effect of PCL:YV scores on conviction frequency in adulthood remained, indicating that the size of a person's negative social network in prison only partially mediated the relationship between PCL:YV scores in adolescence and convictions in the mid- to late-twenties.

Does Substance Use Mediate the Relationship between Psychopathy and Convictions?

Analyses from the previous sections were replicated, this time using substance use issues in early adulthood as the mediator. Unsurprisingly, given the findings from the previous section, in the first phase of the mediation model, PCL:YV scores had a significant direct effect on convictions in adulthood. For the second phase, substance use issues did not significantly increase the rate of reconvictions during the follow-up period. Although analyses in Chapter 6 indicated that psychopathy traits in adolescence increased the odds of substance use issues in early adulthood, this tendency did not translate into increased involvement in criminal behaviour. Thus, there was no evidence that substance use issues mediated the relationship between psychopathy traits and reoffending.

Are the Findings Reliable?

It was necessary to evaluate whether the partial mediation effects observed for the informal social control scale and negative prison network degree centrality were reliable. This section is especially technical, but I want to emphasize why careful attention is needed to ensure that the findings are reliable. A finding of partial mediation has critically important implications for intervention strategies and case formulation. Specifically, if there truly is evidence of partial mediation, then understanding the relationship between psychopathy and offending requires also taking into consideration a person's social environment. Treatment and intervention strategies tailored to enhancing informal social control and modifying prison peer networks may help disrupt involvement in offending for people with psychopathy traits (for similar logic, see Walters & DeLisi, 2015). These recommendations have important implications for professional practice, and therefore, it is essential to evaluate whether these recommendations can be considered reliable.

Reliability was assessed by examining bootstrapped confidence intervals for both informal social control and network mediators. Findings were the same for both measures, and so I only discuss the process of assessing reliability for the informal social control scale. This process involved using the `nlcom` program in Stata to randomly draw 1,000 bootstrapped samples, creating a distribution of all indirect effect coefficient estimates. The 95 percent CI of these estimates did not contain zero, providing further evidence that informal social control partially mediates the relationship between psychopathy and offending.

Can we be confident that the mediating effect of informal social control was not due to an unobserved confounder (i.e., failing to control for other variables)? This refers back to the sequential ignorability assumption and was investigated using the *mediation* package in R (Tingley et al., 2014). This test estimates the proportion of variance an unobserved confounder would need to explain in both informal social control and convictions to nullify the mediation effect. Performing this analysis with 1,000 simulations revealed a rho (ρ) at which mediation = 0 of 0.40 (see Figure 7.2). In other words, for the average causal mediation effect of informal social control to equal zero, it would require a correlation of 0.400 between the error terms of the mediation and outcome models (Imai et al., 2010). Specifically, for ρ to equal zero (i.e., no mediation effect), unobserved covariates would need to simultaneously account for approximately 30 percent of the variance in both the informal social control scale and conviction frequency in adulthood. On its own, this information means little. The key question is whether it is realistic that some unmeasured variable could account for 30 percent of the variance in both measures, thereby rendering the partial mediation effect unreliable.

Figure 7.3 indicates that if an unobserved confounder accounts for approximately 20 percent of the variance in the outcome (y-axis), it would

Are the Findings Reliable?

SEM

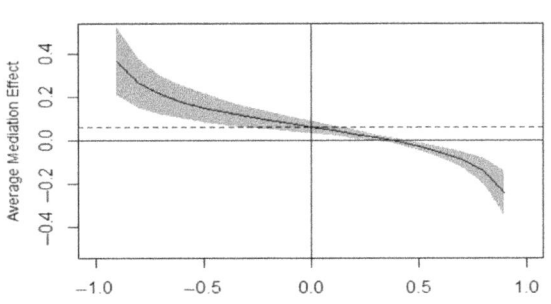

Figure 7.2 Sensitivity analysis of the adult conviction frequency outcome and CRNA informal social control mediator.

Notes. The dotted line represents the estimated mediation effect, the solid line represents the estimated average mediation effect across ρ, and the shaded area represents the 95 percent CI. The average mediation effect (y-axis) reaches zero when the sensitivity parameter ρ equals approximately 0.40 (x-axis).

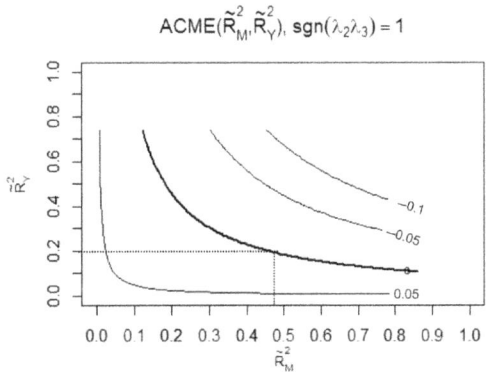

Figure 7.3 Sensitivity analysis of the adult conviction frequency outcome and CRNA informal social control mediator.

Notes. The dark contour line ("0") represents how strong the unobserved confounder must be to nullify the mediation effect. The dotted line shows that if an unobserved confounder accounts for approximately 20 percent of the variance in the outcome (y-axis) it would need to account for approximately 48 percent of the variance in the mediator (x-axis) in order to reduce the mediating effect to zero.

need to account for approximately 48 percent of the variance in the mediator (x-axis) to reduce the mediating effect to zero. By comparison, youth convictions, which is an important mediator in theories of cumulative disadvantage (Nagin & Paternoster, 2000), accounted for only 8.7

percent of variance in informal social control and only 8.8 percent of variance in convictions, which is well below what would be necessary to negate the mediating impact of informal social control. Similar conclusions were reached when examining rho for negative criminogenic networks in prison. In sum, the findings are relatively robust to the influence of other unmeasured variables.

As discussed in Chapters 4 and 5, one criticism of the PCL:YV is that it is over-saturated with measures of prior criminal behaviour, raising tautological concerns when used to predict offending. This criticism was addressed by replicating earlier analyses using (1) the PCL:YV three-factor model that excludes criminal behaviour items and (2) the scale created by summing the 13 items of the PCL:YV that were identified by the item response theory analysis from Chapter 4 as providing meaningful information to the measurement of psychopathy. Regardless of how PCL:YV scores were represented, the same conclusion was reached: both informal social control and negative criminogenic networks in prison partially mediated the relationship between early psychopathy traits and continued offending in adulthood. As substance use issues were unrelated to convictions, it was not necessary to revisit these analyses with different representations of PCL:YV scores.

A Better Understanding of the Relationship between Psychopathy and Offending

The "theory crisis" in psychology (Eronen & Bringmann, 2021) has contributed to a limited understanding of the causal relationship between psychopathy and offending. The goal of this chapter was to integrate psychology's careful attention to construct measurement, exemplified by measures like the PCL:YV, with criminology's emphasis on theoretical models that help more clearly explicate pathways between early risk factors and persistent offending. Some criminological theories offer competing explanations for offending over the life-course. It is therefore necessary to empirically investigate, rather than assume, that a specific theory is helpful in understanding the relationship between psychopathy and persistent offending. The analyses in this chapter facilitated a comparison of state dependence and population heterogeneity meta-theoretical frameworks.

From a state dependence perspective, based on the principle of cumulative disadvantage (Sampson & Laub, 1997), it was anticipated that the relationship between psychopathy and reoffending would be at least partially mediated by the collateral consequences of psychopathy traits in adolescence on social and health outcomes in early adulthood. With respect to population heterogeneity meta-theories, based on the principle of criminal propensity (e.g., Gottfredson & Hirschi, 1990), it was anticipated that psychopathy traits in adolescence would directly influence reoffending throughout adulthood, and that the association between social/health outcomes and offending is spurious because both are caused by psychopathy. Thus, the propensity and cumulative disadvantage perspectives differ regarding whether interventions targeting social and health outcomes in early adulthood would disrupt offending (cumulative disadvantage) or would not disrupt offending (criminal propensity). In this chapter, social outcomes included sources of informal social control, measured via items from the CRNA, and the size of a person's negative criminogenic peer network in prison. Substance use issues, also measured via the CRNA, were used to capture a negative health outcome in early adulthood.

In line with theories that endorse criminal propensity principles, net of control variables, PCL:YV total scores had a significant direct effect on conviction frequency measured over a three-year period in adulthood. The unique contribution of PCL:YV total scores to explained variance in adult conviction frequency was small ($f^2 = 0.02$) per Cohen's (1988) ranking of effect sizes. This reiterates findings from Chapter 5, indicating that although psychopathy traits in adolescence are a significant predictor of persistent offending, they do not guarantee continued offending in adulthood, nor is persistent offending exclusive to people with psychopathy traits.

In line with criminal propensity theory principles, when controlling for psychopathy traits, substance use issues in early adulthood did not significantly influence convictions in adulthood. However, contrary to propensity theory predictions, a person's informal social control and negative criminogenic peer network in prison had a significant direct effect on conviction frequency, even when accounting for the direct effect of PCL:YV total scores on both (1) the social outcome of interest and (2) conviction frequency. In other words, contrary to expectations from propensity theories (Nagin & Paternoster, 2000), the association between adulthood social outcomes and continued offending was not spurious. In fact, based on standardized path coefficients, compared to PCL:YV total scores, early adulthood measures of a person's informal social control and negative criminogenic peer ties in prison had a stronger impact on conviction frequency later in adulthood.

Most notably, consistent with cumulative disadvantage theory principles, separate models examining informal social control and negative ties in prison revealed that these social factors partially mediated the relationship between PCL:YV total scores and conviction frequency in adulthood.

Psychopathy traits in adolescence contribute to weaker social bonds, poorer employment and educational outcomes, and more conflictual relationships with others in prison. As a reminder from Chapter 6, most of these conflictual relationships arise from the person with psychopathy traits victimizing others rather than being victimized. The influence of psychopathy traits on these social outcomes matters for future offending. The partial mediating effects of informal social control and negative criminogenic networks in prison were confirmed using bootstrapping analyses and were robust to concerns about unmeasured confounding variables.

Overall, the findings support a loose rather than a strict interpretation of population heterogeneity theories and criminal propensity principles. On the one hand, theories based on criminal propensity could argue that the significant direct effect of PCL:YV scores on conviction frequency indicates that early predispositions toward offending have a lasting impact on criminal behaviour. Further, only partial mediation was observed, meaning that psychopathy traits in adolescence still directly influenced offending even when accounting for the indirect effects of social outcomes. Therefore, psychopathy does not impact offending only through a process of cumulative disadvantage. In contrast, a strict interpretation of propensity theories assumes that social and health outcomes are unrelated to offending once accounting for psychopathy traits. This assumption held when looking at substance use, but not for measures of informal social control or criminogenic peer networks in prison. It is therefore important that case formulation and intervention strategies integrate insights from both cumulative disadvantage and propensity perspectives.

Implications for Intervention Strategies

These analyses did not directly evaluate whether interventions targeting psychopathy traits vs. interventions targeting social outcomes have a stronger effect on reducing reoffending. In general, there is a lack of psychopathy research addressing these practical questions. I review some of this research in Chapter 10. However, the analyses in this chapter do provide an empirical basis for guiding intervention strategies. An issue with intervention strategies like the Oak Ridge Study discussed in Chapter 2 is that they were developed based on subjective opinions and anecdotal experiences. Although imperfect, the analyses presented here offer insight into why psychopathy traits in adolescence are linked to long-term offending outcomes and inform intervention strategies with respect to which risk factors to target to help disrupt offending outcomes.

Informal social control in early adulthood had a stronger impact on convictions later in adulthood compared to PCL:YV scores in adolescence. Policymakers and practitioners might be tempted to interpret this as evidence that a person's social environment outweighs their personality in influencing offending, and therefore intervention and treatment strategies should prioritize building informal social control and addressing prison-based conflict networks. However, this would be an oversimplification. Psychopathy was measured in adolescence, and social outcomes were measured in early adulthood. It is possible that measuring psychopathy in adulthood would have changed the results. PCL:YV total scores, scores on the three-factor model, and scores on the scale created from core PCL:YV items (based on the item response theory analysis in Chapter 4) were associated with weaker sources of informal social control and larger negative criminogenic prison networks. Thus, although early psychopathy traits were not as predictive of offending as these social environment factors measured in early adulthood, addressing psychopathy traits early in the life-course could help address *both* future offending *and* negative social outcomes. Appropriate interventions should therefore be viewed through a developmental lens, where a person's age helps inform the timing and focus of intervention strategies.

In line with the assortative mating literature, interventions designed to improve sources of informal social control and prison social networks may be less effective if psychopathy traits are not addressed first. People with volatile personality traits tend to self-select into relationships with others who share similar interaction styles (Caspi & Herbener, 1990; Kardum et al., 2017; Krueger et al., 1998; Reale et al., 2020; Salihovic et al., 2012). Chapter 8 explores whether people with psychopathy traits respond to positive social environments in the same way as those without such traits. Psychopathy traits may also indirectly influence self-selection into negative social environments by increasing time spent incarcerated (McCuish et al., 2014). Past research indicates that spending more time incarcerated limits opportunities for developing positive ties to prosocial peers, parents, and teachers (Farrington & Murray, 2014) and limits opportunities for employment, stable housing, and vocational training (Kirk & Wakefield, 2018). Chapter 10 directly examines the impact of incarceration on reoffending for people with psychopathy traits.

Improving social outcomes like informal social control and negative peer networks in prison may help reduce reoffending, but these improvements may not operate as intended if psychopathy traits are not addressed first (de Voegel et al., 2012). One mechanism through which informal social control protects against offending is by spending time with prosocial adults who deter criminal behaviour. However, people with psychopathy traits tend to disregard or even ridicule prosocial social norms and the opinions of others (Logan & Johnstone, 2010) and may use employment positions and relationships as opportunities to be domineering (Forth et al., 2022; Mathieu & Babiak, 2016). Consequently, people with psychopathy traits may have less incentive to associate with or be influenced by prosocial others. Case formulation is especially important for understanding the contexts in which the person offends and for assessing (a) whether the offence is driven primarily by psychopathy traits or by the person's social environment and (b) if the social environment influences criminal behaviour, whether addressing psychopathy traits is a prerequisite for benefiting from improvements in social conditions.

Given that informal social control partially mediated the relationship between psychopathy and reoffending, an apparent recommendation might be to provide people with psychopathy traits the opportunity to participate in employment programs and vocational training as a means of reducing crime. While these programs could have generally positive effects, forensic psychologists and other professionals responsible for case formulation and risk management should consider which types of crimes such interventions are likely to influence. Reviews of empirical research on employment programs and other policies targeting income hardship suggest that such policies have limited impact on reducing violent crime (Ludwig & Schnepel, 2025). Ludwig and Schnepel speculated that violent crime was often driven more by emotions than by profit or material benefit. Therefore, modifying a person's social environment may help reduce certain types of crime, but not violent offences or offences primarily motivated by emotional responses.

Caldwell (2011) reported that, for youth with psychopathy traits, the likelihood of recidivism decreased following participation in a treatment program with a combined focus on the development of social bonds and improvements in interpersonal processes and social skills. It is important to consider that addressing antisocial attitudes and engaging in cognitive restructuring around the value of ties to prosocial individuals may be necessary to ensure that improvements in informal social control and reductions in negative interactions with others in prison effectively contribute to desistance from criminal behaviour.

Chapter Summary

Substantial attention has been given to whether psychopathy measures predict recidivism (Blais et al., 2014; Edens et al., 2007; Leistico et al.,

2008). However, statistical prediction alone does not explain the process connecting psychopathy to reoffending (Wikström, 2020). Thus, there remains a gap in the psychopathy literature regarding *why* psychopathy influences reoffending (Lee & Kim, 2022; Walters & DeLisi, 2015). This gap is particularly evident in understanding why psychopathy traits in adolescence can influence offending that continues into adulthood for more than a decade. Addressing this gap provides a knowledge base for case formulation, risk management, and intervention delivery decisions that require understanding the mechanisms linking psychopathy to offending (Gatner et al., 2022; Wong et al., 2012). It is important to establish whether factors targeted by treatment strategies aimed at reducing offending actually address putative causes. Gatner et al. (2022) recommended that case formulation and intervention be guided by criminology theory. The current chapter compared two meta-theories (and their key principles) routinely considered in criminology (Nagin & Paternoster, 2000): state dependence (cumulative disadvantage) and population heterogeneity (propensity).

The key takeaway from this chapter is that a loose, rather than strict, interpretation of population heterogeneity theoretical principles was supported. A strict interpretation of population heterogeneity principles requires evidence that social outcomes have no relationship with offending once accounting for a person's underlying propensity to offend. This was not supported by the analyses in this chapter. Both informal social control and negative prison networks had direct effects on reoffending. The finding of a significant partial mediation effect for both informal social control and negative prison networks is reliable, unlikely to be explained by unmeasured variables, and robust across different representations of PCL:YV scores. Partial mediation means that although these early adulthood social outcomes helped account for the relationship between psychopathy and reoffending, they did not fully account for this relationship. Psychopathy traits in adolescence continued to directly affect offending even when accounting for the indirect effects of informal social controls and negative criminogenic peer networks in prison.

CHAPTER 8

Psychopathy and Treatment Effect Heterogeneity

Chapter 7 addressed mediating mechanisms by focusing on whether psychopathy influenced persistent offending because of its impact on negative social and health outcomes. In this chapter, I focus on moderating processes by examining whether early adulthood measures of informal social control, prison criminogenic networks (positive and negative), and substance use moderate the relationship between psychopathy traits in adolescence and continued offending in adulthood. Tests of moderation allow for an examination of whether a third variable alters the strength or direction of the relationship between an independent variable like psychopathy and a dependent variable like offending (Baron & Kenny, 1986). Another term for moderation is interaction. Moderation analyses can be used to address questions about whether people with psychopathy traits respond differently to the presence of risk or protective factors hypothesized to influence reoffending (de Vogel et al., 2009). For example, informal social controls are described as protective factors that facilitate desistance (see Laub & Sampson, 2003). Chapter 6 established that people with psychopathy traits were less likely to experience positive sources of informal social control. Chapter 7 established that part of the reason people with psychopathy traits continue offending is due to a lack of informal social control. In this chapter, I examine whether informal social control influences desistance from criminal behaviour even among people with psychopathy traits.

Moderation analysis is a statistical method; it is a vessel for testing certain research questions. However, research questions should be informed by theory. Why should anyone believe that people with psychopathy traits are less responsive to social or health outcomes? The concept of treatment effect heterogeneity provides the theoretical basis for the research questions addressed in this chapter. Treatment effect heterogeneity is sometimes referred to as life-course interdependence (Wright et al., 2001), field theory, or the interactional perspective (Magnusson, 1988).

Despite different terminology, the underlying idea is that people who are faced with similar situations may respond to these situations differently because of individual differences in criminal propensity. Recall from Chapter 7 that criminal propensity refers to a trait or set of traits that emerge in childhood or early adolescence, remain relatively stable over time, and thus have a continued impact on offending over the life-course (Nagin & Paternoster, 2000). Psychopathy is one way of measuring criminal propensity. People with psychopathy traits may respond differently to social and health outcomes compared to people without psychopathy traits. By "respond differently," I mean that the anticipated impact of a person's social environment on offending may vary depending on their personality characteristics (also see Nguyen & Loughran, 2018; Wright et al., 2001). Very little attention has been given to the interrelationship between the characteristics of a person, the nature of their environment, and the implications of this interaction for offending (Hirtenlehner & Schulz, 2021).

Chapter Goals and Analyses

All measures used in this chapter were described in Chapters 4–7. Figure 8.1 outlines the conceptual model under investigation. The four moderators examined include: (1) the informal social control scale derived from six Community Risk Needs Assessment (CRNA) items, (2) criminal social capital (i.e., positive prison criminogenic network degree centrality), (3) prison negative criminogenic network degree centrality, and (4) the CRNA item assessing substance use issues. Like Chapter 5, I used generalized estimating equation models. Given the familiarity with this approach, the key difference in this chapter is that the dependent variable

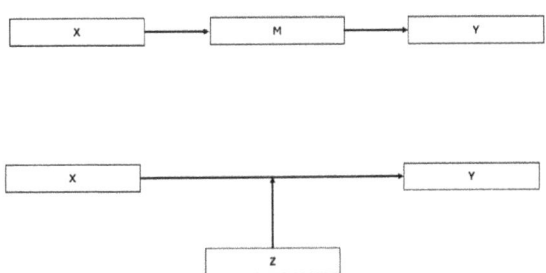

Figure 8.1 Graphical depiction of the difference between mediation (top) and moderation (bottom).

is treated as the number of convictions incurred at each year of age, rather than as a dichotomous indicator of conviction. The measurement of convictions began at the age following measurement of the moderator of interest (i.e., between ages 18 and 23). This approach ensured temporal order among all variables.

Each of the four moderation analyses is interpreted from two perspectives: comparisons between groups and comparisons within groups. The first perspective, which considers between-group differences, examines whether the rate of convictions in adulthood differs for youth who score high vs. low on the Psychopathy Checklist: Youth Version (PCL:YV) but score the same on the moderator. This approach compares groups that differ in their level of psychopathy traits but share similar social or health outcomes. For example, this comparison allows for assessment of whether informal social control influences desistance from offending even among participants with high PCL:YV scores. This comparison also helps to evaluate whether greater levels of criminal social capital have a stronger impact on convictions for youth who score high on the PCL:YV compared to youth who score low on the PCL:YV.

The second perspective, which considers within-group differences, evaluates whether the rate of convictions among youth with high scores on the PCL:YV varies as a function of differences in the level of the moderator. Thus, this comparison focuses only on individuals with elevated psychopathy traits but differing levels of the moderator. This perspective allows for an assessment of whether youth with high PCL:YV scores have similar conviction rates regardless of their level of other risk or protective factors.

For each of the four analyses, I examine whether a significant interaction effect emerges between PCL:YV total scores and the moderator of interest. Although the analyses treat PCL:YV scores as dimensional for ease of interpretation, I present figures that illustrate how the moderator functions at high scores on the PCL:V (i.e., 30 or greater) and at scores on the PCL:YV of less than 30. This categorical approach reflects conventional clinical thresholds and simplifies interpretation, but it should not be interpreted as a preference over dimensional representations of PCL:YV scores. Supplemental analyses examine the consistency of findings by using alternative representations of PCL:YV scores (e.g., three-factor model scores).

Hypotheses Regarding Treatment Effect Heterogeneity

Traditionally, treatment effect heterogeneity has been discussed from three different hypotheses. I discuss each of these hypotheses separately and then propose a fourth hypothesis that considers the potentially unique circumstances of people with psychopathy traits.

Hypothesis #1: Desistance by Default

The first hypothesis rejects the very basis of treatment effect heterogeneity. This perspective, which I will refer to as "desistance by default," asserts that social and health outcomes influence reoffending equally, regardless of a person's criminal propensity. Drs. Robert Sampson and John Laub, who are perhaps most strongly associated with theories about the role of informal social control in influencing desistance from crime, coined the phrase "desistance by default" (Laub & Sampson, 2003, pp. 278–279). They argued that informal social controls influence desistance regardless of background factors like criminal propensity.

Laub and Sampson's (2003) assertions about desistance by default were based on their analyses of boys who spent time in reformatory schools in Massachusetts in the early twentieth century and were subsequently followed into adulthood. Laub and Sampson (2003) suggested that informal social control was a normative part of the life-course for all people, regardless of their personality, values, and beliefs. In contrast to ideas about selection effects and assortative mating, they argued that America's social structure funneled people into informal social controls, even without people necessarily consciously pursuing life-course turning points like employment, marriage, and parenthood. These informal social controls placed constraints on all people, regardless of background, and structured their behaviour in ways that promoted reductions in offending. Laub and Sampson used the phrase "desistance by default" because it was assumed that (1) informal social control was a normative part of adulthood and (2) once informal social controls were in place, they would foster behavioural change even for subgroups with a particularly negative early developmental history (also see Laub et al., 2018; Sampson & Laub, 2016). Since all people experience positive sources of informal social control in adulthood, all people involved in crime eventually desist from criminal behaviour by default.

Hypothesis #2: Social Protection

The second hypothesis regarding treatment effect heterogeneity is based on the concept of social protection. From a social protection perspective, for people with a high propensity for involvement in criminal behaviour, experiencing positive sources of informal social control in early adulthood is anticipated to have a *stronger* influence on reductions in offending. People who are higher in criminal propensity are more prone to antisocial behaviour and are in greater need of deterrence or other constraints on their behaviour, and thus stand to benefit more from positive social and health outcomes (Wright et al., 2001). Conversely, since people with a low propensity for criminal behaviour are already at a low risk of offending, they do not need their family/friends/social environment to disrupt or deter their involvement in crime. Positive and well-intentioned family members cannot strongly influence another family member to stop engaging in criminal behaviour if that person has little inclination toward crime in the first place.

In support of this hypothesis, Boman and Mowen (2018) found that among a sample of formerly incarcerated people, those who came from positive backgrounds experienced only minimal reductions in reoffending following improvements in informal social control. This does not mean these individuals offended at a high rate. Rather, they were already offending at relatively low levels due to their positive background, and so additional improvements in informal social control had little effect. To be clear, the social protection hypothesis does not suggest that people who are low in criminal propensity cannot be influenced by peers involved in delinquent behaviour. The addition of *risk factors* can certainly increase offending among people with low criminal propensity. However, when it comes to the addition of protective factors like informal social control, people who are low in criminal propensity already possess internal constraints, such as altruism or moral values against crime. Thus, they do not need others in their social environment to dissuade them from offending.

Hypothesis #3: Social Amplification

The third hypothesis, referred to as social amplification, is similar to the social protection hypothesis in that people high in criminal propensity are believed to have a more pronounced response to environmental factors. Whereas social protection focuses on protective factors, the social amplification perspective anticipates that people high in criminal propensity are more likely to increase their offending in response to the presence of additional risk factors. This does not mean that people low in criminal propensity do not experience increases in their risk of offending following the addition of other risk factors; rather, it implies that people high in criminal propensity have a stronger response to such risk factors. From a social amplification perspective, people low in criminal propensity may be more resilient in the face of crime-inducing scenarios, such as associating with peers who encourage criminal behaviour.

For people high in criminal propensity, the addition of a criminogenic network reinforces, or even demands, involvement in criminal behaviour (Caspi & Moffitt, 1995). Ousey and Wilcox (2007) reported that people with higher levels of criminal propensity, measured as low self-control, responded more strongly to antisocial peers (i.e., they offended at higher rates) compared to people with lower criminal propensity. Research with youth supports the conclusion that the influence of low self-control on future offending is amplified if that person adopts peers' attitudes and moral views that favour engaging in criminal behaviour (e.g., Hirtenlehner & Kunz, 2016; Hirtenlehner & Schulz, 2021).

Summarizing Studies on Treatment Effect Heterogeneity Responses

Some studies report that factors like informal social control promote desistance from offending regardless of a person's background (Bersani et al., 2009; Doherty, 2006; King et al., 2007) and therefore contradict the principles of treatment effect heterogeneity, supporting the desistance by default hypothesis. Other studies find support for the social protection and social amplification hypotheses (Blokland & Nieuwbeerta, 2005; Reisig et al., 2007). For example, Wang et al. (2014) reported evidence of a social amplification effect in which criminal propensity had a stronger impact on reoffending when youth also lived in areas with high residential mobility. Wright et al. (2001) reported evidence of social protection effects, showing that educational success had a stronger impact on reductions in offending for people high in criminal propensity. Wright et al. (2001) also reported evidence of social amplification because connections to crime-involved peers had a stronger impact on offending among those high in criminal propensity.

There are several reasons for mixed findings across studies. First, studies use different samples, including youth in high schools and youth who have experienced incarceration. The prevalence of criminal propensity differs across these samples and may lead to different interpretations of treatment effect heterogeneity. Second, studies measure criminal propensity in different ways, sometimes relying solely on prior criminal history (e.g., Wang et al., 2014) but most often based on relatively simple, single-item indicators of self-control (e.g., Doherty, 2006). Evidence for treatment effect heterogeneity may be more reliable when using constructs like psychopathy, which better reflect notions of propensity. None of the studies mentioned previously relied on psychopathy to measure propensity.

Psychopathy and Treatment Effect Heterogeneity

In this section, I consider the extent to which descriptions of psychopathy align with the three different hypotheses on treatment effect heterogeneity. I also introduce a fourth hypothesis on treatment effect heterogeneity that may better account for the interplay between psychopathy traits and social/health outcomes, and what this means for the likelihood of persistent offending.

Psychopathy and Desistance by Default

Based on the desistance by default hypothesis, people with psychopathy traits benefit from informal social control just as much as anyone else. Thus, addressing early psychopathy traits is not necessary to increase the likelihood that informal social controls decrease reoffending. Sampson and Laub (2003) argued that "differences in adult criminal trajectories cannot be predicted from childhood" (p. 588). From this perspective, it is reasonable to assume that criminal propensity indicators, like psychopathy, are not informative of persistent offending. Accordingly, the presence of positive social and health outcomes in early adulthood should predict low levels of offending regardless of a person's psychopathy traits.

Psychopathy and Social Protection

Based on the social protection hypothesis, people with psychopathy traits are more prone to involvement in criminal behaviour. Therefore, compared to people who are low in psychopathy traits, those with psychopathy traits are considered to have the most to gain from positive social and health outcomes. For example, reductions in offending following improvements in informal social control are expected to be strongest for people with psychopathy traits.

Psychopathy and Social Amplification

Based on the social amplification hypothesis, people with psychopathy traits are more prone to involvement in criminal behaviour. Therefore, compared to people who are low in psychopathy traits, those with psychopathy traits are expected to be most adversely affected by negative social and health outcomes. For example, increases in offending following the development of a more negative criminogenic network in prison are expected to be strongest for people with psychopathy traits.

Social Resistance as Fourth Hypothesis on Treatment Effect Heterogeneity

None of the perspectives on treatment heterogeneity discussed thus far suggests that people with a high criminal propensity are less responsive to social and health outcomes compared to people with a low criminal propensity. This seems to be an oversight. Others have raised the possibility that people who are unmotivated to change and engage in serious offences might be less likely to respond to adult roles in the same way as people who are motivated to change and engage in minor offences (Hirschi & Gottfredson, 1995; Paternoster et al., 2015; Polaschek, 2019). I refer to this as the social resistance hypothesis. Hoppenbrouwers et al. (2015) use the term response modulation to describe a similar concept in which people with psychopathy traits are hypothesized to lack affective reactivity. This hypothesis implies that *positive* social and health outcomes have less impact on desistance from offending for people who are higher in psychopathy traits. Conversely, *negative* social and health outcomes have less impact on continued criminal behaviour for people who are higher in psychopathy traits. In effect, people with psychopathy traits may be especially resistant to changes to their social and health circumstances. To be clear, the social resistance hypothesis differs from ideas about selection effects and assortative mating. A selection effect describes how people with psychopathy traits are less likely to experience positive social and health outcomes. Social resistance describes how people with psychopathy traits, even when they experience positive social and health outcomes, do not experience the same level of decline in offending compared to people without psychopathy traits.

A social resistance hypothesis is a useful lens through which to view the relationship between psychopathy and the informal social control mechanisms hypothesized to influence desistance. Laub and Sampson (2003) suggested that informal social control would lead to desistance because individuals would not want to jeopardize their social roles. People with psychopathy traits tend to disregard, or even mock, social norms and the opinions of others (Logan & Johnstone, 2010). They, therefore, may be less concerned about whether their behaviour jeopardizes their social roles and relationships. Laub and Sampson (2003) suggested that social roles, such as being employed or married, structure a person's time in ways that reduce opportunities for offending. People with psychopathy traits tend to use relationships and positions of power to victimize others through aggressive, domineering, and manipulative behaviour (Boddy, 2014; Forth et al., 2022; Mathieu & Babiak, 2016). For example, in Chapter 7, I described how Tyler acted violently toward his partner. In theory, a prosocial intimate partner is anticipated to reduce offending. Laub and Sampson (2003) suggested that adult roles influence identity changes. Inherent to certain psychopathy traits, such as cognitive inflexibility, is a resistance to changing attitudes and opinions. Given that people with psychopathy traits tend to feel superior and entitled to privileges not afforded to others (Cooke et al., 2004), it is unlikely that such people will want to change or acknowledge their need to change in response to their social or health circumstances. Identity change may be unlikely for people with psychopathy traits, given that such traits include an uncaring and unempathetic attachment style, cognitive inflexibility, and a sense of entitlement, even in stable relationships with prosocial people (Forth et al., 2022). I am certainly not suggesting that people with psychopathy traits cannot change, but the likelihood of identity change may be lower for people with psychopathy traits compared to the general population. The ideas presented here are meant to reflect general trends rather than absolute rules.

In criminology, routine activity theory describes capable guardians as people who can disrupt offending opportunities by directly or indirectly putting themselves between a motivated offender and the target of their offending. Capable guardians are not typically police; they can include friends, neighbours, and relatives (Cohen & Felson, 1979). Building from this idea, Laub and Sampson (2003) suggested that new social roles increase the amount of time spent with capable guardians who help deter criminal behaviour. However, because psychopathy is negatively associated with perceptions of risk and potential consequences associated with offending (Altikriti et al., 2021), people with psychopathy traits may be less likely to consider the consequences of their actions even when in the presence of capable guardians. In other words, people with psychopathy traits will be relatively resistant to the influence of capable guardians in their social networks.

A social resistance hypothesis also implies that risk factors (e.g., substance use issues, criminogenic social environment) will have less of an influence on the criminal behaviour of people with psychopathy traits compared to people who are low in psychopathy traits. People who would not otherwise be prone to crime may engage in criminal behaviour if they are among friends who encourage such behaviour. There is some evidence supporting this social resistance hypothesis when looking at research on group behaviour. People who do not have a history of offending, and who presumably have a low propensity to offend, tend to be influenced by negative peer groups to join in on criminal behaviour (McGloin & Rowan, 2015). People with prior histories of offending, and who presumably have a higher propensity to offend, are less influenced by negative peer groups to join in on criminal behaviour. For example, college students who have morals opposed to crime (i.e., low criminal propensity) feel less culpable for their criminal behaviour when in the presence of peers who are involved in this behaviour (Rowan et al., 2022).

Granovetter's (1978) concept of a tipping point for collective behaviour helps illustrate how risk factors may have a stronger impact on people low in criminal propensity. In theory, each person has a threshold for the percentage of peers they would need to approve of a crime before joining in on that crime. For some people, 10 percent of peers is enough to meet the threshold for joining in on a crime event. For others, 90 percent of peers must engage in that crime before they join in. Based on Rowan et al.'s (2022) analysis, people with a lower criminal propensity may have a higher tipping point. However, it is also possible that tipping point values are randomly distributed among people high in criminal propensity, which means that there may not be much rhyme or reason when it comes to being motivated by the number of peers already committing a crime. Said differently, increases in the size of a person's criminogenic network may not matter, one way or the other, for someone whose moral beliefs already constrain involvement in crime (Schoepfer & Piquero, 2006).

In sum, contrary to the social protection hypothesis, under a social resistance hypothesis, informal social control and other protective factors will reduce reoffending most strongly for people with low levels of psychopathy traits. The very nature of psychopathy is counterproductive to the development of the causal mechanisms necessary for informal social controls to influence desistance from criminal behaviour. Contrary to the social amplification hypothesis, the social resistance hypothesis assumes that risk factors like large criminogenic networks and substance use promote criminal behaviour most strongly among people with low levels of psychopathy traits. No additional impetus to engage in crime is needed for people with psychopathy traits.

A Case Study Illustration of the Social Resistance Hypothesis

To help illustrate the concepts behind the social resistance hypothesis, I draw upon 20 years of data on a single youth, James. Relative to other members of the PCL:YV Cohort, James had a positive social environment. Yet, relative to other members of the PCL:YV Cohort, James engaged in a much higher rate of offending. It appears that the reason James continued to offend despite the presence of positive sources of informal social control was because of his untreated psychopathy traits.

James' biological parents were married at the time he was born and remained together as of the most recent wave of data collection (i.e., December 2023). Only 11.1 percent of participants reported living with and being raised by both biological parents. Half of ISVYOS participants were in some form of foster care at the time of their incarceration. James' father worked while his mother cared for James and his two younger siblings. Neither of James' parents had a strong understanding of English, but they communicated with James' probation officer through an interpreter. James' probation officer believed the parents to be supportive, caring, and patient. The probation officer also acknowledged that, at times, James' parents enabled his negative behaviour. That said, the enabling was not pervasive. For example, James' mother reported to James' probation officer that she found drugs and large sums of money in his bedroom and hoped that the criminal legal system would intervene because James was not listening to his parents' concerns and was not responsive to their disciplinary actions (e.g., grounding and taking away video game consoles).

James became involved with the criminal legal system at age 15. He was involved in an assault against a sibling, which led to family members calling the police. James was ordered by the court not to be in the upstairs portion of his home. Still at age 15, James assaulted his mother. As a result, he was temporarily placed in a transition bed. James returned home within a few days. A month later, James assaulted another female member of his family. Another incident occurred when James screamed at his mother and then pushed her after arguing about playing video games. On one occasion, James threatened to kill a family member and then punched them in the face. In this instance, multiple family members were required to restrain James. The assault occurred because James' parents told him he was not allowed to leave the home at night because of his court-ordered curfew. James' parents were therefore trying to act as capable guardians who would deter criminal behaviour, but James ignored deterrence warnings. Following this event, James' sister reported to James' probation officer that her family lived in fear of James. James' family sought help through mental health services. A clinician diagnosed James with attention deficit hyperactivity disorder, oppositional defiant disorder, and conduct disorder. James was prescribed Ritalin for hyperactivity, but was not otherwise involved in counselling or other treatment.

James was involved in drug trafficking at age 17. His family observed him with large sums of money, multiple cell phones, and drug-dealing paraphernalia (e.g., weight scales). At age 18, James' mother reported that James was a bully at home and suspected that he was using ecstasy and steroids. James told his probation officer that rival drug dealers had kidnapped him. He considered this to be an exciting part of his lifestyle. At age 19, James was attacked by a group of peers at a party and beaten to the point of requiring hospitalization, where he received stitches.

At age 20, James reported to his probation officer that he was aware that he had been upsetting his family, that his family wanted him to change, and that he also wanted to change. However, less than one year later, James was described by his probation officer as an expert at deflecting responsibility and minimizing his negative behaviour. During the period that James suggested that he wanted to change, James claimed that he was working with his father. However, it was discovered that James was using his claimed work with his father as a cover story while he resumed his involvement in drug trafficking. In effect, James' father was either not a suitable guardian, or James overlooked the risks of detection and did not care about his father's opinion or the potential consequences of losing his job. Although James attended treatment for people with histories of violent offending, his presence at group counseling sessions was disruptive because he was manipulative, controlling, and bullied and intimidated other participants. Such observations align with what has been written about the heightened tendency for people with psychopathy traits to disrupt the treatment progress of others (Olver, 2022). However, it also must be kept in mind that this is a single case study and so James' lack of meaningful participation in treatment should not be generalized to all youth with psychopathy traits. This case study is simply an illustrative example of social resistance; it does not confirm the robustness of this hypothesis across incarcerated youth scoring high on the PCL:YV.

At age 23, James received a lengthy sentence for a violent assault and kidnapping and was not released from custody until age 25. When discussing this offence with his probation officer, James made disparaging remarks about the victim and claimed that he would do it again if provoked. While living with his parents and sister, James gained employment working six days a week for a unionized construction company. One evening after work, he entered the room of his female cousin, started screaming at her, took off his shirt, threatened to punch her in the face, and then spat on her.

Between the ages 25 and 26, James became involved in a relationship with Jill. James told his probation officer that Jill had experienced severe abuse by family members growing up and that this abuse continued with her intimate partners. James suggested that he was committed to helping her and giving her a sense of family. One month into their relationship, the police were called to Jill's home. Police observed Jill with multiple injuries to her face, her cellphone was broken, and she reported that James had locked her inside her apartment and refused to let her leave. At age 26, James reported that he felt ashamed that his family was afraid of him. He blamed his aggression on his use of steroids. He eventually resumed his relationship with Jill, and they moved in together. Shortly thereafter, he explained to his probation officer that he did not like living with her. He reported that Jill was annoying him because she kept telling him whom not to hang out with. Again, someone in James' life was acting in the role of a capable guardian, but James ignored their requests. Two weeks later, James told his probation officer that Jill was smothering him and getting on his nerves, and that he did not want to go back to jail because of her. The probation officer interpreted this as James insinuating that he would assault Jill if she continued this behaviour. The probation officer informed James that he was responsible for managing his behaviour and emotions. James responded by muttering that he would break Jill's legs. This information was reported to the police. One week later, James and Jill got into another argument, and Jill informed James that he was no longer welcome in her apartment. That same evening, James moved in with a woman named Sarah and her young child.

Less than a week after moving in with Sarah, James resumed his relationship with Jill. Within a day of their reconciliation, Jill informed James' probation officer that he was not allowed to stay at her place because he had been threatening her and her property. The probation officer contacted the police, who were dispatched to Jill's residence and arrested James. The next day, Jill called James' probation officer to say that James had pushed her and threatened to damage her car. James met with his probation officer the following day. James was accompanied by a former gang member who wanted to mentor James to help him avoid criminal behaviour. Although this was viewed as a positive source of peer support, within a week, James grew tired of living with this person and moved back in with Jill.

After another breakdown in his relationship with Jill, James returned to living at Sarah's house. Shortly thereafter, James attended Jill's residence and initiated an argument, which resulted in neighbours calling the police. En route, police observed James repeatedly striking Jill. She suffered a broken nose, and several items from her house were either damaged or stolen by James. James was once again arrested, but this time he was held in custody. When released on bail several months later, James complained to his probation officer about how the criminal legal system had given him a reputation as someone who assaults women. While James was in custody, his peers became aware of his intimate partner violence offences. James blamed the criminal legal system for the trouble he was receiving from peers. While on bail, James moved back in with Sarah and her child. Police met with Sarah and asked her to keep James out of her home because he was a risk to her and her child. Rather than have James leave the home, Sarah indicated that she preferred to have her child move back in with the child's father instead. It was suspected that Sarah's decision was motivated by James paying Sarah's rent and supplying her with drugs. James and Sarah were eventually arrested by the police for drug trafficking. Police investigated James for assault and sexual assault against both Sarah and her child, though charges were ultimately not filed.

Two days after being arrested for drug trafficking, James told his probation officer that he was no longer living with Sarah because she was misinterpreting their relationship as being more serious than it was. Six days after this, James reported to his probation officer that he was back living with Sarah. Two weeks into this arrangement, police were called as Sarah was threatening to self-harm. James moved to a new apartment where he appeared to live alone. Within a month, police were called to Jill's residence because a neighbour heard screaming coming from the apartment. Police attended the residence where they found Jill bleeding and her face swollen. Jill's roommates reported that James had choked Jill, confined her to a bedroom, choked her cat, and threatened Jill that he would kill her cat. James was arrested, held in custody without bail, and eventually given a lengthy sentence. He remains in custody as of the most recent wave of data collection.

Explaining James' Case History through the Social Resistance Hypothesis

To review, James presented with multiple personality traits consistent with psychopathy. In addition to being diagnosed with conduct disorder, which is considered a precursor to antisocial personality disorder, James was consistently unempathetic toward his family members, reckless in his behaviour, and manipulative and duplicitous. A criminal legal system practitioner who completed the Spousal Assault Risk Assessment (Kropp et al., 1994) indicated that James displayed traits of jealousy and obsessiveness and engaged in victim blaming and displacement of responsibility (i.e., consistent with interpersonal and affective traits of psychopathy). At age 27, James claimed that he wanted to get married, start a family, and find a job. When asked about why he wanted these things, he mentioned that it would look good to the judge presiding over his intimate partner violence charges. Criminologists often refer to the "respectability package" as an indicator that a person is on the pathway to desistance (Giordano et al., 2002). James seemed to be interested in acquiring indicators of respectability but did not want these new social roles and responsibilities to affect his lifestyle. Readers may recall the case study of Justin (see Chapter 3), where Justin did not actually care about the well-being of his partner. Much like a car or other perceived status symbol, Justin cared about his girlfriend because of how she reflected upon him. James appeared to have similar attitudes.

When it came to James' social environment, there were a variety of reasons for optimism. James' family, although sometimes enabling, clearly cared about James and wanted to see his behaviour change. By all accounts, they certainly did not have positive attitudes toward crime. James' mother especially focused on helping him follow the conditions of his probation order, was willing to punish James' negative behaviour, and provided James with a place to stay when he got into trouble. In general, James always had housing. He experienced some residential instability, but this was primarily of his own choosing, as he moved at will between different intimate partners' residences. Changes in residency did not appear to be due to financial difficulties. Although he earned income through drug trafficking, James was often also gainfully employed. He received on-the-job training and mentorship, including working with and for his father. Although most of James' peers were involved in the criminal legal system, James also had older peers who were willing to mentor him and help keep him from continuing to be involved in criminal behaviour. James was also involved in intimate partner relationships with women who were, at least prior to meeting James, not involved in criminal behaviour.

Despite these sources of social support, few members of the ISVYOS sample were more criminally active than James. Between the ages of 12 and

25, James incurred more than three dozen convictions and spent 5 years in prison. Although employment is supposed to prevent opportunities for offending and alter one's identity, James' employment was used as a cover for his involvement in drug trafficking. His employment did not prevent him from engaging in criminal behaviour, including assaults against his intimate partners and family members. While James always had places to live, those with whom he lived were commonly the target of his violent outbursts. Although intimate partner relationships are considered a source of social bonds that deter involvement in criminal behaviour, many of James' convictions came from perpetrating intimate partner violence. Several other violent offences were perpetrated against vulnerable family members. In summary, James' sources of informal social control were not a turning point. In fact, at times, informal social controls provided additional opportunities for violence. James' violence toward intimate partners and family members, yet his reliance on those same family members for housing, in many ways resembles how Cleckley (1976) described "Max" as his prototypical example of the manifestation of psychopathy traits.

James' case history illustrates an example of the social resistance hypothesis and why intervening on psychopathy traits may be necessary before positive social outcomes have their desired effect. Failing to address the types of risk factors James presented with (e.g., psychopathy traits, criminogenic lifestyle, misogynistic attitudes) implies that informal social controls will not act as turning points that promote desistance. There was no evidence of the "desistance by default" hypothesis (Laub & Sampson, 2003). Informal social controls did not have their anticipated effect. However, this is just one case. The analyses in the remainder of this chapter examine whether evidence of the social resistance hypothesis observed in James' background generalized across the PCL:YV Cohort.

Testing the Interaction between Psychopathy and Social/Health Outcomes

Treatment effect heterogeneity was examined by performing a series of generalized estimating equations (see Chapter 5) that included interaction effects between PCL:YV total scores and early adulthood measures of: informal social control, positive criminogenic networks in prison (i.e., criminal social capital), negative criminogenic networks in prison, and substance use issues. Each interaction effect was examined in terms of both between-group differences (i.e., differences between high and low scores on the PCL:YV) and within-group differences (i.e., differences among ISVYOS participants who scored high on the PCL:YV). The between-group analyses facilitated comparisons of, for example, whether informal social control influences reductions in reoffending regardless of a person's score on the PCL:YV. The within-group analyses facilitated evaluations of, for example, whether youth with high PCL:YV scores reoffended at a similar rate regardless of differences in their level of other risk/protective factors.

The Interaction between Psychopathy and Informal Social Control

Beginning with informal social control, in terms of main effects (i.e., not considering moderation), consistent with Chapters 5–7, PCL:YV scores had a significant and positive influence on the rate of convictions in adulthood. CRNA informal social control scale scores had a significant and negative influence on the rate of convictions in adulthood. Most relevant to the questions addressed in this chapter, a significant interaction effect was observed between PCL:YV total scores and the CRNA informal social control scale on the average yearly rate of convictions in adulthood. Figure 8.2 helps visualize this interaction. Figure 8.2 provides separate plots of the relationship between informal social control and the average yearly rate of convictions for (1) participants who scored less than 30 on the PCL:YV and (2) participants who scored 30 or greater.

Interpreting the analyses from a between-group perspective, the association between higher CRNA informal social control scale scores and fewer convictions was stronger for participants with lower scores on the PCL:YV. People with psychopathy traits were more resistant to the impact of informal social control on offending. The right-hand side of the x-axis in Figure 8.2 shows participants with high levels of informal social control. Those who scored less than 30 on the PCL:YV (dark shading) had nearly zero convictions. However, those who scored 30 or higher (light shading) averaged nearly two convictions per year of age during the follow-up period, despite also having high levels of informal social control.

Looking at the analyses from a within-group perspective, among those who scored high on the PCL:YV, the number of convictions incurred per year is nearly identical across the full range of scores on the informal social control scale.[1] For the line in Figure 8.2 representing high PCL:YV scores, whether looking at the very left of the x-axis (lack of informal social

---

[1] Chapter 7 demonstrated that informal social control partially mediated the relationship between psychopathy traits and convictions. The findings here imply that this mediation effect may not be equal across different levels of PCL:YV scores (i.e., there is stronger evidence of mediation at lower rather than higher PCL:YV scores).

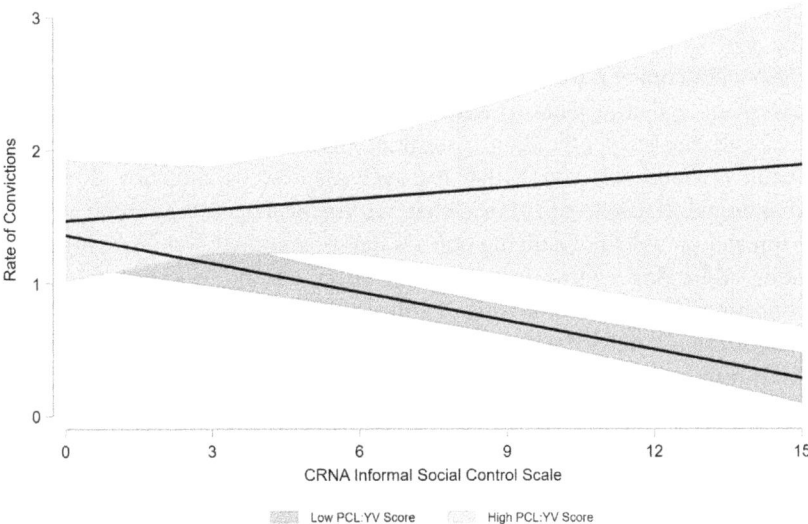

Figure 8.2 Examining the interaction effect of psychopathy traits and informal social control on the rate of convictions in adulthood.

Notes. Psychopathy traits measured in adolescence via the PCL:YV. A high score represents a score of 30 or greater. A low score represents a score of less than 30. Informal social control is measured in early adulthood via the CRNA. Convictions over the follow-up period are measured beginning in the year of age following the measurement of informal social control.
The shaded area represents a 95 percent confidence interval.

control) or very right of the x-axis (high informal social control), the rate of offending in adulthood is virtually the same. Looking within the high PCL:YV group, the line is nearly flat. Looking within the low PCL:YV group, the line clearly slopes downward. Informal social control influences lower rates of offending within the group that scored low on the PCL:YV. However, informal social control did not influence lower rates of offending within the group that scored high on the PCL:YV.

The examination of the interaction between PCL:YV total scores and the CRNA informal social control scale provides evidence supporting the social resistance hypothesis. For Robert, acquiring a stable job was insufficient to act as a turning point or to promote desistance. Robert worked as a heavy-duty mechanic and was paid well above the minimum wage. However, he also felt that selling drugs was more profitable. He mismanaged his finances and regularly used cocaine. His drug of choice eventually shifted from cocaine to crack cocaine. He subsequently quit his job and went on disability. Anger control problems that emerged in adolescence continued in adulthood. Robert incurred 13 convictions in adolescence and 47 convictions between the ages 18 and 35. He spent over 3,000 days incarcerated between the ages 18 and 35. For individuals like Robert, making assumptions that they will acquire a job and then desist by default neglects the complex treatment and intervention needs associated with psychopathy, substance use, and persistent offending. Assertions that desistance occurs by default (Laub & Sampson, 2003), that the assessment of psychopathy should be abandoned (Larsen, 2019), or that treatment is unnecessary (Laub & Sampson, 2003) risk justifying policies that prematurely terminate interventions addressing substance use issues, anger control, and mental health concerns influencing offending. Laub and Sampson's (2003) perspective that nothing is needed when it comes to correctional intervention resembles Martinson's (1974) now-debunked (Gendreau & Ross, 1983) report that developmental treatment programs in corrections are ineffective.

The Interaction between Psychopathy and Other Social/Health Outcomes

The remaining interaction analyses (see Figures 8.3 to 8.5) were not significant and are therefore described jointly. The absence of significant

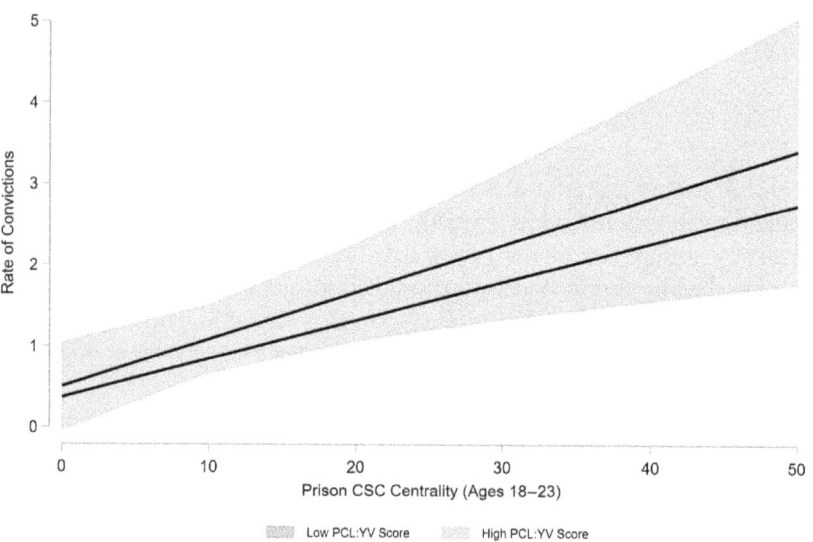

Figure 8.3 Relationship between PCL:YV scores and positive tie degree centrality.
Notes. Psychopathy traits measured in adolescence via the PCL:YV. A high score represents a score of 30 or greater. A low score represents a score of less than 30. Positive ties represent different types of prison-based criminal social capital (CSC), including mutual conflict or where one party was the clear aggressor (e.g., where an ego victimized an alter or where an alter victimized an ego). Convictions measured at each year of age from ages 24 to 29. The shaded area represents a 95 percent confidence interval.

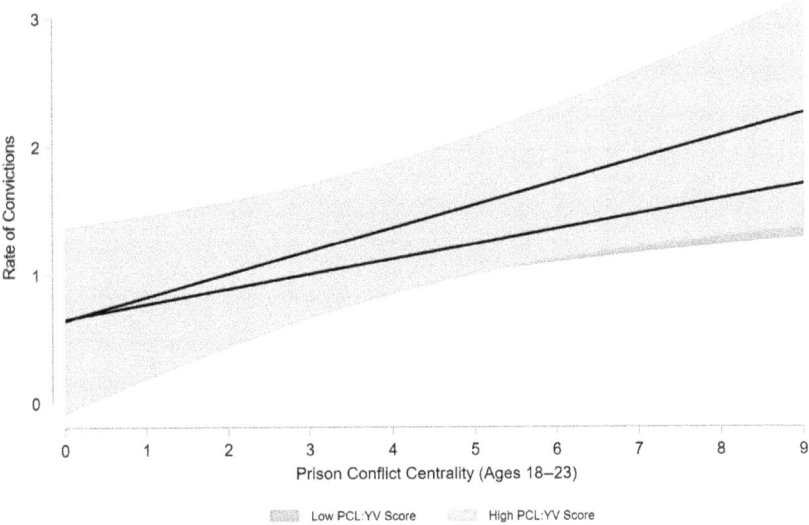

Figure 8.4 Relationship between PCL:YV scores and negative tie degree centrality.
Notes. Psychopathy traits measured in adolescence via the PCL:YV. A high score represents a score of 30 or greater. A low score represents a score of less than 30. Negative ties represent different types of prison-based conflict, including mutual conflict or where one party was the clear aggressor (e.g., where an ego victimized an alter or where an alter victimized an ego). The shaded area represents a 95 percent confidence interval. Convictions measured at each year of age from ages 24 to 29.

interaction effects indicates that the measures of criminogenic networks (both prison social capital and negative networks) and substance use issues related to reconvictions similarly across different levels of PCL:YV scores. Thus, for example, from a between-group perspective, high levels of prison social capital did not significantly increase the frequency of convictions for people with high PCL:YV scores compared to those with low scores. The same interpretation applies to negative criminogenic prison networks and substance use issues as well.

From a within-group perspective, the interpretation differs somewhat from the between-group perspective. It was not the case that individuals with high PCL:YV scores were fully resistant to the impact of moderators. For example, those with high PCL:YV scores who also had substance use issues averaged higher rates of convictions compared to their counterparts with high PCL:YV scores but without substance use issues. The same interpretation applies to the other two moderators. From this within-group perspective, the three analyses provide evidence consistent with the social

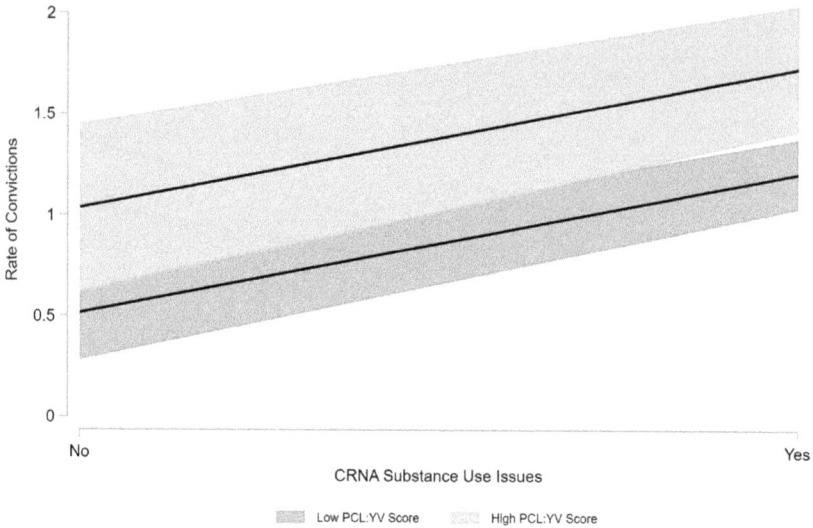

Figure 8.5 The relationship between PCL:YV total scores and a person's CRNA-based substance use rating in early adulthood.

Notes. Psychopathy traits measured in adolescence via the PCL:YV. High score represents a score of 30 or greater on the PCL:YV. A low score represents a score of less than 30 on the PCL:YV. Informal social control is measured in early adulthood via the CRNA. Convictions over the follow-up period are measured beginning in the year of age following the measurement of informal social control. The shaded area represents a 95 percent confidence interval.

amplification hypothesis. Among ISVYOS participants with a score of at least 30 on the PCL:YV, substance use issues, high levels of prison-based criminal social capital, and high levels of negative ties within prison amplified rates of offending compared to counterparts with lower levels on these moderators. The key to interpreting the within-group comparisons in Figures 8.3 to 8.5 is to examine the slope of the "High PCL:YV" score line. A noticeable change in the slope across values of the x-axis indicates that not all people with a high PCL:YV score have the same level of offending. This contrasts with Figure 8.2, where the rate of convictions is nearly identical across different levels of informal social control for the high PCL:YV group.

Consistency of Findings across Different Representations of PCL:YV Scores

I did not test interaction effects between the 4 moderators and the 4 factors of the PCL:YV, as this would have required 16 different analyses and raised concerns about Type I error (i.e., rejecting a null hypothesis when it is actually true). However, I reran analyses using the three-factor model and reached the same conclusions. I also reran analyses with the 13 core PCL: YV items, as identified by the item response theory analyses in Chapter 4, and again reached the same conclusions.

Chapter Summary

Treatment effect heterogeneity implies that, when compared to people without psychopathy traits, people with psychopathy traits respond differently to the same social and health circumstances. Understanding whether the influence of informal social control on lower rates of offending is limited to persons who are relatively low risk (e.g., those without psychopathy traits) is a critical gap to address in studies of offending over the life-course (Nguyen & Loughran, 2018). Examining the relationship between psychopathy and offending through the lens of treatment effect heterogeneity can help identify whether treatment strategies that are effective with lower risk populations will also have a similar impact on people with psychopathy traits.

The desistance by default hypothesis posits that social or health factors influence desistance from criminal behaviour similarly, regardless of the presence or absence of psychopathy traits. By contrast, treatment effect heterogeneity suggests that the interplay between psychopathy traits and social/health factors has implications for the likelihood of offending. There are different hypotheses about the mechanisms through which treatment effect heterogeneity operates. According to the social amplification hypothesis, the co-occurrence of psychopathy traits and social/health risk factors increases the likelihood of reoffending. According to the social protection hypothesis, the co-occurrence of psychopathy traits and social or health protective factors increases the likelihood of desistance from criminal behaviour. According to the social resistance hypothesis, the co-occurrence of psychopathy traits and social/health factors has a weaker or negligible impact on reoffending compared to the impact of the same factors for individuals with low psychopathy traits. The social resistance hypothesis implies that underlying psychopathy traits may need to be addressed before positive social/health factors can influence desistance from offending.

This chapter examined four social/health consequences, previously discussed in Chapter 6, that could have implications for the strength of the relationship between psychopathy and convictions. These four measures included informal social control, criminal social capital, the size of negative criminogenic prison ego networks, and substance use issues. In line with a social resistance perspective, only people who scored low on the PCL:YV benefited from positive sources of informal social control. People with low PCL:YV scores and high levels of informal social control were convicted of fewer offences compared to people with low PCL:YV scores who had low levels of informal social control. Conversely, among people with high PCL:YV scores, level of informal social control had little bearing on their rate of convictions. This finding is also consistent with the risk assessment literature's emphasis that protective factors may not operate as anticipated for youth with psychopathy traits (de Vogel et al., 2009). This observation contrasts with the social protection hypothesis, which posits that people with psychopathy traits would have more to gain (e.g., a larger impact on reductions in reoffending) from a positive social environment. With respect to the other three measures, there was evidence of a social amplification effect, in which the presence of these risk factors (prison ego networks and substance use issues) combined with high scores on the PCL:YV was associated with higher levels of offending compared to high scores on the PCL:YV but low levels of the aforementioned risk factors.

It is not especially surprising that people with psychopathy traits were resistant to positive sources of informal social control. Personality disorders are associated with maladaptive social and identity functioning (Cooke et al., 2004; Sharp & Wall, 2021), even in positive social environments (Forth et al., 2022). Psychopathy is associated with a tendency to act in socially inappropriate ways while in adult roles like marriage and employment (Brazil & Volk, 2022). Qualitative interviews with adults who previously partnered with individuals exhibiting psychopathy traits have documented experiences of financial abuse, social isolation, and emotional, professional, and physical harm (Forth et al., 2022). Additionally, employees of people with psychopathy traits have reported decreased job satisfaction (Boddy, 2014).

The mechanisms linking informal social controls to desistance, such as altering identities, forming close bonds, and knifing off from negative peers (Laub & Sampson, 2003), may not elicit the presumed uniform response when psychopathy traits are present (also see Polaschek & Skeem, 2018). Through manipulation, grandiosity, and pathological lying, people with psychopathy traits may exploit their adult roles and relationships to avoid punishment by projecting the appearance of a "respectability package" (Giordano et al., 2002, p. 311). Rather than acting as a hook for change, at least in the shortterm, people with psychopathy traits may establish adult roles and leverage perceptions of a "respectability package" to create opportunities for offending and avoid punishment (Forth et al., 2022).

This is consistent with descriptions of the relationship between psychopathy and a fast life history strategy that prioritizes mating effort over long-term relationships (Kardum et al., 2017). This does not imply that treatment strategies are ineffective; rather, it suggests that interventions may need to concurrently focus on reducing psychopathy traits and improving a person's social environment (Caldwell, 2011).

CHAPTER 9

Birth Cohort and Period Effects
Implications for the Relationship between Psychopathy and Offending

To this point in the book, I have only considered the individual-level characteristics of Incarcerated Serious and Violent Young Offender Study (ISVYOS) participants. Some of these individual-level characteristics are internal to the individual (e.g., psychopathy traits). Others reflect their immediate social environment (e.g., family background, peer network, informal social control). A fair criticism of research on psychopathy is that too much focus is placed on the individual and their immediate social environment (see Verona & Fox, 2025). For example, Chapter 8 focuses solely on the interaction between psychopathy traits and other individual-level characteristics. It is also possible that broader contextual factors beyond the individual may influence the relationship between psychopathy and offending.

The focus of this chapter is on whether birth cohort membership and exposure to different youth justice system philosophies have implications for the relationship between psychopathy traits and offending. Social structures have changed, and these changes have shaped the development of successive generations born into different historical contexts. An overlooked issue in criminal legal system decision-making is whether risk assessment instruments continue to serve as valid predictors of future offending for new generations and those exposed to different criminal legal system policies. Addressing such questions is important because risk assessment tools are regularly used to make decisions about sentencing severity. Although the PCL:YV is not a risk assessment tool, the assessment of psychopathy is typically included in risk assessment protocols. Although the question of birth cohort differences in the relationship between psychopathy and offending has not been addressed empirically, there are a variety of reasons, detailed later in this chapter, for why researchers should consider whether the impact of psychopathy traits on offending remains consistent across different generations and historical periods.

Studies have emphasized the importance of examining the relationship between psychopathy traits and offending across gender (Klein Haneveld et al., 2022), ethnicity (Hawes et al., 2018), and culture (Pechorro et al., 2017). This research has shown, for example, that the statistical association between Psychopathy Checklist: Youth Version (PCL:YV) scores and reoffending is similar between Indigenous youth and White youth (McCuish et al., 2018b). Less attention has been given to broader structural contexts, such as whether younger generations, who were not included in the original validation samples of measures like the PCL:YV and risk assessments like the Historical–Clinical–Risk Management–20 (HCR-20), exhibit higher levels of offending if they score higher on psychopathy measures.

Chapter Goals and Analyses

The analyses in this chapter respond to calls for a more ecological approach to research on personality and offending by considering both individual characteristics and the broader social environment in which individuals are embedded (e.g., beyond proximal relationships with friends and family members; see Verona & Fox, 2025). The analyses in this chapter address two questions using generalized estimating equations. First, I test whether birth cohort membership moderates the relationship between psychopathy traits in adolescence and offending that persists through adulthood (see Chapter 8 for an overview of moderation analysis). The study of birth cohorts is premised on the idea that the era in which someone is born shapes exposure to different structural contexts that may influence behaviour (Ryder, 1965). Second, I test whether criminal legal system legislation represents a unique period effect that conditions the relationship between psychopathy traits in adolescence and offending that persists through adulthood. A period effect is a specific structural context that may apply across people born at different times. In all analyses, I control for demographic characteristics and risk/protective factors described in Chapter 3. I also control for informal social control in emerging adulthood to account for more proximal environmental circumstances.

Measuring Cohort and Period Effects

With respect to birth cohort membership, ISVYOS participants were born between 1979 and 1998. The median birth year for the sample is 1984. Birth cohorts are sometimes defined by the decade in which they were born. However, it is difficult to argue that someone born in 1989 (an eighties kid) experienced a historical context that more closely resembled the experience of someone born in 1980 than someone born in 1990 (a nineties kid). For the main analyses, I treated birth cohort status as an interval-level variable ranging from 1979 to 1998. One limitation with this approach is that macro-level events and historical contexts do not necessarily improve or worsen in a linear fashion. For example, unemployment may increase from 1998 to 1999, but by 2000, unemployment may be lower than in 1998. In regression analyses, it is assumed that each one-unit increase in year of birth has the same impact on the dependent variable. This assumption may hold for a measure of psychopathy, but is less plausible for birth cohort status. Thus, to examine the reliability of findings, I also created birth cohort groups that resembled those used by Neil and Sampson (2021). The birth cohort groupings represented participants who were born within five-year intervals that captured the following periods: 1979–1983 ($n = 229$); 1984–1988 ($n = 124$); 1989–1993 ($n = 141$); and 1994–1998 ($n = 24$).[1]

Figure 9.1 shows differences in macro-level environmental circumstances in the Province of British Columbia. For each cohort group, I examine conditions in British Columbia when cohort members were 12 years old.[2] Although not perfectly linear, the data indicate a general improvement in quality of life. Younger generations of ISVYOS participants tended to come of age during periods of greater prosperity. For example, Figure 9.1 shows that the average maternal age at childbirth has increased over time in British Columbia. A younger maternal age at childbirth is associated with an increased likelihood of the child's physical aggression (Tzoumakis et al., 2014) and a variety of other negative outcomes (Tzoumakis et al., 2018). Members of more recent birth cohorts therefore came of age during periods in which their peers' mothers tended to be older at childbirth. Therefore, even if an individual's own mother was relatively young at childbirth, their peers tended to be born into comparatively positive circumstances, reflecting broader structural improvements and a relatively lower likelihood of aggression and other difficult behaviours.

To capture period effects, I determined whether an ISVYOS participant was incarcerated under Canada's Young Offenders Act or Youth Criminal Justice Act. Differences between the two acts are described later in the

---

[1] I excluded 18 participants who, for reasons that were outlined in Chapter 5 (e.g., mortality), were missing follow-up data regarding convictions.
[2] For each participant, I identified the year in which they turned 12 years old and then pulled data from Statistics Canada for that corresponding year.

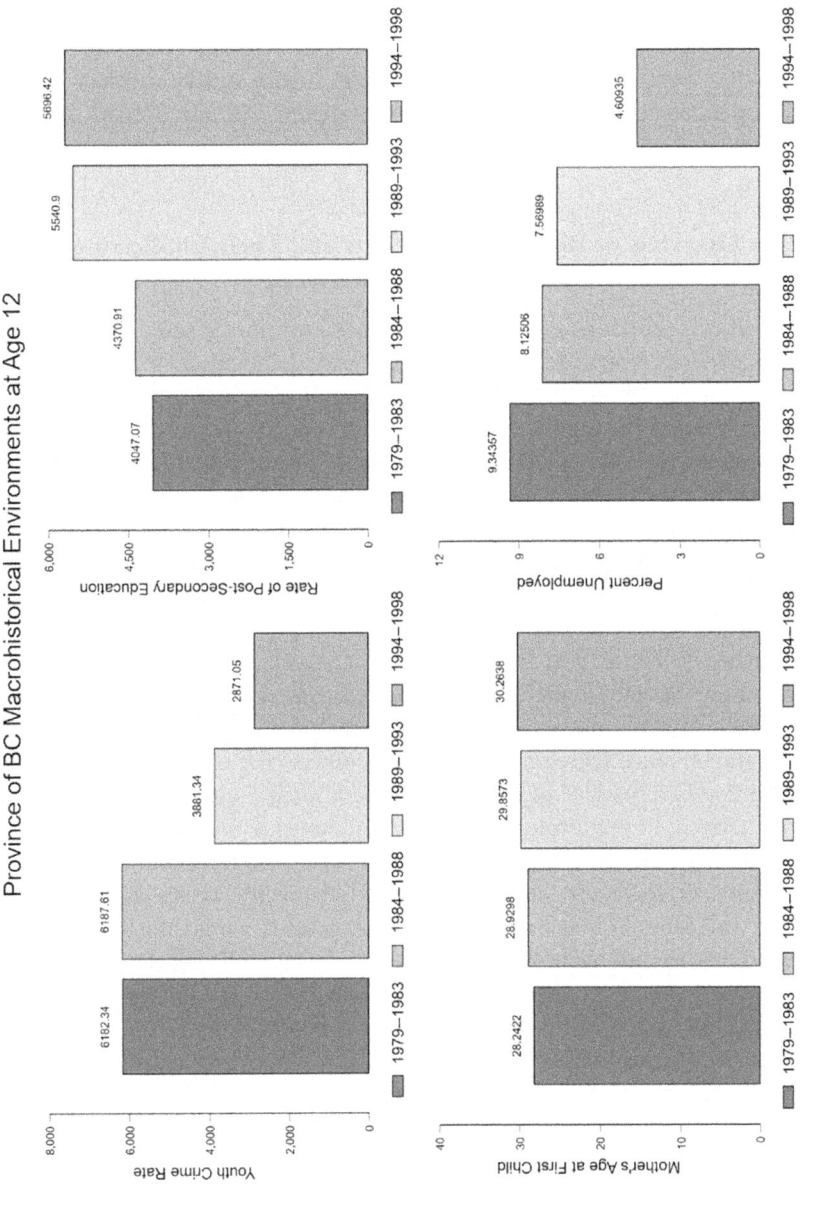

Figure 9.1 Macro-historical environmental characteristics in the Province of British Columbia, Canada.

Notes: Each bar chart reflects the provincial average or rate for each cohort grouping when a member within that cohort was 12 years old. For example, for the 1994–1998 birth cohort, the youth crime rate represents the average crime rate (arrests) in British Columbia per 100,000 between 2006 and 2010.

chapter. The ISVYOS began data collection in 1998 and took a data collection hiatus starting in 2002 and ending in 2005. Participants recruited between 1998 and 2002 were adjudicated under the Young Offenders Act ($n = 351$). Participants recruited between 2005 and 2011 were adjudicated under the Youth Criminal Justice Act ($n = 184$). The data collection hiatus ensured that no participant was adjudicated under both acts.

An Overview of Birth Cohort Effects and Their Implications for Psychopathy Research

Birth cohorts represent groups of individuals born in the same year or era who experience macro-level events (e.g., wars, pandemics, recessions) at the same or similar ages. Ryder (1965) was among the first to describe how birth cohorts can be used to help understand individual-level differences in development over the life-course. Differences in individual-level development occur when certain cohorts are exposed to unique historical events. For example, the Silent Generation (1928–1945) directly experienced the impact of World War II during childhood. No other generation's childhood included this experience. This is not to say that all members of the Silent Generation had identical experiences during World War II or that the impact of World War II was identical across all members of the Silent Generation. People of the same birth cohort do not necessarily respond identically to the same social shifts or historical contexts (Ryder, 1965). For example, racial segregation impacts members of the same birth cohort differently. The practice of redlining in the United States restricted mortgage financing in predominantly Black neighbourhoods (Bradford, 1979). This practice was a direct attempt to curtail wealth accumulation for Black Americans. Accordingly, although anyone born in the 1920s came of age during redlining, White Americans in such cohorts would not have been harmed, and in fact were likely to have benefited, while Black Americans born at this time were clearly negatively impacted (see Linning and Eck, 2023). Thus, accounting for intracohort differences in factors such as gender, race, and criminal propensity[3] is also important to fully understand the impact of macro-level structural changes and policies.

---

[3] Ryder (1965) might disagree with this position, given that he emphasized that a person "arrives on the social scene literally without sociopsychological configuration ... agencies of socialization and social control are designed to give the new member a shape appropriate to the societal design" (p. 844).

For several decades, Ryder's emphasis on birth cohorts received minimal attention in research on criminal behaviour. The limited research has mostly examined differences in the aggregate age–crime curve across different eras (Farrington, 1986; Steffensmeier et al., 1989). The age–crime curve, which plots rates of offending across age groups, typically shows that crime rates rise in mid-adolescence, peak sharply in late adolescence, and then swiftly decline. Data from the United States and Australia indicate that the aggregate age–crime curve's traditionally sharp peak in adolescence has flattened for more recent cohorts (Payne & Piquero, 2020; Tuttle, 2023). More recent birth cohorts thus appear to have lower peak rates of criminal legal system involvement. Declining crime rates have implications for tests of the relationship between risk assessment instruments, individual items from risk assessment instruments (e.g., psychopathy), and reoffending. Specifically, base rates of reoffending impact statistical prediction. If reoffending base rates are lower for younger generations, then there is the possibility of overestimating their risk of reoffending if relying on older data.

Actuarial risk assessment instruments operate on the basis that people with high and low propensities for violent recidivism can be distinguished. Targeting high propensity individuals with effective interventions should lead to reductions in recidivism. Conversely, the ability to identify people with a low likelihood of recidivism helps avoid imposing restrictions or requirements on individuals unlikely to threaten public safety (Imrey & Dawid, 2015). The issue is that risk assessment instruments that create categories of low, medium, and high risk based on samples born in the 1970s may not be valid indicators of the risk of recidivism for people born in the 1990s. The concern is that someone with a high propensity for criminal behaviour who was born in 2005 has a likelihood of recidivism at age 18 that is comparable to the risk of recidivism at age 18 for a person born in 1995 who has a low propensity for criminal behaviour. Helmus et al. (2009) reported that people with the same risk assessment score but sampled from different years or locations had different probabilities of recidivism. To extend this logic to psychopathy, two individuals with the same PCL:YV score may differ in their probability of recidivism depending on when they were born or where they were detained and punished. If reoffending rates vary dramatically across time, widely different conclusions could be drawn about the risk of reoffending for two people, even if those two people received the same PCL:YV score (see the discussion by Helmus et al., 2012 for similar logic).

Addressing whether being born in a specific era has implications for the strength of the relationship between risk factors and offending is difficult.

Rarely does a single dataset include (1) people born in different time periods, (2) the same risk factor measured in the same way, and (3) offending measured at the same ages across cohorts. For example, it is common to have a dataset where people are born in different years, and the same risk assessment instrument is administered for each participant. However, the third criterion is often not satisfied. For the follow-up period, some participants are in their forties, others in their thirties, others in their twenties. Given what we know about the age–crime curve, it becomes difficult to compare cohort effects when offending is examined at different periods of the life-course. With such research designs, it is not possible to examine whether the influence of psychopathy on offending during a specific age or developmental stage varies across birth cohorts.

The Project on Human Development in Chicago Neighborhoods (PHDCN+) is one of the few studies suited to examining the relationship between criminal propensity and offending across different birth cohorts. The PHDCN+ includes a behaviour-based measure of self-control derived from Achenbach's Child Behavioural Checklist (CBCL; Achenbach, 1997), repeated measures of arrest from adolescence into adulthood, and a variety of other individual-level and community-level risk factors (Sampson et al., 2022). A trio of studies using data from the PHDCN+ provided a framework for examining birth cohort differences in the relationship between criminal propensity (measured via low self-control) and offending (Montana et al., 2023; Neil et al., 2021; Neil & Sampson, 2021). These studies reported that participants born in the 1990s averaged lower arrest rates than participants born in the 1980s. The difference between cohorts in arrest rates was so dramatic that younger cohorts with low self-control had arrest rates comparable to older cohorts with high self-control (Neil & Sampson, 2021).

Based on findings from the PHDCN+, Sampson and Smith (2021, p. 19) suggested that "when a person is" (i.e., the sociohistorical period a person is born into) is more informative of their offending trajectory than "who the person is" (i.e., their level of criminal propensity). Growing up in eras with lower crime rates has been referred to as winning "the birth lottery of history" (Neil & Sampson, 2021) because doing so decreases one's risk of involvement in criminal behaviour (Shen et al., 2020), including violent offences like homicide (Lu et al., 2024). Conversely, being involved in crime during eras with lower crime rates may imply that criminal legal system decision-making will be more biased. Specifically, contemporary cohorts who are high in criminal propensity may be wrongly viewed through the same lens as older cohorts with the same level of criminal propensity. However, similarities in risk factors do not imply an equal likelihood of reoffending when comparing across cohorts. Relying on information about the likelihood of reoffending that was derived from older cohorts when making decisions about individuals from contemporary cohorts could lead to overestimating the likelihood of offending.

Montana et al. (2023) found that the predictive accuracy of markers of criminal propensity was lower for younger generations compared to older ones. The research by Montana et al. has important implications for whether psychopathy continues to be relevant to the prediction of offending among contemporary cohorts. It also has implications for the appropriateness of risk assessment ratings that are not updated with data from contemporary birth cohorts.

There are two caveats to the PHDCN+ research design that justify further examination of the relationship between birth cohorts, criminal propensity, and offending. First, different birth cohorts from the PHDCN+ received different versions of the CBCL used to measure self-control (Neil & Sampson, 2021). It is possible that differences in the relationship between propensity and offending across birth cohorts resulted from differences in how propensity was measured. The ISVYOS avoids this issue by using the PCL:YV for all participants, regardless of birth cohort. Second, self-control is only one of several constructs used to measure criminal propensity. The relationship between criminal propensity and reoffending varies depending on how propensity is measured (e.g., psychopathy vs. low self-control; see Wiebe, 2003). Additional research is therefore needed to examine different measures of criminal propensity, especially those routinely included in risk assessment instruments.

An Overview of Period Effects and Their Implications for Psychopathy Research

A period effect reflects a macro-level event that influences people born in different generations. For example, the coronavirus disease 2019 (COVID-19) pandemic may represent a key period impacting criminal behaviour (Hodgkinson & Andresen, 2020). Although the COVID-19 pandemic was experienced by everyone from Baby Boomers to Gen Z, it is plausible that period effects are experienced more strongly by specific birth cohorts. The same historical event can amplify generational differences in development because individuals respond to events differently depending on their age (Ryder, 1965; Yang & Land, 2013). For instance, a recession may have a stronger impact on younger generations seeking employment compared to older generations who are in retirement.

The analyses in this chapter considered exposure to unique criminal legal system legislation as a specific type of period effect. Among the PCL:YV Cohort, 351 participants were exposed to the Young Offenders Act (1984–2003), whereas 184 participants were exposed to the Youth Criminal Justice Act (2003–present). The differences in these legal systems, summarized in the next section, may reflect a period-specific effect that moderates the relationship between psychopathy and reoffending.

The Young Offenders Act vs. The Youth Criminal Justice Act

The Young Offenders Act (YOA) and the Youth Criminal Justice Act (YCJA) both specified rehabilitation and punishment as goals of the youth justice system. However, the YOA lacked a clear hierarchy in its organizing principles, and the result was substantial variability in judicial decisions regarding sentencing. The YOA lacked clear guidelines for when to use incarceration vs. when to use community-based sentencing options like probation. Faced with ambiguity, Canadian judges appeared to err on the side of incarceration as a sentencing option (Bala et al., 2009). In contrast, the YCJA's guiding principles made it clear when to prioritize diversionary measures or community-based sentences over more punitive custody sentences. The YCJA emphasized that holding youth accountable through meaningful (i.e., proportionate) consequences was the best way to protect the public. These different philosophies contributed to higher rates of incarceration under the YOA compared to the YCJA. This idea bears out in the ISVYOS data. Participants adjudicated under the YOA were incarcerated for less serious offences and had fewer risk factors compared to participants adjudicated under the YCJA (McCuish et al., 2021).

The YOA and the YCJA assign different weights to the relevance of recidivism sentencing premiums,[4] proportionality, and deterrence. This implies that youth with psychopathy traits under the YOA were punished according to different sentencing principles compared to youth with psychopathy traits who were adjudicated under the YCJA. Compared to the YOA, sentencing under the YCJA was more attuned to issues of proportionality. The YCJA mandated that youth receive shorter sentences

---

[4] Recidivism sentencing premiums reflect policies where an individual is given a lengthier sentence on the basis of their prior criminal behaviour (Roberts, 2008).

than an adult would receive for the same offence. In contrast, welfare-based decision-making under the YOA resulted in a tendency to give youth more punitive sanctions compared to what an adult would receive for the same offence. The goal of the YOA was to use a short, sharp, shock approach to sentencing to deter youth from future offending (Cesaroni & Bala, 2008). In contrast, deterrence was explicitly absent from sentencing policies under the YCJA. YCJA sentencing instead emphasized proportionality and rehabilitation, even when incarceration sentences were used (Bala et al., 2009). Under the YCJA, case law decisions from the Supreme Court of Canada determined that judges could not rely on deterrence as part of their reasons for sentencing (see R. v. B.W.P and R. v. D.P). Thus, for offences like simple assault, youth with psychopathy traits likely received more punitive sanctions under the YOA compared to the YCJA.

The differences in justice system principles between the two acts are correlated with differences in crime rates. Under the YCJA, the rate of incarceration was about 10 times lower compared to the peak rate of incarceration under the YOA (i.e., approximately 70 per 100,000 youth; Statistics Canada, 2024a). Based on research in the United States, growing up in eras with higher rates of incarceration increases the likelihood of one's own involvement in the criminal legal system (Shen et al., 2020). If such findings generalize to British Columbia, ISVYOS participants with psychopathy traits who were adjudicated under the YOA would be expected to have higher rates of reoffending compared to participants with psychopathy traits who were adjudicated under the YCJA. If risk assessment instruments and associated risk factors overestimate the likelihood of reoffending in eras with lower crime rates (e.g., Montana et al., 2023), then the predictive validity of the PCL:YV may be weaker for participants adjudicated under the YCJA. This idea was empirically tested in later sections of this chapter.

Does Birth Cohort Membership Moderate the Relationship between Psychopathy and Offending?

Bivariate analyses were performed as a starting point for understanding the underlying data. When cohorts were defined as each birth year ranging from 1979 to 1998, a significant and positive correlation was observed between PCL:YV scores and year of birth ($r = 0.158$; $p < 0.001$). Being born more recently was associated with higher PCL:YV scores. Figure 9.2 shows the distribution of PCL:YV total scores across birth cohort groupings. According to an analysis of variance (ANOVA) comparing means

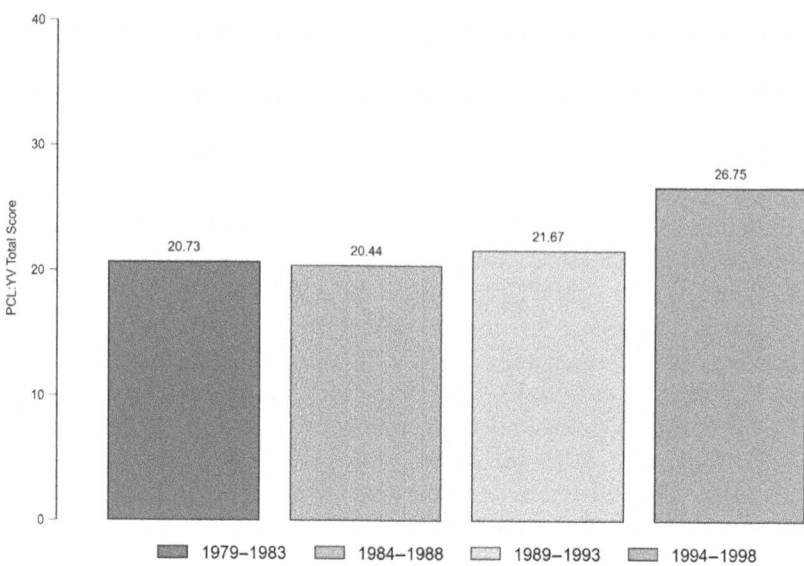

Figure 9.2 The distribution of PCL:YV total scores across participants from different birth cohorts.

across the four cohort groups indicated that the youngest birth cohort had significantly higher PCL:YV scores compared to each of the other three cohort groups. In terms of birth cohorts and convictions, a significant relationship was not observed when examining the correlation between birth cohort year and the annual rate of convictions ($r = 0.080$; $p = 0.074$). However, when looking at cohort subgroups, per an ANOVA analysis, the youngest birth cohort averaged a significantly higher annual rate of convictions compared to each of the other birth cohort groupings. Mean differences are shown in Figure 9.3. As mentioned earlier, it is possible that the relationship between birth cohort membership and convictions is not linear. The ANOVA analysis reiterates the importance of defining birth cohorts in different ways, as improvements in macro-level environmental circumstances may not increase linearly over time.

Figures 9.2 and 9.3 reiterate that psychopathy traits and offending tended to be higher in younger cohort groupings. It could be tempting to view these findings as supporting John Dilulio's (1995) claims that a wave of youth "superpredators" would emerge in more recent birth cohorts. Keep in mind that more recent ISVYOS birth cohorts were incarcerated under the YCJA. A goal of the YCJA was to reserve custody

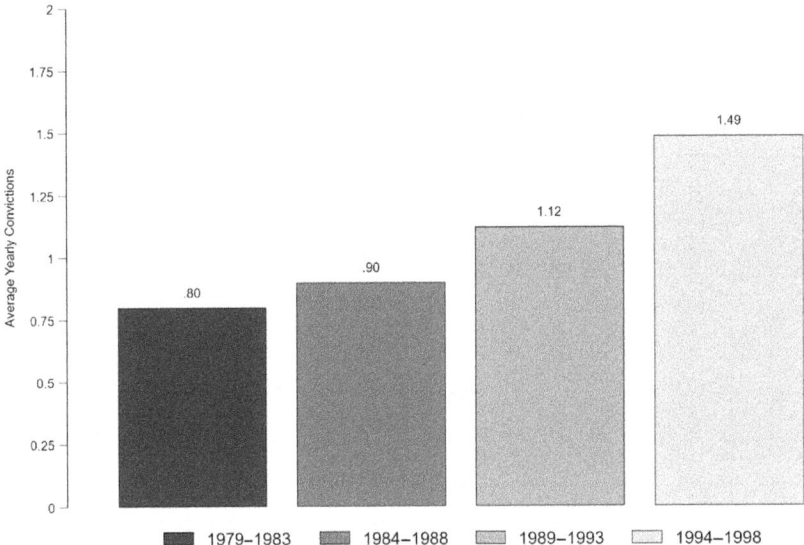

Figure 9.3 The distribution of convictions across participants from different birth cohorts.

sentences for youth involved in serious or violent offences.[5] Selection effects, discussed in Chapter 6, are again relevant. These findings do not imply that younger generations are more psychopathic; instead, differences in who is incarcerated across generations account for the observed patterns. Younger generations were incarcerated under the YCJA, which had a higher threshold than the YOA for determining whether an offence warranted incarceration. Thus, younger generations of ISVYOS participants are likely drawn from a population with a higher proportion of youth involved in serious and violent offences. This reiterates the importance of looking at period effects (see next section) because *who* gets incarcerated, and thus included in research sampling from custody populations, can cloud the interpretation of birth cohort differences.

Separate generalized estimating equation models were performed to examine different ways of representing birth cohort measures. All analyses

---

[5] Section 39 of the YCJA specified that custody sentences could only be used under the following conditions: (1) a violent offence, (2) an administrative offence, (3) an indictable offence and prior findings of guilt, or (4) an indictable offence with aggravating circumstances present. Even when such conditions were met, judges are required to consider all other alternatives before ordering a custody sentence (Bala et al., 2009).

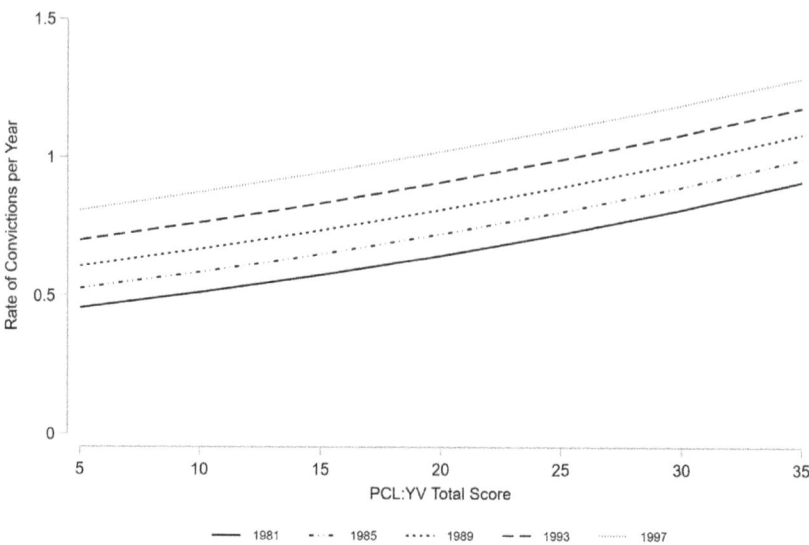

Figure 9.4 The relationship between PCL:YV total scores and convictions across birth year.

Notes. The 95 percent confidence intervals were excluded in order to more clearly visualize the slopes of each birth year. Although the year of birth ranged from 1979 to 1998, I only show years 1981, 1985, 1989, 1993, and 1997 to avoid cluttering the graph.

accounted for demographic characteristics and other risk factors mentioned in Chapter 3. Consistent with findings from Chapters 5 and 8, increases in PCL:YV total scores were associated with significant increases in the average rate of convictions during the follow-up period. Of greater relevance, when birth cohort was treated as an interval level variable, a one-unit increase (i.e., being born one year later) was associated with a significant 0.027 unit increase in the average number of convictions within a given year of the follow-up period ($p = 0.033$). When examining birth cohort groups, both the 1979–1983 and 1984–1988 birth cohort groups averaged significantly fewer convictions during the follow-up period compared to the 1994–1998 birth cohort groups ($p = 0.020$ and $p = 0.024$, respectively). Thus, regardless of how birth cohort groups were defined, cohorts born more recently were involved in a greater number of offences.

Of principal interest was whether birth cohort membership moderated the relationship between PCL:YV scores and offending. Figure 9.4 shows the results of a moderation analysis with birth cohort treated as an interval-level variable. The x-axis shows PCL:YV total scores, and the y-axis shows the average number of convictions per year of age during the follow-up

Birth Cohort Membership Moderate Psychopathy?

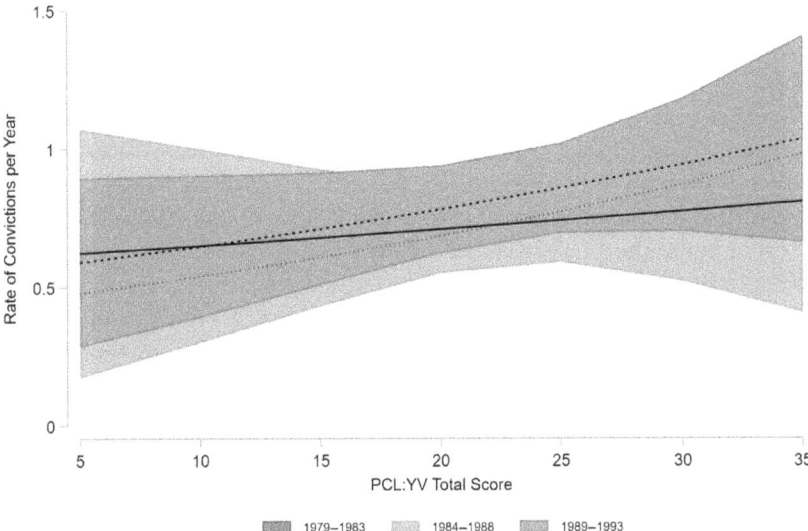

Figure 9.5 The relationship between PCL:YV total scores and convictions across different birth cohorts.

Notes. The 1994–1998 birth cohort grouping had a confidence interval that obfuscated the rest of the graph and thus was excluded. The two dotted lines reflect the two younger cohorts (1984–1988 and 1989–1993). The solid line represents the 1979–1983 cohort.

period. Intercepts in this graph represent the average number of convictions when PCL:YV scores equal five. Although intercepts differ between cohorts, more importantly, the slopes (indicating the rate of increase in convictions with changes in PCL:YV scores) do not. Across the different birth years, there is a similar rise in convictions with increases in PCL:YV score. The influence of PCL:YV total scores on convictions during the follow-up period does not vary as a function of when someone was born.

Figure 9.5 shows the results of a moderation analysis with birth cohort subgrouping. Once again, the interaction effect was not significant. In other words, controlling for demographic characteristics, risk factors from adolescence, and scores on the informal social control scale, the impact of PCL:YV total scores on average convictions during each year of the follow-up period did not vary depending on when a participant was born. Like Figure 9.4, this finding can be understood by looking at the slopes of the different birth cohort groups. Figure 9.5 shows that across the different cohort groups, increases in PCL:YV scores have a similar effect on convictions.

Do Period Effects Moderate the Relationship between Psychopathy and Offending?

The birth cohort analyses were replicated, this time looking at exposure to specific youth justice legislation (i.e., YOA or YCJA) as a specific period effect. Figure 9.6 shows the distribution of PCL:YV scores by youth justice legislation. An independent samples t-test indicated that participants adjudicated under the YCJA averaged significantly higher PCL:YV total scores compared to participants adjudicated under the YOA ($p = 0.004$). Figure 9.7 shows the distribution of the average yearly number of convictions over the follow-up period across the youth justice legislation. An independent samples t-test indicated that the mean number of convictions during the follow-up period was significantly higher for participants who were adjudicated under the YCJA compared to those adjudicated under the YOA ($p < 0.001$).

Based on generalized estimating equation models that controlled for demographic characteristics, adolescent risk factors, and adulthood informal social control scale scores, increases in PCL:YV total scores remained

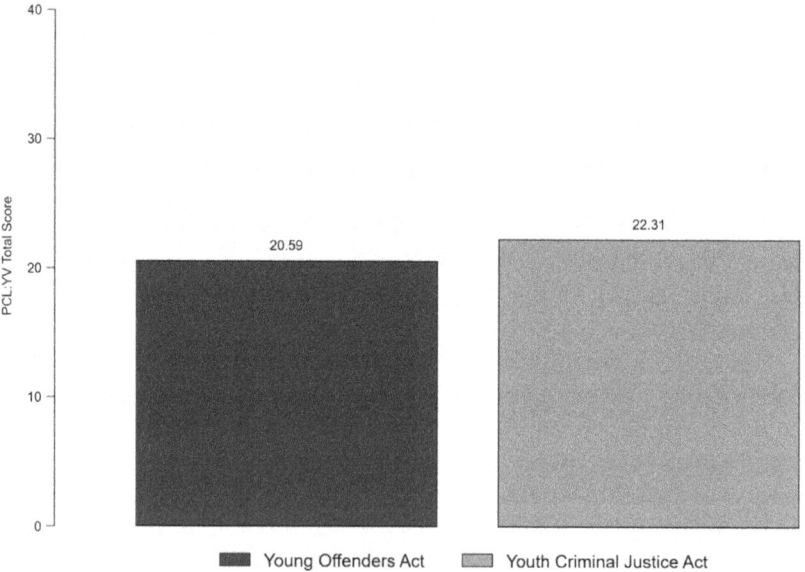

Figure 9.6 The distribution of PCL:YV total scores across participants who were incarcerated under either the Young Offenders Act (left) or the Youth Criminal Justice Act (right).

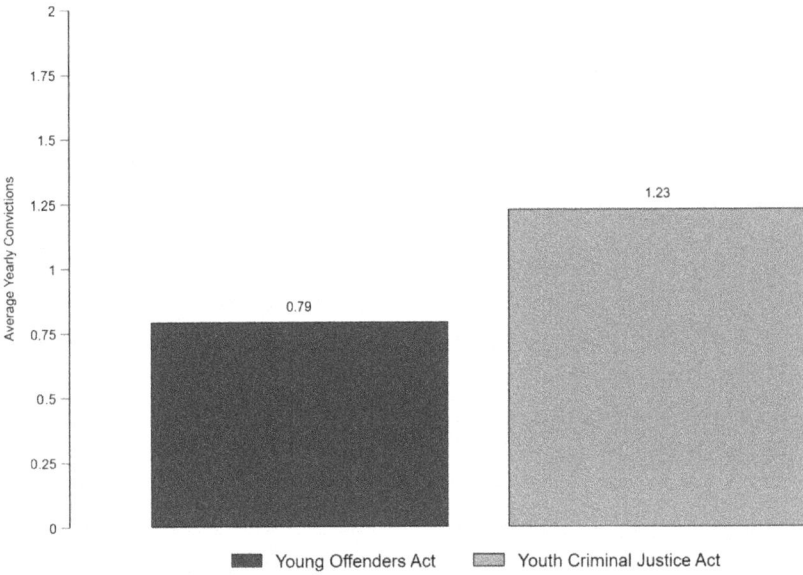

Figure 9.7 The distribution of convictions across exposure to specific youth justice legislation.

significantly associated with the rate of convictions during the follow-up period ($p = 0.023$). For period effects, the generalized estimating equation model indicated that those who were incarcerated under the YCJA averaged 0.23 more convictions for each year of the follow-up period compared to those who were incarcerated under the YOA ($p = 0.035$). The YCJA aimed to reserve incarceration for youth involved in especially serious and violent offences. These youth generally had a greater level of risk to reoffend compared to ISVYOS participants adjudicated under the YOA. Thus, the finding that those who were incarcerated under the YCJA averaged a higher rate of reconviction over the follow-up period aligns with expectations. This does not mean that the YCJA was less effective at preventing offending in adulthood, but rather reflects that these youth were higher-risk compared to youth adjudicated under the YOA.

Figure 9.8 helps visualize the results from the main question in this section: Does youth justice system exposure impact the relationship between psychopathy traits in adolescence and continued offending in adulthood? Based on the generalized estimating equation models, the youth justice-specific period effect did not moderate the relationship

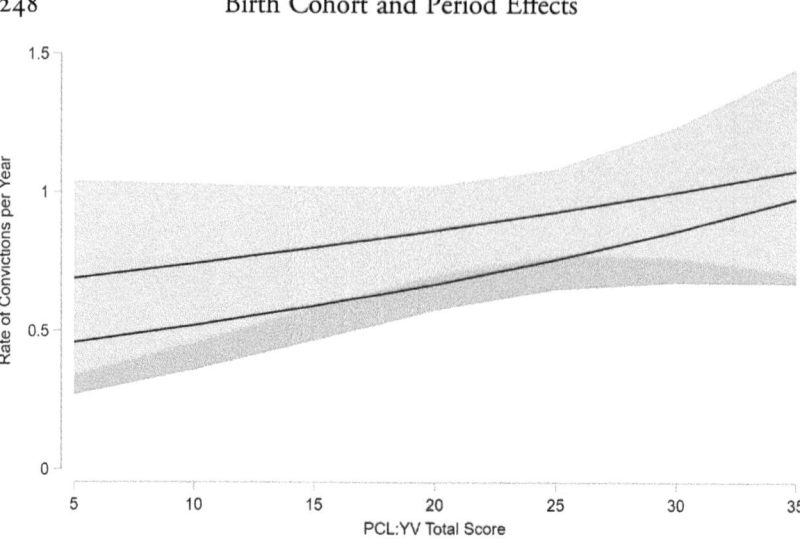

Figure 9.8 The relationship between PCL:YV total scores and convictions across exposure to specific youth justice legislation.

between PCL:YV total scores and offending. For participants with higher PCL:YV scores, whether they were adjudicated under the YOA or YCJA did not affect the number of convictions incurred over the follow-up period. Although the PCL:YV was developed in the era of the YOA (Forth et al., 2003), its predictive validity extends to those adjudicated under the YCJA.

Psychopathy, the Ecological Context, and Implications for Criminal Legal System Practice

Criminal legal system decision-making may be biased against generations who came of age in eras where crime rates were lower and macro-level structural contexts were more positive. Montana et al.'s (2023) examination of youth from Chicago illustrated that indicators of criminal propensity, like low self-control, were stronger predictors of offending among older generations exposed to more adverse social contexts, including higher crime rates and lower employment rates. Said differently, Montana et al. (2023) found that criminal propensity is a weaker predictor of future offending among younger cohorts.

One implication from Montana et al.'s (2023) research is that criminal legal system decision-making may be biased against younger generations. Risk assessment tools that guide legal system decision-making may have limited generalizability if they were validated and calibrated using data on older generations. In older generations, base rates of recidivism tend to be higher. Per Montana et al.'s (2023) analyses, a "high-risk" person from an older generation is more likely to reoffend compared to a "high-risk" person from a younger generation (also see Neil & Sampson, 2021). Legal system professionals should be concerned that risk assessment tools may overestimate the risk of recidivism for younger generations. Actuarial risk assessment tools are premised on the idea that individuals classified as "high" risk are more likely to recidivate compared to those classified as "low" risk (Imrey & Dawid, 2015). Montana et al.'s (2023) research challenges this premise and implies that risk assessment instruments may systematically overestimate the risk of reoffending for more recent generations.

Psychopathy assessments are commonly used to aid criminal legal system decision-making (Viljoen et al., 2010b), a practice that has recently come under scrutiny (Larsen, 2025). It therefore seemed especially important to examine whether Montana et al.'s (2023) findings generalized to the PCL:YV. For ISVYOS participants, the era in which participants were born did not moderate the relationship between PCL:YV scores and the frequency of convictions. Although these findings differ from those of Montana et al. (2023), it would be a mistake to view these studies as contradictory. The two studies used different measures of criminal propensity. Compared to self-control, which was examined in Montana et al.'s (2023) analyses of PHDCN+ data, psychopathy may be less sensitive to changing social contexts. This interpretation aligns with findings from Chapter 8, which indicated that proximal social context (i.e., informal social control) did not influence offending for people with psychopathy traits. The PHDCN+ and ISVYOS also sampled from different populations. The PHDCN+ sampled from neighbourhoods/communities and, therefore, is more generalizable to the broader population. The ISVYOS, by contrast, is more representative of incarcerated populations, where extremely difficult life circumstances are more common. For this marginalized population, variation in macro-level social climates may matter less for offending.

Finally, the PHDCN+ sample lived in Chicago, Illinois in the United States, whereas ISVYOS participants lived in British Columbia, Canada. It is possible that macro-level social changes in Canada occur more gradually compared to the United States. For ISVYOS participants growing up in Canada, the fact that birth cohort membership and legislative changes did not impact the relationship between psychopathy traits and reoffending may be evidence that Canada is in a "settled period" (see Swidler, 1986). In settled periods, it is difficult to discern an independent influence of cultural factors on individual behaviour because major macro-level structural changes unfold slowly. Policy changes in Canada tend to be incremental rather than dramatic (Doob & Webster, 2016; Roberts, 2012), especially when compared to the United States (Tonry, 2013b). The YCJA may not have exerted a unique impact on the relationship between psychopathy and reoffending compared to the YOA because there were also some similarities between the two acts (McCuish et al., 2021), and incarceration rates in British Columbia were declining even prior to the enactment of the YCJA.

Chapter Summary

Until this chapter, this book has focused on individual-level risk and protective factors and a person's immediate social environment. Neil and Sampson's (2021) paper transformed my perspective on the relationship between individual-level risk factors and offending. Neil and Sampson (2021) noted that "when" we are (i.e., the era in which we come of age) is as important, or even more important, than "who" we are (i.e., individual-level risk factors) in determining the likelihood of justice system involvement. This idea has critical implications for criminal legal systems, especially in terms of whether risk assessment tools are biased against people born into specific eras with unique macro-level social contexts (e.g., lower crime rates) or exposed to different types of justice system philosophies. Sampson and Smith (2021) further emphasized the need for more careful consideration of the role of social change as a situational context moderating the relationship between criminal propensity and offending. Two ways of capturing social change are through the examination of birth cohorts (i.e., specific groups born in similar eras and exposed to similar circumstances) and the examination of period effects (i.e., macro-level events that may shape future behaviour, such as changes to justice system principles).

Forensic psychology has traditionally focused on the individual and their proximal social environment, often neglecting broader structural contexts and macro-level circumstances (Verona & Fox, 2025). To address this gap, this chapter examined whether being born during a particular era impacted the strength of the relationship between psychopathy and offending. Analyses also included an examination of whether exposure to a particular youth justice legislation acted as a period effect that impacted the relationship between psychopathy and offending. The key takeaway is that, in this sample of incarcerated Canadian youth, PCL:YV scores were informative of persistent convictions through adulthood, regardless of when someone was born (1979–1998) and regardless of whether they were adjudicated under legislation with more of an emphasis on punishment and deterrence (YOA) or rehabilitation and community sentences (YCJA).

CHAPTER 10

Psychopathy Traits and Responses to Incarceration

Chapters 5–9 established that psychopathy traits in adolescence are informative of a variety of negative outcomes in later stages of the lifecourse. A natural follow-up question relates to how to disrupt the relationship between psychopathy traits in adolescence and negative outcomes, like persistent offending. When it comes to psychopathy, there has been a long-standing belief, mostly among the general public, but also among some researchers, that people with psychopathy traits do not respond to punishment. Some, like Ronson (2011), have misattributed treatment pessimism to Cleckley's (1976) initial work. However, reading the first chapter of *The Mask of Sanity* reveals that Cleckley was actually advocating for more attention to psychopathy to support the development of specialized treatment strategies.

The perspective that psychopathy is inherently untreatable is one way that psychopathy research has been misinterpreted and misrepresented. However, there are also very real concerns that people with psychopathy traits are less likely than others to consider the consequences of their actions and have difficulty learning from their mistakes and the associated punishment response (e.g., incarceration). In a longitudinal study of over 1,000 youth incarcerated in Philadelphia and Phoenix, Altikriti et al. (2021) found that participants with elevated psychopathy traits had lower perceptions of the riskiness of offending behaviour (e.g., risk of getting arrested). Laboratory-based studies indicate that people with psychopathy traits are less sensitive to cues regarding retribution (Aharoni et al., 2007). The heightened tendency for risk-taking behaviour, a lack of consideration for the consequences of punishment, and a diminished responsivity to punishment may be due to deficits in the prefrontal cortex and amygdala (Umbach et al., 2015). Other laboratory studies, however, indicate that people with psychopathy traits are capable of discerning what is considered morally appropriate or inappropriate behaviour (Aharoni et al., 2012).

It would be unethical to, for example, randomly assign people to experience harsher punishments, like incarceration instead of probation just to see how they would respond. Due to these ethical constraints, Simourd and Hoge (2000) noted that the literature on psychopathy and punishment/treatment responses is "short on quantity and long on lore" (p. 270). In other words, there are many opinions about whether criminal legal system interventions reduce reoffending for people with psychopathy traits. Yet, there are only a few studies that actually empirically test this question. Part of the reason that there is so much "lore" about the treatment of psychopathy traits stems from of unethical treatment practices, like the Oak Ridge Study, that get widely cited despite being based on incredibly weak research designs. Perhaps relatedly, agencies that provide funding for mental health research rarely support work on psychopathy (Gatner et al., 2023). It is possible that some of the hesitancy to fund research on psychopathy and treatment relates to pessimism that such research would be fruitful.

Chapter Goals and Analyses

In this chapter, I examine whether people with psychopathy traits reduce their level of offending (measured via convictions) after spending more time in custody. The analyses do not assess individuals who all experienced the same program, the same treatment, or even incarceration at the same custody center. The data are unable to clarify whether any observed reductions in reoffending were due to specific deterrence (e.g., not wanting to reoffend due to the threat of being reincarcerated) or rehabilitation (e.g., being exposed to treatment programs while in custody). Participants were incarcerated at different times, in different institutions, and undoubtedly were exposed to different programs. This chapter therefore focuses broadly on the general custody experience and represents a starting point for understanding responsivity to incarceration among people with psychopathy traits.

A strength of the analyses in this chapter is the technique used to address selection bias. Selection bias is the biggest threat to the reliability of research on incarceration and reoffending, and most studies poorly address this issue (Nagin et al., 2009). Selection bias threatens the reliability of research on incarceration and reoffending because confounding factors (e.g., age, gender, race, current offence, and prior offending) are associated with both the likelihood of incarceration and the likelihood of reoffending (Wakefield, 2018). People who are given a custody sentence tend to have more risk factors than people given, for example, a probation sentence. So, studies often are unable to answer a very basic question: Is the relationship observed between incarceration and reoffending actually due to incarceration, or does it simply reflect that people who are incarcerated already have a greater range of risk factors that increase their likelihood of reoffending?

Why not simply compare probation and custody samples while controlling for other risk factors? One problem is that there are hundreds of risk factors to account for to address selection bias (Nagin et al., 2009). An even greater problem is that even if all of these risk factors are measured, controlling for them in regression analyses or using quasi-experimental methods like propensity score matching may still produce unreliable results (Loeffler & Nagin, 2022). Traditional analytic strategies are not suitable for examining the relationship between incarceration and reoffending.

In some of my earlier work, my colleagues and I relied on a less commonly used analytic technique to study the relationship between incarceration and reoffending (see McCuish et al., 2025). We focused on within-individual change rather than between-group differences. So far, the analyses in this book have looked at between-group differences. For example, bivariate analyses in Chapter 9 compared average PCL:YV total scores between groups of different birth cohorts. Analyses of within-individual change make use of longitudinal data and examine whether individuals change over the course of a study as opposed to whether some groups of individuals are different from other groups of individuals.

A major motivation for focusing on within-individual change is that doing so accounts for selection bias by controlling for all time-invariant confounders (Allison, 2009). This means that any factor that does not change (e.g., race, age of onset of offending, history of abuse) is accounted for because each person acts as their own control. When measuring change from one point to the next, all time-invariant factors (i.e., variables that do not change) are accounted for. For example, the age of onset of offending is a key predictor of future offending, but it does not vary once established. If someone's age of onset of offending is age 14, the change in age of onset of offending from age 21 to age 22 will be zero (i.e., $14 - 14 = 0$). Time spent incarcerated between ages 21 and age 22 can change, as can convictions, allowing studies to reliably measure whether within-individual change in the amount of time spent incarcerated results in within-individual change in the number of crimes committed.

For this within-individual analysis, I used a first-differenced fixed-effect estimator to examine the relationship between year-over-year change in the number of days spent incarcerated and future year-over-year change in the number of convictions. First-differencing detrends data[1] by subtracting values at time $t - 1$ (e.g., Wave 1) from values at time t (e.g., Wave 2). First-differencing means that change is evaluated from one follow-up period to the next (e.g., change is examined from ages 12 to 13, 13 to 14, 14 to 15, etc.). In a fixed-effect analysis, time-invariant factors like race do not need to be measured and controlled for, but there is an assumption that the effect of incarceration on reoffending is the same (i.e., "fixed") across different racial groups. This assumption may not necessarily be true, which is a limitation of fixed-effect analyses. This has implications for the current chapter. What if the relationship between incarceration and offending varies across levels of psychopathy traits? To address this possibility, I ran separate analyses to examine, for both low and high scores on the PCL:YV, the relationship between year-over-year changes in the amount of time incarcerated and future year-over-year changes in convictions.

The measurement of incarceration included both time remanded (i.e., denied bail) and time sentenced to custody. In British Columbia, the same custody facilities are used for remanded and sentenced youth. However, the adult system has separate facilities. There are more services available in adult sentencing facilities than in remand facilities. It was not possible to distinguish between the amount of time spent remanded vs. sentenced. The Incarcerated Serious and Violent Young Offender Study (ISVYOS) directly measured each date a participant was admitted to a custody center and each date they were released from a custody center. Days incarcerated were summed for each year of age.

The Origins of the Pessimism Regarding Psychopathy and Responsivity to Punishment

As discussed in Chapter 2, a lot of the pessimism surrounding whether people with psychopathy traits respond to intervention strategies, whether punishment-oriented or treatment-oriented, stems from the Oak Ridge Study. This program involved forcing "patients," including women and teenagers, to sleep together in a large, brightly-lit room while they

---

[1] Detrending is needed to remove between-person differences in level of incarceration and level of convictions that may be tied to time-invariant factors. Between-person differences in time-varying measures can be removed by detrending the data. First-differencing produces unbiased estimates and reflects the degree and direction of within-person change rather than the magnitude of between-person differences. The detrending method should be chosen based on its appropriateness for the underlying theory or research question being evaluated (Waldfogel, 1997).

underwent experimental treatments, including receiving doses of lysergic acid diethylamide (LSD). Men were sometimes stripped naked and forced to spend lengthy periods of time together while eating from wall-mounted feeding tubes designed to represent a woman's breast. The Oak Ridge Study never intended to systematically measure psychopathy. Instead, it was wrongly assumed that if someone was at Oak Ridge, they must be a psychopath (Ronson, 2011).

The Oak Ridge Study was not designed to examine whether the program reduced recidivism for people with psychopathy traits. This did not stop some researchers from using the program as evidence that people with psychopathy traits do not benefit from treatment. For example, Harris and Rice (2017) reported that Oak Ridge patients reoffended at a high rate and therefore argued that psychopathy should be considered untreatable. Their conclusion is dubious given that (a) psychopathy was assessed retrospectively (i.e., after the program) using only file-based information[2] and (b) only a small number of patients scored high on file-based measurements of the Psychopathy Checklist – Revised (PCL-R). Overall, the pessimism surrounding the treatment and punishment responsivity of people with psychopathy traits likely stems from research conducted in eras where psychopathy was measured unreliably, punishment strategies were disconnected from research evidence, and criminal legal system policies emphasized mass incarceration, deterrence, and punitive eye-for-an-eye justice.

Treatment engagement refers to whether someone meaningfully participates in and completes treatment. Some studies report concerns about whether people with psychopathy traits are less likely to meaningfully engage with treatment programs and may even disrupt others' treatment progress (Sewall & Olver, 2019; Vasaturo et al., 2024). However, this challenge is not unique to psychopathy. A variety of factors influence treatment engagement, including characteristics of the person, but also characteristics of the program and the treatment provider (Holdsworth et al., 2014). It would therefore be a mistake to view psychopathy as uniquely detrimental to treatment engagement or to assume that people with psychopathy traits should not be included in treatment programs. Difficulties with treatment engagement are so common that an entire branch of the Risk–Need–Responsivity Model (RNR) model (the

---

[2] There is evidence that assessing psychopathy solely through file-based information is generally reliable (Grann et al., 1998). There is far less reason to believe that file-based assessments would be reliable in the Oak Ridge data, given the poor quality of the program.

responsivity component) was developed having in mind that some people benefit more from certain types of treatment programs than others (Bonta & Andrews, 2007). Accordingly, when it comes to psychopathy traits, emphasis should be placed on identifying programs that are more likely to increase the chance of engagement as opposed to ruling out programs altogether. Importantly, even reliable studies that show that individuals with psychopathy traits are less likely to meaningfully participate in treatment do not conclude that no individuals with psychopathy traits meaningfully participate in treatment.

Psychopathy, Treatment, and Reasons for Optimism

Research since the Oak Ridge Study generally supports the conclusion that individuals with psychopathy traits benefit from treatment. What seems to work when treating people with psychopathy traits is the use of intensive cognitive behavioural therapy programs delivered by highly skilled and well-trained staff, combined with efforts to address additional underlying risk/needs factors (Olver, 2018). Cognitive behavioural therapy aims to help individuals identify problem behaviours or thought patterns and then develop skills and strategies to change and/or manage them. Pairing cognitive behavioural therapy with strategies for changing criminogenic attitudes and beliefs also enhances treatment effectiveness (Lewis, 2018; Salekin, 2002).

There is a small body of empirical evidence indicating that people with psychopathy traits who successfully complete treatment are just as likely to reduce their reoffending as people who complete treatment but do not present with psychopathy traits (Olver et al., 2013; Wong et al., 2012). Programs like the Mendota Juvenile Treatment Centre, which offer intensive treatment services for high-risk youth, appear to reduce reoffending for youth with psychopathy traits (Caldwell et al., 2006, 2007). A cost-benefit analysis of this program estimated that every one dollar spent was associated with seven dollars in savings to state welfare systems (Caldwell et al., 2006). In Germany, social therapy facilities have been constructed to provide support to people involved in persistent offending. Social therapy involves integrating cognitive behavioural and psychoanalytic approaches to improve personal insight into behaviour. Such programs also include educational and occupational programming and consideration of the environment that an individual finds themself in when living in the community. Studies of men sentenced to these facilities identified reliable decreases in PCL-R test scores, including reductions in core interpersonal and affective personality traits (Moosburner et al., 2024).

The Incarceration Experience and Its Impact on Reoffending

Can prison be an effective place to promote positive change? It probably is not the ideal setting, as there are challenges in implementing treatment programs in settings where people feel at risk of experiencing victimization (Vaswani & Paul, 2019). The level of conflict in prison social networks (see Chapter 6) reiterates this point. However, there have been substantial improvements to Canada's correctional system since the Oak Ridge Study. I am not suggesting that these improvements have fully addressed concerns about sentencing practices and conditions within custody facilities. The quality and availability of Canada's rehabilitative efforts have received sustained criticism (Zinger, 2022). Compared to countries like Norway, persons incarcerated in Canada, especially women, report accessing fewer services (Bucerius & Sandberg, 2022). Canada's correctional system also has been scrutinized for failing to address issues related to victimization in custody, the overreliance on solitary confinement, and the overrepresentation of Indigenous Persons in custody (Zinger, 2022). However, to suggest that improvements in the incarceration experience have not been made since the Oak Ridge Study would be to overlook evidence-based changes to incarceration policies in Canada. The fact that Canada has a "prison watchdog" to hold correctional services accountable is an important difference from 50 years ago (Zinger, 2024).[3]

Not all prison contexts are the same. Canada's incarceration practices and policies differ from those in the United States. Compared to the United States, Canada's youth and adult incarceration policies center around the use of shorter sentences that are more individualized, focused on rehabilitation (Tonry, 2013b), and mostly unaffected by political agendas (Neil & Carmichael, 2015). Over the last 30 years, compared to the United States, Canada's correctional philosophy has shifted away from punishment severity in favor of using the RNR model to create individualized and evidence-based service delivery plans that aim to reduce the pains of imprisonment and promote rehabilitation (Bonta & Andrews, 2007; Tonry, 2013a, 2022; Webster et al., 2019). The transition from the Young Offenders Act to the Youth Criminal Justice Act (YCJA; see Chapter 9) reflects another example of a move toward the perspective that

---

[3] I am not suggesting that attempts to change correctional practices in Canada have always been successful, nor am I suggesting that correctional services in Canada have always been fully responsive to recommendations. Issues in corrections persist. However, to suggest that Canada today is in the same place it was in 1965, at the time of the Oak Ridge Study, would be to undermine a lot of progress and effort to implement, for example, attention to cultural differences and experiences of trauma (Muir & Viljoen, 2022).

incarceration should prioritize rehabilitation, service delivery, and detailed community reentry plans (McCuish et al., 2021). During the ISVYOS recruitment period, youth in British Columbia were incarcerated at rates ranging from approximately 40 to 80 per 100,000 (Statistics Canada, 2024a). During a similar period, youth in the United States were incarcerated at rates ranging from 196 to 355 per 100,000 (OJJDP, 2019). Unlike most jurisdictions in the United States (Bishop, 2000), juvenile transfers are not part of the Canadian youth criminal legal system, meaning that youth involved in the most serious and violent offences were not excluded from the ISVYOS because all youth are incarcerated in youth facilities, regardless of the severity of their index offence.

Unlike the United States, custody facilities in British Columbia are not privatized. Physical and mental health services are delivered by the provincial government. Each custody facility has a mental health professional who coordinates services. Incarcerated youth have access to high school education that is part of the British Columbia Public School District system and have daily programming opportunities for drug and alcohol counseling, mental health support, life skills coaching, and employment readiness (Government of British Columbia, 2024). In line with principles of behavioural conditioning, youth custody centers in British Columbia use a token economy system in which positive behaviours are rewarded in multiple ways (e.g., financial incentives, additional privileges, extra recreational programs).

When youth were recruited to participate in the study, ISVYOS Research Assistants could only conduct interviews during periods when the participant was not involved in schooling or a rehabilitative program. We were unable to interview youth between the hours of 9 a.m. and 3 p.m., and even in the evenings we often could not interview specific youth because they were involved in a program. In other words, youth spent much of their time in custody participating in programs conducive to rehabilitation. Albeit anecdotal, one thing that stood out to me during the hundreds of hours I spent at the Burnaby Youth Custody Centre was how positive teachers were about their job. Whereas teachers in public schools might face a student-to-teacher ratio of 30:1, in the custody center the ratio was an estimated 7–10 students for every teacher.

Evaluating the Impact of Incarceration on Reoffending for Youth with Psychopathy Traits

The main analysis in this chapter applied a first-differenced fixed-effect estimator for data spanning ages 12 to 25. Over this period, the PCL:YV Cohort averaged 22.27 convictions (standard deviation (SD) = 15.25) and

33.38 months in custody (SD = 28.47). This analysis allowed for the examination of year-over-year change in incarceration (i.e., between time $t-2$ and time $t-1$) in relation to year-over-year change in convictions (i.e., between time $t-1$ and time t). In this case, t reflects a participant's age. There were no between-participant differences in age because all participants were the same age during each wave. All analyses controlled for linear and quadratic effects of ageing, but for parsimony, these are excluded from Eq. 10.1.

$$Con_{it} - Con_{it-1} = \left(\beta_0 + \beta_1 Inc_{it-1} + a_i + u_{it}\right) - \left(\beta_0 + \beta_1 Inc_{it-2} + a_i + u_{it-1}\right)$$

(10.1)

Con represents the number of convictions for individual i at age t, and *Inc* represents the number of days spent incarcerated for individual i at age t.[4]

I begin by examining, for all members of the PCL:YV Cohort, the relationship between the year-over-year change in the number of days spent incarcerated and future year-over-year change in the number of convictions. I then replicate these analyses for those who scored high on the PCL:YV (i.e., a score of 30 or greater) to assess whether results generalize to psychopathy traits.[5] Model 1 of Table 10.1 shows the results of a first-differenced fixed-effect estimator investigating, between ages 12 and 25, the effect of year-over-year within-person change in incarceration between time $t-2$ and time $t-1$ on year-over-year within-person change in convictions between time $t-1$ and time t.

Model 1 of Table 10.1 indicates that each additional day incarcerated from two years ago to one year ago results in a 0.063 unit decrease in the number of convictions from one year ago to the present. In simpler terms, spending more time incarcerated was associated with fewer convictions.

The same analysis was repeated, but this time I only included participants with a score of 30 or higher on the PCL:YV. By restricting the analysis to this group, it was possible to investigate whether findings were consistent with Model 1 of Table 10.1 or whether there was no evidence that people with psychopathy traits respond to longer periods of incarceration by reoffending less often. Model 2 of Table 10.1 reflects the findings

---

[4] The subtraction of each component in the equation differences out all unobserved time-invariant factors (a_i). What remains is the effect of differences in incarceration ($\beta_1 Inc_{it-1} - \beta_1 Inc_{it-2}$) and the error term ($u_{it} - u_{it-1}$). Robust (clustered) standard errors (SEs) were specified to address serial correlation (Nichols & Schaffer, 2007).

[5] To reiterate past statements in this book, I view psychopathy traits as dimensional rather than categorical. I categorize psychopathy traits in this chapter as "high" or "not high" because of the requirements of the type of analytic approach being performed.

Table 10.1 *The effect of changes in incarceration on changes in reconvictions*

	Model 1 PCL:YV cohort b (SE) [95% CI]	Model 2 High PCL:YV only b (SE) [95% CI]
Change in Age	1.47 (0.13)*** [1.22; 1.72]	1.76 (0.45)*** [0.87; 2.65]
Change in (Age)²	−0.04 (0.003)*** [−0.05; −0.03]	−0.05 (0.01)*** [−0.07; −0.03]
Change in incarceration	−0.010 (0.001)*** [−0.01; −0.01]	−0.010 (0.002)*** [−0.01; −0.004]
Model fit	$F(3, 517) = 80.88$, $p < 0.001$; $R^2 = 0.04$	$F(3, 666) = 75.36$, $p < 0.001$; $R^2 = 0.04$

Notes. Standard errors (SE) clustered within participants. *** $p < 0.001$. High PCL:YV test score = 30 or greater. Change in (Age)² represented a quadratic effect in which age was multiplied by itself to account for the nonlinear relationship between age and offending, as depicted by the age–crime curve (i.e., crime increases with age in adolescence but declines with age in adulthood).

from Model 1. Between ages 12 and 25, ISVYOS participants who scored high on the PCL:YV experienced decreases in their rate of convictions following increases in the number of days spent incarcerated. The confidence intervals (CIs) overlap between models. This implies that the effect of incarceration on reoffending did not differ between the full sample and the small subsample of participants who scored high on the PCL:YV. R^2 indicates the proportion of variance accounted for in the model. In both models, R^2 is only 4 percent. This reiterates the complexity of explaining offending; prior incarceration accounted for only a small proportion of variance in future convictions. Nevertheless, the results indicate that in prison systems where the RNR model is emphasized, people with psychopathy traits reduce their level of offending following longer periods of time in custody.

Implications for Treatment and Intervention

The findings should not be interpreted as support for expanding the use of incarceration. In fact, the findings from this chapter may reflect what happens when incarceration is reserved for a small group of youth involved in particularly serious or violent offences. It would be a mistake to interpret these findings as a reason for Canada's correctional system to maintain the status quo (Zinger, 2022). Nevertheless, and of relevance to the central theme of this book, youth scoring high on the PCL:YV were responsive to longer periods of time spent incarcerated. Careful consideration should be given to whether findings generalize to other jurisdictions. For example, unlike Canada's youth justice system, in the United States, the 1980s marked the beginning of crime control models that focused on responding to perceived out-of-control youth through punishment rather than rehabilitation (Cauffman & Steinberg, 2012). Some US States mandate youth transfers to adult court. Canada currently prohibits such practices, and youth are never incarcerated with adults (McCuish et al., 2021). Especially since the 1990s, Canadian correctional psychology researchers working in policy positions have voiced concerns about punitive components of incarceration (Gendreau et al., 1999), promoted effective correctional practices (Gendreau & Ross, 1983), and developed the RNR model to help identify who should be incarcerated and how to address treatment needs (Bonta & Andrews, 2007). It is within this context that the findings from this chapter might generalize to other jurisdictions.

Hypotheses for Why Longer Periods of Incarceration Reduced Reoffending

There are at least three possibilities for why people with psychopathy traits decreased their level of offending following increases in the amount of time spent incarcerated. First, it is possible that more time incarcerated afforded more opportunity to access rehabilitative services. In British Columbia, there is a wide range of rehabilitative services offered to youth and adults while in custody. Several of these specific programs are associated with reductions in reoffending (Gress, 2009), and most persons report satisfaction with service delivery (Gress, 2010). The RNR model and the Community Risk Needs Assessment (CRNA) include a focus on criminogenic attitudes. Walters (2025) showed that targeting criminogenic attitudes has a positive impact on reductions in reoffending.

A second potential explanation for why people with psychopathy traits experienced reductions in reoffending following longer periods of time spent incarcerated is related to specific deterrence. Canada's legal system relies on the concept of recidivism sentencing premiums in which people are given harsher punishments compared to prior punishments (Roberts, 2008). Although the YCJA did not explicitly include specific deterrence as a sentencing principle, incarcerated youth may nevertheless have been deterred from reoffending when their experience of punishment escalated from one year to the next. Although this is a possibility, if specific deterrence reduced the likelihood of reoffending, it is unclear why numerous studies in the United States, where specific deterrence is a mainstay of sentencing philosophies, failed to observe a relationship between incarceration and reduced levels of offending (Petrich et al., 2021). It would be a mistake to interpret findings from this chapter as justification for expanding the use of custody sentences. In British Columbia, concerted effort was made to prohibit the use of incarceration for youth not involved in serious/violent offences. It may be that this intentional effort to reserve custody sentences for the most at-risk youth explains why the findings in this chapter contradict research from the United States (Petrich et al., 2021). Expanding the use of incarceration might simply undo the success of these policies.

A third potential explanation for reductions in reoffending among people with psychopathy traits is not incarceration itself, but rather the policies surrounding community reentry following release. These policies include closer supervision and monitoring by a probation/parole office and/or access to additional rehabilitative services. Closer supervision and monitoring refer to conditions of probation or parole, such as curfew, no-contact orders, and requirements regarding schooling or employment. Closer supervision and monitoring may have deterred reoffending by creating a perception that there was a high likelihood of detection and that a new offence perpetrated while on probation/parole would result in harsher-than-average punishment. However, this perspective contradicts empirical research indicating that people with psychopathy traits have lower perceptions of the riskiness of offending and the likelihood of getting caught.

Youth in British Columbia who are released from custody receive a variety of community-based social supports designed to reduce reoffending. Some of these services are described as wrap around programs that address multiple needs of people exiting custody. Such services are meant to be intensive, holistic, and to involve family members and community supports (Public Safety Canada, 2021). Although appealing as an explanation for why incarceration reduced reoffending, the empirical literature evaluating wrap-around services is mixed. A major concern is that wrap-around services are too intensive and try to do too much all at once rather than prioritize specific needs (Doleac, 2019). This does not imply that rehabilitation programs do not work, only that intensive interventions may drain a person's time and energy, reduce motivation to change, and ultimately be an inefficient use of resources.

The potential for wrap around services to be ineffective due to being too intensive raises important questions beyond the scope of ISVYOS data. Per the RNR model, those who are at the highest risk to reoffend, such as people with psychopathy traits, require more intensive services and treatment (Reidy et al., 2015; Simourd & Hoge, 2000). Future research should examine how to find the right balance between providing greater resources without influencing burnout, treatment dropout, and declining motivation to change. It may be important for treatment and intervention strategies to more precisely identify which needs should be prioritized first, as opposed to addressing multiple needs simultaneously.

In-Custody Treatment Programs for People with Psychopathy Traits

The analyses in this chapter provided evidence that youth with psychopathy traits who spent more time incarcerated subsequently reduced their reoffending. A plausible hypothesis, given British Columbia's approach to youth incarceration, is that ISVYOS participants benefited from the treatment programs that were available to them while incarcerated. Unfortunately, the ISVYOS did not directly evaluate specific treatment programs. In the absence of program-level data, I describe existing programs that reflect the types of services that ISVYOS participants reported that they received while in custody.

Recognizing the intensive needs of people with psychopathy traits, Wong et al. (2012) used the structure of PCL-based measures of psychopathy to develop a two-component treatment model. The first component, designed to address interpersonal and affective traits, addresses issues that may emerge when it comes to responsivity to treatment (e.g., willingness to participate or engage). For example, being manipulative, callous, unempathic, and persistent lying may act as barriers to the therapeutic alliance between practitioner and client. Under this component, effective programming involves training staff to anticipate and respond in safe and ethical ways to treatment-interfering behaviours (Olver, 2022). Component one, therefore, focuses on how to adapt program delivery and maximize program effectiveness to improve treatment engagement.

The second component, designed to address social deviance traits of psychopathy, emphasizes the use of treatment strategies to directly address criminogenic needs (e.g., substance use, sensation seeking, and impulsivity). This component is not just about addressing psychopathy traits but also about acknowledging that people with psychopathy traits typically present with more risk factors and fewer protective factors (Simourd &

Hoge, 2000). The logic of this approach is supported by analyses from Chapter 6 indicating that people with psychopathy traits tended to have lower levels of informal social control, more criminogenic peer networks, and a greater likelihood of substance use issues. The higher level of risk does not imply an inability to change, just that more intensive intervention and treatment may be required (Lovatt et al., 2025). The need for more intensive intervention must be balanced against Doleac's (2019) finding that wrap around services may have poor treatment fidelity and may drain participants' energy and motivation, thereby limiting their effectiveness in reducing reoffending.

Another type of treatment program is schema therapy, which was developed with personality disorders like psychopathy in mind (see Young et al., 2003 for a review). Like the two-component model, schema therapy integrates multiple treatment modalities to help motivate patients (e.g., component 1), treat personality disorder traits, address risk factors, and promote strength factors (e.g., component 2), and develop structured plans for community reentry (Bernstein et al., 2023). Schema therapy overlaps with principles from the YCJA that emphasize that the purpose of incarceration is to promote public safety through rehabilitation and treatment. This approach includes individualized case management plans to target risk/need factors, build strengths, and improve the success of community reentry by having the final third of a person's custody sentence served under community supervision (McCuish et al., 2021).

Bernstein et al. (2023) found that, among people with personality disorder traits, those who underwent schema therapy showed greater evidence of rehabilitation than those who underwent treatment as usual, as indicated by an increased likelihood of being approved for unsupervised leaves of absence from inpatient facilities. Bernstein et al. (2023) also found that treatment participation was associated with reductions in personality disorder traits that overlap with psychopathy.

Schema therapy was not developed with youth in mind, nor was it developed specifically for people with psychopathy traits. Similarly, the two-component model was not developed specifically for youth. The PSYCHOPATHY.COMP program was designed for youth with psychopathy traits (Riberio da Silva et al., 2019). It is based on a Compassion-Focused Therapy model in which time is taken to explain how the human mind works in reaction to threats and situations outside of one's control. The program then emphasizes developing responsibility for actions and learning strategies for coping with shame and frustration. Compassion-Focused Therapy acknowledges that people have multiple working identities that they must balance in different situations. The program calls for participants to demonstrate compassion toward oneself and others and to access their compassionate self during periods of turmoil to maintain control over their own behaviour. To remain in control of their behaviour, the program aims to equip participants with tools for making responsible choices. Overall, PSYCHOPATHY.COMP aims to help youth process difficult memories and emotions, develop skills to become more self-aware and in control, and use compassionate alternatives to coping with difficult life circumstances (see Riberio da Silva et al., 2019).

An initial evaluation of the PSYCHOPATHY.COMP program indicated promising reductions in reducing psychopathy traits compared to a treatment as usual approach. There was no evidence of relapse: changes in psychopathy traits were maintained after a six-month period following the completion of treatment (Ribeiro da Silva et al., 2021). As with most evaluations of treatment programs for people with psychopathy traits, a limitation of research on the PSYCHOPATHY.COMP program is the absence of randomized controlled designs that more reliably evaluate treatment effects. A strength of the PSYCHOPATHY.COMP program is its focus on the full spectrum of youth psychopathy traits. In contrast, other programs are often only focused on CU traits and conduct problems/conduct disorder (for reviews, see Almas & Lordos, 2025; Waschbusch et al., 2024). This means that, for these other programs, certain core traits of psychopathy like pathological lying are not accounted for when considering (1) who should be included in the treatment program and (2) whether psychopathy traits change following treatment.[6]

Chapter Summary

If people with psychopathy traits are inflexible, uncaring toward others, manipulative, and difficult to get along with, the suggestion that treatment strategies will be ineffective may sound intuitive. However, what is intuitive and what is accurate do not always align. The analyses in this chapter

---

[6] There has been growing emphasis on looking beyond callous–unemotional (CU) traits when measuring psychopathy (Salekin et al., 2018). The *Diagnostic and Statistical Manual of Mental Disorders – Fifth Edition* (DSM-5) (American Psychiatric Association, 2013) uses the term limited prosocial emotions as a specifier when assessing conduct disorder. Limited prosocial emotions include a lack of remorse, CU traits, shallow affect, and a lack of concern for performance. Some have questioned whether limited prosocial emotion items fully capture the broader construct of psychopathy traits (McCuish et al., 2019; Salekin, 2016). However, consideration of limited prosocial emotions is at least an improvement over treatment programs that focus only on CU traits.

added to research indicating that people with psychopathy traits can change and respond to intervention strategies as expected (Bernstein et al., 2023; Wong et al., 2012). Specifically, the analyses in this chapter indicated that even for participants who scored 30 or higher on the PCL:YV, within-individual increases in the amount of time spent incarcerated from one period to the next were associated with future within-individual decreases in the number of convictions from one period to the next.

I believe that these findings do not reflect the impact of specific deterrence or the benefits of a punitive justice system. ISVYOS participants were exposed to a youth justice system that emphasized treatment and rehabilitation. Spending longer periods of time in custody may have afforded greater opportunities for treatment. This sample reflects some of the highest-risk offenders in British Columbia. The RNR model that guides youth justice in Canada emphasizes delivering higher-intensity intervention strategies (e.g., custody sentences) only to people at a high risk of reoffending. The ISVYOS subsample of youth who scored high on the PCL:YV and who were involved in serious and violent offences is a clear example of high-risk youth who received intensive intervention through custody sentences that prioritized rehabilitation over deterrence.

Reacting to the types of youth in the ISVYOS once they are in custody may be less efficient than developing proactive, humanistic intervention strategies that are initiated before criminal legal system involvement. More proactive approaches are needed to intervene prior to the perpetration of serious and harmful offences. Caution is needed before generalizing the findings from this chapter to jurisdictions with higher incarceration rates or more punitive sentencing philosophies.

CHAPTER 11

Concluding Thoughts

I restricted the focus of this book to psychopathy traits among incarcerated youth because I did not want to speak about topics beyond my training, experience, and program of research. Since 2008, I have been part of a team involved in interviewing incarcerated youth. These interviews led to 535 youth from the Incarcerated Serious and Violent Young Offender Study (ISVYOS) receiving a rating on the Psychopathy Checklist: Youth Version (PCL:YV). I focused on incarcerated youth rather than youth in high schools because this was my experience. I focused on the PCLYV because this was the tool I was trained to use when assessing psychopathy. I focused on criminological theories because my BA, MA, and PhD were completed in criminology. In short, the topics covered in this book were selected not necessarily because they are the most important, but because they reflect areas where I am best positioned to make a meaningful contribution.

What Is Missing from the Book?

The training I received and the data available influenced the questions addressed in this book. There are plenty of important topics that this book failed to address through empirical analysis. Before summarizing and integrating key findings across chapters, I begin by describing themes that I failed to address, why they are important, and how they could be addressed in future research.

Person-Oriented Analyses

Most of the analyses in this book looked at the impact of increases in PCL:YV scores on various dependent variables. This approach is consistent with variable-centered analyses, where it is assumed that, for example, all people with a score of 30 or higher on the PCL:YV are the same. There are limitations to this approach. Bergman and Magnusson (1997) explain that "the modeling/description of variables over individuals can be very difficult to translate into properties characterizing single individuals because the information provided by the statistical method is variable oriented, not individual oriented" (p. 292). As opposed to methods like structural equation modeling (Chapter 7), which rely on sample means that may not reflect the nature of individual persons, person-centered analyses have the individual as the central object of study (Bergman & Magnusson, 1997). Person-centered research on psychopathy (e.g., Garofalo et al., 2020) explores whether there are subgroups of people defined by differences in psychopathy traits. Model-based cluster analysis can contribute to the need for person-oriented research by examining whether there are different profiles of psychopathy traits and whether such profiles differentially relate to external outcomes (e.g., offending).

A common theoretical view on psychopathy that fits person-oriented theories involves the distinction between primary and secondary psychopathy. I did not investigate questions about primary vs. secondary psychopathy because this area of research is so convoluted that an entire book might be needed to clarify the meaning of these two terms. Definitional disagreements are not necessarily problematic, but when it comes to the literature on primary and secondary psychopathy, researchers are so divided that the terms can be nearly meaningless (for reviews, see Craig et al., 2021; Yildrim & Derksen, 2015). Some researchers view primary and secondary psychopathy as distinct trait clusters of the same disorder, where primary mainly reflects interpersonal/affective deficits and secondary mainly reflects lifestyle/antisocial deficits (Levenson et al., 1995). Some researchers distinguish the two based on etiological differences, where primary psychopathy is genetically influenced and secondary psychopathy is environmentally influenced (Frazier et al., 2019). Some differentiate the two based on unique brain structures (Deljou et al., 2022). Others distinguish primary and secondary psychopathy based on external factors, such as considering a lack of anxiety to be specific to primary psychopathy (Kimonis et al., 2012). In Chapter 1, I discussed disagreement in the literature regarding the conceptualization of psychopathy, but at least there was general agreement that personality traits represented the core of psychopathy. The literature on primary and secondary psychopathy is much murkier. Future research is needed to help address whether primary and secondary psychopathy meaningfully distinguish people based on traits, causes, brain structure, external criteria, or a combination thereof.

Proactive Treatment Programs

The empirical chapters in this book failed to address whether a specific treatment program influenced changes in psychopathy traits or in other risk factors common to people with psychopathy traits. The small body of research on psychopathy and treatment tends to focus on inpatient facilities that react to youth already involved in the justice system (e.g., the Mendota Juvenile Treatment Center (Caldwell et al., 2007); the PSYCHOPATHY.COMP program (Ribeiro da Silva et al., 2021)). This is not a criticism of those specific programs, but additional research is needed on preventative programs initiated prior to criminal legal system involvement.

The Summer Treatment Program is intended for youth under 13 and focuses on reductions in risk through parent training, behavioural therapy, and skill building (Waschbusch et al., 2024). Programs that focus on early parent-child interactions have had lasting success in reducing CU traits (for a review, see Almas & Lordos, 2025). Further research is needed that uses randomized controlled trials, larger samples that are more reflective of ethnic and gender diversity, and longer follow-up periods to evaluate whether reductions in psychopathy traits are sustained. Measures of psychopathy should not be restricted to callous–unemotional (CU) traits. Research should also consider the unintended negative consequences (e.g., stigmatization) of these programs and whether program impact varies across subgroups. Surveys of forensic psychologists highlight the importance of culturally informed treatment programs (Fanniff et al., 2023). However, it is difficult to know what such programs should look like, given that research on psychopathy is almost exclusively conducted in Western, Educated, Industrialized, Rich, and Democratic (WEIRD) jurisdictions. Before treatment practices can be culturally informed it is important to understand how psychopathy traits develop and manifest in non-WEIRD cultures (e.g., Nijdam-Jones et al., 2020) and whether existing measures of psychopathy can be implemented reliably in these contexts (McCuish et al., 2018b).

The Etiology of Psychopathy

ISVYOS data were not suitable for questions about the etiology of psychopathy traits. Theories on the origins of psychopathy traits typically recognize the importance of both environmental and biological pathways (Farrington et al., 2010; Kiehl et al., 2001; Viding et al., 2005). It is difficult to implement the research designs and nuanced data collection required to empirically test these theoretical ideas in a reliable manner. For example, unless longitudinal data are collected very early in the life-course, it is not possible to determine whether abusive experiences in childhood influenced psychopathy traits or whether psychopathy traits from birth influenced parental hostility, which in turn influenced abusive experiences (Backman et al., 2021). When investigating the causes of psychopathy traits, it is critical to rule out risk factors that are actually *consequences* of psychopathy traits. The financial costs associated with implementing the necessary research design are prohibitive. At least in Canada, grants in the health sciences tend to be larger than those in the social sciences. It may be useful to frame psychopathy as a public health issue to obtain grants large enough to implement more rigorous research designs.

The Adolescent Brain Cognitive Development (ABCD) Study provides a solid example of the research design needed to examine the etiology of psychopathy. The ABCD Study includes self-report measures of psychopathy, brain imaging, and various social and environmental factors that may be relevant to the development of psychopathy traits (e.g., Waller et al., 2020). However, ABCD participants were recruited in late childhood, which may miss critical earlier developmental stages important for understanding the development of psychopathy traits. One way to capture earlier periods is through large-scale multigenerational studies in which the first generation of participants is in early adulthood. A second generation of participants can be recruited that represents the children of the original participants (see Farrington & Bergstrøm, 2022). Focusing on would-be parents prior to childbirth offers an opportunity to initiate nurse-family partnerships that promote physical and mental health during pregnancy (Olds, 2002). Such programs help reduce the types of prenatal and perinatal complications linked to psychopathy traits (Fowler et al., 2009). Thus, there are ways to study the etiology of psychopathy traits that can inform prevention efforts and move beyond more reactive intervention strategies.

Preregistration

The replication crisis in the social sciences (Lilienfeld & Strother, 2020) is partly attributable to the failure of researchers to preregister their studies. The analyses in this book were not preregistered. Preregistration involves researchers uploading documents detailing their data collection strategy and planned analyses to a publicly available repository that time-stamps each document. By making the research design publicly available, independent researchers can verify that results described in a particular paper were based on planned analyses rather than post hoc adjustments (Benning & Smith, 2023). Outlining planned analyses before data collection ensures that researchers are not engaging in questionable research practices like "p-hacking." P-hacking involves conducting multiple unplanned statistical analyses that are not driven by theory but rather are merely intended to improve the chances of observing a significant relationship between variables. In such cases, the relationship is due to statistical noise rather than a true relationship. Rarely is psychopathy research preregistered. However, Verschuere et al. (2021) provided a useful framework for how preregistration practices can be implemented in psychopathy research. A good template for other researchers is Sharpe et al. (2023), who followed Verschuere et al.'s (2021) guidelines in their own preregistered analyses, offering a strong model for other researchers to follow.

The analyses in this book were not preregistered because it was too late in the research process. The ISVYOS began in 1998, and by the time of this book, data were already collected and variables of interest (e.g., the PCL:YV) had been analyzed in prior work (e.g., Vincent, 2002). To present the ISVYOS data as if they were preregistered would constitute fraud (Verschuere et al., 2021). In the absence of preregistration, I relied on Benning and Smith's (2023) guidelines for postregistration. A copy of the ISVYOS codebook is publicly available on ResearchGate, and the code used to perform the analyses described in this book is available on my GitHub page.[1] Chapter 3 outlines the extent of ISVYOS data used, specifies that I focused specifically on participants with a PCL:YV, and clarifies that I did not eliminate from consideration any members of the PCL:YV cohort (except in instances of early mortality which subsequently meant that data after mortality were unavailable). Verschuere et al. (2021) reported concerns that researchers measure psychopathy in multiple ways and then retain whichever measure relates most strongly to the outcome of interest. Aside from the examination of concurrent validity in Chapter 4, I did not run the same analyses with multiple measures of psychopathy to increase the chance of observing evidence of predictive validity. Another concern in the psychopathy literature is the use of arbitrary cut-points on dimensional measures to improve the chance of a significant relationship (Verschuere et al., 2021). I used a standard cut-point of 30 on the PCL:YV across all analyses; moreover, I only dichotomized PCL:YV scores to help communicate research findings in a more intuitive way for readers less

---

[1] Search "EvanMcCuish+GitHub" and navigate to the PsychopathyBook repository (https://github.com/EvanMcCuish).

familiar with specific statistical analyses, rather than as part of hypothesis testing or as a substitute for examining dimensional scores.

Summarizing and Synthesizing the Chapters

The Preface of this book introduced a case study that described Michael's involvement in two homicides committed several years apart. Despite the seriousness of these offences, Michael scored relatively low on the PCL:YV. Too often, popular culture sources approach things backwards by beginning with an assumption that if the crime in question involved extreme violence, then the perpetrator must be a psychopath. The identification of psychopathy begins with an interview and a focus on personality traits as opposed to starting with an assumption that certain offences could only be perpetrated by psychopaths. Assessing psychopathy requires a clear understanding of the traits that define the disorder, which I attempted to clarify in Chapters 1 and 2 of this book.

A History of Psychopathy Definitions, Debates, and Misrepresentations

Chapters 1 and 2 called for subject-matter experts to be less private and more public about their perspectives on psychopathy. Subject-matter experts do not need to agree on a universal definition of psychopathy. However, Wittgenstein's Beetle in a Box experiment indicates that shared language is important for communication. The four contemporary perspectives on psychopathy discussed in this book (Cleckleyan, the Comprehensive Assessment of Psychopathic Personality (CAPP), the triarchic model, and psychopathy as extreme personality traits) tend to share the perspective that interpersonal, affective, and behavioural domains define the core elements of psychopathy. Although not as firmly agreed upon in the academic literature, there is support for the views that (1) criminal behaviour is a consequence of psychopathy rather than a specific trait of psychopathy, (2) psychopathy is a dimensional rather than categorical construct, (3) successful psychopathy is an oxymoron given the association between psychopathy and dysfunctional interpersonal interactions, (4) expert-rating measures are preferred to self-report instruments, and (5) psychopathy traits are malleable over the life-course.

Another source of agreement for subject-matter experts is the view that popular culture depictions of psychopathy poorly reflect the academic literature. This belief is supported by empirical research indicating that learning about psychopathy from the media does not improve comprehension of its definition (Keesler & DeMatteo, 2017). My biggest concern is not that television and film fictionalize psychopathy; this should be expected given that these sources typically do not claim to directly inform their viewers about the academic literature on psychopathy. The issue arises when journalists and others present their work as an honest assessment of the psychopathy literature. In reality, whether knowingly or due to ignorance, they sacrifice accuracy in favour of entertainment. Jon Ronson's TED Talk is perhaps the most viewed source of information on psychopathy (TED, 2012). Ronson's lecture and associated book have been repeatedly scrutinized by subject-matter experts for perpetuating harmful myths about psychopathy and how it is assessed (Society for the Scientific Study of Psychopathy, 2012). Contrary to Ronson, the practice of assessing psychopathy does not start with an assumption that psychopathy traits are present and then proceed to search for evidence to support this assumption. The goal is to assess whether and to what extent psychopathy traits are present. Despite what True Crime podcasts, TikTokers (even the ones claiming to have degrees in psychology), and YouTube tutorial videos tell their audiences, psychopathy is not something that is spotted through body language and verbal cues. I hope that this book helps readers develop an understanding of psychopathy from an academic perspective so that they can better evaluate the veracity of claims about psychopathy that are ever-present in daily life.

Can Readers Trust the Data?

The ISVYOS has been ongoing since 1998. Some participants are now in their forties. The longitudinal design of the study allowed me to examine the adult outcomes of over 500 youth who were assessed for psychopathy traits using the PCL:YV. Examining the relationship between psychopathy traits in adolescence and negative outcomes in adulthood means nothing in the absence of quality data, including a reliable and valid measure of psychopathy.

Chapters 3 and 4 addressed questions about the process of data collection and the reliability and validity of the PCL:YV. As illustrated in Chapter 3, some of the expressions of psychopathy traits among ISVYOS participants overlapped with Cleckley's (1976) observations of adult clinical patients from decades ago. Examples of such overlap included a tendency to overinflate knowledge or ability. Justin, an ISVYOS participant, bragged about his knowledge of Mark Twain. Max, one of Cleckley's patients (1976; see Chapter 5 of his book), did the same with Shakespeare.

Although this overlap was interesting, it is important not to read too much into similarities in the expression of a single trait in a single instance. Evidence of psychopathy traits requires establishing that the trait has been present over time and across different social contexts. Assessing psychopathy is thus complex and requires strong interview skills (e.g., rapport, active listening, and preparation) to probe the depth and robustness of personality traits across time and social context. Background knowledge of psychopathy is also critical for differentiating between traits, thereby ensuring that evidence of one trait (e.g., lack of empathy) is not also used as evidence of another trait (e.g., lack of remorse).

Chapter 4 established that the ISVYOS research team's efforts to conduct detailed interviews and careful scoring resulted in evidence of PCL:YV interrater reliability and internal consistency. A high degree of reliability does not imply perfection. Understanding youth psychopathy traits has been likened to an impressionist painting. From further away, the distinction between psychopathy and other youth characteristics (e.g., moral disengagement, low self-control, and criminogenic attitudes) might seem clear. However, like an impressionist painting, once you are in the interview room and face-to-face with a young person, the ability to distinguish psychopathy traits from other developmental difficulties becomes less clear. As indicated in the discussion of false positive cases in Chapter 5, it is possible to get things wrong. People are not measured in test tubes.

Construct validity relates to whether the PCL:YV is measuring psychopathy as intended. Confirmatory factor analyses supported both a four-factor model and a three-factor model, with slightly more evidence for a hierarchical three-factor model. A hierarchical model means that the correlation between factors is spurious (i.e., not real) because the overarching psychopathy construct is a common cause of each factor and its associated traits. The three-factor model implies that the Antisocial factor of the PCL:YV did not improve model fit compared to a model that only included items from the Interpersonal, Affective, and Lifestyle factors. Aligning with this observation, item response theory and psychopathology network analyses indicated that items from the Antisocial factor were among the least relevant to PCL:YV-measured psychopathy. Core psychopathy traits primarily emerged from interpersonal and affective domains of functioning, including impression management, grandiosity, pathological lying, manipulation, lack of remorse, shallow affect, callous/lack of empathy, and failure to accept responsibility.

Although there were different ways of representing PCL:YV scores (e.g., three-factor model, four-factor model, or summing core traits), the different representations of scores were all highly correlated (e.g., >0.800), which implied that predictive validity analyses would reach the same conclusion regardless of how PCL:YV scores were totalled. This expectation was confirmed across the empirical chapters in this book. It was rare to reach a conclusion with PCL:YV total scores that was not also reached when examining scores on the three-factor model or the sum of core traits per the item response theory analysis. With respect to convergent validity, the PCL:YV was only moderately correlated with two other measures of psychopathy: the Comprehensive Assessment of Psychopathic Personality – Institutional Rating Scale (CAPP-IRS) and the Millon Adolescent Clinical Inventory (MACI) Psychopathy Content Scale. This reflects the fact that the three measures were developed with different perspectives of psychopathy in mind as well as the fact that the MACI is a self-report survey.

Psychopathy Traits in Adolescence and Their Consequences in Adulthood

Chapters 5 and 6 were written to better understand the relationship between psychopathy traits in adolescence and negative outcomes in adulthood. The goal was to gain clarity about whether some of the consequences of assessing psychopathy (e.g., expending time and resources, the potential for stigmatization) would be at least partly offset by evidence that ignoring psychopathy would result in missed opportunities to prevent future harm. Compared to other mental health disorders, psychopathy research receives minimal funding from government agencies (Gatner et al., 2023). This may be attributed, in part, to stigma surrounding psychopathy (Reidy et al., 2015) and to myths perpetuated by some academics, such as the claim that people with psychopathy traits do not benefit from treatment (Harris & Rice, 2017). Framing psychopathy as a public health issue rather than a criminal legal system issue, and debunking long-held misperceptions, may be helpful for improving funding for psychopathy research. Another reason psychopathy research is underfunded may be because researchers tend to be too narrow in their focus on offending outcomes, which is why I also examined social and health outcomes in adulthood.

Chapters 5 and 6 indicated that psychopathy traits in adolescence were associated with significant increases in the likelihood of persistent offending and serious crimes like sex offences and firearm offences. They were also linked to lower levels of informal social control (e.g., positive relationships, employment, and stable housing), conflict with peers in prison, substance use issues, and mortality. Contrary to earlier research that questioned whether the Interpersonal and Affective factors were informative of future offending (Walters, 2004), each of the four factors of the PCL:YV was individually informative of persistent offending. Interpersonal and Affective factors were also informative of low levels of informal social control in adulthood, which is consistent with theories of assortative mating and research with those who report experiencing victimization by people with psychopathy traits. Lifestyle and Antisocial factors of the PCL:YV were most informative of health outcomes like substance use and mortality. My hope is that the diversity of negative outcomes associated with psychopathy traits illustrates that psychopathy is not just a criminal legal system problem. It is also possible that the criminal legal system is not the best place to address psychopathy traits, especially if the goal is to avoid stigma. The idea that the assessment of psychopathy serves no benefit because people with psychopathy traits do not differ from others in their level of dangerousness or psychological functioning (Larsen, 2025) was not supported here. One reason why the empirical analyses in this book differ from Larsen's (2025) narrative is that Larsen conflated recidivism with dangerousness, even though recidivism is a far broader concept than dangerousness because it includes minor and administrative offences that poorly reflect dangerousness.

Chapters 5 and 6 also highlighted that there are many factors beyond psychopathy that relate to offending, social relationships, and health; psychopathy traits alone are insufficient to fully explain these issues. Furthermore, psychopathy traits are not a harbinger for persistent offending and other negative outcomes. In Chapter 5, a set of case studies was used to better understand why youth who scored high on the PCL:YV nevertheless were not involved in persistent offending in adulthood. Sometimes there were concerns about accurate ratings on the PCL:YV or the appropriateness of the PCL:YV in distinguishing psychopathy from other disorders. In some cases, youth truly desisted from offending in adulthood due to changes in psychopathy traits. In other cases, it appeared that the absence of official convictions was merely evidence of an ability to avoid detection and punishment.

Understanding the Relationship between Psychopathy and Offending

The results of analyses performed elsewhere (e.g., McCuish & Lussier, 2018) support the conclusion that psychopathy traits are not as stable between adolescence and adulthood as originally thought. This observation poses a challenge for interpreting the results from Chapter 5. Specifically, if some youth scoring high on the PCL:YV experience changes in psychopathy traits yet continue to offend at a high rate in adulthood, what accounts for their persistence in offending? As I reported in Chapter 6, psychopathy traits in adolescence influenced a variety of negative outcomes in adulthood. One possible explanation for this paradox is that psychopathy traits in adolescence have negative ramifications, in the short term, for social roles, relationships, and health, which in turn are risk factors for persistent offending.

Studies that show that psychopathy statistically predicts offending are not able to clarify whether there is a causal relationship between psychopathy and offending, even if other risk factors are controlled for. This is because statistical prediction is not informative of the process that connects a putative cause (psychopathy) to an expected outcome (offending; Wikström, 2020). In lieu of this, forensic psychologists often rely on a process of case formulation to identify the contexts and motivations that lead to offending and to better understand why specific risk factors influence reoffending (Hart et al., 2011). Case formulation involves decision-making for a single person. However, much of what is known about the relationship between psychopathy and offending is based on studies that either only examined whether psychopathy statistically predicts offending, or relied on a clinician's anecdotal experiences or expertise.

To help provide more evidence-based support for case formulation practices, analyses in Chapter 7 used structural equation modeling to examine pathways from psychopathy traits to offending. Analyses addressed whether the relationship between psychopathy traits in adolescence and persistent offending in adulthood was direct, entirely indirect (e.g., fully mediated by a person's social context, such as their level of informal social control), or a combination of both (i.e., partial mediation). Reliably addressing this question requires a research design where the measurement of psychopathy precedes adult social/health outcomes and where the measurement of these social/health outcomes precedes the measurement of offending. The right analytic strategy is also needed. Based on a mediation model with bootstrapped indirect effects, Chapter 7 indicated that part of the reason why psychopathy traits in adolescence were associated with persistent offending in adulthood was because of the influence of psychopathy traits on, in early adulthood (ages 18 to 23), low levels of informal social control and a high level of conflict within participants' prison-based social networks. Early developmental experiences have a cascading impact on a person's social environment, and this environment matters for future offending.

Case formulation also recognizes the possibility that protective factors like informal social control may not function as anticipated for people with psychopathy traits (de Vogel et al., 2009). Chapter 8 introduced the idea of a social resistance hypothesis, which proposes that people with psychopathy traits will be more resistant to the impact of positive social/health outcomes on desistance from criminal behaviour. For example, informal social control is thought to promote desistance through stronger bonds to friends and family, which in turn deters criminal behaviour. However, for people with psychopathy traits who are callous, lacking in empathy, and prone to manipulating others, there are reasons to believe that they will be resistant to informal social control because they do not fear losing their bonds to others due to their involvement in criminal behaviour. A case study describing James' developmental history illustrated how offending can continue even when positive sources of informal social control are present. James often offended against people who were meant to be positive sources of informal social control. Cleckley (1976) reported a similar observation regarding Max's perpetration of intimate partner violence against his wife.

James' circumstances were not unique. The idea of a social resistance hypothesis was formally tested in a moderation analysis that examined the interaction between PCL:YV scores and social/health outcomes. Only people who scored low on the PCL:YV experienced reduced levels of offending when positive sources of informal social control were present. Said differently, people with low PCL:YV scores and high levels of informal social control were convicted of fewer offences compared to people with low PCL:YV scores who nevertheless had low levels of informal social control. Conversely, among people with high PCL:YV scores, positive sources of informal social control in adulthood did not improve the chances of desistance from criminal behaviour. This finding aligns with clinical research and associated theories suggesting that personality disorders like psychopathy are associated with maladaptive social and identity functioning (Cooke et al., 2004; Sharp & Wall, 2021), even in positive social environments (Forth et al., 2022).

Psychopathy, Social Institutions, and Offending

Psychopathy research has been criticized (fairly) for being overly concerned with the individual and their immediate environment (Verona & Fox, 2025). Chapters 9–10 departed from this tradition by investigating the role of historical contexts and formal institutions in shaping repeated offending. Recent research on birth cohorts revealed that it is important to situate individual-level characteristics in their appropriate historical context. Analyses of data from the PHDCN+ study in Chicago found that people with low levels of self-control (i.e., high risk for offending) who were born in eras with lower crime rates were involved in similar levels of offending compared to people with high self-control (i.e., low risk for offending) who were born in eras with higher crime rates. In other words, high-risk and low-risk persons had similar levels of offending, and the reason appears to be that people who were low-risk came of age when crime was more prevalent (Montana et al., 2023). It is therefore important to look beyond a person's immediate social environment and consider the historical context in which a person grows up.

Research from the PHDCN+ reflects the idea that "when" someone is born can be just as important as "who" they are when it comes to risk for reoffending (Neil & Sampson, 2021). However, for ISVYOS participants, PCL:YV total scores were informative of persistent convictions in adulthood regardless of when they were born (1979–1998) and regardless of whether they were incarcerated under legislation with more of an emphasis on punishment and deterrence or rehabilitation. Youth who scored high on the PCL:YV but were born in eras with lower crime rates and more emphasis on rehabilitation still had higher levels of offending compared to youth who scored low on the PCL:YV but were born in eras with higher crime rates and a stronger punitive focus. The difference in findings between this study, based on participants from Canada, and the studies from the PHDNC+, based on participants from the United States, may reflect the fact that Canada experiences less dramatic changes in its social environment and political climate compared to the United States (e.g., Neil & Carmichael, 2015; Roberts, 2012; Tonry, 2013b). Thus, having participants born between 1979 and 1998 may have been too small a gap to detect an impact of changes in Canada's macro-level social structure.

The analyses from Chapter 10 addressed long-standing assumptions that people with psychopathy traits do not respond to treatment or punishment (Harris & Rice, 2017). To evaluate this assumption, I used a first-differenced fixed-effect estimator to examine the relationship between year-over-year change in the number of days spent incarcerated and future year-over-year change in the number of convictions. Among youth who scored high on the PCL:YV, controlling for changes in age, year-over-year increases in the amount of time spent incarcerated were associated with subsequent year-over-year *decreases* in convictions between adolescence and adulthood. Given British Columbia's emphasis on providing rehabilitation programs for incarcerated youth, it is possible that these findings reflect the efficacy of the Risk–Need–Responsivity Model (RNR) model. The RNR model emphasizes higher intensity intervention strategies (e.g., custody sentences) only for those people who represent a high risk of reoffending.

Psychopathy directly influences negative outcomes in adulthood. Moreover, people with psychopathy traits often present with multiple co-occurring risk factors that further increase the likelihood of negative outcomes (Skeem et al., 2011). Given the diversity of treatment needs among people with psychopathy traits, higher-intensity wrap-around treatment services addressing different needs simultaneously may seem ideal. However, there are concerns that wrap-around services are too intensive and lead to burnout, treatment dropout, and declining motivation to change (Doleac, 2019). This does not imply that no services should be provided, nor does it imply that wrap-around services will not be effective for people with psychopathy traits. Rather, it is important to evaluate, rather than just assume, that wrap-around services have a positive impact on the lives of people with psychopathy traits. An alternative strategy would be to precisely identify which risk factors to prioritize for intervention instead of addressing multiple needs simultaneously.

The mediation and moderation analyses in Chapters 7–9 illustrate why one-size-fits-all treatment strategies may not be useful given the unique circumstances of people with psychopathy traits. For example, Chapter 7 showed that although psychopathy traits in adolescence increased the likelihood of substance use issues in adulthood, substance use issues did not mediate the relationship between psychopathy and offending. Thus, for people with psychopathy traits, even if they present with serious substance use issues, interventions that only address substance use issues may not reduce reoffending. Evidence in Chapter 8 supporting the social resistance hypothesis indicates that it may be important to first address psychopathy traits before attempting to improve positive sources of informal social control. PSYCHOPATHY.COMP, the Mendota Juvenile Treatment Center, schema therapy (see Bernstein et al., 2023), and Wong et al.'s (2012) two-component model are examples of programs that appear to find the right balance between addressing psychopathy traits and other needs-based factors without being too intensive or overbearing.

Final Thoughts

Larsen (2019, 2025) argued in favor of eliminating the assessment of psychopathy to avoid stigmatization and because he believed that people with psychopathy traits are not meaningfully different from others involved in criminal behaviour. I agree with parts of this perspective. The Oak Ridge Study's stigmatization of psychopathy provides clear support for Larsen's argument. The Oak Ridge Study had a long-term impact on shaping inaccurate perceptions, whether of laypersons (Ronson, 2011) or academics (Harris & Rice, 2017; Rice et al., 1992), that treatment did not work for people with psychopathy traits.

I agree with Larsen about the issue of stigmatization. However, I disagree that stigmatization arises merely from the assessment of psychopathy. If the formal assessment of psychopathy in forensic practice and in research were to end, stigmatization may in fact worsen because there would be no research to combat misconceptions of psychopathy. Without ongoing research, the vacuum would be filled by groups and individuals who perpetuate myths about psychopathy through sensationalized case studies. For example, research has shown that youth psychopathy traits change over time, which has helped contribute to the argument that labels like "psychopath" should be avoided (McCuish & Lussier, 2018). Even when assessment reveals that psychopathy is associated with negative consequences, it is not the assessment that causes stigma. The cause of stigma comes from reactions to this assessment by clinicians, criminal justice system personnel, researchers, jurors, and others. Researchers and clinicians should improve how they communicate psychopathy research to help avoid stigmatization. Stigma arises less from the structured assessment process and more from how assessment results are interpreted and operationalized.

Calls to stop assessing for psychopathy are often premised on outdated research or mischaracterizations of contemporary research (e.g., American Society of Criminology, 2024; Larsen, 2019, 2025). For example, Larsen (2025) misinterpreted odds ratio effect sizes when psychopathy was treated as a dimensional rather than categorical construct[2], failed to differentiate false positives from false negatives when evaluating the utility of psychopathy, conflated legal biases with limitations of psychopathy as a construct, and inappropriately equated recidivism with dangerousness or crime severity. Based on findings from this book and reported elsewhere, psychopathy traits are associated with a variety of negative social and health outcomes. It may be important for people to know whether they have psychopathy traits so that they can take steps (e.g., seeking treatment) to mitigate the risk of early mortality and other types of negative social and health outcomes such as low relationship quality and satisfaction. (see Shipley & Arrigo, 2001). Despite being rare in the general population, psychopathy is associated with billions of dollars in costs to the welfare, criminal legal, and health care systems (Gatner et al., 2023). In the ISVYOS PCL:YV cohort, major social and health consequences in adulthood did not occur randomly. Psychopathy traits in adolescence were helpful for understanding, but certainly did not fully explain, the occurrence of negative life events in

---

[2] It is appropriate to treat psychopathy test scores as dimensional rather than categorical, but given how odds ratios are calculated and the wide range of possible test scores on measures of psychopathy, dimensional representations of test scores will virtually always produce lower odds ratios compared to categorical representations of test scores. Odds ratios must be interpreted with the scale of the measure in mind.

adulthood. Proactive strategies that help achieve more positive forms of life success without creating stigmatizing labels are needed. In line with this, part of avoiding stigma involves communicating that people who score high on psychopathy measures in adolescence are not destined continue scoring high in adulthood (McCuish & Lussier, 2018).

Although I disagree with Larsen that the assessment of psychopathy should be abandoned, I do think that assessment practices can be improved. Assessing psychopathy is not always straightforward, and sometimes assessments are inaccurate. When it comes to research, inaccurate assessments lead to weaker predictive validity and lower explained variance in offending and other outcomes. In practical settings, the consequences of inaccurate assessments are more severe, given that decisions are made about, for example, parole eligibility. Misinterpretation of emotional responses is one mechanism through which inaccurate assessments may arise. Lachapelle et al.'s (2024) interviews with people experiencing incarceration indicated that some criminal legal system professionals misinterpreted imprisoned people's emotions when preparing for community reentry. It is important not to mistake situational emotions for psychopathy traits. If medical practitioners are acknowledged for their ability to temporarily suppress empathic responding in high-stress situations (Decety et al., 2010), the same level of understanding should be extended to incarcerated individuals who may also be dealing with stressful situations. Especially in instances where court processes are long and increase the chances of exposure to situational stressors, multiple interviews and assessments may be advisable because single assessments may be more vulnerable to misclassification. Multiple assessments would allow for an evaluation of the consistency of traits and test scores. Additionally, improved training in distinguishing situational distress from personality traits may reduce inaccurate assessments.

Psychopathy traits in adolescence are associated with long-term patterns of offending as well as a variety of negative social and health outcomes in early adulthood, including weaker social bonds, a higher degree of conflict in prison, substance use issues, and even early mortality. To ignore the existence of psychopathy traits because some researchers, politicians, and policymakers have co-opted the term for ideological purposes or to further specific policy agendas (Dilulio, 1995) ignores the reality that certain personality traits can be harmful to both the individual and others. Acknowledging this does not preclude the possibility of change. Instead, it acknowledges the potential benefit of early, humanistic intervention and treatment strategies that can improve the likelihood of positive outcomes over the life-course and reduce the broader social harms associated with untreated psychopathy traits.

References

Achenbach, T. (1997). *Manual of the young adult self-report and young adult behaviour checklist*. University of Vermont, Department of Psychiatry.

Aharoni, E., Sinnott-Armstrong, W., & Kiehl, K. (2012). Can psychopathic offenders discern moral wrongs? A new look at the moral/conventional distinction. *Journal of Abnormal Psychology*, 121(2), 484–497.

Aharoni, E., Weintraub, L., & Fridlund, A. (2007). No skin off my back: Retribution deficits in psychopathic motives for punishment. *Behavioural Sciences & the Law*, 25(6), 869–889.

Allard, T., McCarthy, M., & Stewart, A. (2020). The costs of Indigenous and non-Indigenous offender trajectories. *Trends and Issues in Crime and Criminal Justice*, 594, 1–18.

Allison, P. (2009). *Fixed effects regression models*. Sage.

Almas, I., & Lordos, A. (2025). A narrative review of psychopathy research: Current advances and the argument for a qualitative approach. *The Journal of Forensic Psychiatry & Psychology*, 36(3), 1–51.

Altikriti, S., Nedelec, J., & Silver, I. (2021). The role of arrest risk perception formation in the association between psychopathy and aggressive offending. *Youth Violence and Juvenile Justice*, 19(4), 402–422.

Amato, J., Cornell, D., & Fan, X. (2008). Adolescent psychopathy: Factor structure and correspondence with the Millon Adolescent Clinical Inventory. *Criminal Justice and Behaviour*, 35(3), 294–310.

American Cancer Society. (2024). *What is cancer?* Retrieved from https://www.cancer.org/cancer/understanding-cancer/what-is-cancer.html

American Psychiatric Association. (2013). *Diagnostic and statistical manual of mental disorders* (5th Ed.). APA.

American Society of Criminology. (2024). *ASC 2023 Presidential Address – Shadd Maruna* [Video]. YouTube. https://www.youtube.com/watch?v=VR9cJMgstb8

Andershed, H., Kerr, M., Stattin, H., & Levander, S. (2002). Psychopathic traits in non-referred youths: A new assessment tool. In E. Blau & L. Sheridan (Eds.), *Psychopaths: Current international perspectives* (pp. 131–158). Elsevier.

Arrigo, B., & Shipley, S. (2001). The confusion over psychopathy (I): Historical considerations. *International Journal of Offender Therapy and Comparative Criminology*, 45(3), 325–344.

Ashworth, P. D. (2009). William James's "psychologist's fallacy" and contemporary human science research. *International Journal of Qualitative Studies on Health and Well-being*, 4(4), 195–206.

Augimeri, L., Walsh, M., Donato, A., Blackman, A., & Piquero, A. (2018). SNAP (Stop Now And Plan): Helping children improve their self-control and externalizing behaviour problems. *Journal of Criminal Justice*, 56, 43–49.

Babiak, P., & Hare, R. (2007). *Snakes in suits: When psychopaths go to work*. Harper.

Backman, H., Laajasalo, T., Jokela, M., & Aronen, E. T. (2021). Parental warmth and hostility and the development of psychopathic behaviors: A longitudinal study of young offenders. *Journal of Child and Family Studies*, 30(4), 1–11.

Baglivio, M. T., Wolff, K. T., Piquero, A. R., & Epps, N. (2015). The relationship between Adverse Childhood Experiences (ACE) and juvenile offending trajectories in a juvenile offender sample. *Journal of Criminal Justice*, 43, 229–241.

Baker, F. (2001). *The basics of item response theory*. ERIC Clearinghouse.

Bala, N., Carrington, P., & Roberts, J. (2009). Evaluating the Youth Criminal Justice Act after five years: A qualified success. *Canadian Journal of Criminology and Criminal Justice*, 51(2), 131–167.

Bandura, A., Barbarnelli, C., Caprara, G. V., & Pastorelli, C. (1996). Mechanisms of moral disengagement in the exercise of moral agency. *Journal of Personality and Social Psychology*, 71, 364–374.

Baron, R., & Kenny, D. (1986). The moderator–mediator variable distinction in social psychological research: Conceptual, strategic, and statistical considerations. *Journal of Personality and Social Psychology*, 51(6), 1173–1182.

Baron, S. (1999). Street youths and substance use: The role of background, street lifestyle, and economic factors. *Youth & Society*, 31(1), 3–26.

Bayer, P., Hjalmarsson, R., & Pozen, D. (2009). Building criminal capital behind bars: Peer effects in juvenile corrections. *The Quarterly Journal of Economics*, 124(1), 105–147.

Beauregard, E., & Proulx, J. (2007). A classification of sexual homicide against men. *International Journal of Offender Therapy and Comparative Criminology*, 51(4), 420–432.

Beaver, K., Nedelec, J., da Silva Costa, C., Poersch, A., Stelmach, M., Freddi, M., & Boccio, C. (2014). The association between psychopathic personality traits and health-related outcomes. *Journal of Criminal Justice*, 42(5), 399–407.

Becker, E. (2001). As ex-theorist on young "Superpredators": Bush aide has regrets. *New York Times*, 9.

Becker, H. (1963). *Outsiders: Studies in the sociology of deviance*. Free Press of Glencoe.

Bellair, P., & Browning, C. (2010). Contemporary disorganization research: An assessment and further test of the systemic model of neighborhood crime. *Journal of Research in Crime and Delinquency*, 47, 496–521.

Belzak, L., & Halverson, J. (2018). Evidence synthesis – The opioid crisis in Canada: A national perspective. *Health Promotion and Chronic Disease Prevention in Canada: Research, Policy and Practice*, 38(6), 224–233.

Bennett, W., Dilulio, J., & Walters, J. (1996). *Body count: Moral poverty – And how to win America's war against crime and drugs*. Simon & Schuster.

Benning, S., & Smith, E. (2023). The registration continuum in personality disorder studies: Theory, rationale, and template. *Personality Disorders: Theory, Research, and Treatment*, 14(1), 5–18.

Bergman, L. R., & Magnusson, D. (1997). A person-oriented approach in research on developmental psychopathology. *Development and Psychopathology*, 9, 291–319.

Berluti, K., Ploe, M. L., Doherty, H., Jones, D. N., Patrick, C. J., & Marsh, A. A. (2025). Prevalence and correlates of psychopathy in the general population. *Journal of Personality Disorders*, 39(1), 1–21.

Bernstein, D. P., Keulen-de Vos, M., Clercx, M., De Vogel, V., Kersten, G. C., Lancel, M., & Arntz, A. (2023). Schema therapy for violent PD offenders: A randomized clinical trial. *Psychological Medicine*, 53(1), 88–102.

Berryessa, C. (2016). Behavioural and neural impairments of frontotemporal dementia: Potential implications for criminal responsibility and sentencing. *International Journal of Law and Psychiatry*, 46, 1–6.

Bersani, B., Laub, J. H., & Nieuwbeerta, P. (2009). Marriage and desistance from crime in the Netherlands: Do gender and socio-historical context matter? *Journal of Quantitative Criminology*, 25(1), 3–24.

Bhuller, M., Dahl, G., Løken, K., & Mogstad, M. (2020). Incarceration, recidivism, and employment. *Journal of Political Economy*, 128(4), 1269–1324.

Bishop, D. (2000). Juvenile offenders in the adult criminal justice system. *Crime and Justice*, 27, 81–167.

Blais, J., Solodukhin, E., & Forth, A. E. (2014). A meta-analysis exploring the relationship between psychopathy and instrumental versus reactive violence. *Criminal Justice and Behaviour*, 41(7), 797–821.

Blokland, A., & Nieuwbeerta, P. (2005). The effects of life circumstances on longitudinal trajectories of offending. *Criminology*, 43, 1203–1240.

Blumstein, A., Cohen, J., & Farrington, D. P. (1988). Criminal career research: Its value for criminology. *Criminology*, 26(1), 1–35.

Boddy, C. (2014). Corporate psychopaths, conflict, employee affective well-being and counterproductive work behaviour. *Journal of Business Ethics*, 121(1), 107–121.

Boduszek, D., & Debowska, A. (2016). Critical evaluation of psychopathy measurement (PCL-R and SRP-III/SF) and recommendations for future research. *Journal of Criminal Justice*, 44, 1–12.

Bolt, D. (2017). Analyzing the Psychopathy Checklist—Revised using factor analysis and item response theory. In H. Herve & J. C. Yuille (Eds.), *The psychopath* (pp. 105–139). Routledge.

Bolt, D., Hare, R. D., Vitale, J., & Newman, J. P. (2004). A multigroup item response theory analysis of the psychopathy checklist-revised. *Psychological Assessment*, 16(2), 155–168.

Boman, J., & Mowen, T. (2018). The role of turning points in establishing baseline differences between people in developmental and life-course criminology. *Criminology*, 56(1), 191–224.

Bonta, J., & Andrews, D. (2007). Risk-need-responsivity model for offender assessment and rehabilitation. *Rehabilitation*, 6(1), 1–22.

Bonta, J., Bourgon, G., Rugge, T., Pedneault, C., & Lee, S. (2021). *Large-scale implementation and evaluation of the Strategic Training Initiative in Community Supervision (STICS)*. Public Safety Canada.

Book, A., Holden, R., Starzyk, K., Wasylkiw, L., & Edwards, M. (2006). Psychopathic traits and experimental induced deception in self report assessment. *Personality and Individual Differences*, 41, 601–608.

Borgatti, S., Everett, M., & Johnson, J. (2013). *Analyzing social networks*. Sage.

Borsboom, D., & Cramer, A. O. J. (2013). Network analysis: An integrative approach to the structure of psychopathology. *Annual Review of Clinical Psychology*, 9, 91–121.

Borum, R., Bartel, P., & Forth, A. (2002). *SAVRY: Manual for the structured assessment of violence risk in youth*. Florida Mental Health Institute, University of South Florida.

Bouchard, M. (2020). Collaboration and boundaries in organized crime: A network perspective. *Crime and Justice*, 49(1), 425–469.

Bradford, C. (1979). Financing home ownership: The federal role in neighborhood decline. *Urban Affairs Quarterly*, 14, 313–335.

Brazil, K., & Volk, A. (2022). Cads in dads' clothing? Psychopathic traits and men's preferences for mating, parental, and somatic investment. *Evolutionary Psychological Science*, 8(3), 299–315.

Bruineman, M. (2021). Psychiatric patients awarded nearly $10M in lawsuit over experimental treatments. *The Toronto Star*. Retrieved from https://www.thestar.com/news/canada/psychiatric-patients-awarded-nearly-10m-in-lawsuit-over-experimental-treatments/article_60b39dd0-5920-510c-b2a6-3dd5ef959e4e.html

Bucerius, S., & Sandberg, S. (2022). Women in prisons. *Crime and Justice*, 51(1), 137–186.

Burchett, D., Sellbom, M., & Bagby, R. (2023). Assessment of response bias in personality disorder research. *Personality Disorders: Theory, Research, and Treatment*, 14, 93–104.

Burgess, L. (2021). What happens when you turn a psychopath into a therapist? *CBC News*. Retrieved from https://newsinteractives.cbc.ca/longform/oak-ridge-st-thomas-psychiatric-treatment/

Bushway, S., Piquero, A. R., Broidy, L. M., Cauffman, E., & Mazerolle, P. (2001). An empirical framework for studying desistance as a process. *Criminology*, 39(2), 491–516.

Bushway, S. D., & Denver, M. (2025). The myth that most people recidivate. *The Criminologist*, 51, 1–7.

Butsang, T., Owl, N., Butler, A., Sabourin, H., Croxford, R., Gislason, L., & Kouyoumdjian, F. G. (2025). Opioid toxicity deaths in Indigenous people who experienced incarceration in Ontario, Canada 2015–2020: A whole population retrospective cohort study. *The Lancet Regional Health – Americas*, 41, 1–9.

Cain, S. (2013). *Quiet: The power of introverts in a world that can't stop talking*. Crown.

Caldwell, M. F. (2011). Treatment-related changes in behavioural outcomes of psychopathy facets in adolescent offenders. *Law and Human Behaviour*, 35, 275–287.

Caldwell, M. F., McCormick, D. J., Umstead, D., & Van Rybroek, G. J. (2007). Evidence of treatment progress and therapeutic outcomes among adolescents with psychopathic features. *Criminal Justice and Behaviour*, 34(5), 573–587.

Caldwell, M. F., Skeem, J., Salekin, R., & Van Rybroek, G. J. (2006). Treatment response of adolescent offenders with psychopathy features: A 2-year follow-up. *Criminal Justice and Behaviour*, 33(5), 571–596.

Cantor, D., & Land, K. (1985). Unemployment and crime rates in the post-World War II United States: A theoretical and empirical analysis. *American Sociological Review*, 50(3), 317–332.

Caspi, A., & Herbener, E. S. (1990). Continuity and change: Assortative marriage and the consistency of personality in adulthood. *Journal of Personality and Social Psychology*, 58, 250–258.

Caspi, A., & Moffitt, T. E. (1995). The continuity of maladaptive behaviour: From description to understanding in the study of antisocial behaviour. In D. Cicchetti & D. Cohen (Eds.), *Manual of developmental psychology* (pp. 472–511). Wiley.

Caspi, A., & Roberts, B. W. (2001). Personality development across the life course: The argument for change and continuity. *Psychological inquiry*, 12(2), 49–66.

Caspi, A., Roberts, B. W., & Shiner, R. L. (2005). Personality development: Stability and change. *Annual Review of Psychology*, 56, 453–484.

Cauffman, E., & Steinberg, L. (2012). Emerging findings from research on adolescent development and juvenile justice. *Victims & Offenders*, 7(4), 428–449.

Cauffman, E., Skeem, J., Dmitrieva, J., & Cavanagh, C. (2016). Comparing the stability of psychopathy scores in adolescents versus adults: How often is "fledgling psychopathy" misdiagnosed? *Psychology, Public Policy, and Law*, 22, 77–91.

Cesaroni, C., & Bala, N. (2008). Deterrence as a principle of youth sentencing: No effect on youth, but a significant on judges. *Queen's Law Journal*, 34, 447–482.

Chan, H. C., Myers, W. C., & Heide, K. M. (2010). An empirical analysis of 30 years of US juvenile and adult sexual homicide offender data: Race and age differences in the victim–offender relationship. *Journal of Forensic Sciences*, 55(5), 1282-1290.

Cleckley, H. (1941). *The mask of sanity* (1st Ed.). Mosby.

(1976). *The mask of sanity* (5th Ed.). Mosby.

Clemmer, D. (1950). Observations on imprisonment as a source of criminality. *Journal of Law and Criminology*, 41(3), 311–319.

Cogburn, R. (1993). *A study of psychopathy and its relation to success in interpersonal deception*. University of Oregon.

Cohen, J. (1988). *Statistical power analysis for the behavioural sciences*. Lawrence Erlbaum.

(2020, July). A Teenager didn't do her online schoolwork so a judge sent her to juvenile detention. *ProPublica*. Retrieved from https://www.propublica.org/article/a-teenager-didnt-do-her-online-schoolwork-so-a-judge-sent-her-to-juvenile-detention

Cohen, L. E., & Felson, M. (1979). Social change and crime rate trends: A routine activity approach. *American Sociological Review*, 44(4), 588–608.

Cohen, M., & Piquero, A. R. (2009). New evidence on the monetary value of saving a high risk youth. *Journal of Quantitative Criminology*, 25, 25–49.

Cohen, M., Piquero, A. R., & Jennings, W. G. (2010). Studying the costs of crime across offender trajectories. *Criminology & Public Policy*, 9, 279–305.

Coid, J., Yang, M., Ullrich, S., Roberts, A., & Hare, R. D. (2009). Prevalence and correlates of psychopathic traits in the household population of Great Britain. *International Journal of Law and Psychiatry*, 32(2), 65–73.

Colins, O., Van Damme, L., Hendriks, A. M., & Georgiou, G. (2020). The DSM-5 with limited prosocial emotions specifier for conduct disorder: A systematic literature review. *Journal of Psychopathology and Behavioural Assessment*, 42, 248–258.

Cooke, D., & Logan, C. (2018). Capturing psychopathic personality: Penetrating the mask of sanity through clinical interview. In C. Patrick (Ed.), *Handbook of psychopathy* (pp. 189–210). Guilford Press.

Cooke, D., & Michie, C. (1997). An item response theory analysis of the Hare Psychopathy Checklist–Revised. *Psychological Assessment*, 9(1), 3–14.

(2001). Refining the construct of psychopathy: Towards a hierarchical model. *Psychological Assessment*, 13(2), 171–188.

Cooke, D., Hart, S., Logan, C., & Michie, C. (2004). *Comprehensive Assessment of Psychopathic Personality – Institutional Rating Scale (CAPP-IRS)*. Department of Psychology, Glasgow Caledonian University.

Cooke, D., Hart, S. D., Logan, C., & Michie, C. (2012). Explicating the construct of psychopathy: Development and validation of a conceptual model, the Comprehensive Assessment of Psychopathic Personality (CAPP). *International Journal of Forensic Mental Health*, 11(4), 242–252.

Cooke, D. J., Hart, S. D., Logan, C., & Michie, C. (2022). Evaluating the test validity of the comprehensive assessment of psychopathic personality symptom rating Sale (CAPP SRS). *Journal of Personality Assessment*, 104(6), 711–722.

Cooke, D. J., Michie, C., & Skeem, J. (2007). Understanding the structure of the Psychopathy Checklist–Revised: An exploration of methodological confusion. *The British Journal of Psychiatry*, 190(S49), s39–s50.

Corrado, R., & McCuish, E. C. (2015). The development of early onset, chronic, and versatile offending: The role of fetal alcohol spectrum disorder and mediating factors. *International Journal of Child and Adolescent Health*, 8(2), 241–250.

Corrado, R., Vincent, G. M., Hart, S. D., & Cohen, I. M. (2004). Predictive validity of the Psychopathy Checklist: Youth Version for general and violent recidivism. *Behavioural Sciences & the Law*, 22(1), 5–22.

Craig, S., Goulter, N., & Moretti, M. (2021). A systematic review of primary and secondary callous-unemotional traits and psychopathy variants in youth. *Clinical Child and Family Psychology Review*, 24(1), 65–91.

Cramer, A. O., Waldorp, L. J., Van Der Maas, H. L., & Borsboom, D. (2010). Comorbidity: A network perspective. *Behavioural and Brain Sciences*, 33(2–3), 137–150.

Crego, C., & Widiger, T. A. (2015). Psychopathy and the DSM. *Journal of Personality*, 83(6), 665–677.

Cunha, O., Braga, T., Gomes, H., & Abrunhosa Gonçalves, R. (2020). Psychopathy checklist-revised (PCL-R) factor structure in male perpetrators of intimate partner violence. *Journal of Forensic Psychology Research and Practice*, 20(3), 241–263.

Damm, A. P., & Gorinas, C. (2020). Prison as a criminal school: Peer effects and criminal learning behind bars. *The Journal of Law and Economics*, 63(1), 149–180.

Dawson, K. (2021). *Capital gains: Examining the role of gang members personal networks and criminal careers*. Unpublished doctoral dissertation, Simon Fraser University, Burnaby.

Dawson, S., McCuish, E., Hart, S., & Corrado, R. (2012). Critical issues in the assessment of adolescent psychopathy: An illustration using two case studies. *International Journal of Forensic Mental Health*, 11(2), 63–79.

Day, D. M., & Koegl, C. J. (2019). The monetary costs of criminal trajectories for a sample of offenders in Ontario, Canada. *Journal of Developmental and Life-Course Criminology*, 5(2), 203–219.

De Brito, S. A., Forth, A. E., Baskin-Sommers, A. R., Brazil, I. A., Kimonis, E. R., Pardini, D., & Viding, E. (2021). Psychopathy. *Nature Reviews Disease Primers*, 7(1), 49.

Decety, J., Yang, C. Y., & Cheng, Y. (2010). Physicians down-regulate their pain empathy response: An event-related brain potential study. *Neuroimage*, 50(4), 1676–1682.

DeLisi, M. (2016). *Psychopathy as unified theory of crime*. Palgrave Macmillan.

DeLisi, M., & Piquero, A. (2011). New frontiers in criminal careers research, 2000–2011: A state-of-the-art review. *Journal of Criminal Justice*, 39, 289–301.

DeLisi, M., Angton, A., Vaughn, M. G., Trulson, C. R., Caudill, J. W., & Beaver, K. M. (2014a). Not my fault: Blame externalization is the psychopathic feature most associated with pathological delinquency among confined delinquents. *International Journal of Offender Therapy and Comparative Criminology*, 58(12), 1415–1430.

DeLisi, M., Hochstetler, A., Jones-Johnson, G., Caudill, J. W., & Marquart, J. W. (2011). The road to murder: The enduring criminogenic effects of juvenile confinement among a sample of adult career criminals. *Youth Violence and Juvenile Justice*, 9(3), 207–221.

DeLisi, M., Peters, D. J., Dansby, T., Vaughn, M. G., Shook, J. J., & Hochstetler, A. (2014b). Dynamics of psychopathy and moral disengagement in the etiology of crime. *Youth Violence and Juvenile Justice*, 12(4), 295–314.

DeLisi, M., Vaughn, M. G., Beaver, K. M., & Wright, J. P. (2010). The Hannibal Lecter myth: Psychopathy and verbal intelligence in the MacArthur violence risk assessment study. *Journal of Psychopathology and Behavioural Assessment*, 32, 169–177.

Deljou, B., Rudsari, A. B., & Farnam, A. (2022). Structural equation modelling of primary and secondary vulnerability of psychopathic disorder based on behavioral brain systems in medical students. *Depiction of Health*, 13(2), 234–243.

DeMatteo, D., Hart, S. D., Heilbrun, K., Boccaccini, M. T., Cunningham, M. D., Douglas, K. S., & Reidy, T. J. (2020). Statement of concerned experts on the use of the Hare Psychopathy Checklist–Revised in capital sentencing to assess risk for institutional violence. *Psychology, Public Policy, and Law*, 26(2), 133–144.

Dillard, C. L., Salekin, R. T., Barker, E. D., & Grimes, R. D. (2013). Psychopathy in adolescent offenders: An item response theory study of the antisocial process screening device – Self report and the Psychopathy Checklist: Youth Version. *Personality Disorders: Theory, Research, and Treatment*, 4(2), 101–120.

Dilulio, J. (1995, December). Moral poverty: The coming of the Superpredators should scare us into wanting to get to the root causes of crime a lot faster. *Chicago Tribune*, Section 1, p. 31.

Doherty, E. E. (2006). Self-control, social bonds, and desistance: A test of life-course interdependence. *Criminology*, 44(4), 807–833.

Doleac, J. L. (2019). Wrap-around services don't improve prisoner reentry outcomes. *Journal of Policy Analysis and Management*, 38(2), 508–514.

Doob, A., & Webster, C. (2016). Weathering the storm? Testing long-standing Canadian sentencing policy in the twenty-first century. *Crime and Justice*, 45(1), 359–418.

Dotterer, H., Waller, R., Cope, L., Hicks, B. M., Nigg, J. T., Zucker, R., & Hyde, L. W. (2017). Concurrent and developmental correlates of psychopathic traits using a triarchic psychopathy model approach. *Journal of Abnormal Psychology*, 126(7), 859–876.

Douglas, K. S., Guy, L. S., & Hart, S. D. (2009). Psychosis as a risk factor for violence to others: A meta-analysis. *Psychological Bulletin*, 135(5), 679–706.

Douglas, K. S., Hart, S. D., Webster, C. D., & Belfrage, H. (2013). *HCR-20V3: Assessing risk of violence – User guide*. Mental Health, Law, and Policy Institute, Simon Fraser University.

Drefahl, S., Wallace, M., Mussino, E., Aradhya, S., Kolk, M., Brandén, M., & Andersson, G. (2020). A population-based cohort study of sociodemographic risk factors for COVID-19 deaths in Sweden. *Nature Communications*, 11(1), Article 5097.

Dyck, H. L., Campbell, M. A., Schmidt, F., & Wershler, J. L. (2013). Youth psychopathic traits and their impact on long-term criminal offending trajectories. *Youth Violence and Juvenile Justice*, 11(3), 230–248.

Edens, J., Campbell, J., & Weir, J. (2007). Youth psychopathy and criminal recidivism: A meta-analysis of the psychopathy checklist measures. *Law & Human Behaviour*, 31, 53–75.

Edens, J., Clark, J., Smith, S. T., Cox, J., & Kelley, S. E. (2013a). Bold, smart, dangerous and evil: Perceived correlates of core psychopathic traits among jury panel members. *Personality and Mental Health*, 7(2), 143–153.

Edens, J. F., Magyar, M. S., & Cox, J. (2013b). Taking psychopathy measures "out of the lab" and into the legal system: Some practical concerns. In K. A. Kiehl & W. P. Sinnott-Armstrong (Eds.), *Handbook on psychopathy and law* (pp. 250–272). Oxford University Press.

Eichenbaum, A. E., Marcus, D. K., & French, B. F. (2019). Item response theory analysis of the Psychopathic Personality Inventory–Revised. *Assessment*, 26(6), 1046–1058.

(2021). Item response theory analysis of the Triarchic Psychopathy Measure. *Psychological Assessment*, 33(8), 766–776.

Eisenbarth, H., Hart, C., Zubielevitch, E., Keilor, T., Wilson, M., Bulbulia, J., & Sedikides, C. (2022). Aspects of psychopathic personality relate to lower subjective and objective professional success. *Personality and Individual Differences*, 186, Article 111340.

Elder, G. H. (1994). Time, human agency, and social change: Perspectives on the life course. *Social Psychology Quarterly*, 57(1), 4–15.

Ellard, J. (1988). The history and present status of moral insanity. *Australian and New Zealand Journal of Psychiatry*, 22, 383–389.

Epskamp, S., & Fried, E. I. (2018). Package "bootnet." CRAN. Retrieved from https://cran.r-project.org/web/packages/bootnet/bootnet.pdf

Epskamp, S., Borsboom, D., & Fried, E. I. (2017). Estimating psychological networks and their accuracy: A tutorial paper. *Behaviour Research Methods*, 50(1), 195–212.

Epskamp, S., Cramer, A. O., Waldorp, L. J., Schmittmann, V. D., & Borsboom, D. (2012). qgraph: Network visualizations of relationships in psychometric data. *Journal of Statistical Software*, 48, 1–18.

Eronen, M. I., & Bringmann, L. F. (2021). The theory crisis in psychology: How to move forward. *Perspectives on Psychological Science*, 16(4), 779–788.

Fanniff, A., York, T., & Gutierrez, R. (2023). Developing consensus for culturally informed forensic mental health assessment: Experts' opinions on best practices. *Law and Human Behavior*, 47(3), 385–402.

Farrington, D. (1986). Age and crime. *Crime and Justice*, 7, 189–250.

Farrington, D., & Bergstrøm, H. (2022). The development of psychopathy through the lifespan and its relation to offending. In P. B. Marques, M. Paulino, & L. Alho (Eds.), *Psychopathy and criminal behavior* (pp. 105–125). Academic Press.

Farrington, D., & Welsh, B. (2008). *Saving children from a life of crime: Early risk factors and effective interventions*. Oxford University Press.

Farrington, D. P., & Murray, J. (Eds.). (2014). *Labeling theory: Empirical tests*. Transaction.

Farrington, D. P., Loeber, R., & Berg, M. T. (2012). Young men who kill: A prospective longitudinal examination from childhood. *Homicide Studies*, 16, 99–128.

Farrington, D. P., Ullrich, S., & Salekin, R. T. (2010). Environmental influences and child and adolescent psychopathy. In R. T. Salekin & D. R. Lynam (Eds.), *Handbook of child and adolescent psychopathy* (pp. 202–230). Guilford.

Flexon, J. L., & Meldrum, R. C. (2013). Adolescent psychopathic traits and violent delinquency: Additive and nonadditive effects with key criminological variables. *Youth Violence and Juvenile Justice*, 11(4), 349–369.

Ford, J. D. (2012). Indigenous health and climate change. *American Journal of Public Health*, 102, 1260–1266.

Forouzan, E., & Cooke, D. J. (2005). Figuring out la femme fatale: Conceptual and assessment issues concerning psychopathy in females. *Behavioral Sciences & the Law*, 23(6), 765–778.

Forsman, J. (2024). "If I am going to have a past, I prefer it to be multiple choice": The Joker, madness, and metafiction. In Massimiliano L. Cappuccio, George A. Dunn, & Jason T. Eberl (Eds.), *Joker and philosophy: Why so serious?* (pp. 106–116). John Wiley & Sons.

Forsman, M., Lichtenstein, P., Andershed, H., & Larsson, H. (2008). Genetic effects explain the stability of psychopathic personality from mid-to late adolescence. *Journal of Abnormal Psychology*, 117, 606–617.

Forth, A., Kosson, D., & Hare, R. (2003). *The Hare Psychopathy Checklist: Youth Version*. Multi-Health Systems.

Forth, A., Sezlik, S., Lee, S., Ritchie, M., Logan, J., & Ellingwood, H. (2022). Toxic relationships: The experiences and effects of psychopathy in romantic relationships. *International Journal of Offender Therapy and Comparative Criminology*, 66(15), 1627–1658.

Fowler, T., Langley, K., Rice, F., Whittinger, N., Ross, K., van Goozen, S., & Thapar, A. (2009). Psychopathy traits in adolescents with childhood attention-deficit hyperactivity disorder. *The British Journal of Psychiatry*, 194(1), 62–67.

Fowles, D. C. (2018). Temperament risk factors for psychopathy. In C. Patrick (Ed.), *Handbook of psychopathy* (2nd Ed., pp. 94–126). Guilford Press.

Fox, B., & DeLisi, M. (2019). Psychopathic killers: A meta-analytic review of the psychopathy-homicide nexus. *Aggression and Violent Behaviour*, 44, 67–79.

Fox, K., Zambrana, K., & Lane, J. (2011). Getting in (and staying in) when everyone else wants to get out: 10 lessons learned from conducting research with inmates. *Journal of Criminal Justice Education*, 22(2), 304–327.

Frazier, A., Ferreira, P. A., & Gonzales, J. E. (2019). Born this way? A review of neurobiological and environmental evidence for the etiology of psychopathy. *Personality Neuroscience*, 2, 1–16.

Gacono, C. B. (2000). Suggestions for implementation and use of the Psychopathy Checklists in forensic and clinical practice. In C. B. Gacono (Ed.), *The clinical and forensic assessment of psychopathy: A practitioner's guide* (pp. 175–202). Lawrence Erlbaum Associates.

(2021). *A clinical and forensic interview schedule for the Hare psychopathy checklist: Revised and screening version*. Routledge.

Gacono, C. B., & Hutton, H. (1994). Suggestions for the clinical and forensic use of the Hare Psychopathy Checklist-Revised (PCL-R). *International Journal of Law and Psychiatry*, 17(3), 303–317.

Gadermann, A., Guhn, M., & Zumbo, B. (2012). Estimating ordinal reliability for Likert-type and ordinal item response data: A conceptual, empirical, and practical guide. *Practical Assessment, Research & Evaluation*, 17(3), 1–13, n3.

Gao, Y., & Raine, A. (2010). Successful and unsuccessful psychopaths: A neurobiological model. *Behavioural Sciences & the Law*, 28(2), 194–210.

Garofalo, C., Neumann, C. S., & Mark, D. (2020). Associations between psychopathy and the Trait Meta-Mood Scale in incarcerated males: A combined latent variable-and person-centered approach. *Criminal Justice and Behavior*, 47(3), 331–351.

Gatner, D. (2019). *How much does that cost? Examining the economic costs of crime in North America attributable to people with psychopathic personality disorder*. SFU thesis repository.

Gatner, D. T., Douglas, K., & Hart, S. (2016). Examining the incremental and interactive effects of boldness with meanness and disinhibition within the triarchic model of psychopathy. *Personality Disorders: Theory, Research, and Treatment*, 7(3), 259–268.

Gatner, D. T., Douglas, K. S., Almond, M. F. E., Hart, S. D., & Kropp, P. (2023). How much does that cost? Examining the economic costs of crime in North America attributable to people with psychopathic personality disorder. *Personality Disorders: Theory, Research, and Treatment*, 14(4), 391–400.

Gatner, D. T., Douglas, K. S., Hart, S. D., & Kropp, P. (2022). Structured professional judgment (SPJ) violence risk case formulation and psychopathic personality disorder. *International Journal of Forensic Mental Health*, 21, 20–36.

Geis, G. (1955). Pioneers in Criminology VII – Jeremy Bentham (1748–1832). *Journal of Criminal Law, Criminology and Police Science*, 46, 159–171.

Gendreau, P., & Ross, R. (1983). Correctional treatment: Some recommendations for effective intervention. *Juvenile and Family Court Journal*, 34, 31–39.

Gendreau, P., Cullen, F. T., & Goggin, C. (1999). *The effects of prison sentences on recidivism* (pp. 4–5). Solicitor General Canada.

Giordano, P., Cernkovich, S., & Rudolph, J. (2002). Gender, crime, and desistance: Toward a theory of cognitive transformation. *American Journal of Sociology*, 107(4), 990–1064.

Gottfredson, M., & Hirschi, T. (1990). *The general theory of crime*. Stanford University Press.

Gough, H. G. (1948). A sociological theory of psychopathy. *American Journal of Sociology*, 53(5), 359–366.

Government of British Columbia. (2024). *Youth custody in BC*. Retrieved from https://www2.gov.bc.ca/gov/content/justice/criminal-justice/bcs-criminal-justice-system/youth-justice/youth-justice-in-british-columbia/serving-a-youth-sentence/youth-custody

Grann, M., Langstrom, N., Tengstrom, A., & Stalenheim, E. (1998). Reliability of file-based retrospective ratings of psychopathy with the PCL-R. *Journal of Personality Assessment*, 70(3), 416–426.

Granneman, J. (2020). Can you stop being an introvert? Probably not, according to science. *Introvert, Dear*. Retrieved from https://introvertdear.com/news/introvert-genetic-dna/

Granovetter, M. (1978). Threshold models of collective behaviour. *American Journal of Sociology*, 83(6), 1420–1443.

Greenwood, P., & Abrahamse, A. *Selective incapacitation*. Rand, 1982.

Gress, C. (2009). Corrections Branch Performance, Research and Evaluation Unit. *BC Corrections*. Retrieved from https://www2.gov.bc.ca/assets/gov/law-crime-and-justice/criminal-justice/corrections/research-evaluation/issue-1.pdf

(2010a). Advancing offender programs. *BC Corrections*. Retrieved from https://www2.gov.bc.ca/assets/gov/law-crime-and-justice/criminal-justice/corrections/research-evaluation/issue-2.pdf

(2010b). Revealing research & evaluation. *BC Corrections*. Retrieved from https://www2.gov.bc.ca/assets/gov/law-crime-and-justice/criminal-justice/corrections/research-evaluation/issue-3.pdf

Gretton, H. M., Hare, R. D., & Catchpole, R. E. (2004). Psychopathy and offending from adolescence to adulthood: A 10-year follow-up. *Journal of Consulting and Clinical Psychology*, 72(4), 636–645.

Guay, J., Knight, R., Ruscio, J., & Hare, R. (2018). A taxometric investigation of psychopathy in women. *Psychiatry Research*, 261, 565–573.

Guay, J., Ruscio, J., Knight, R., & Hare, R. (2007). A taxometric analysis of the latent structure of psychopathy: Evidence for dimensionality. *Journal of Abnormal Psychology*, 116(4), 701–716.

Guy, L. S., Douglas, K. S., & Hendry, M. C. (2010). The role of psychopathic personality disorder in violence risk assessments using the HCR-20. *Journal of Personality Disorders*, 24(5), 551–580.

Hanneman, R. A., & Riddle, M. (2005). *Introduction to social network methods*. University of California, Riverside.

Hardin, J., & Hilbe, J. (2007). *Generalized linear models and extensions*. Stata Press.

Hare, R. (2022). Foreword. In P. B. Marques, M. Paulino, & L. Alho (Eds.), *Psychopathy and criminal behaviour: Current trends and challenges* (pp. xxix–xxxv). Academic Press.

Hare, R., & Neumann, C. (2010). Psychopathy: Assessment and forensic implications. In L. Malatesti & J. McMillan (Eds), *Responsibility and psychopathy: Interfacing law, psychiatry and philosophy* (pp. 93–123). Oxford University Press.

Hare, R. D. (1980). A research scale for the assessment of psychopathy in criminal populations. *Personality and Individual Differences*, 1, 111–117.

(1996). Psychopathy: A clinical construct whose time has come. *Criminal Justice and Behaviour*, 23, 25–54.

(2001). Psychopaths and their nature: Some implications for understanding human predatory violence. In A. Raine & J. Sanmartin (Eds.), *Violence and psychopathy* (pp. 5–34). Kluwer Academic Publishers.

(2003). *The Hare Psychopathy Checklist-Revised* (2nd Ed.). Multi-Health Systems Inc.

Hare, R. D., & Cox, D. (1978). Clinical and empirical conceptions of psychopathy, and the selection of subjects for research. In R. Hare & D. Schalling (Eds.), *Psychopathic behaviour: Approaches to research* (pp. 1–21). Wiley.

Hare, R. D., & Neumann, C. S. (2010). The role of antisociality in the psychopathy construct: Comment on Skeem and Cooke (2010). *Psychological Assessment*, 22(2), 446–454.

Hare, R. D., McPherson, L M., & Forth, A. E. (1988). Male psychopaths and their criminal careers. *Journal of Consulting and Clinical Psychology*, 56(5), 710–714.

Harris, G., & Rice, M. E. (2017). Psychopathy research at Oak Ridge: Skepticism overcome. In H. Herve & J. C. Yuille (Eds.), *The Psychopath: Theory, research, and practice* (pp. 57–76). Routledge.

Harris, G. T., Rice, M. E., & Quinsey, V. L. (1993). Violent recidivism of mentally disordered offenders: The development of a statistical prediction instrument. *Criminal Justice and Behaviour*, 20, 315–355.

Hart, S. (2016). Culture and violence risk assessment: The case of Ewert v. Canada. *Journal of Threat Assessment and Management*, 3(2), 76–96.

Hart, S. D. (1998). The role of psychopathy in assessing risk for violence: Conceptual and methodological issues. *Legal and Criminological Psychology*, 3, 121–137.

Hart, S. D., & Cook, A. N. (2012). Current issues in the assessment and diagnosis of psychopathy (psychopathic personality disorder). *Neuropsychiatry*, 2(6), 497–508.

Hart, S. D., & Hare, R. D. (1997). Psychopathy: Assessment and association with criminal conduct. In D. M. Stoff, J. Breiling, & J. D. Maser (Eds.), *Handbook of antisocial behaviour* (pp. 22–35). Wiley.

Hart, S. D., Sturmey, P., Logan, C., & McMurran, M. (2011). Forensic case formulation. *International Journal of Forensic Mental Health*, 10, 118–126.

Harter, S. (1990). Self and identity development. In S. S. Feldman & G. R. Elliott (Eds.), *At the threshold: The developing adolescent* (pp. 352–387). Harvard University Press.

Haslam, N. (2003). The dimensional view of personality disorders: A review of the taxometric evidence. *Clinical Psychology Review*, 23(1), 75–93.

Hawes, S. W., Byrd, A. L., Kelley, S. E., Gonzalez, R., Edens, J. F., & Pardini, D. A. (2018). Psychopathic features across development: Assessing longitudinal invariance among Caucasian and African American youths. *Journal of Research in Personality*, 73, 180–188.

Hawes, S. W., Mulvey, E. P., Schubert, C. A., & Pardini, D. A. (2014). Structural coherence and temporal stability of psychopathic personality features during emerging adulthood. *Journal of Abnormal Psychology*, 123(3), 623–633.

Hayes, A. F. (2013). *Introduction to mediation, moderation, and conditional process analysis: A regression-based approach*. Guilford Press.

Helfgott, J. B. (2013a). The popular conception of the psychopath: Implications for criminal justice practice. In J. B. Helfgott (Ed.), *Criminal psychology* (pp. 515–546). Praeger/ABC-CLIO.

Helmus, L., Hanson, R. K., & Thornton, D. (2009). Reporting Static-99 in light of new research on recidivism norms. *The Forum*, 21(1), 38–45.

Helmus, L., Hanson, R. K., Thornton, D., Babchishin, K. M., & Harris, A. J. (2012). Absolute recidivism rates predicted by Static-99R and Static-2002R sex offender risk assessment tools vary across samples: A meta-analysis. *Criminal Justice and Behaviour*, 39(9), 1148–1171.

Helmus, L. M., & Babchishin, K. M. (2017). Primer on risk assessment and the statistics used to evaluate its accuracy. *Criminal Justice and Behavior*, 44(1), 8–25.

Hemphälä, M., Kosson, D., Westerman, J., & Hodgins, S. (2015). Stability and predictors of psychopathic traits from mid-adolescence through early adulthood. *Scandinavian Journal of Psychology*, 56, 649–658.

Hinton, E. (2019). How the Central Park Five changed the history of American Law. *The Atlantic*. Retrieved from https://www.theatlantic.com/entertainment/archive/2019/06/when-they-see-us-shows-cases-impact-us-policy/590779/

Hirschi, T., & Gottfredson, M. (1995). Control theory and the life-course perspective. *Studies on Crime and Crime Prevention*, 4, 131–142.

Hirtenlehner, H., & Kunz, F. (2016). The interaction between self-control and morality in crime causation among older adults. *European Journal of Criminology*, 13(3), 393–409.

Hirtenlehner, H., & Schulz, S. (2021). Deterrence and the moral context: Is the impact of perceived sanction risk dependent on best friends' moral beliefs? *Criminal Justice Review*, 46(1), 53–79.

Hodgkinson, T., & Andresen, M. A. (2020). Show me a man or a woman alone and I'll show you a saint: Changes in the frequency of criminal incidents during the COVID-19 pandemic. *Journal of Criminal Justice*, 69, 101706.

Hoff, H. A., Rypdal, K., Hystad, S. W., Hart, S. D., Mykletun, A., Kreis, M. K., & Cooke, D. (2014). Cross-language consistency of the Comprehensive Assessment of Psychopathic Personality (CAPP) model. *Personality Disorders: Theory, Research, and Treatment*, 5(4), 356–368.

Hoff, H. A., Rypdal, K., Mykletun, A., & Cooke, D. J. (2012). A prototypicality validation of the Comprehensive Assessment of Psychopathic Personality model (CAPP). *Journal of Personality Disorders*, 26(3), 414–427.

Hoffmann, A., & Verona, E. (2021). Psychopathic traits and sexual coercion against relationship partners in men and women. *Journal of Interpersonal Violence*, 36, 1788–1809.

Holden, R. R., & Jackson, D. N. (1985). Disguise and the structured self-report assessment of psychopathology: I. An analogue investigation. *Journal of Consulting and Clinical Psychology*, 53(2), 211–222.

Holdsworth, E., Bowen, E., Brown, S., & Howat, D. (2014). Client engagement in psychotherapeutic treatment and associations with client characteristics, therapist characteristics, and treatment factors. *Clinical Psychology Review*, 34(5), 428–450.

Hoppenbrouwers, S. S., Van der Stigchel, S., Slotboom, J., Dalmaijer, E. S., & Theeuwes, J. (2015). Disentangling attentional deficits in psychopathy using visual search: Failures in the use of contextual information. *Personality and Individual Differences*, 86, 132–138.

Hu, L. T., & Bentler, P. M. (1999). Cutoff criteria for fit indexes in covariance structure analysis: Conventional criteria versus new alternatives. *Structural Equation Modeling: A Multidisciplinary Journal*, 6, 1–55.

Imai, K., Keele, L., & Tingley, D. (2010). A general approach to causal mediation analysis. *Psychological Methods*, 15, 309–334.

Imrey, P. B., & Dawid, A. P. (2015). A commentary on statistical assessment of violence recidivism risk. *Statistics and Public Policy*, 2(1), 1–18.

Irtelli, F., & Vincenti, E. (2017). Successful psychopaths: A contemporary phenomenon. In Federico Durbano (Ed.), *Psychopathy – New Updates on an old phenomenon* (pp. 185–193). InTech.

Ismail, G., & Looman, J. (2018). Field inter-rater reliability of the Psychopathy Checklist–Revised. *International Journal of Offender Therapy and Comparative Criminology*, 62(2), 468–481.

Israel, M. (1997). "all...not". *Alt.usage.English*. Retrieved from https://www.alt-usage-english.org/excerpts/fxallnot.html, April 16, 2025

Jewell, T., & Raypole, C. (2024). *What it actually means to be a "sociopath."* Heathline.com. Retrieved from https://www.healthline.com/health/mental-health/sociopath

Johansson, P., & Kerr, M. (2005). Psychopathy and intelligence: A second look. *Journal of Personality Disorders*, 19(4), 357–369.

Johnson, V., & Pandina, R. J. (1991). Effects of the family environment on adolescent substance use, delinquency, and coping styles. *The American Journal of Drug and Alcohol Abuse*, 17(1), 71–88.

Johnstone, L., & Cooke, D. (2004). Psychopathic-like traits in childhood: Conceptual and measurement concerns. *Behavioral Sciences & the Law*, 22(1), 103–125.

Jones, S., Cauffman, E., Miller, J. D., & Mulvey, E. (2006). Investigating different factor structures of the psychopathy checklist: Youth version: Confirmatory factor analytic findings. *Psychological Assessment*, 18(1), 33–48.

Jones, S., Dinkins, B., Sleep, C. E., Lynam, D. R., & Miller, J. D. (2021). The Add Health psychopathy scale: Assessing its construct validity. *Journal of Criminal Justice*, 72, Article 101779.

Kagan, J., & Snidman, N. (2009). *The long shadow of temperament*. Harvard University Press.

Kardum, I., Hudek-Knezevic, J., Gračanin, A., & Mehic, N. (2017). Assortative mating for psychopathy components and its effects on the relationship quality in intimate partners. *Psihologijske Teme*, 26, 211–239.

Karpman, B. (1948). The myth of the psychopathic personality. *American Journal of Psychiatry*, 104(9), 523–534.

 (1951). The sexual psychopath. *Journal of the American Medical Association*, 146(8), 721–726.

Kavish, N., Bailey, C., Sharp, C., & Venta, A. (2018). On the relation between general intelligence and psychopathic traits: An examination of inpatient adolescents. *Child Psychiatry & Human Development*, 49, 341–351.

Keesler, M. E., & DeMatteo, D. (2017). How media exposure relates to laypersons' understanding of psychopathy. *Journal of Forensic Sciences*, 62(6), 1522–1533.

Kelm, M. E., & Smith, K. (2018). *Talking back to the Indian Act: Critical readings in settler colonial histories*. University of Toronto Press.

Kemp, E. C., Picou, P., Vaughan, E. P., Robertson, E. L., Walker, T. M., Frick, P. J., ... & de Back, J. (2023). The association between Callous-Unemotional (CU) traits and suicidal behavior in a psychiatric inpatient adolescent sample. *Journal of Applied Research on Children*, 14(1), 1–25.

Kempf-Leonard, K., Tracy, P., & Howell, J. (2001). Serious, violent, and chronic juvenile offenders: The relationship of delinquency career types to adult criminality. *Justice Quarterly*, 18, 449–478.

Kennealy, P. J., Skeem, J. L., Walters, G. D., & Camp, J. (2010). Do core interpersonal and affective traits of PCL-R psychopathy interact with antisocial behaviour and disinhibition to predict violence? *Psychological Assessment*, 22(3), 569–580.

Kiehl, K. A. (2015). *The psychopath whisperer: The science of those without conscience*. Crown.

Kiehl, K. A., Smith, A. M., Hare, R. D., Mendrek, A., Forster, B. B., Brink, J., & Liddle, P. F. (2001). Limbic abnormalities in affective processing by criminal psychopaths as revealed by functional magnetic resonance imaging. *Biological Psychiatry*, 50(9), 677–684.

Kimonis, E. R., Frick, P. J., Cauffman, E., Goldweber, A., & Skeem, J. (2012). Primary and secondary variants of juvenile psychopathy differ in emotional processing. *Development and Psychopathology*, 24(3), 1091–1103.

King, R., Massoglia, M., & Macmillan, R. (2007). The context of marriage and crime: Gender, the propensity to marry, and offending in early adulthood. *Criminology*, 45, 33–66.

Kirk, D. (2006). Examining the divergence across self-report and official data sources on inferences about the adolescent life-course of crime. *Journal of Quantitative Criminology*, 22, 107–129.

Kirk, D. S., & Wakefield, S. (2018). Collateral consequences of punishment: A critical review and path forward. *Annual Review of Criminology*, 1(1), 171–194.

Klein Haneveld, E., Molenaar, D., de Vogel, V., Smid, W., & Kamphuis, J. H. (2022). Do we hold males and females to the same standard? A measurement invariance study on the Psychopathy Checklist-Revised. *Journal of Personality Assessment*, 104(3), 368–379.

Kline, R. B. (2010). Promise and pitfalls of structural equation modeling in gifted research. In B. Thompson & R. F. Subotnik (Eds.), *Methodologies for conducting research on giftedness* (pp. 147–169). American Psychological Association.

Koch, J. L. A. (1892). *Die psychopathischen Minderwertigkeiten* (Vol. 2). O. Maier.

Kosson, D., Gacono, C., Klipfel, K., & Bodholdt, R. (2016). Understanding and assessing psychopathy. In C. Gacono (Ed.), *The clinical and forensic assessment of psychopathy: A practitioner's guide* (2nd Ed., pp. 252–275). Routledge.

Krabbe, P. (2017). *The measurement of health and health status concepts, methods and applications from a multidisciplinary perspective.* Academic Press.

Krafft-Ebing, R. von. (1904). *Textbook of insanity* (C. G. Chaddock, Trans.). F. A. Davis.

Kranefeld, I., & Blickle, G. (2022). The good, the bad, and the ugly? A triarchic perspective on psychopathy at work. *International Journal of Offender Therapy and Comparative Criminology*, 66(15), 1498–1522.

Kranefeld, I., Schilbach, M., Baethge, A., & Rigotti, T. (2024). Workplace indicators: Job satisfaction, turnover, and productivity. In Marie-Line Germain (Ed.), *Psychopathy in the workplace: Coping strategies for employees* (pp. 73–85). Palgrave Macmillan.

Kropp, P. R., Hart, S. D., Webster, C. D., & Eaves, D. (1994). *Manual for the Spousal Assault Risk Assessment Guide.* British Columbia Institute on Family Violence.

Krueger, R. F., Moffitt, T. E., Caspi, A., Bleske, A., & Silva, P. A. (1998). Assortative mating for antisocial behaviour: Developmental and methodological implications. *Behaviour Genetics*, 28, 173–186.

Lachapelle, S., Gelbard, S. B., & Kilty, J. M. (2024). "It's like you're still in jail": Exploring the subjugation of emotional knowledge in prison-to-community reintegration in Canada. *Current Issues in Criminal Justice*, online first, 1–16.

Larsen, R. R. (2019). Psychopathy treatment and the stigma of yesterday's research 1. In Fritz Allhoff & Sandra Borden (Eds.), *Ethics and error in medicine* (pp. 262–287). Routledge.

(2025). *Psychopathy unmasked: The rise and fall of a dangerous diagnosis*. MIT.

Larsen, R. R., Koch, P., Jalava, J., & Griffiths, S. (2022). Are psychopathy assessments ethical? A view from forensic mental health. *Journal of Threat Assessment and Management*, 9(4), 260–286.

Larsen, R. R., McLaren, S. A., Griffiths, S., & Jalava, J. (2024). Do psychopathic persons lack empathy? An exploratory systematic review of empathy assessment and emotion recognition studies in psychopathy checklist samples. *Psychology, Public Policy, and Law*. Advance online publication. https://psycnet.apa.org/record/2025-35838-001

Laub, J., & Sampson, R. (2003). *Shared beginnings, divergent lives: Delinquent boys to age 70*. Harvard University Press.

Laub, J., Rowan, Z., & Sampson, R. (2018). The age-graded theory of informal social control. In David P. Farrington, Lila Kazemian, & Alex R. Piquero (Eds.), *The Oxford handbook of developmental and life-course criminology* (pp. 295–322). Oxford Press.

Lauritsen, J. (1999). Limitations in the use of longitudinal self-report data. *Criminology*, 37(3), 687–694.

Le Blanc, M., Frechette, M., & McDuff, P. (1991). *MASPAQ: Manuel sure des mesures de l'adaptation sociale et personnelle pour les adolescents Québécois: [manuel et guide d'utilisation]*. École de psychoéducation, Groupe de recherche sur les adolescents en difficulté, Université de Montréal.

Lee, Y., & Kim, J. (2022). Psychopathic traits and different types of criminal behaviour: An assessment of direct effects and mediating processes. *Journal of Criminal Justice*, 80, Article 101772.

Leedom, L. (2017). The impact of psychopathy on the family. In Federico Durbano (Ed.), *Psychopathy – New updates on an old phenomenon* (pp. 139–167). InTech.

Leistico, A., Salekin, R., DeCoster, J., & Rogers, R. (2008). A large-scale meta-analysis relating the Hare measures of psychopathy to antisocial conduct. *Law and Human Behaviour*, 32, 28–45.

Levenson, M. R., Kiehl, K. A., & Fitzpatrick, C. M. (1995). Assessing psychopathic attributes in a noninstitutionalized population. *Journal of Personality and Social Psychology*, 68(1), Article 151158.

Lewis, M. (2018). Treatment of psychopathy: A conceptual and empirical review. *Journal of Criminological Research, Policy and Practice*, 4(3), 186–198.

Lilienfeld, S. O. (2013). Is psychopathy a syndrome? Commentary on Marcus, Fulton, and Edens. *Personality Disorders: Theory, Research, and Treatment*, 4, 85–86.

(2018). The multidimensional nature of psychopathy: Five recommendations for research. *Journal of Psychopathology and Behavioral Assessment*, 40, 79–85.

Lilienfeld, S. O., & Fowler, K. A. (2006). The self-report assessment of psychopathy: Problems, pitfalls, and promises. In C. J. Patrick (Ed.), *Handbook of psychopathy* (pp. 107–132). Guilford Press.

Lilienfeld, S. O., & Strother, A. N. (2020). Psychological measurement and the replication crisis: Four sacred cows. *Canadian Psychology/Psychologie Canadienne*, 61(4), 281–288.

Lilienfeld, S. O., & Widows, M. R. (2005). *Psychopathic Personality Inventory Revised (PPI-R): Professional manual.* Psychological Assessment Resources.

Lilienfeld, S. O., Patrick, C. J., Benning, S. D., Berg, J., Sellbom, M., & Edens, J. F. (2012). The role of fearless dominance in psychopathy: Confusions, controversies, and clarifications. *Personality Disorders: Theory, Research, and Treatment*, 3(3), 327–340.

Lilienfeld, S. O., Smith, S. F., Sauvigné, K. C., Patrick, C. J., Drislane, L. E., Latzman, R. D., & Krueger, R. F. (2016). Is boldness relevant to psychopathic personality? Meta-analytic relations with non-Psychopathy Checklist-based measures of psychopathy. *Psychological Assessment*, 28(10), 1172–1185.

Lilienfeld, S. O., Watts, A. L., Murphy, B., Costello, T. H., Bowes, S. M., Smith, S. F., & Tabb, K. (2019). Psychopathy as an emergent interpersonal syndrome: further reflections and future directions. *Journal of Personality Disorders*, 33(5), 645–652.

Lilienfeld, S. O., Watts, A. L., & Smith, S. F. (2015). Successful psychopathy: A scientific status report. *Current Directions in Psychological Science*, 24(4), 298–303.

Lilienfeld, S. O., Watts, A. L., Smith, S. F., & Latzman, R. D. (2018a). Boldness: Conceptual and methodological issues. In C. J. Patrick (Ed.), *Handbook of psychopathy* (2nd Ed., pp. 165–188). Guilford Press.

Lilienfeld, S. O., Watts, A. L., Smith, S. F., Patrick, C. J., & Hare, R. D. (2018b). Hervey Cleckley (1903–1984): Contributions to the study of psychopathy. *Personality Disorders: Theory, Research, and Treatment*, 9(6), 510–520.

Linning, S. J., & Eck, J. E. (2025). Race-based real estate practices and spuriousness in community criminology: Was the Chicago school part of a self-fulfilling prophecy? *Criminal Justice Review*, 50(2), 117–142.

Livesley, W. J. (2007). Introduction to special feature on the structure of psychopathy. *Journal of Personality Disorders*, 21(2), 99–101.

Loeber, R., & Farrington, D. P. (2011). *Young homicide offenders and victims: Risk factors, prediction, and prevention from childhood.* Springer.

Loeber, R., Pardini, D., Homish, D. L., Wei, E. H., Crawford, A. M., ... & Rosenfeld, R. (2005). The prediction of violence and homicide in young men. *Journal of Consulting and Clinical Psychology*, 73, 1074–1088.

Loeffler, C., & Nagin, D. (2022). The impact of incarceration on recidivism. *Annual Review of Criminology*, 5, 133–152.

Logan, C., & Johnstone, L. (2010). Personality disorder and violence: Making the link through risk formulation. *Journal of Personality Disorders*, 24, 610–633.

Lovatt, K. M., Stockdale, K. C., & Olver, M. E. (2025). The intersection of juvenile psychopathy, protective factors, treatment change, and diversity in justice-involved youth. *Criminal Justice and Behaviour*, 52(3), 364–390.

Lu, Y., Luo, L., & Santos, M. R. (2024). Social change and race-specific homicide trajectories: An age-period-cohort analysis. *Journal of Research in Crime and Delinquency*, 61(2), 224–267.

Ludwig, J., & Schnepel, K. (2025). Does nothing stop a bullet like a job? The effects of income on crime. *Annual Review of Criminology*, 8(1), 269–289.

Lussier, P., McCuish, E. C., & Cale, J. (2021). *Understanding sexual offending: An evidence-based response to myths and misconceptions*. Springer.

Lykken, D. T. (1995). *The antisocial personalities*. Erlbaum.

(2018). Psychopathy, sociopathy, and antisocial personality disorder. In C. J. Patrick (Ed.), *Handbook of psychopathy* (2nd Ed., pp. 22–38). Guilford Press.

Lynam, D. R. (1998). Early identification of the fledgling psychopath: Locating the psychopathic child in the current nomenclature. *Journal of Abnormal Psychology*, 107, 566–575.

Lynam, D. R., & Miller, J. D. (2015). Psychopathy from a basic trait perspective: The utility of a five-factor model approach. *Journal of Personality*, 83(6), 611–626.

Lynam, D. R., & Vachon, D. D. (2012). Antisocial personality disorder in DSM-5: Missteps and missed opportunities. *Personality Disorders: Theory, Research, and Treatment*, 3(4), 483–495.

Lynam, D. R., Caspi, A., Moffitt, T. E., Loeber, R., & Stouthamer-Loeber, M. (2007). Longitudinal evidence that psychopathy scores in early adolescence predict adult psychopathy. *Journal of Abnormal Psychology*, 116(1), 155–165.

Lynam, D. R., Gaughan, E. T., Miller, J. D., Miller, D. J., Mullins-Sweatt, S., & Widiger, T. A. (2011). Assessing the basic traits associated with psychopathy: Development and validation of the Elemental Psychopathy Assessment. *Psychological Assessment*, 23(1), 108–124.

Magnusson, D. (1988). *Individual development from an interactional perspective: A longitudinal study*. Lawrence Erlbaum Associates Inc.

Martinson, R. (1974). What works? Questions and answers about prison reform. *The Public Interest*, 35, 22–54.

Maruna, S. (2025). Redeeming desistance: From individual journeys to a social movement. *Criminology*, 63(1), 5–25.

Mathieu, C., & Babiak, P. (2016). Corporate psychopathy and abusive supervision: Their influence on employees' job satisfaction and turnover intentions. *Personality and Individual Differences*, 91, 102–106.

Maurer, J. M., Gullapalli, A. R., Milillo, M. M., Allen, C. H., Rodriguez, S. N., Edwards, B. G., & Kiehl, K. A. (2024). Adolescents with elevated psychopathic traits are associated with an increased risk for premature mortality. *Research on Child and Adolescent Psychopathology*, 53(1), 17–28.

McCarthy, B., & Hagan, J. (2001). When crime pays: Capital, competence, and criminal success. *Social Forces*, 79(3), 1035–1060.

McCormick, A. (2007). *Interrater reliability of the Comprehensive Assessment of Psychopathic Personality Disorder among a sample of incarcerated serious and violent young offenders*. SFU thesis repository.

(2015). *Validity of the comprehensive assessment of psychopathic personality disorder – Institutional rating scale in a Canadian sample of incarcerated serious and violent young offenders*. SFU thesis repository.

McCuish, E. C., & Corrado, R. R. (2018). Do risk and protective factors for chronic offending vary across Indigenous and White youth followed prospectively through full adulthood? *Crime & Delinquency*, 64(10), 1247–1270.

McCuish, E. C., & Gushue, K. (2022). Maturation as a promoter of change in features of psychopathy between adolescence and emerging adulthood. *Youth Violence and Juvenile Justice*, 20(1), 3–21.

McCuish, E. C., & Lussier, P. (2018). A developmental perspective on the stability and change of psychopathic personality traits across the adolescence–adulthood transition. *Criminal Justice and Behaviour*, 45(5), 666–692.

(2021). Describing changes in features of psychopathy via an individual-level measure of P(Δ). *Journal of Quantitative Criminology*, 37, 891–913.

(2023). Twenty years in the making: Revisiting Laub and Sampson's version of life-course criminology. *Journal of Criminal Justice*, 88, Article 102117.

(2025). From prediction to explanation: Is the relationship between youth psychopathy traits and continued offending in adulthood mediated by social environment? *Personality Disorders: Theory, Research, and Treatment*, 16(1), 69–79.

McCuish, E. C., Bouchard, M., & Corrado, R. R. (2015). The search for suitable homicide co-offenders among gang members. *Journal of Contemporary Criminal Justice*, 31(3), 319–336.

McCuish, E. C., Bushway, S., Lussier, P., & Gushue, K. (2025). The impact of incarceration on reoffending: A period-to-period analysis of Canadian youth followed into adulthood. *Journal of Criminal Justice*, 96, Article 102335.

McCuish, E. C., Corrado, R., Lussier, P., & Hart, S. D. (2014). Psychopathic traits and offending trajectories from early adolescence to adulthood. *Journal of Criminal Justice*, 42, 66–76.

McCuish, E. C., Hanniball, K., & Corrado, R. (2019). The assessment of psychopathic personality disturbance among adolescent male offenders: Interview strategies and recommendations. *International Journal of Forensic Mental Health*, 18, 35–49.

McCuish, E. C., Lussier, P., & Corrado, R. (2018a). Incarceration as a turning point? The impact of custody experiences and identity change on community reentry. *Journal of Developmental and Life-Course Criminology*, 4, 427–448.

McCuish, E.C, Lussier, P., & Corrado, R. (2021). *The life-course of serious and violent youth grown up: A twenty-year longitudinal study*. Routledge.

(2022). Cohort Profile: The Incarcerated Serious and Violent Young Offender Study. *Journal of Developmental and Life-Course Criminology*, 8(2), 315–335.

McCuish, E. C., Lussier, P., & Rocque, M. (2020). Maturation beyond age: Interrelationships among psychosocial, adult role, and identity maturation and their implications for desistance from crime. *Journal of Youth and Adolescence*, 49(2), 479–493.

McCuish, E. C., Mathesius, J., Lussier, P., & Corrado, R. (2018b). The cross-cultural generalizability of the Psychopathy Checklist: Youth Version for adjudicated Indigenous youth. *Psychological Assessment*, 30(2), 192–203.

McGloin, J. M., & Kirk, D. S. (2010). Social network analysis. In A. R. Piquero & D. Weisburd (Eds.), *Handbook of quantitative criminology* (pp. 209–224). Springer.

McGloin, J. M., & Rowan, Z. R. (2015). A threshold model of collective crime. *Criminology*, 53(3), 484–512.

McGuire, M. (2022). Reflections on decolonization and X_aaydaG_a Tll Yahda TllG_uhlG_a: A Haida Justice System. *Decolonization of Criminology and Justice*, 4(1), 31–56.

McKnight, C., Weng, C., Reynoso, M., Kimball, S., Thompson, L., & Des Jarlais, D. (2023). Understanding intentionality of fentanyl use and drug overdose risk: Findings from a mixed methods study of people who inject drugs in New York City. *International Journal of Drug Policy*, 118, Article 104063.

Milledge, S. V., Cortese, S., Thompson, M., McEwan, F., Rolt, M., Meyer, B., & Eisenbarth, H. (2019). Peer relationships and prosocial behaviour differences across disruptive behaviours. *European Child & Adolescent Psychiatry*, 28, 781–793.

Miller, J. (2012). Five-factor model personality disorder prototypes: A review of their development, validity, and comparison to alternative approaches. *Journal of Personality*, 80(6), 1565–1591.

Miller, J. D., Widiger, T. A., & Campbell, W. K. (2010). Narcissistic personality disorder and the DSM-V. *Journal of Abnormal Psychology*, 119(4), 640–649.

Millon, T. (1981). *Disorders of personality: DSM-III, Axis II*. John Wiley.

Millon, T., & Davis, R. (1993). The Millon Adolescent Personality Inventory and the Millon Adolescent Clinical Inventory. *Journal of Counseling and Development*, 71, 570–574.

Millon, T., Simonsen, E., & Birket-Smith, M. (1998). Historical conceptions of psychopathy in the United States and Europe. In T. Millon, E. Simonsen, M. Birket-Smith, & R. D. Davis (Eds.), *Psychopathy: Antisocial, criminal, and violent behaviour* (pp. 3–31). Guilford Press.

Moffitt, T. (1993). "Life-course-persistent" and "adolescent-limited" antisocial behaviour: A developmental taxonomy. *Psychological Review*, 100, 674–701.

Mokros, A., Osterheider, M., Hucker, S. J., & Nitschke, J. (2011). Psychopathy and sexual sadism. *Law and Human Behaviour*, 35, 188–199.

Monahan, J. (2006). *Comments on cover jacket of C. J. Patrick (ed.), Handbook of psychopathy*. Guilford Press.

Monroe, S. M., & Anderson, S. F. (2015). Depression: The shroud of heterogeneity. *Current Directions in Psychological Science*, 24(3), 227–231.

Montana, E., Nagin, D., Neil, R., & Sampson, R. J. (2023). Cohort bias in predictive risk assessments of future criminal justice system involvement. *Proceedings of the National Academy of Sciences*, 120(23), Article e2301990120.

Moosburner, M., Etzler, S., Brunner, F., Briken, P., & Rettenberger, M. (2024). Is psychopathy a dynamic risk factor? An empirical investigation of changes in psychopathic personality traits over the course of correctional treatment. *Criminal Justice and Behaviour*, 51(2), 230–246.

Muir, N. M., & Viljoen, J. L. (2022). Adverse childhood experiences and recidivism in Indigenous and white female and male adolescents on probation. *Child Abuse & Neglect*, 126, Article 105512.

Murrie, D. C., & Cornell, D. G. (2000). The Millon Adolescent Clinical Inventory and psychopathy. *Journal of Personality Assessment*, 75(1), 110–125.

Murrie, D. C., Boccaccini, M. T., Johnson, J. T., & Janke, C. (2008). Does interrater (dis) agreement on Psychopathy Checklist scores in sexually violent predator trials suggest partisan allegiance in forensic evaluations? *Law and Human Behaviour*, 32, 352–362.

Murrie, D. C., Cornell, D. G., Kaplan, S., McConville, D., & Levy-Elkon, A. (2004). Psychopathy scores and violence among juvenile offenders: A multi-measure study. *Behavioural Sciences & the Law*, 22(1), 49–67.

Murrie, D. C., Cornell, D. G., & McCoy, W. K. (2005). Psychopathy, conduct disorder, and stigma: Does diagnostic labeling influence juvenile probation officer recommendations? *Law and Human Behaviour*, 29, 323–342.

Muthén, L. K., & Muthén, B. O. (2011). *Mplus user's guide* (6th Ed.) Muthén & Muthén.

Myers, W. C., Chan, H. C., Vo, E. J., & Lazarou, E. (2010). Sexual sadism, psychopathy, and recidivism in juvenile sexual murderers. *Journal of Investigative Psychology and Offender Profiling*, 7(1), 49–58.

Nagin, D., & Land, K. (1993). Age, criminal careers and population heterogeneity: Specification and estimation of nonparametric mixed poisson model. *Criminology*, 31, 327–354.

Nagin, D., & Paternoster, R. (2000). Population heterogeneity and state dependence: State of the evidence and directions for future research. *Journal of Quantitative Criminology*, 16, 117–144.

Nagin, D., Cullen, F., & Jonson, C. (2009). Imprisonment and reoffending. *Crime and Justice*, 38, 115–200.

Nai, A. (2019). Disagreeable narcissists, extroverted psychopaths, and elections: A new dataset to measure the personality of candidates worldwide. *European Political Science*, 18(2), 309–334.

Neil, R., & Carmichael, J. (2015). The use of incarceration in Canada: A test of political and social threat explanations on the variation in prison admissions across Canadian provinces, 2001–2010. *Sociological Inquiry*, 85, 309–332.

Neil, R., & Sampson, R. J. (2021). The birth lottery of history: Arrest over the life course of multiple cohorts coming of age, 1995–2018. *American Journal of Sociology*, 126(5), 1127–1178.

Neil, R., Sampson, R. J., & Nagin, D. S. (2021). Social change and cohort differences in group-based arrest trajectories over the last quarter-century. *Proceedings of the National Academy of Sciences*, 118(31), Article e2107020118.

Nelson, L. D. & Foell, J. (2018). Externalizing proneness and psychopathy. In C. J. Patrick (Ed.), *Handbook of psychopathy* (2nd Ed., pp. 127–143). Guilford Press.

Neumann, C. S., Hare, R. D., & Pardini, D. A. (2015). Antisociality and the construct of psychopathy: Data from across the globe. *Journal of Personality*, 83(6), 678–692.

Nguyen, H. (2020). On the conceptualization of criminal capital. *Journal of Research in Crime and Delinquency*, 57(2), 182–216.

Nguyen, H., & Loughran, T. (2018). On the measurement and identification of turning points in criminology. *Annual Review of Criminology*, 1, 335–358.

Nguyen, H., Loughran, T. A., Paternoster, R., Fagan, J., & Piquero, A. R. (2017). Institutional placement and illegal earnings: Examining the school of crime hypothesis. *Journal of Quantitative Criminology*, 33(2), 207–235.

Nichols, A., & Schaffer, M. (2007, September). Clustered errors in Stata. In *United Kingdom Stata Users' Group Meeting* (pp. 133–138). https://www.stata.com/meeting/13uk/nichols_crse.pdf

Nijdam-Jones, A., García-López, E., Aparcero, M., & Rosenfeld, B. (2020). How do Latin American professionals approach violence risk assessment? A qualitative exploratory study. *International Journal of Forensic Mental Health*, 19(3), 227–240.

Ogonah, M. G., Seyedsalehi, A., Whiting, D., & Fazel, S. (2023). Violence risk assessment instruments in forensic psychiatric populations: A systematic review and meta-analysis. *The Lancet Psychiatry*, 10(10), 780–789.

OJJDP. (2019). Easy access to the census of juveniles in residential placement: 1997–2017. Retried from https://www.ojjdp.gov/ojstatbb/ezacjrp/asp/State_Race.asp?state=&topic=State_Race&year=2001&percent=rate

Olds, D. L. (2002). Prenatal and infancy home visiting by nurses: From randomized trials to community replication. *Prevention Science*, 3, 153–172.

Olver, M. (2018). Can psychopathy be treated? What the research tells us. In E. Jeglic & C. Calkins (Eds.), *New frontiers in offender treatment* (pp. 287–306). Springer.

Olver, M., Lewis, K., & Wong, S. (2013). Risk reduction treatment of high-risk psychopathic offenders: The relationship of psychopathy and treatment change to violent recidivism. *Personality Disorders: Theory, Research, and Treatment*, 4, 160–167.

Olver, M., Stockdale, K., Neumann, C., Hare, R., Mokros, A., Baskin-Sommers, A., ... & Yoon, D. (2020). Reliability and validity of the Psychopathy Checklist-Revised in the assessment of risk for institutional violence: A cautionary note on DeMatteo et al. (2020). *Psychology, Public Policy, and Law*, 26(4), 490–510.

Olver, M. E. (2022). Treatment of psychopathic offenders: A review of research, past, and current practice. In P. B. Marques, M. Paulino, & L. Alho (Eds.), *Psychopathy and criminal behaviour: Current trends and challenges* (pp. 469–481). Academic Press.

Olver, M. E., & Wong, S. C. (2009). Therapeutic responses of psychopathic sexual offenders: Treatment attrition, therapeutic change, and long-term recidivism. *Journal of Consulting and Clinical Psychology*, 77(2), 328–336.

Opsahl, T., Agneessens, F., & Skvoretz, J. (2010). Node centrality in weighted networks: Generalizing degree and shortest paths. *Social Networks*, 32, 245–251.

Ostapchuk, N. (2018). *Lay theories and attitudes about psychopathy*. Doctoral dissertation, Carleton University.

Ouellet, F., & Bouchard, M. (2017). Only a matter of time? The role of criminal competence in avoiding arrest. *Justice Quarterly*, 34, 699–726.

Ousey, G. C., & Wilcox, P. (2007). The interaction of antisocial propensity and life-course varying predictors of delinquent behaviour: Differences by method of estimation and implications for theory. *Criminology*, 45(2), 313–354.

Papachristos, A. V., Wildeman, C., & Roberto, E. (2015). Tragic, but not random: The social contagion of nonfatal gunshot injuries. *Social Science & Medicine*, 125, 139–150.

Paternoster, R., Bachman, R., Bushway, S., Kerrison, E., & O'Connell, D. (2015). Human agency and explanations of criminal desistance: Arguments for a rational choice theory. *Journal of Developmental and Life-Course Criminology*, 1(3), 209–235.

Patrick, C., Drislane, L., & Strickland, C. (2012). Conceptualizing psychopathy in triarchic terms: Implications for treatment. *International Journal of Forensic Mental Health*, 11(4), 253–266.

Patrick, C. J. (2010a). Conceptualizing the psychopathic personality: Disinhibited, bold,...Or just plain mean? In R. T. Salekin & D. R. Lynam (Eds.), *Handbook of Child and Adolescent Psychopathy* (pp. 15–48). Guilford Press.

(2010b). *Operationalizing the triarchic conceptualization of psychopathy: Preliminary description of brief scales for assessment of boldness, meanness, and disinhibition*. Unpublished test manual, Florida State University, Tallahassee, FL, pp. 1110–1131.

(2018). *Handbook of psychopathy* (2nd Ed.). Guilford Press.

(2022). Psychopathy: Current knowledge and future directions. *Annual Review of Clinical Psychology*, 18(1), 387–415.

Patrick, C. J., Fowles, D. C., & Krueger, R. F. (2009). Triarchic conceptualization of psychopathy: Developmental origins of disinhibition, boldness, and meanness. *Development and Psychopathology*, 21, 913–938.

Pauls, N. (2019). *Pathways to early mortality for serious and violent young offenders*. SFU thesis repository.

Payne, J., & Piquero, A. (2020). *Developmental criminology and the crime decline: A comparative analysis of the criminal careers of two New South Wales birth cohorts*. Cambridge Elements.

Pechorro, P., Da Silva, D. R., Rijo, D., Gonçalves, R. A., & Andershed, H. (2017). Psychometric properties and measurement invariance of the youth psychopathic traits inventory-short version among Portuguese youth. *Journal of Psychopathology and Behavioural Assessment*, 39, 486–497.

Persson, B. N., & Lilienfeld, S. O. (2019). Social status as one key indicator of successful psychopathy: An initial empirical investigation. *Personality and Individual Differences*, 141, 209–217.

Petrich, D., Pratt, T., Jonson, C., & Cullen, F. (2021). Custodial sanctions and reoffending: A meta-analytic review. *Crime and Justice*, 50, 353–424.

Petrila, J., & Skeem, J. L. (2003). An introduction to the special issues on juvenile psychopathy and some reflections on the current debate. *Behavioural Sciences & the Law*, 21(6), 689–694.

Phillips, T. (2019). *Joker* [Film]. Warners Bros. Pictures.

Pickersgill, M. (2012). Standardising antisocial personality disorder: The social shaping of a psychiatric technology. *Sociology of Health & Illness*, 34(4), 544–559.

Piquero, A. R., Farrington, D. P., Fontaine, N. M., Vincent, G., Coid, J., & Ullrich, S. (2012). Childhood risk, offending trajectories, and psychopathy at age 48 years in the Cambridge Study in Delinquent Development. *Psychology, Public Policy, and Law*, 18(4), 577–598.

Piquero, A. R., Jennings, W. G., & Farrington, D. (2013). The monetary costs of crime to middle adulthood: Findings from the Cambridge study in delinquent development. *Journal of Research in Crime and Delinquency*, 50, 53–74.

Ploe, M. L., Berluti, K., Ibonie, S. G., Villanueva, C. M., Marsh, A., & Gruber, J. (2023). Psychopathy and associations with reward responsiveness and social networks in emerging adults. *Journal of Research in Personality*, 103, Article 104357.

Polaschek, D. (2019). The psychology of desistance. In D. L. L. Polaschek, A. Day, & C. R. Hollin (Eds.), *The Wiley international handbook of correctional psychology* (pp. 315–336). Wiley.

Polaschek, D. & Skeem, J. (2018). Treatment of adults and juveniles with psychopathy. In C. P. Patrick (Ed.), *Handbook of psychopathy* (2nd Ed., pp. 710–773). Guilford Press.

Polaschek, D., Bell, R., Casey, A., Dickson, S., & Yesberg, J. (2022). Do triarchic psychopathy components of New Zealand high-risk parolees predict probation officer relationship quality, quality of life on parole, and recidivism? *International Journal of Offender Therapy and Comparative Criminology*, 66(15), 1682–1702.

Polaschek, D. L., & Daly, T. E. (2013). Treatment and psychopathy in forensic settings. *Aggression and Violent Behavior*, 18(5), 592–603.

Pornpitakpan, C. (2004). The persuasiveness of source credibility: A critical review of five decades' evidence. *Journal of Applied Social Psychology*, 34(2), 243–281.

Preszler, J., Marcus, D. K., Edens, J. F., & McDermott, B. E. (2018). Network analysis of psychopathy in forensic patients. *Journal of Abnormal Psychology*, 127, 171–182.

Prosecution Service. (2019). Information sheet: High-risk offenders and high-risk accused. Retrieved from https://www2.gov.bc.ca/assets/gov/law-crime-and-justice/criminal-justice/prosecution-service/information-sheets/infosheet_high-risk_offenders.pdf

Public Safety Canada. (2018, January 24). *The investigation, prosecution and correctional management of high-risk offenders: A national guide*. Public Safety Canada.

(2021). Wraparound: Program snapshot. Government of Canada. Retrieved from https://www.publicsafety.gc.ca/cnt/cntrng-crm/crm-prvntn/nvntr/dtls-en.aspx?i=10068

(2022). Parliamentary Committee notes: Nova Scotia mass shooting incident – Chronology of events. Retrieved from https://www.publicsafety.gc.ca/cnt/trnsprnc/brfng-mtrls/prlmntry-bndrs/20221122/03-en.aspx

Quinn, M. M., Rutherford, R. B., Leone, P. E., Osher, D. M., & Poirier, J. M. (2005). Youth with disabilities in juvenile corrections: A national survey. *Exceptional Children*, 71, 339–345.

R Core Team. (2018). *R: A language and environment for statistical computing*. Vienna: R Foundation for Statistical Computing. Retrieved from https://www.R-project.org/

Rafter, N. H. (1997). *Creating born criminals*. University of Illinois Press.

Raphael, S. (2021). The intended and unintended consequences of ban the box. *Annual Review of Criminology*, 4(1), 191–207.

Reale, K. S., Bouchard, M., Lim, Y. L., Cook, A. N., & Hart, S. D. (2020). Are psychopathic traits associated with core social networks? An exploratory study in university students. *Social Psychology Quarterly*, 83(4), 423–442.

Reidy, D. E., Kearns, M. C., DeGue, S., Lilienfeld, S. O., Massetti, G., & Kiehl, K. A. (2015). Why psychopathy matters: Implications for public health and violence prevention. *Aggression and Violent Behaviour*, 24, 214–225.

Reisig, M. Bales, W., Hay, C., & Wang, X. (2007). The effect of racial inequality on Black male recidivism. *Justice Quarterly*, 24(3), 408–434.

Ribeiro da Silva, D., Rijo, D., Brazão, N., Paulo, M., Miguel, R., Castilho, P., ... & Salekin, R. T. (2021). The efficacy of the PSYCHOPATHY. COMP program in reducing psychopathic traits: A controlled trial with male detained youth. *Journal of Consulting and Clinical Psychology*, 89(6), 499–513.

Ribeiro da Silva, D., Rijo, D., Castilho, P., & Gilbert, P. (2019). The efficacy of a Compassion Focused Therapy-based intervention in reducing psychopathic traits and disruptive behavior: A clinical case study with a juvenile detainee. *Clinical Case Studies*, 18, 323–343.

Ribeiro da Silva, D., Rijo, D., & Salekin, R. T. (2012). Child and adolescent psychopathy: A state-of-the-art reflection on the construct and etiological theories. *Journal of Criminal Justice*, 40(4), 269–277.

Rice, M. E., Harris, G. T., & Cormier, C. A. (1992). An evaluation of a maximum security therapeutic community for psychopaths and other mentally disordered offenders. *Law and Human Behaviour*, 16(4), 399–412.

Rigg, K., & Kusiak, E. (2023). Perceptions of fentanyl among African Americans who misuse opioids: Implications for risk reduction. *Harm Reduction Journal*, 20(1), Article 179.

Roberts, J. (2008). Punishing persistence: Explaining the enduring appeal of the recidivist sentencing premium. *The British Journal of Criminology*, 48, 468–481.

(2012). Structuring sentencing in Canada, England and Wales: A tale of two jurisdictions. *Criminal Law Forum*, 23, 319–345.

Robins, L. N. (1978). Sturdy childhood predictors of adult antisocial behaviour: Replications from longitudinal studies. *Psychological Medicine*, 8(4), 611–622.

Rodriguez, N., Smith, H., & Zatz, M. S. (2009). "Youth is enmeshed in a highly dysfunctional family system": Exploring the relationship among dysfunctional families, parental incarceration, and juvenile court decision making. *Criminology*, 47(1), 177–208.

Ronson, J. (2011). *The psychopath test*. Picador.

Rose, L., Carter, N. T., Lynam, D. R., Miller, J. D., & Oltmanns, T. F. (2024). Validity, stability, and change in psychopathic traits in older adults: A registered report. *Clinical Psychological Science*, 13(3), 664–679.

Rose, S. (2019). "He is a psychopath": Has the 2019 Joker gone too far? *The Guardian*. Retrieved from https://www.theguardian.com/film/2019/sep/28/he-is-a-psychopath-has-the-2019-joker-gone-too-far

Roth, N. (1952). Factors in the motivation of sexual offenders. *The Journal of Criminal Law, Criminology, and Police Science*, 42(5), 631–635.

Rowan, Z. R., Kan, E., Frick, P. J., & Cauffman, E. (2022). Not (entirely) guilty: The role of co-offenders in diffusing responsibility for crime. *Journal of Research in Crime and Delinquency*, 59(4), 415–448.

Rush, B. (1812). *Medical inquiries and observations upon the diseases of the mind*. Kimber & Richardson.

Russell, C., Ali, F., Imtiaz, S., Butler, A., Greer, A., & Rehm, J. (2024). The decriminalization of illicit drugs in British Columbia: A national evaluation protocol. *BMC Public Health*, 24(1), 1–17.

Ryder, N. (1965). The cohort as a concept in the study of social change. *American Sociological Review*, 30(6), 843–861.

Ryu, H., & McCuish, E. C. (2022). Exploring the reciprocal relationship between serious victimization and criminogenic networks. *Canadian Journal of Criminology and Criminal Justice*, 64(2), 82–100.

Sakki, H., St Clair, M., Hwang, S., & Allen, J. L. (2023). The association between callous-unemotional traits and substance use in childhood and adolescence: A systematic review and meta-analysis. *Journal of Affective Disorders*, 338, 502–517.

Salekin, R. (2008). Psychopathy and recidivism from mid-adolescence to young adulthood: Cumulating legal problems and limiting life opportunities. *Journal of Abnormal Psychology*, 117(2), 386–395.

(2016). Psychopathy in childhood: Toward better informing the DSM–5 and ICD-11 conduct disorder specifiers. *Personality Disorders: Theory, Research, and Treatment*, 7, 180–191.

Salekin, R. T. (2002). Psychopathy and therapeutic pessimism Clinical lore or clinical reality? *Clinical Psychology Review*, 22, 79–112.

Salekin, R., Worley, C., & Grimes, R. D. (2010). Treatment of psychopathy: A review and brief introduction to the mental model approach for psychopathy. *Behavioural Sciences & the Law*, 28(2), 235–266.

Salekin, R. T., Andershed, H., Batky, B. D., & Bontemps, A. P. (2018). Are callous unemotional (CU) traits enough? *Journal of Psychopathology and Behavioral Assessment*, 40, 1–5.
Salihovic, S., Kerr, M., Özdemir, M., & Pakalniskiene, V. (2012). Directions of effects between adolescent psychopathic traits and parental behaviour. *Journal of Abnormal Child Psychology*, 40, 957–969.
Sampson, R. J., & Laub, J. H. (1997). A life-course theory of cumulative disadvantage and the stability of delinquency. *Developmental Theories of Crime and Delinquency*, 7, 133–161.
  (2003). Life-course desisters? Trajectories of crime among delinquent boys followed to age 70. *Criminology*, 41, 555–592.
  (2016). Turning points and the future of life-course criminology: Reflections on the 1986 criminal careers report. *Journal of Research in Crime and Delinquency*, 53, 321–335.
Sampson, R. J., & Smith, L. A. (2021). Rethinking criminal propensity and character: Cohort inequalities and the power of social change. *Crime and Justice*, 50(1), 13–76.
Sampson, R. J., Kirk, D. S., & Bucci, R. (2022). Cohort profile: Project on human development in Chicago neighborhoods and its additions (PHDCN+). *Journal of Developmental and Life-Course Criminology*, 8(3), 516–532.
Sanz-García, A., Gesteira, C., Sanz, J., & García-Vera, M. P. (2021). Prevalence of psychopathy in the general adult population: A systematic review and meta-analysis. *Frontiers in Psychology*, 12, Article 661044.
Savolainen, J. (2009). Work, family and criminal desistance: Adult social bonds in a Nordic welfare state. *The British Journal of Criminology*, 49(3), 285–304.
van Schie, C. C., Matthews, E. L., Marceau, E. M., Römer, S., & Grenyer, B. F. S. (2024). Affective and neural mechanisms of how identity dysfunction in borderline personality disorder may interfere with building positive relationships. *Personality Disorders: Theory, Research, and Treatment*. Advance online publication. https://doi.org/10.1037/per0000697
Schmidt, F., Campbell, M. A., & Houlding, C. (2011). Comparative analyses of the YLS/CMI, SAVRY, and PCL:YV in adolescent offenders: A 10-year follow-up into adulthood. *Youth Violence and Juvenile Justice*, 9(1), 23–42.
Schneider, A., & Ervin, L. (1990). Specific deterrence, rational choice, and decision heuristics: Applications in juvenile justice. *Social Science Quarterly*, 71(3), 585–601.
Schneider, A. L. (1990). *Deterrence and juvenile crime*. Springer.
Schoepfer, A., & Piquero, A. R. (2006). Self-control, moral beliefs, and criminal activity. *Deviant Behaviour*, 27(1), 51–71.
Seabrook, J. (2008). Suffering souls. *The New Yorker*. Retrieved from https://www.newyorker.com/magazine/2008/11/10/suffering-souls
Seagrave, D., & Grisso, T. (2002). Adolescent development and the measurement of juvenile psychopathy. *Law and Human Behaviour*, 26, 219–239.
Sellbom, M., & Bromberg, D. S. (2019). The assessment and diagnosis of "mental abnormalities," personality disorders, and psychopathy in sexually

violent predator evaluations. In William T. O'Donohue & Daniel S. Bromberg (Eds.), *Sexually violent predators: A clinical science handbook* (pp. 153–165). Springer.

Sellbom, M., Cooke, D. J., & Shou, Y. (2019). Development and initial validation of the Comprehensive Assessment of Psychopathic Personality–Self-Report (CAPP-SR). *Psychological Assessment*, 31(7), 878–894.

Sellbom, M., Lilienfeld, S., Fowler, K., & McCrary, K. (2018). The self-report assessment of psychopathy: Challenges, pitfalls, and promises. In C. J. Patrick (Ed.), *Handbook of psychopathy* (pp. 211–258). Guilford Press.

Seto, E., & Davis, W. (2021). Authenticity predicts positive interpersonal relationship quality at low, but not high, levels of psychopathy. *Personality and Individual Differences*, 182, 1–6.

Sewall, L. A., & Olver, M. E. (2019). Psychopathy and treatment outcome: Results from a sexual violence reduction program. *Personality Disorders: Theory, Research, and Treatment*, 10(1), 59–69.

Shaffer, C. S., McCuish, E. C., Corrado, R. R., Behnken, M. P., & DeLisi, M. (2015). Psychopathy and violent misconduct in a sample of violent young offenders. *Journal of Criminal Justice*, 43(4), 321–326.

Sharp, C., & Wall, K. (2021). DSM-5 level of personality functioning: Refocusing personality disorder on what it means to be human. *Annual Review of Clinical Psychology*, 17, 313–337.

Sharpe, B. M., Van Til, K., Lynam, D. R., & Miller, J. D. (2023). Incremental and interactive relations of triarchic psychopathy measure scales with antisocial and prosocial correlates: A preregistered replication of Gatner et al. (2016). *Personality Disorders: Theory, Research, and Treatment*, 14(2), 237–248.

Shen, Y., Bushway, S. D., Sorensen, L. C., & Smith, H. L. (2020). Locking up my generation: Cohort differences in prison spells over the life course. *Criminology*, 58, 645–677.

Shi, D., Maydeu-Olivares, A., & Rosseel, Y. (2020). Assessing fit in ordinal factor analysis models: SRMR vs. RMSEA. *Structural Equation Modeling: A Multidisciplinary Journal*, 27(1), 1–15.

Shipley, S., & Arrigo, B. A. (2001). The confusion over psychopathy (II): Implications for forensic (correctional) practice. *International Journal of Offender Therapy and Comparative Criminology*, 45(4), 407–420.

Sierra-Arevalo, M., & Papachristos, A. V. (2015). Social network analysis and gangs. In Scott H. Decker & David C. Pyrooz (Eds.), *The handbook of gangs* (pp. 157–177). Wiley.

Simourd, D. J., & Hoge, R. D. (2000). Criminal psychopathy: A risk-and-need perspective. *Criminal Justice and Behaviour*, 27(2), 256–272.

Skardhamar, T. (2010). Distinguishing facts and artifacts in group-based modeling. *Criminology*, 48(1), 295–320.

Skeem, J. L., & Cooke, D. J. (2010). Is criminal behaviour a central component of psychopathy? Conceptual directions for resolving the debate. *Psychological Assessment*, 22(2), 433–445.

Skeem, J. L., & Mulvey, E. P. (2001). Psychopathy and community violence among civil psychiatric patients: Results from the MacArthur Violence Risk Assessment Study. *Journal of Consulting and Clinical Psychology*, 69(3), 358–374.

Skeem, J. L., Mulvey, E. P., & Grisso, T. (2003). Applicability of traditional and revised models of psychopathy to the Psychopathy Checklist: Screening version. *Psychological Assessment*, 15(1), 41–55.

Skeem, J. L., Polaschek, D. L., Patrick, C. J., & Lilienfeld, S. O. (2011). Psychopathic personality: Bridging the gap between scientific evidence and public policy. *Psychological Science in the Public Interest*, 12(3), 95–162.

Skryabin, V. Y. (2021). Analysing Joker: An attempt to establish diagnosis for a film icon. *BJPsych Bulletin*, 45(6), 329–332.

Slaney, K., Storey, J., & Barnes, J. (2011). Is my test valid? Guidelines for the practicing psychologist for evaluating the psychometric properties of measures. *International Journal of Forensic Mental Health*, 10(4), 261–283.

Slovenko, R. (2006). Remorse. *Journal of Psychiatry and Law*, 34, 397–432.

Smith, S. F., & Lilienfeld, S. O. (2013). Psychopathy in the workplace: The knowns and unknowns. *Aggression and Violent Behaviour*, 18(2), 204–218.

Smith, S. T., Edens, J. F., Clark, J., & Rulseh, A. (2014). "So, what is a psychopath?" Venire person perceptions, beliefs, and attitudes about psychopathic personality. *Law and Human Behavior*, 38, 490–500.

Society for the Scientific Study of Psychopathy. (2012). General Ronson commentary. Retrieved from https://psychopathysociety.org/page/RonsonCommentary

Stam, M., Wermink, H., Blokland, A., & Been, J. (2023). The effects of imprisonment length on recidivism: A judge stringency instrumental variable approach. *Journal of Experimental Criminology*, 20(3), 973–1004.

StataCorp. (2019). *Stata statistical software: Release 16*. StataCorp LLC, College Station, TX.

Statistics Canada. (2013). *British Columbia (Code 59) (table). National Household Survey (NHS) Aboriginal Population Profile. 2011 National Household Survey*. Statistics Canada Catalogue no. 99-011-X2011007. Ottawa.

(2024a). *Average counts of young persons in provincial and territorial correctional services (Table: 35-10-0003-01 (formerly CANSIM 251-0008)*, Retrieved from https://www150.statcan.gc.ca/t1/tbl1/en/tv.action?pid=3510000301

Statistics Canada. (2024b). *Mortality rates, by age group (Table: 13-10-0710-01 (formerly CANSIM 102-0504))*, Retrieved from https://www150.statcan.gc.ca/t1/tbl1/en/tv.action?pid=1310071001

Steffensmeier, D. J., Allan, E. A., Harer, M. D., & Streifel, C. (1989). Age and the distribution of crime. *American Journal of Sociology*, 94(4), 803–831.

Sturup, J., Edens, J. F., Sörman, K., Karlberg, D., Fredriksson, B., & Kristiansson, M. (2014). Field reliability of the Psychopathy Checklist-Revised among life sentenced prisoners in Sweden. *Law and Human Behaviour*, 38(4), 315–324.

Sutherland, E. (1949). The sexual psychopath laws. *Journal of Criminal Law & Criminology*, 40, 543–554.

———(1972). The theory of differential association. In David Dressler (Ed.), *Readings in criminology and penology* (pp. 365–371). Columbia University Press.

Swidler, A. (1986). Culture in action: Symbols and strategies. *American Sociological Review*, 51, 273–286.

Taasoobshirazi, G., & Wang, S. (2016). The performance of the SRMR, RMSEA, CFI, and TLI: An examination of sample size, path size, and degrees of freedom. *Journal of Applied Quantitative Methods*, 11(3), 31–39.

TED. (2012, August 12). *Strange answers to the psychopathy test* [Video] YouTube. https://www.youtube.com/watch?v=xYemnKEKxoc&ab_channel=TED

Tennenbaum, D. (1977). Personality and criminality: A summary and implications of the literature. *Journal of Criminal Justice*, 5, 225–235.

Tingley, D., Yamamoto, T., Hirose, K., Keele, L., & Imai, K. (2014). Mediation: R package for causal mediation analysis. *Journal of Statistical Software*, 59(5), 1–38.

Toch, H. (1998). Psychopathy or antisocial personality disorder in forensic settings. In T. Millon, E. Simonsen, M. Birket-Smith, & R. D. Davis (Eds.), *Psychopathy: Antisocial, criminal, and violent behaviour* (pp. 144–158). Guilford Press.

Tonry, M. (2013a). Sentencing in America, 1975–2025. *Crime and Justice*, 42(1), 141–198.

———(2013b). "Nothing" works: Sentencing "Reform" in Canada and the United States. *Canadian Journal of Criminology and Criminal Justice*, 55(4), 465–480.

———(2022). Punishments, politics, and prisons in Western countries. *Crime and Justice*, 51, 7–57.

Tremblay, P. (1993). Searching for suitable co-offenders. In R. V. Clarke & M. Felson (Eds.), *Routine activity and rational choice: Advances in criminological theory* (pp. 17–36). Transaction Publishers.

Tremblay, P., & Paré, P. (2003). Crime and destiny: Patterns in serious offenders' mortality rates. *Canadian Journal of Criminology and Criminal Justice*, 45(3), 299–326.

Tsang, S., Schmidt, K. M., Vincent, G. M., Salekin, R. T., Moretti, M. M., & Odgers, C. L. (2015). Assessing psychopathy among justice involved adolescents with the PCL:YV: An item response theory examination across gender. *Personality Disorders: Theory, Research, and Treatment*, 6, 22–31.

Tuttle, J. (2023). The end of the age-crime curve? A historical comparison of male arrest rates in the United States, 1985–2019. *The British Journal of Criminology*, 64(3), 638–655.

Twisk, J. (2013). *Applied longitudinal data analysis for epidemiology: A practical guide*. Cambridge University Press.

Tyrer, P. (2012). *The Psychopath Test* by Jon Ronson. *The British Journal of Psychiatry*, 20(2), 167.

Tzoumakis, S., Carr, V. J., Dean, K., Laurens, K. R., Kariuki, M., Harris, F., & Green, M. J. (2018). Prenatal maternal smoking, maternal offending, and offspring behavioural and cognitive outcomes in early childhood. *Criminal Behaviour and Mental Health*, 28(5), 397–408.

Tzoumakis, S., Lussier, P., & Corrado, R. (2014). The persistence of early childhood physical aggression: Examining maternal delinquency and offending, mental health, and cultural differences. *Journal of Criminal Justice*, 42(5), 408–420.

Ullrich, S., Farrington, D., & Coid, J. (2008). Psychopathic personality traits and life-success. *Personality and Individual Differences*, 44(5), 1162–1171.

Umbach, R., Berryessa, C. M., & Raine, A. (2015). Brain imaging research on psychopathy: Implications for punishment, prediction, and treatment in youth and adults. *Journal of Criminal Justice*, 43(4), 295–306.

Vachon, D. D., Lynam, D. R., Loeber, R., Stouthamer-Loeber, M. (2012). Generalizing the nomological network of psychopathy across populations differing on race and conviction status. *Journal of Abnormal Psychology*, 121(1), 263–269.

Vasaturo, A., Krstic, S., & Knight, R. A. (2024). The effects of psychopathy facets on treatment involvement. *International Journal of Offender Therapy and Comparative Criminology*, online first, 1–17. https://doi.org/10.1177/0306624X241270593

Vaswani, N., & Paul, S. (2019). "It's knowing the right things to say and do": Challenges and opportunities for trauma-informed practice in the prison context. *The Howard Journal of Crime and Justice*, 58(4), 513–534.

Vaughn, M. G., & DeLisi, M. (2008). Were Wolfgang's chronic offenders psychopaths? On the convergent validity between psychopathy and career criminality. *Journal of Criminal Justice*, 36, 33–42.

Vaughn, M. G., Howard, M. O., & DeLisi, M. (2008). Psychopathic personality traits and delinquent careers: An empirical examination. *International Journal of Law and Psychiatry*, 31(5), 407–416.

Vaurio, O., Lähteenvuo, M., Kautiainen, H., Repo-Tiihonen, E., & Tiihonen, J. (2022). Female psychopathy and mortality. *Frontiers in Psychiatry*, 13, Article 831410.

Vaurio, O., Repo-Tiihonen, E., Kautiainen, H., & Tiihonen, J. (2018). Psychopathy and mortality. *Journal of forensic sciences*, 63(2), 474–477.

Veal, R., & Ogloff, J. R. (2022). The concept of psychopathy and risk assessment: Historical developments, contemporary considerations, and future directions. In P. B. Marques, M. Paulino, & L. Alho (Eds.), *Psychopathy and criminal behaviour: Current trends and challenges* (pp. 169–192). Academic Press.

Verona, E., & Fox, B. (2025). Pathways to crime and antisocial behavior: A critical analysis of psychological research and a call for broader ecological perspectives. *Annual Review of Clinical Psychology*, 21(1), 439–464.

Verona, E., McKinley, S. J., Hoffmann, A., Murphy, B. A., & Watts, A. L. (2023). Psychopathy facets, perceived power, and forms of aggression. *Personality Disorders: Theory, Research, and Treatment*, 14(3), 259–273.

Verschuere, B., & Te Kaat, L. (2020). What are the core features of psychopathy? A prototypicality analysis using the Psychopathy Checklist-Revised (PCL-R). *Journal of Personality Disorders*, 34(3), 410–419.

Verschuere, B., van Ghesel Grothe, S., Waldorp, L., Watts, A., Lilienfeld, S., Edens, J., & Noordhof, A. (2018). What features of psychopathy might be central? A network analysis of the Psychopathy Checklist-Revised (PCL-R) in three large samples. *Journal of Abnormal Psychology*, 127(1), 51–65.

Verschuere, B., Yasrebi-de Kom, F. M., van Zelm, I., & Lilienfeld, S. O. (2021). A plea for preregistration in personality disorders research: The case of psychopathy. *Journal of Personality Disorders*, 35(2), 161–176.

Viding, E., & Kimonis, E. R. (2018). Callous-unemotional traits. In C. J. Patrick (Ed.), *Handbook of psychopathy* (2nd Ed., pp. 144–164). Guilford Press.

Viding, E., Blair, R. J. R., Moffitt, T. E., & Plomin, R. (2005). Evidence for substantial genetic risk for psychopathy in 7-year-olds. *Journal of Child Psychology and Psychiatry*, 46(6), 592–597.

Viljoen, J., & Vincent, G. M. (2020). Risk assessments for violence and reoffending: Implementation and impact on risk management. *Clinical Psychology: Science and Practice*, 31(2), 119–131.

Viljoen, J., McLachlan, K., & Vincent, G. M. (2010a). Assessing violence risk and psychopathy in juvenile and adult offenders: A survey of clinical practices. *Assessment*, 17(3), 377–395.

Viljoen, J. L., MacDougall, E., Gagnon, N., & Douglas, K. (2010b). Psychopathy evidence in legal proceedings involving adolescent offenders. *Psychology, Public Policy, & Law*, 16, 254–283.

Viljoen, J. L., Shaffer, C. S., Muir, N., Cochrane, D., & Brodersen, E. (2019). Improving case plans and interventions for adolescents on probation: The implementation of the SAVRY and a structured case planning form. *Criminal Justice and Behaviour*, 46, 42–62.

Vincent, G. (2002). *Investigating the legitimacy of adolescent psychopathy assessments: Contributions of item response theory*. Unpublished doctoral dissertation, Simon Fraser University, Burnaby.

Vincent, G. M., Odgers, C. L., McCormick, A. V., & Corrado, R. (2008). The PCL: YV and recidivism in male and female juveniles: A follow-up into young adulthood. *International Journal of Law and Psychiatry*, 31(3), 287–296.

de Vogel, V., de Ruiter, C., Bouman, Y., & de Vries Robbé, M. (2012). *SAPROF manual: Assessment of protective factors for violence risk*. Van der Hoeven Kliniek.

Vogt, W. (2007). *Quantitative research methods for professionals*. Pearson Education.

Wahl, O., Wood, A., & Richards, R. (2002). Newspaper coverage of mental illness: Is it changing? *Psychiatric Rehabilitation Skills*, 6(1), 9–31.

Wahl, O. F. (1995). *Media madness: Public images of mental illness*. Rutgers University Press.

Wakefield, S. (2018). Sentence length and recidivism: Evidence and the challenges of criminal justice reform in the carceral state. *Criminology & Public Policy*, 17, 771–777.

Waldfogel, J. (1997). The effect of children on women's wages. *American Sociological Review*, 62(2), 209–217.

Waller, R., Hawes, S. W., Byrd, A. L., Dick, A. S., Sutherland, M. T., Riedel, M. C., & Gonzalez, R. (2020). Disruptive behavior problems, callous-unemotional traits, and regional gray matter volume in the adolescent brain and cognitive development study. *Biological Psychiatry: Cognitive Neuroscience and Neuroimaging*, 5(5), 481–489.

Wall-Wieler, E., Roos, L. L., Bolton, J., Brownell, M., Nickel, N. C., & Chateau, D. (2017). Maternal health and social outcomes after having a child taken into care: Population-based longitudinal cohort study using linkable administrative data. *Journal of Epidemiology and Community Health*, 71(12), 1145–1151.

Walsh, Z., Swogger, M. T., & Kosson, D. S. (2004). Psychopathy, IQ, and violence in European American and African American county jail inmates. *Journal of Consulting and Clinical Psychology*, 72(6), 1165–1169.

Walters, G., Gray, N., Jackson, R., Sewell, K., Rogers, R., Taylor, J., & Snowden, R. (2007). A taxometric analysis of the Psychopathy Checklist: Screening Version (PCL: SV): Further evidence of dimensionality. *Psychological Assessment*, 19(3), 330–339.

Walters, G. D. (2004). The trouble with psychopathy as a general theory of crime. *International Journal of Offender Therapy and Comparative Criminology*, 48(2), 133–148.

(2025). The effect of direct interventions for antisocial cognition on recidivism in antisocial populations: A meta-analysis. *Journal of Experimental Criminology*, (online first), 1–17. https://link.springer.com/article/10.1007/s11292-025-09675-8

Walters, G. D., & DeLisi, M. (2015). Psychopathy and violence: Does antisocial cognition mediate the relationship between the PCL: YV factor scores and violent offending? *Law and Human Behaviour*, 39(4), 350–359.

Wang, X., Hay, C., Todak, N., & Bales, W. (2014). Criminal propensity, social context, and recidivism: A multilevel analysis of interactive relationships. *Criminal Justice and Behaviour*, 41(3), 300–317.

Waschbusch, D. A., Bansal, P. S., & Willoughby, M. T. (2024). A review of the Summer Treatment Program (STP) for youth with callous-unemotional (CU) traits: Moving past the "untreatable" hypothesis. *Evidence-Based Practice in Child and Adolescent Mental Health*, 10(2), 360–375.

Webster, C. D., Douglas, K. S., Eaves, D., & Hart, S. D. (1997). *HCR-20: Assessing risk for violence (version 2)*. Mental Health Law and Policy Institute, Simon Fraser University.

Webster, C. M., Sprott, J. B., & Doob, A. N. (2019). The will to change: Lessons from Canada's successful decarceration of youth. *Law & Society Review*, 53(4), 1092–1131.

Welsh, E. C. O., & Lenzenweger, M. F. (2021). Psychopathy, charisma, and success: A moderation modeling approach to successful psychopathy. *Journal of Research in Personality*, 95, Article 104146.
Westen, D., & Weinberger, J. (2004). When clinical description becomes statistical prediction. *American Psychologist*, 59, 595–613.
Widiger, T. A., & Lynam, D. R. (1998). Psychopathy and the Five-Factor Model of personality. In T. Millon, E. Simonsen, M. Birket-Smith, & R. D. Davis (Eds.), *Psychopathy: Antisocial, criminal, and violent behaviors* (pp. 171–187). Guilford Press.
Wiebe, R. (2003). Reconciling psychopathy and low self-control. *Justice Quarterly*, 20(2), 297–336.
Wikström, P. O. (2020). Explaining crime and criminal careers: The DEA model of situational action theory. *Journal of Developmental and Life-Course Criminology*, 6, 188–203.
Wikström, P. O., & Treiber, K. (2009). Violence as situational action. *International Journal of Conflict and Violence*, 3, 75–96.
Wiley, S., Slocum, L., O'Neill, J., & Esbensen, F. (2020). Beyond the breakfast club: Variability in the effects of suspensions by school context. *Youth & Society*, 52(7), 1259–1284.
Wilkinson, S., Waller, R., & Viding, E. (2016). Practitioner review: Involving young people with callous unemotional traits in treatment – Does it work? A systematic review. *Journal of Child Psychology and Psychiatry*, 57(5), 552–565.
Wittgenstein, L. (1993). *Philosophical occasions, 1912–1951*. Hackett Publications.
Wolfgang, M., Figlio, R., & Sellin, T. (1972). *Delinquency in a birth cohort*. University of Chicago Press.
Wong, S., Gordon, A., Gu, D., Lewis, K., & Olver, M. (2012). The effectiveness of violence reduction treatment for psychopathic offenders: Empirical evidence and a treatment model. *International Journal of Forensic Mental Health*, 11(4), 336–349.
Wright, B., Caspi, A., Moffitt, T. E., & Silva, P. A. (1999). Low self-control, social bonds, and crime: Social causation, social selection, or both? *Criminology*, 37(3), 479–514.
  (2001). The effects of social ties on crime vary by criminal propensity: A life-course model of interdependence. *Criminology*, 39(2), 321–348.
Yang, J., McCuish, E., & Corrado, R. (2017). Foster care beyond placement: Offending outcomes in emerging adulthood. *Journal of Criminal Justice*, 53, 46–54.
Yang, Y., & Land, K. C. (2013). *Age-period-cohort analysis: New models, methods, and empirical applications*. Taylor & Francis.
Yildrim, B., & Derksen, J. (2015). Clarifying the heterogeneity in psychopathic samples: Towards a new continuum of primary and secondary psychopathy. *Aggression and Violent Behavior*, 24, 9–41.
Yildrim, B. O. (2015). *What makes a psychopath? Neuro-developmental pathways to immoral and antisocial behaviour*. PhD thesis Belge Yayinlari – Istanbul.

Retrieved from https://repository.ubn.ru.nl/bitstream/handle/2066/150752/150752.pdf
Young, J., Klosko, J. S., & Weishaar, M. E. (2003). *Schema therapy: A practitioner's guide.* Guilford Press.
Zinger, I. (2022). Annual report 2021–2022. Office of the Correctional Investigator.
⸻ (2024). Annual report 2023–2024. Office of the Correctional Investigator.
Zylbersztejn, A., Gilbert, R., Hjern, A., Wijlaars, L., & Hardelid, P. (2018). Child mortality in England compared with Sweden: A birth cohort study. *The Lancet,* 391(10134), 2008–2018.

Cases and Legislation Cited

Criminal Code, R.S.C. 1985, c. C-46, s. 16(1)
Criminal Code, R.S.C. 1985, c. C-46, s. 718
Ewert v. Canada, 2016 FCA 203 (CanLII)
R. v. B.W.P.; R. v. B.V.N., [2006] 1 S.C.R. 941, 2006 SCC 27
R. v. D.B., [2008] 2 S.C.R. 3, 2008 SCC 25
Youth Criminal Justice Act, S.C. 2002. c. 1

Index

antisocial personality disorder, 12, 14
anxiety, 17, 20, 37, 42

birth cohort, 233, 236, 238, 240
birth cohorts, 234, 236–239, 242, 250
boldness, 17, 20–21, 27, 37, 42, 89, 161

CAPP, 19, 22–23, 25, 27–28, 35, 40, 71–73, 87, 90–91, 93, 112–113
classical syndrome, 34–37
Cleckley, xviii, 12–13, 17, 20–21, 24, 89–90
Comprehensive Assessment of Psychopathic Personality. *See* CAPP
configural construct, 35
Confirmatory factor analysis, 93, 101
correctional psychology, 116, 185–186
criminal social capital, 156, 166, 168–171, 174, 209, 226

desistance, 60, 117, 130, 206, 211, 215, 217, 222–223
Diagnostic and Statistical Manual of Mental Disorders. *See* DSM
DSM, xxi, 11–12, 14, 16

Elemental Psychopathy Assessment. *See* EPA
emergent interpersonal syndrome, 37
EPA, 24, 40, 42
expert rating tools, 40, 42, 56, 58, 112

five factor model.forensic psychology, xvi–xvii, 1, 116, 185–186

Hare, 3, 14, 18, 29, 56, 69, 118, 128, 147, 175
heterotypic continuity, 4, 69
High Risk Offender Intervention Program. *See* HROIP
homicide, xiii–xiv, 55, 60, 63, 77, 120, 127, 138, 157, 165, 179
HROIP, xxi, 140

informal social control, 60, 108, 151–152, 159–160, 162–164, 184, 186, 188–192, 195–198, 200–201, 203–205, 207–209, 211–212, 215, 223–225, 228
interrater reliability, 40, 91–92, 112, 114, 275
item response theory, 93, 104, 108, 110, 134, 205

Jon Ronson, 1, 6, 54–56, 58, 72
latent construct, 33–36, 134, 182
life-course criminology, 165
life-course interdependence. *See* treatment effect heterogeneity

mediation, 186, 188, 191, 193–196, 198–201, 204, 207–209, 224
Mendota Juvenile Treatment Center, 46
meta-analysis, 130, 176
moderation, 209–210
mortality, xvii, 2–3, 130, 151, 157, 179–182, 184, 188

Oak Ridge Study, 44, 204

Pathways to Desistance Study, 48
PCL-R, xxi, 18, 20–22, 28–29, 32–33, 40, 43, 45–46, 56, 90–91, 179
period effect, 233, 239–240, 247, 251
period effects, 232, 239, 243, 246–247, 250
Pinel, 8–9, 11–12
PPI-R, 20
Psychopathic Personality Inventory-Revised. *See* PPI-R
psychopathology network, 109
Psychopathy Content Scale, 71, 87, 93, 112–113
psychosis, 45, 52
public health, 178, 182–183

recidivism, 29, 116, 120, 148, 151, 185, 206
risk assessment, xvii, 1, 42, 66–67, 116, 143, 185–187, 230, 241
risk assessment instruments, 42, 241
risk-need-responsivity. *See* RNR model
RNR, xxi, 151, 258
RNR model, 151, 267
Ronson. *See* Jon Ronson

schizophrenia, 13, 45, 55, 58
self-report measures, 24, 40, 56, 161
sex offences, 139
Sexual Psychopath Laws, 10
SNA, xxi, 153
social network analysis. *See* SNA
sociopathic personality disturbance. *See* sociopathy
sociopathy, 12
stability, xviii, 24, 46, 110, 142, 152, 160, 195, 197
substance use, 65–66, 68, 86, 144, 147, 151–152, 156–157, 163–164, 175–176, 178, 186–188, 190, 193, 199, 203–204, 209, 228
Successful psychopathy, 36

therapeutic alliance, 264
treatment effect heterogeneity, 159, 210, 213–214
triarchic model, 20–21, 27, 89
Triarchic Psychopathy Model. *See* TriPM
TriPM, 21
True Crime, xv, 1, 25, 57

validity, 24, 87, 96, 112, 114, 117, 175
  convergent validity, 91, 93
  predictive validity, 117

wrap-around services, 264

Young Offenders Act, xxi, 64, 240
Youth Criminal Justice Act, xxi, 64, 240
Youth Psychopathic Traits Inventory. *See* YPI
YPI, xxi, 49

For EU product safety concerns, contact us at Calle de José Abascal, 56–1°, 28003 Madrid, Spain or eugpsr@cambridge.org.

www.ingramcontent.com/pod-product-compliance
Ingram Content Group UK Ltd.
Pitfield, Milton Keynes, MK11 3LW, UK
UKHW020050230326
469195UK00017B/184